Personal and organizational effectiveness

Editor: **Richard Hacon**

Senior Manpower Development Consultant,
International Computers Limited

London · New York · St Louis · San Francisco · Düsseldorf
Johannesburg · Kuala Lumpur · Mexico · Montreal · New Delhi
Panama · Rio de Janeiro · Singapore · Sydney · Toronto

Published by

McGRAW-HILL Book Company (UK) Limited

MAIDENHEAD · BERKSHIRE · ENGLAND

07 094237 4

PRINTED AND BOUND IN GREAT BRITAIN

Personal and organizational effectiveness

Contents

The contributors

Howard Baumgartel
Professor of Psychology and Human Relations, University of Kansas.

Warren G. Bennis
President, Cincinnati University

Leland P. Bradford
Executive Director, NTL Institute for Applied Behavioral Science, Washington (until his retirement in 1970).

Harold Bridger
Programme Director, Career Development and Institutional Change, Tavistock Institute of Human Relations, London.

Raymond B. Caldwell
Lecturer in Administration, Department of Business Studies, Trinity College, Dublin.

William J. Crockett
Vice-president, Human Relations, Saga Corporation, California. His chapter refers to the period 1961-1967 when he was Deputy Under-secretary of State for Administration, US Government.

Samuel A. Culbert
NTL Institute for Applied Behavioral Science, associated with the National Education Association, Washington, DC.

Sheldon A. Davis
Vice-president, Industrial Relations, TRW Systems Group, California.

William B. Eddy
Professor of Administration, University of Missouri, Kansas City.

Paul Grabbe
Dartmouth Eye Institute, Dartmouth College, New Hampshire.

Richard Hacon (editor)
Senior Manpower Development Consultant, International Computers Ltd, London. Formerly, Director of Management Development, British Institute of Management.

Roger Harrison
Vice-president and London-based representative, Development Research Associates Inc., Cambridge, Mass.

Geoffrey Holroyde
Senior Training Specialist, British Leyland Motor Corporation.

Peter Honey
Management consultant (UK).

Colin Hutchinson
Management and Organization Development Adviser, British-American Tobacco Company Ltd.

Kurt Lewin
Deceased, ex-Director of Research Centre, Group Dynamics, Massachusetts Institute of Technology.

Alistair D. Mant
Advisor on Management Development, IBM (UK) Ltd, Office Products Division.

Hugh B. Marlow
Senior Consultant, Associated Industrial Consultants Ltd, London.

Matthew B. Miles
Professor of Psychology and Education, Teachers College, Columbia University, New York.

Seamus Roche
A management development consultant whose connection with Coverdale Training dates from 1964 when he initiated the first Coverdale organization development project.

Herbert A. Shepard
Visiting Professor, School of Medicine, Yale University.

Robert Tannenbaum
Professor of Behavioural Science, University of California, Los Angeles.

Rein van der Vegt
Lecturer in Social Psychology, Institute of Social Psychology, University of Utrecht, The Netherlands. Part-time lecturer, Department of Business Studies, Trinity College, Dublin.

Stephanie White
Formerly on the staff of the Human Resources Centre, Tavistock Institute of Human Relations, London.

1. Introduction
Richard Hacon

To any student of contemporary society, it is disturbingly obvious that most industrialized countries are now in the grip of an inflation of expectations.

Throughout the 'sixties managements have operated within a framework of more or less constant high demand, low unemployment, and paper money inflation. There has also been a rapid rise in psychological expectations by most employees. Such expectations have bounded ahead of promotion opportunities. Hence the sharp interest of managers in how more individuals can achieve job satisfaction. Furthermore, the rate of the rate of change is causing many companies to ask themselves whether they are structured in a way best calculated to take advantage of the available technological know-how. At the same time they recognize that their workforce is more educated and seeks to be treated as such.

All these pressures, social, technological and educational, are forcing perceptive senior managers to question their own assumptions regarding what makes for an effective organization. Formerly organizations were hierarchical. Early retirements were infrequent. Middle and lower management knew or felt that they would be shielded from the outside environment through clear upwards reporting procedures. Now there is need for far more personal contacts, both outside the company and inside the organization, across formerly well-demarcated departmental boundaries. Such interactions and mutual interdependence are to be seen in the growth of project groups and temporary taskforces made up of a man from each of several interested functions. One man one boss is in many ways outmoded. Matrix management, which involves one man working on more than one task and beholden to more than one boss, or function, is becoming much more necessary. But whether individuals have the attitudes and requisite skills to work in these new-style collaborative ways, is the question that now has to be asked by senior managers. The 20 articles in this book bear on this theme; they are a mixture of old and new. They have all been chosen for their usefulness to thoughtful busy managers. Twelve have been published before in various books and journals, and some can be described as classics in the sense that they opened up new ways of thought and action. Eight are original articles and were sought out because it seemed to me that

1

their authors had something special to offer. Indeed, it is fair to say that some of these contributors were a trifle reluctant to put pen to paper.

Looking again at the mix of authors, I find it hard to say exactly why I chose those particular articles. At a time when periodicals and journals are being spawned at a frightening rate, any selection is bound to be somewhat arbitrary. The choice gets harder every month. In the circumstances it is probably more honest to admit that this selection can best be viewed as no more than a personal choice. Even so, it has been most difficult to leave out a number of obvious contributors. Fifteen of the authors are known personally to me, some I have worked with over a period of years and I believe that their message, and their approach, deserve to be more widely considered by those thoughtful practising managers keen to improve the overall performance of their own organization.

The book has a common theme in spite of the seemingly disparate subject matter of the different contributions. It is the effectiveness of organizations seen from a people-centred as opposed to, say, a financial, manufacturing, or operations research, point of view. As will be explained later, the articles have been grouped into 7 sections, each focuses on particular facets of the problem. Since the subject matter is managers in organizations, it means that the focus is twofold. Always there are two aspects: what is happening to individuals as employees in organizational settings and what is happening to those organizations that employ them. An organization is not a monolith whose productivity is unaffected by the expectations of those that it employs. Indeed, there is a very real but overlooked cost sometimes paid by those organizations that do not pay sufficient attention to how its members feel—the cost is that many of the bright and dissatisfied ones leave. Organizations need to learn. There is, in a sense, an organization learning process. This is somehow connected with the growth of the behavioural sciences. But how? And how relevant is that way of thinking to the manager and his world? Managers think in terms of

seeking opportunities for the business;
defining objectives;
setting policies;
looking at problems;
allocating resources between competing desirable ends.

They settle issues in the light of profitability. Their frame of reference is action and effectiveness in situations of uncertainty.

Behavioural scientists think in terms of

roles;
needs of individuals and organizations;
expectations,
attitudes,
nature of social relationships—conflict or cooperation.

They see human behaviour in terms of fact-gathering, descriptions, and hypotheses that explain. Their frame of reference is analysis rather than, or certainly prior to, action.

2

Can these two streams of thinking and activity so different in perspective benefit from each other? I believe they can. And though it is not stated explicitly by all the contributors, I feel sure that they all subscribe to that belief. Two illustrations may suffice to show how these viewpoints are coming closer together even if they remain asymptotic.

1 The polarity between needs of individuals and needs of organizations, as posed in the literature of the behavioural sciences in the 'forties and 'fifties, was sometimes typified as a win-lose situation. It received obvious publicity in W. H. Whyte's *Organisation Man*. Since then, instead of thinking in terms of individuals *versus* the organization, the emphasis has swung decisively to viewing individuals *in* organizations.

2 In the 'fifties, one of the major problems facing management research workers in the United Kingdom, and, perhaps, elsewhere, was how to gain access to companies to carry out research. But there were two difficulties. The first was due to some of their colleagues in the late 'forties and early 'fifties adopting the line: 'Research, publish, and damn the consequences for the organizations into which we researched.' That is, they were not really bothered with the aftermath of their questioning on the managers and workers in those organizations that kindly gave them access to company information. Though such researchers were very few in number, their impact on managerial thinking was most unfortunate. It stunted for more than five years the growth of collaborative ventures between companies and university research departments.

Dr A. T. M. Wilson wrote a paper listing some points needed for a professional ethic in social research, which alleviated the position somewhat.[1] The British Institute of Management later published a set of helpful guidelines for its member companies entitled 'Management Research: Notes for Guidance'. More than 3000 have been asked for. This handout has helped to make the industrial climate more open to proposals from *bona fide* research workers developing their first contacts with a company.

The second difficulty was simply that companies often could not see any direct advantages to be gained from the new survey material. They thought they were providing access for research workers to gather research material to be incorporated into lectures, rather perhaps, along the lines that 'that which was of interest to an academic could not be practical'; an attitude which died some time ago. But, keeping a sense of perspective, it must be remembered that less than 10 years ago there were far fewer management courses and no business schools of international standing in the UK.

Now there has been a coming together of viewpoints. Such phrases as, 'management of conflict', 'group pressures', 'job satisfaction', 'change agent', may just as easily be said by a manager as an academic. It is no accident that, of the 23 contributors, 5 are employed full time in industry or commerce and 8 others are consultants. Put another way, only 10 are full-time academics.

Why have companies become so interested in the behavioural sciences? The answer must be as varied as the number of companies. A few executives in some

3

companies may have been attracted out of curiosity, 'Let's see what is in it for us', or 'If X organization finds it useful to employ Professor P, then maybe we should, too'. However, it would appear from casual conversations, that most organizations turn to the behavioural sciences because they have a really pressing management problem, which they know they cannot solve in traditional ways. This business need is so powerful that it has overridden any feelings that they may have had about 'academics'. For most companies, their interest has been pragmatic and utilitarian. There is a world of difference between how the behavioural sciences can be used and whether a particular business problem can be alleviated through any insights from the behavioural sciences.

In a recent survey,[2] the National Industrial Conference Board asked 302 large, medium, and small North American companies for their comments. Out of 302 (251 American and 51 Canadian) companies 241 (80 per cent) reported some interest in the subject, 85 (35 per cent) used experiential learning and sensitivity training courses conducted by the NTL Institute for Applied Behavioural Science (12 of the authors in this book are members of NTL). Eighty additional firms used the managerial grid which can be regarded as a spin-off of sensitivity training. The degree of interest in the behavioural sciences was more related to company size than to the advanced state of its technology. Only 50 per cent of companies of under 1000 employees showed any interest; all the companies with over 100 000 employees reported 'moderate' or 'great' interest. In 94 companies (39 per cent) it was the chief executive and 113 companies (47 per cent) it was the personnel officer who spearheaded the Company's interest.[2]

There have been no comparable surveys in the UK, but I should imagine that the percentage figures would be lesser in every case. Yet the feel of the problem is the same. In the UK, as in America, there has been a growing recognition that the target of change should at times be the organization rather than the individual. Exclusive attention to the individual as the unit to be improved has meant too little attention has been paid to the work environment from which he has been temporarily detached for training purposes. When the organization is accepted as the frame of reference for improvement new perspectives soon come into focus and new training designs become necessary. These include:

re-entry of individuals to back-home work environment;
in-company team training;
organization development programmes.[3]

So much by way of general Introduction. I do not propose to try to define 'effective organizations', 'sensitivity training', 'interpersonal competence', or 'organization development'. Too many people enter the thicket of terminology, get scratched to pieces and are often no further forward in terms of 'action'. Managers live in the world of deeds, and operate in conditions of risk and uncertainty. Better performance means more to them than verbal clarity. Words, and yet more words, can never communicate a 'gut' experience. This is the paradox of telling. Yet sometimes something is gained from the telling. Perhaps it leads to a willingness to 'have a go' oneself.

4

In June 1969, I organized a four day course for 32 senior British managers keen to learn of the behavioural science applications in one technologically advanced company, TRW Systems of California.[4] At the evening introductory session, there developed a sustained discussion on the methods to be employed during the workshop. Two people, on fully appreciating that they would be taking part in a form of sensitivity training, rather felt that they had been conned into coming: had they known that the conference was going to take this form they might not have come. . . . Two days later one of those two said that he had always run away from this kind of conference and he could not think why. He was enjoying himself hugely and was so glad that he had come. Both confirmed later that I had in fact given them sufficient advance information about the purpose and methods to be used. They knew that they were going to learn about personal experience training in TRW, but they had not fully appreciated that the only way to understand experiential training was to take part in an experiential learning exercise themselves.

I mention this case simply because the bias of this book is on the value of learning from personal experience and from 'here and now' situations. Experiential learning, though but a small portion of the behavioural science field, can offer managers a range of useful insights about the *process* of their interaction with other persons as well as about the *content* of their contacts. The kinds of learning to be gained about oneself as an interacting person, what may be called issues of identity—what sort of a person I really am—need to be tied into more formal business management education and into real life issues of actually running a business. This is to be inferred in the last two chapters by Alistair Mant and William Crockett.

As mentioned earlier in this Introduction, the 20 chapters have been grouped to give point and emphasis to their selection. Briefly, part 1, 'Focus on the Future', contains a single chapter that points to trends and values that may well become more common in pacemaking organizations. They are, however, unlikely to become commonplace across industry and commerce because of the high degree of interactive skills necessary in the managerial population first to bring such modes of behaviour and values into existence and then to sustain them in the face of everday pressures.

Part 2, 'Focus on Methods and Phases of Development', aims to give some theoretical background to the many courses that have now been held based on 'here and now' learning and learning from experience. This approach does not shun cognitive inputs and the value of head knowledge. It does, however, affirm strongly that such knowledge is only really 'received' when a person can relate it to an actual experience he has, preferably, recently undergone.

Part 3, 'Focus on Systematic Task Performance', is a group of chapters that enables the reader to sense the utility of this way of thinking and action. The emphasis turns more on action than discussion, and on conditions for effective performance rather than individual and group introspection on current feelings and experience *per se.*

Part 4, 'Focus on Applications in Organizations', takes this mode of thinking and action a stage further. What has been experienced and attempted in a training

5

situation can so easily wither away when faced with the insistent pressures of the real job. These two articles drawn from British organizations have the merit of showing how insights into interpersonal behaviour have been translated into the work place and can be seen as work improvement exercises rather than training sessions.

Part 5, 'Focus on the Inner Man', takes a brief look at the man behind the executive mask. It takes two to shake hands. For a man to be given honest feedback about how he comes over to others is a tribute to the climate of candour and trust that has been built up between the individuals concerned. For that man to be helped to appreciate what is being said, and for him then to work on improving his own behaviour in some specific aspect, is one of the real hallmarks and rewards of sensitivity training.

Part 6, 'Focus on Context of Learning and Motivation', builds on the preceding part, in that it makes a number of points explicit concerning what needs to be done for learning to take place. While the focus is still on the person, there is considerably more attention paid to the context in which he is embedded.

In the final part, part 7, the emphasis shifts perceptibly. All the authors in this part, to a greater or lesser degree, see that the unit to be changed is the organization as a whole, rather than a particular individual in that organization. When the unit of change envelops such a complex of interacting variables, the task becomes much more testing.

These articles more than hint at the way in which some pacemaking organizations and institutions are tackling the problem of anticipating change rather than reacting to it. In this sense, we have come full-circle to the issues raised in part 1, 'Values, Man, and Organization'.

It is my belief and hope, and I am sure of all the contributors, that something of value out of their own experience, set down in words, will be of use to the reader, to be applied in their own organizations.

References

1. WILSON, A. T. M., A Note on the Social Sanctions of the Social Sciences'. *Sociological Review,* Vol. 3, No. 5, 1955, pp. 109-16.
2. NATIONAL INDUSTRIAL CONFERENCE BOARD, Behavioural Science Concepts and Management Application'. *Studies in Personal Policy*, No. 216, 1969.
3. For further development of this idea, see the series on organization development published by Addison-Wesley (London).
   BECKHARD, R., *Organization Development: Strategies and Models,* 1969.
   BENNIS, WARREN G., *Organization Development: Its Origins, Nature, and Prospects,* 1969.
   BLAKE, R. R., and MOUTON, JANE, *Building a Dynamic Corporation through Grid Organization Development,* 1969.
   LAWRENCE, PAUL R. and LORSCH, JAY W., *Developing Organizations Diagnosis and Action,* 1970.
   SCHEIN, EDGAR H., *Process Consultation: Its Role in Organization Development,* 1969.
   WALTON, RICHARD E., *Interpersonal Peacemaking: Confrontations and Third Party Consultation,* 1969.
4. Entitled 'Strategies and Skills for Change Workshop', held at the British Institute of Management, 15-19 June 1969. Staff members were Professor Herbert Shepard and Sheldon Davis, assisted by Harold Bridger, Tom Byers, Richard Hacon, and Bruce Neale.

PART ONE : Focus on the future

It proved most difficult to select the opening contribution. It needed to meet several stringent criteria. It had to speak from current success, point to emergent issues, indicate ways of overcoming those problems, be optimistic in tone and above all ring true to managers.

I believe this article 'Values, Man and Organizations' by Robert Tannenbaum and Sheldon Davis meets all those criteria. Most managers will recognize the kinds of situations reported on, and would be only too pleased if they had the skills to deal with them as successfully. The article indicates directions to travel in rather than final goals.

It offers an approach, not a set of packaged programmes. The skills that they deploy have been learnt over a number of years. The authors are not offering a placebo in terms of managing men and situations. Nor do they believe there are any short cuts to a lot of hard work of a face to face nature. What they are saying is that the pay-off can be profound as far as the quality of personal relationships at work is concerned. Furthermore, they are saying the man most likely to succeed in working through these tricky work situations will be someone who is in touch with his own feelings. He will come over to others as genuine, or 'authentic' as the Americans have it.

2. Values, man, and organizations

Robert Tannenbaum and Sheldon A. Davis

. . . we are today in a period when the development of theory within the social sciences will permit innovations which are at present inconceivable. Among these will be dramatic changes in the organization and management of economic enterprise. The capacities of the average human being for creativity, for growth, for collaboration, for productivity (in the full sense of the term) are far greater than we have recognized . . . it is possible that the next half century will bring the most dramatic social changes in human history.[1]

For those concerned with organization theory and with organizational development work, this is an exciting and challenging time. Probably never before have the issues at the interface between changing organizations and maturing man been so apparent, so compelling, and of such potentially critical relevance to both. And to a considerable extent, the sparks at the interface reflect differences in values both within organizations and within man—human values which are coming loose from their moorings, whose functional relevance is being reexamined and tested, and which are without question in transition.

Many organizations today, particularly those at the leading edge of technology, are faced with ferment and flux. In increasing instances, the bureaucratic model—with its emphasis on relatively rigid structure, well-defined functional specialization, direction and control exercised through a formal hierarchy of authority, fixed systems of rights, duties, and procedures, and relative impersonality of human relationships—is responding inadequately to the demands placed upon it from the outside and from within the organization. There is increasing need for experimentation, for learning from experience, for flexibility and adaptability, and for growth. There is a need for greater inventiveness and creativity, and a need for collaboration among individuals and groups. Greater job mobility and the effective use of temporary systems seem essential. An environment must be created in which people will be more fully utilized and challenged and in which people can grow as human beings.

In his book, *Changing Organizations,* Warren Bennis pointed out that the bureaucratic form of organization 'is becoming less and less effective, that it is hopelessly out of joint with contemporary realities, and that new shapes, patterns, and models . . . are emerging which promise drastic changes in the conduct of the corporation and in managerial practices in general.'[2] At least one of the newer models, the one with which our recent experience is most closely connected, is organic and systems-oriented. We feel that, for the present at least, this model is one which can suggest highly useful responses to the newer demands facing organizations.

At this historical juncture, it is not just organizations which are in flux. Man, perhaps to an extent greater than ever before, is coming alive; he is ceasing to be an object to be used, and is increasingly asserting himself, his complexity, and his importance. Not quite understanding why or how, he is moving slowly but ever closer to the center of the universe.

The factors underlying man's emergence are complex and inter-related. They include higher levels of educational attainment, an increased availability of technology which both frees man from the burdens of physical and routine labor and makes him more dependent on society, an increasing rate of change affecting his environment which both threatens and challenges him, and higher levels of affluence which open up opportunities for a variety and depth of experiences never before so generally available.

The evidences of this trend are many. They are to be found, for example, in the gropings within many religions for more viable modes and values. They are to be found in the potent thrusts for independence of minorities everywhere, and in the challenges of our youth who find our values phony and often materialistically centered. They are to be found in the involvement of so many people in psychotherapy, in sensitivity training, and in self-expression activities in the arts and elsewhere. They are also to be found in the continuing and growing interest in writings and ideas in the general direction of the humanistic-existential orientation to man.

Organizations are questioning and moving away from the bureaucratic model, in part because man is asserting his individuality and his centrality, in part because of growing dissatisfaction with the personally constraining impact of bureaucracies. In this flux, organizations and man must find a way with each other. In our view, this way will be found through changing values—values which can hopefully serve the needs for effectiveness and survival of organizations and the needs for individuality and growth of emergent man. Those concerned with organization theory and with organizational development have, in our judgement, a most important role to play in this quest.

Values in transition

Deeply impressed with the managerial and organizational implications of the increasing accumulation of knowledge about human behavior, Professor Douglas McGregor formulated his assumptions of theory Y. According to him, these assumptions were essentially his interpretations, based upon the newer knowledge and on his extensive experience, of the nature of man and of man's motivation. In our view, McGregor was overly cautious and tentative in calling the theory Y tenets 'assumptions', and in limiting them to being his 'interpretations'. In trying to be 'scientific', he seemed reluctant in his writing to assert explicity as *values* those elements (including the theory Y assumptions) which so much affected his organizational theory and practice. He was not alone in his reluctance. Perhaps the most pervasive common characteristic among people in laboratory training and in organizational development work is their values, and yet, while organizational development academicians and practitioners are generally aware of their shared values and while these values implicitly guide much of what they do, they too have usually been reluctant to make them explicit.

We want here not only to own our values, but also to state them openly. These values are consistent with McGregor's assumptions and in some instances go beyond his. They are not scientifically derived nor are they new, but they are compatible with relevant 'findings' emerging in the behavioral sciences. They are deeply rooted in the nature of man and are therefore basically humanistic. As previously suggested, many of the values underlying the bureaucratic model and its typical implementation have been inconsistent with the nature of man, with the result that he has not been fully utilized, his motivation has been reduced, his growth as a person stunted, and his spirit deadened. These outcomes sorely trouble us, for we believe organizations can in the fullest sense serve man as well as themselves.

Growing evidence strongly suggests that humanistic values not only resonate with an increasing number of people in today's world, but also are highly consistent with the effective functioning of organizations built on the newer organic model. As we discuss a number of these values, we will provide some face validity for their viability by illustrating them with cases or experiences taken from our involvements with or knowledge of a number of organizations which recently have been experimenting with the interface between the organizational and humanistic frontiers described above. The illustrations come primarily from TRW Systems, with which we have had a continuing collaboration for more than four years. Other organizations with which one or both of us have been involved include Aluminum Company of Canada, Ltd, US Department of State, and the Organizational Behavior Group of Case Institute of Technology.

We clearly recognize that the values to which we hold are not absolutes, that they represent directions rather than final goals. We also recognize that the degree of their short-run application often depends upon the people and other variables involved. We feel that we are now in a period of transition, sometimes slow and sometimes rapid, involving a movement away from older, less personally meaningful and organizationally relevant values toward these newer values.

Away from a view of man as essentially bad toward a view of him as basically good—At his core, man is not inherently evil, lazy, destructive, hurtful, irresponsible, narrowly self-centered, and the like. The life experiences which he has, including his relationships with other people and the impact on him of the

11

organizations with which he associates, can and often do move him in these directions. On the other hand, his more central inclination toward the good is reflected in his behavior as an infant, in his centuries-long evolution of ethical and religious precepts, and in the directions of his strivings and growth as a result of experiences such as those in psychotherapy and sensitivity training. Essentially man is internally motivated toward positive personal and social ends; the extent to which he is not motivated results from a process of demotivation generated by his relationships and/or environment.

We have been impressed with the degree to which the fairly pervasive cultural assumption of man's badness has led to organizational forms and practices designed to control, limit, push, check upon, inhibit, and punish. We are also increasingly challenged by the changes in behavior resulting from a growing number of experiments with organizational forms and practices rooted in the view of man as basically good.

Within an organization it is readily apparent to both members and perceptive visitors whether or not there is, in general, an atmosphere of respect for the individual as a person. Are people treated arbitrarily? Are there sinister coups taking place? How much of the time and energy of the members of the organization is devoted to constructive problem-solving rather than to playing games with each other, back-biting, politicing, destructive competition, and other dysfunctional behavior? How does management handle problems such as the keeping of time records? (Some organizations do not have time clocks and yet report that employees generally do not abuse this kind of a system.) One of the authors can remember a chain of retail stores which fired a stock clerk because he had shifty eyes, although he was one of the best stock boys in that chain. There are all kinds of negative assumptions about man behind such an incredible action.

For a long period of time, two senior engineers, Taylor and Durant, had real difficulty in working together. Each had a negative view of the other; mutual respect was lacking. Such attitudes resulted in their avoiding each other even though their technical disciplines were closely related. A point in time was reached when Taylor sorely needed help from Durant. Caught up in his own negative feelings, however, he clearly was not about to ask Durant for help. Fortunately, two of Taylor's colleagues who did not share his feelings prodded him into asking Durant to work with him on the problem. Durant responded most positively, and brought along two of his colleagues the next day to study the problem in detail. He then continued to remain involved with Taylor until the latter's problem was solved. Only a stereotype had kept these men apart; Taylor's eventual willingness to approach Durant opened the door to constructive problem-solving.

Away from avoidance or negative evaluation of individuals towards confirming them as human beings—One desire frequently expressed by people with whom we consult is: 'I wish I knew where I stand with my boss (with this organization) (with my colleagues) (with my subordinates). I'd really like to know what they think of me personally.' We are not referring to the excessively neurotic needs of

12

some persons for attention and response, but rather to the much more pervasive and basic need to know that one's existence makes a difference to others.

Feedback that is given is generally negative in character and often destructive of the individual instead of being focused on the perceived shortcomings of a given performance. It seems to be exceedingly difficult for most of us to give positive feedback to others—and, more specifically, to express genuine feelings of affection and caring.

When people are seen as bad, they need to be disciplined and corrected on the issue only; when they are seen as good, they need to be confirmed. Avoidance and negative evaluation can lead individuals to be cautious, guarded, defensive. Confirmation can lead to personal release, confidence, and enhancement.

A senior executive reported to one of us that he did not get nearly as much feedback as he wanted about how people thought about him as a person and whether or not they cared for him. He reported that one of the most meaningful things that had happened to him in this regard occurred when the person he reported to put his arm around him briefly at the end of a working session, patted him on the shoulder, and said, 'Keep up the good work', communicating a great deal of warmth and positive feeling towards the person through this behavior. This event had taken place two years ago and lasted about five seconds, yet it was still fresh in the senior executive's memory and obviously has had a great deal of personal meaning for him. In our culture, most of us are grossly undernourished and have strong need for the personal caring of others.

Away from a view of individuals as fixed, toward seeing them as being in process—The traditional view of individuals is that they can be defined in terms of given interests, knowledge, skills, and personality characteristics: they can gain new knowledge, acquire additional skills, and even, at times, change their interests, but it is rare for people really to change. This view, when buttressed by related organizational attitudes and modes, insures a relative fixity of individuals, with crippling effects. The value to which we hold is that people can constantly be in flux, groping, questing, testing, experimenting, and growing. We are struck by the tremendous untapped potential in most individuals yearning for discovery and release. Individuals may rarely change in core attributes, but the range of alternatives for choice can be widened, and the ability to learn how to learn more about self can be enhanced.

Organizations at times question whether it is their responsibility to foster individual growth. Whether or not it is, we believe that for most organizations, especially those desiring long-term survival through adaptability, innovation, and change, it is an increasing necessity. Further, evidence suggests that to have people in process requires a growth-enhancing environment. Personal growth requires healthy organizations. This value, then, carries with it great implications for work in organizational development. In organizations, people continuously experience interpersonal difficulties in relating to the other people with whom they must work. Some reasons for the difficulties are that people listen very badly to each other, attribute things of a negative nature to another person, and make all kinds of

13

paranoid assumptions, with the result that communication breaks down rather severely.

There have been many instances within TRW Systems of people, who, in the eyes of others around them, produce some fairly significant changes in their own behavior. Most of these changes have been reported quite positively. In some cases there have been rather dramatic changes with respect to how a person faces certain kinds of problems—how he handles conflicts, how he conducts staff meetings. In those cases an individual, who is perceived as having changed, quite often reports that these changes are personally rewarding, that he feels better about himself and more optimistic and expansive about life.

TRW Systems is committed to a continuation and improvement of its Career Development program, which places considerable emphasis on the personal and professional growth of its members. Although the original commitment was perhaps largely based on faith, experience gained in recent years strongly suggests that one of the most productive investments the organization can make is in the continuing growth of its members and in the health of the environment in which they work.

Away from resisting and fearing individual differences toward accepting and utilizing them—The pervasive and long-standing view of man as bad takes on even more serious implications when individual differences among men appear— differences in race, religion, personality (including personal style), specialties, and personal perceptions (definitions of truth or reality). A bad man poses sufficient problems, but a strange bad man often becomes impossible.

Organizations and individuals are frequently threatened by what they consider questioning of or challenge to their existing values and modes, represented by the presence of alternative possibilities. And they choose to avoid the challenge and the related and expected conflicts, discomforts, and the like, which might follow. As a result, they achieve drabness, a lack of creativity, and a false sense of peace and security. We firmly believe that the existence of differences can be highly functional. There is no single truth, no one right way, no chosen people. It is at the interface of differences that ferment occurs and that the potential for creativity exists. Furthermore, for an organization to deny to itself (in the name of 'harmony' or some similar shibboleth) the availability of productive resources simply because they do not conform to an irrelevant criterion is nothing short of madness. To utilize differences creatively is rarely easy, but our experience tells us that the gains far outweigh the costs.

In the play *Right You Are*, Pirandello makes the point that truth in a particular human situation is a collection of what each individual in the situation sees. Each person will see different facets of the same event. In a positive sense, this would lead us to value seeing all the various facets of an issue or problem as they unfold in the eyes of all the beholders and to place a positive value on our interdependence with others, particularly in situations where each of us can have only part of the answer or see part of the reality.

An organization recently faced the problem of filling a key position. The man whose responsibility it was to fill the position sat down with five or six people who,

14

due to their various functional roles, would have a great deal of interaction with the person in that position and with his organization. The man asked them to help him identify logical candidates. The group very quickly identified a number of people who ought to be considered and the two or three who were the most logical candidates. Then the group went beyond the stated agenda and came up with a rather creative new organizational notion, which was subsequently implemented and proved to be very desirable. After this took place, the executive, who had called the meeting in order to get the help for the decision he had to make, reported that it was very clear to him that doing the job became much easier by getting everyone together to share their varying perceptions. This meant that he had more relevant data available to him in making his decision. Furthermore, the creative organizational concept only came about as a result of the meeting's having taken place.

In most organizations persons and groups with markedly different training, experience, points of view, and modes of operating frequently bump into each other. Project managers face functional performers, mechanical engineers face electrical engineers, designers face hardware specialists, basic researchers face action-oriented engineers, financial specialists face starry-eyed innovators. Each needs to understand and respect the world of the other, and organizations should place a high value upon and do much to facilitate the working through of the differences which come into sharp focus at interfaces such as these.

Away from utilizing an individual primarily with reference to his job description toward viewing him as a whole person—People get pigeon-holed very easily, with job description (or expectations of job performance) typically becoming the pigeon hole. A cost accountant is hired, and from then on he is seen and dealt with as a cost accountant. Our view is that people generally have much more to contribute and to develop than just what is expected of them in their specific positions. Whole persons, not parts of persons, are hired and available for contribution. The organizational challenge is to recognize this fact and discover ways to provide outlets for the rich, varied, and often untapped resources available to them.

One of many personal examples that could be cited within TRW Systems is that of a person trained as a theoretical physicist. Having pursued this profession for many years, he is now effectively serving also as a part-time behavioral science consultant (a third-party process facilitator) to the personnel organization within the company. This is an activity for which he had no previous formal training until a new-found interest began asserting itself. The organization has supported him in this interest, has made a relevant learning opportunity available to him, and has opened the door to his performing an additional function within the organization.

An organizational example involves the question of charters that are defined for particular sub-elements of the organization: divisions, staffs, labs, etc. What are their functions? What are they supposed to do? To state the extreme, an organizational unit can have very sharply defined charters so that each person in it knows exactly what he is supposed to do and not do. This can lead to very clean functional relationships. Another approach, however, is to say that the *core* of the charter will

15

be very clear with discrete responsibilities identified, but the outer edges (where one charter interacts with others) will not be sharply defined and will deliberately overlap and interweave with other charters. The latter approach assumes that there is a potential synergy within an organization which people can move toward fully actualizing if they can be constructive and creative in their interpersonal and intergroup relations. Very different charters are produced in this case, with very different outcomes. Such charters must, by definition, not be clean and sharply described, or the innovative and coordinated outcomes that might come about by having people working across charter boundaries will not occur.

Away from walling-off the expression of feelings towards making possible both appropriate expression and effective use—In our culture, there is a pervasive fear of feelings. From early childhood, children are taught to hide, repress, or deny the existence of their feelings, and their learnings are reinforced as they grow older. People are concerned about 'losing control', and organizations seek rational, proper, task-oriented behavior, which emphasizes head-level as opposed to gut-level behavior. But organizations also seek high motivation, high morale, loyalty, team work, commitment, and creativity, all of which, if they are more than words, stem from personal feelings. Further, an individual cannot be a whole person if he is prevented from using or divorced from his feelings. And the energy dissipated in repression of feelings is lost to more productive endeavors.

We appreciate and are not afraid of feelings, and strongly believe that organizations will increasingly discover that they have a reservoir of untapped resources available to them in the feelings of their members, that the repression of feelings in the past has been more costly, both to them and to their members, than they ever thought possible.

One of the relevant questions to ask within an organization is how well problems stay solved once they are apparently solved. If the feelings involved in such problems are not directly dealt with and worked through, the problem usually does not remain solved for very long. For example, if two subordinates are fighting about something, their supervisor can either intervene and make the decision for them or arbitrate. Both methods can solve the immediate difficulty, but the fundamental problem will most likely again occur in some other situation or at some other time. The supervisor has dealt only with the symptoms of the real problem.

The direct expression of feelings, no matter what they are, does typically take place somewhere along the line, but usually not in the relevant face to face relationship. A person will attend a staff meeting and experience a great deal of frustration with the meeting as a whole or with the behaviour of one or more persons in it. He will then talk about his feelings with another colleague outside the meeting or bring them home and discuss them with or displace them on his wife or children, rather than talking about them in the meeting where such behavior might make an important difference. To aid communication of feelings, participants at a given staff meeting could decide that one of the agenda items will be: 'How do we feel about this meeting; how is it going; how can it be improved?' They could then talk with

16

each other while the feeling was immediately relevant to the effective functioning of the staff group. The outcomes of the face to face confrontation can be far more constructive than the 'dealing with symptoms' approach.

Away from maskmanship and game-playing towards authentic behavior—Deeply rooted in existing organizational lore is a belief in the necessity or efficacy of being what one is not, both as an individual and as a group. Strategy and out-maneuvering are valued. Using diplomacy, wearing masks, not saying what one thinks or expressing what one feels, creating an image—these and other deceptive modes are widely utilized. As a result, in many interpersonal and intergroup relations, mask faces mask, image faces image, and much energy is employed in dealing with the other persons's game. That which is much more basically relevant to the given relationship is often completely avoided in the transaction.

To be that which one (individual or group) truly is—to be authentic—is a central value to us. Honesty, directness, and congruence, if widely practiced, create an organizational atmosphere in which energies get focused on the real problems rather than on game-playing and in which individuals and groups can genuinely and meaningfully encounter each other.

Recently, two supervisors of separate units within an organization got together to resolve a problem that affected both of them. At one point in their discussion, which had gone on for some time and was proving not to be very fruitful, one of them happened to mention that he had recently attended a sensitivity training laboratory conducted by the company. At that point, the other one mentioned that sometime back he had also attended a laboratory. They both quickly decided 'to cut out the crap', stop the game they were playing, and really try to solve the problem they had come to face. Within a very short period of time, they dramatically went from a very typical organizational mode of being very closed, wearing masks, and trying to outmaneuver each other, to a mode of being open and direct. They found that the second mode took less energy and that they solved the problem in much less time and were able to keep it solved. But, somehow, at least one of them had not felt safe in taking off his mask until he learned that the other one had also gone through a T Group.

When people experience difficulty with others in organizations, they quite often attribute the difficulty to the fact that the other person or group is not trustworthy. This attitude, of course, justifies their behavior in dealing with the other. On numerous occasions within TRW Systems, groups or individuals who are experiencing distrust are brought together and helped to articulate how they feel about each other. When the fact that 'I do not trust you' is out on the table, and only then, can it be dealt with. Interestingly, it turns out that when the feeling is exposed and worked through, there are not really very many fundamentally untrustworthy people. There certainly are all kinds of people continuously doing things that create feelings of mistrust in others. But these feelings and the behavior that triggers them are rarely explored in an effort to work them through. Instead, the mistrust escalates, continues to influence the behavior of both parties, and becomes self-fulfilling. Once the locked-in situation is broken through and the

17

people involved really start talking to each other authentically, however, trust issues, about which people can be very pessimistic, become quite workable. This has happened many, many times in organizational development efforts at TRW Systems.

Away from use of status for maintaining power and personal prestige toward use of status for organizationally relevant purposes—In organizations, particularly large ones, status and symbols of status can play an important role. In too many instances, however, they are used for narrowly personal ends, both to hide behind and to maintain the aura of power and prestige. One result is that dysfunctional walls are built and communication flow suffers.

We believe that status must always be organizationally (functionally) relevant. Some people know more than others, some can do things others cannot do, some carry more responsibility than others. It is often useful for status to be attached to these differences, but such status must be used by its holder to further rather than to wall off the performance of the function out of which the status arises. An organization must be constantly alert to the role that status plays in its functioning.

It is relatively easy to perceive how status symbols are used within an organization, how relatively functional or dysfunctional they are. In some organizations, name-dropping is one of the primary weapons for accomplishing something. A person can go to a colleague with whom he is having a quarrel about what should be done and mention that he had a chat with the president of the organization yesterday. He then gets agreement. He may or may not have talked with the president, he may or may not have quoted him correctly; but he is begging the question by using a power figure in order to convince the other person to do it his way. In other organizations, we have observed that people very rarely work a problem by invoking the name of a senior executive, and that, in fact, those who do name-drop are quickly and openly called to task.

At TRW Systems, with only minor exceptions, middle- and top-level executives, as well as key scientists and engineers, are typically available for consultation with anyone in the organization on matters of functional relevance to the organization. There is no need to use titles, to 'follow the organization chart', to obtain permission for the consultation from one's boss or to report the results to him afterwards. As a result, those who can really help are sought out, and problems tend to get worked at the point of interface between need on the one hand and knowledge, experience, and expertise on the other.

Away from distrusting people toward trusting them—A corollary of the view that man is basically bad is the view that he cannot be trusted. And if he cannot be trusted, he must be carefully watched. In our judgement, many traditional organizational forms exist, at least in part, because of distrust. Close supervision, managerial controls, guarding, security, sign-outs, carry with them to some extent the implication of distrust.

The increasing evidence available to us strongly suggests that distrusting people often becomes a self-confirming hypothesis—distrusting another leads to behavior

18

consciously or unconsciously designed by the person or group not trusted to 'prove' the validity of the distrust. Distrust begets distrust. On the other hand, the evidence also suggests that trust begets trust; when people are trusted, they often respond in ways to merit or justify that trust.

Where distrust exists, people are usually seen as having to be motivated 'from the outside in', as being responsive only to outside pressure. But when trust exists, people are seen as being motivated 'from the inside out', as being at least potentially self-directing entities. One motivational device often used in the outside-in approach involves the inculcation of guilt. Rooted in the Protestant ethic, this device confronts the individual with 'shoulds', 'oughts', or 'musts' as reasons for behaving in a given way. Failure to comply means some external standard has not been met. The individual has thus done wrong, and he is made to feel guilty. The more trustful, inside-out approach makes it possible for the individual to do things because they make sense to him, because they have functional relevance. If the behavior does not succeed, the experience is viewed in positive terms as an opportunity to learn rather than negatively as a reason for punishment and guilt.

Organizations which trust go far to provide individuals and groups with considerable freedom for self-directed action backed up by the experience-based belief that this managerial value will generate the assumption of responsibility for the exercise of that freedom.

In California, going back about 27 years, a forward-looking director of one of our state prisons got the idea of a 'prison without walls'. He developed and received support for an experiment that involved bringing prisoners to the institution where correctional officers, at that time called guards, carried no guns or billy clubs. There were no guards in the towers or on the walls. The incoming prisoners were shown that the gate was not locked. Under this newer organizational behavior, escape rates decreased, and the experiment has become a model for many prisons in this country and abroad.

An organizational family embarked upon a two-day team-development lab shortly after the conclusion was reached from assessment data that the partial failure of a space vehicle had resulted from the non-functioning of a subsystem developed by this team. At the outset of the lab, an aura of depression was present, but there was no evidence that the team had been chastised by higher management for the failure. Further, in strong contrast with what most likely would have been the case if they had faced a load of guilt generated from the outside, there was no evidence of mutual destructive criticism and recriminations. Instead, the team was able, in time, to turn its attention to a diagnosis of possible reasons for the failure and to action steps which might be taken to avoid a similar outcome in the future.

During a discussion which took place between the head of an organization and one of his subordinates (relating to goals and objectives for that subordinate for the coming year), the supervisor said that one of the things he felt very positive about with respect to that particular subordinate was the way he seemed to be defining his own set of responsibilities. This comment demonstrated the large degree of trust that was placed in the subordinates of this particular supervisor. While the supervisor certainly made it clear to this individual that there were some specific things expected of him, he consciously created a large degree of freedom within which the subordinate would be able to determine for himself how he should spend his time, what priorities he ought to have, what his function should be. This is in great contrast to other organizations which define very clearly and elaborately what they expect from people. Two very different sets of assumptions about people underlie these two approaches.

Away from avoiding facing others with relevant data towards making appropriate confrontation—This value trend is closely related to the one of 'from maskmanship toward authenticity', and its implementation is often tied to moving 'from distrust toward trust'.

In many organizations today, there is an unwillingness to 'level' with people, particularly with respect to matters which have personal implications. In merit reviews, the 'touchy' matters are avoided. Often, incompetent or unneeded employees are retained much longer than is justified either from the organizations's or their own point of view. Feelings toward another accumulate and, at times, fester, but they remain unexpressed. 'Even his best friends won't tell him.'

Confrontation fails to take place because 'I don't want to hurt Joe', although, in fact, the non-confronter may be concerned about being hurt himself. We feel that a real absurdity is involved here. While it is widely believed that to 'level' is to hurt and, at times, to destroy the other, the opposite may often be the case. Being left to live in a 'fool's paradise' or being permitted to continue with false illusions about self is often highly hurtful and even destructive. Being honestly confronted in a context of mutual trust and caring is an essential requirement for personal growth. In an organizational setting, it is also an important aspect of 'working the problem'.

A quite dramatic example of confrontation and its impact occurred in a sensitivity training laboratory when one executive giving feedback to a colleague said to him that he and others within the organization perceived him as being ruthless. This came as a tremendous jolt to the person receiving the feedback. He had absolutely no perception of himself as ruthless and no idea that he was doing doing things which would cause others to feel that way about him. The confrontation was an upending experience for him. As a result, he later began to explore with many people in the organization what their relationship with him was like and made some quite marked changes in his behavior after getting additional data, which tended to confirm what he had recently heard. In the absence of these data (previously withheld because people might not want to hurt him), he was indeed living in a fool's paradise. A great deal of energy was expended by other people in dealing with his 'ruthlessness', and a considerable amount of avoidance took place, greatly influencing the productivity of everyone. Once this problem was exposed and worked through, this energy became available for more productive purposes.

Away from avoidance of risk-taking toward willingness to risk—A widely discernible attribute of large numbers of individuals and groups in organizations today is the

20

unwillingness to risk, to put one's self or the group on the line. Much of this reluctance stems from not being trusted, with the resulting fear of the consequences expected to follow close upon the making of an error. It often seems that only a reasonable guarantee of success will free an individual or group to take a chance. Such a stance leads to conformity, to a repetition of the past, to excessive caution and defensiveness. We feel that risk-taking is an essential quality in adaptable, growthful organizations; taking a chance is necessary for creativity and change. Also, individuals and groups do learn by making mistakes. Risk-taking involves being willing 'to take the monkey on my back', and it takes courage to do so. It also takes courage and ingenuity on the part of the organization to foster such behavior.

At TRW Systems, the president and many of the senior executives were until recently located on the fifth floor of one of the organization's buildings, and part of the language of the organization was 'the fifth floor', meaning that place where many of the power figures resided. This phrase was used quite often in discussion: 'The fifth floor feels that we should . . . .' In working with groups one or two levels below the top executives to explore what they might do about some of the frustrations they were experiencing in getting their jobs done, one of the things that dominated the early discussions was the wish that somehow 'the fifth floor' would straighten things out. For example, a group of engineers of one division was having problems with a group of engineers of another division, and they stated that 'the fifth floor' (or at least one of its executives) ought to go over to the people in the other division and somehow 'give them the word'. After a while, however, they began to realize that it really was not very fruitful or productive to talk about what they wished someone else would do, and they began to face the problem of what they could do about the situation directly.

The discussion then became quite constructive and creative, and a number of new action items were developed and later successfully implemented—even though there was no assurance of successful outcomes at the time the action items were decided upon.

Away from a view of process work as being unproductive effort toward seeing it as essential to effective task accomplishment—In the past and often in the present, productive effort has been seen as that which focused directly on the production of goods and services. Little attention has been paid to the processes by which such effort takes place; to do so has often been viewed as a waste of time. Increasingly, however, the relevance to task accomplishment of such activities as team maintenance and development, diagnosis and working through of interpersonal and intergroup communication barriers, confrontation efforts for resolution of organizationally dysfunctional personal and interpersonal hangups, and assessment and improvement of existing modes of decision-making is being recognized. And, in fact, we harbor growing doubts with respect to the continued usefulness of the notion of a task-process dichotomy. It seems to us that there are many activities which can make contributions to task accomplishment and that the choice from among these is essentially an economic one.

21

Within TRW Systems, proposals are constantly being written in the hope of obtaining new projects from the Department of Defense, NASA, and others. These proposals are done under very tight time constraints. What quite often happens is that the request for the proposal is received from the customer and read very quickly by the principals involved. Everybody then charges off and starts working on the proposal because of the keenly felt time pressure. Recently, on a very major proposal, the proposal manager decided that the first thing he should do was spend a couple of days (out of a three-month period of available time) meeting with the principals involved. In this meeting, they would not do any writing of the proposal but would talk about how they were going to proceed, make sure they were all making the same assumptions about who would be working on which subsystem, how they would handle critical interfaces, how they woud handle critical choice points during the proposal period, and so on. Many of the principals went to the meeting with a great deal of skepticism, if not impatience. They wanted to get 'on with the job', which to them meant writing the proposal. Spending a couple of days talking about 'how things were to be done' was not defined by them as productive work. After the meeting, and after the proposal had been written and delivered to the customer, a critique was held on the process used. Those involved in general reported very favorably on the effects of the meeting which took place at the beginning of the proposal-writing cycle. They reported things such as 'The effect of having spent a couple of days as we did meant that at that point when we then charged off and started actually writing the proposal, we were able to function as if we had already been working together for perhaps two months. We were much more effective with each other and much more efficient, so that in the final analysis, it was time well spent.' By giving attention to their ways of getting work done, they clearly had facilitated their ability to function well as a team.

Away from a primary emphasis on competition towards a much greater emphasis on collaboration—A pervasive value in the organizational milieu is competition. Competition is based on the assumption that desirable resources are limited in quantity and that individuals or groups can be effectively motivated through competing against one another for the possession of these resources. But competition can often set man against man and group against group in dysfunctional behavior, including a shift of objectives from obtaining the limited resource to blocking or destroying the competitor. Competition inevitably results in winners and losers, and at least some of the hidden costs of losing can be rather high in systemic terms.

Collaboration, on the other hand, is based on the assumption that the desirable limited resources can be shared among the participants in a mutually satisfactory manner and, even more important, that it is possible to increase the quantity of the resources themselves.

As organizational work becomes more highly specialized and complex, with its accomplishment depending more and more on the effective interaction of individuals and groups, and as the organic or systems views of organizational functioning become more widely understood, the viability of collaboration as an organizational mode becomes ever clearer. Individuals and groups are often highly interdependent, and such interdependency needs to be facilitated through collaborative behavior rather than walled off through competition. At the same time, collaborative behavior must come to be viewed as reflecting strength rather than weakness.

In organizations which have a high degree of interdependency, one of the problems people run into regarding the handling of this interdependency is that they look for simple solutions to complex problems. Simple solutions do not produce very good results because they deal with the symptoms, rather than with the real problems.

A major reorganization recently took place within TRW Systems. The president of the organization sketched out the broad, general directions of the reorganization, specifying details only in one or two instances. He assigned to a large number of working committees the development of the details of the new organization. The initial reaction of some people was that these were things that the president himself should be deciding. The president, however, did not feel he had enough detailed understanding and knowledge to come up with many of the appropriate answers. He felt strongly that those who had the knowledge should develop the answers. This was an explicit, conscious recognition on his part of the fact that he did indeed need very important inputs from other people in order to effect the changes he was interested in making. These working committees turned out to be very effective. As a result of the president's approach, the reorganization proceeded with far less disruption and resistance than is typically the case in major reorganizations.

Another example involved a major staff function which was experiencing a great deal of difficulty with other parts of the organization. The unit having the trouble made the initial decision to conduct briefings throughout the organization to explain what they were really trying to accomplish, how they were organized, what requirements they had to meet for outside customers, and so on. They felt that their job would be easier if they could solicit better understanding. What actually took place was quite different. Instead of conducting briefings to convince the 'heathen', the people in this unit revised their plan and met with some key people from other parts of the company who had to deal with them to ask what the unit was doing that was creating problems at the interface. After receiving a great deal of fairly specific data, the unit and the people with whom they consulted developed joint collaborative action items for dealing with the problems. This way of approaching the problem quickly turned interfaces that had been very negative and very hostile into ones that were relatively cooperative. The change in attitude on both sides of the interface provided a positive base for working toward satisfactory solutions to the problems.

Some implications of these values in transition

Many people would agree with the value trends stated in this paper and indeed claim that they use these guidelines in running their own organizations. However, there is often quite a gap between saying that you believe in these values and actually practicing them in meaningful, important ways. In many organizations, for example, there is a management by objectives process which has been installed and used for several years—an approach which can involve the implementation of some of the values stated earlier in this paper. If, however, one closely examines how this process takes place in many organizations, it is in fact a very mechanical one, one which is used very defensively in some cases. What emerges is a statement of objectives which has obtained for the boss what he really wants, and, at the end of the year, protects the subordinate if he does not do everything that his boss thought he might do. It becomes a 'Pearl Harbor file'. The point that needs emphasis is that the payoff in implementing these values by techniques is not in the techniques themselves but in how they are applied and in what meaning their use has for the people involved.

To us, the implementation of these values clearly involves a bias regarding organizational development efforts. Believing that people have vast amounts of untapped potential and the capability and desire to grow, to engage in meaningful collaborative relationships, to be creative in organizational contexts, and to be more authentic, we feel that the most effective change interventions are therapeutic in nature. Such interventions focus directly on the hangups, both personal and organizational, that block a person from realizing his potential. We are referring to interventions which assist a person in breaking through the neurotic barriers in himself, in others around him, and in the ongoing culture.

We place a strong emphasis on increasing the sanity of the individuals in the organization and of the organization itself. By this we mean putting the individuals and the organization more in touch with the realities existing within themselves and around them. With respect to the individual, this involves his understanding the consequences of his behavior. How do people feel about him? How do they react to him? Do they trust him? With respect to the organization, it involves a critical examination of its culture and what that culture produces: the norms, the values, the decision-making processes, the general environment that it has created and maintained over a period of time.

There are obviously other biases and alternatives available to someone approaching organizational development work. One could concentrate on structural interventions: How should we organize? What kind of charters should people in various functional units have? The bias we are stating does not mean that structure, function, and charters are irrelevant, but that they are less important and have considerably less leverage in the early stages of organizational development efforts than working with the individuals and groups in a therapeutic manner. Furthermore, as an individual becomes more authentic and interpersonally competent, he becomes far more capable of creative problem-solving. He and his associates have within them more resources for dealing with questions of structure, charters, and operating procedures, in more relevant and creative ways, than does someone from outside their system. Such therapeutic devices include the full range of laboratory methods usually identified with the NTL Institute: sensitivity training, team-building, intergroup relationship-building, and so on. They also include individual and group counseling within the organization, and the voluntary involvement of individuals in various forms of psychotherapy outside the organization.

In order to achieve a movement towards authenticity, focus must be placed on developing the whole person and in doing this in an organic way. The program cannot be something you crank people through; it must be tailored in a variety of ways to individual needs as they are expressed and identified. In time, therapy and individual growth (becoming more in touch with your own realities) become values in and of themselves. And as people become less demotivated and move toward authenticity, they clearly demonstrate that they have the ability to be creative about organization matters, and this too becomes a value shared within the organization. Once these values are introduced and people move towards them, the movement in and of itself will contain many forces that make for change and open up new possibilities in an organization. For example, as relationships become more trustworthy, as people are given more responsibility, as competition gives way to collaboration, people experience a freeing up. They are more apt to challenge all the given surroundings, to test the limits, to try new solutions, and to rock the boat. This can be an exciting and productive change, but it can also be troublesome, and a variety of responses to it must be expected.

Therapeutic efforts are long-term efforts. Movement towards greater authenticity, which leads to an organization's culture becoming more positive, creative, and growthful, is something that takes a great deal of time and a great deal of energy. In this kind of approach to organizational development, there is more ambiguity and less stability than in other approaches that might be taken. Patience, persistence, and confidence are essential through time if significant change is to occur and be maintained.

For the organizational development effort to have some kind of permanency, it is very important that it becomes an integral part of the line organization and its mode of operating. Many of the people involved in introducing change in organizations are in staff positions, typically in personnel. If, over time, the effort continues to be mainly one carried out by staff people, it is that much more tenuous. Somehow the total organization must be involved, particularly those people with line responsibility for the organization's success and for its future. They must assimilate the effort and make it a part of their own behavior within the organization. In other words, those people who have the greatest direct impact on and responsibility for creating, maintaining, and changing the culture of an organization must assume direct ownership of the change effort.

In the transition and beyond it, these changes can produce problems for the organization in confronting the outside world with its traditional values. For example, do you tell the truth to your customers when you are experiencing problems building a product for them, or do you continue to tell them that everything is going along fine? For the individual, there can be problems in other relationships around him, such as within his family at home. We do not as yet have good methods developed for dealing with these conflicts, but we can certainly say that they will take place and will have to be worked out.

As previously stated, the Career Development program at TRW Systems, now in its fifth year of operation, is an effort in which both authors have been deeply involved. We feel it is one of the more promising examples of large-scale, long-term, systematic efforts to help people move toward the values we have outlined.

One question that is constantly raised about efforts such as the Career Development program at TRW Systems relates to assessing their impact. How does one know there has been a real payoff for the organization and its members? Some behavioral scientists have devised rather elaborate, mechanical tools in order to answer this question. We feel that the values themselves suggest the most relevant kind of measurement. The people involved have the capacity to determine the relevance and significance to them and to their organizational units of what they are doing. Within TRW Systems, a very pragmatic approach is taken. Questions are asked such as: Do we feel this has been useful? Are these kinds of problems easier to resolve? Are there less hidden agenda now? Do we deal more quickly and effectively with troublesome intergroup problems? The payoff is primarily discussed in qualitative terms, and we feel this is appropriate. It does not mean that quantitative judgements are not possible, but to insist on reducing the human condition to numbers, or to believe that it can be done, is madness.

The role of the person introducing change (whether he is staff or in the line) is a very tough, difficult, and, at times, lonely one. He personally must be as congruent as he can with the values we have discussed. If people perceive him to be outside the system of change, they should and will reject him. He must be willing and able to become involved as a person, not merely as the expert who will fix everybody else up. He, too, must be in process. This is rewarding, but also very difficult.

Introducing change into a social system almost always involves some level of resistance to that change. Accepting the values we have described means that one will not be fully satisfied with the here and now because the limits of man's potential have certainly not been reached. All we know for sure is that the potential is vast. Never accepting the *status quo* is a rather lonely position to take. In effect, as one of our colleagues has put it, you are constantly saying to yourself, 'Fifty million Frenchmen are wrong!' From our own experience, we know that this attitude can produce moments when one doubts one's sanity: 'How come nobody else seems to feel the way I do, or to care about making things better, or to believe that it is possible to seek improvements?' Somehow, these moments must be worked through, courage must be drawn upon, and new actions must follow.

We are struck with and saddened by the large amounts of frustration, feelings of inadequacy, insecurity, and fear that seem to permeate groups of behavioral science practitioners when they meet for seminars or workshops. Belief in these values must lead to a bias towards optimism about the human condition. 'Man does have the potential to create a better world, and I have the potential to contribute to that effort.' But in addition to this bias towards optimism, there has to be a recognition of the fundamental fact that we will continuously have to deal with resistance to change, including resistances within ourselves. People are not standing in line outside our doors asking to be freed up, liberated, and upended. Cultures are not saying: 'Change us, we can no longer cope, we are unstable.' Commitment to trying

26

to implement these values as well as we can is not commitment to an easy, safe existence. At times, we can be bone weary of confrontation, questioning, probing, and devil's-advocating. We can have delightful fantasies of copping out on the whole mess and living on some island. We can be fed up with and frightened by facing someone's anger when we are confronting him with what is going on around him. We can be worn out from the continuous effort to stretch ourselves as we try to move towards living these values to the fullest.

On the other hand, the rewards we experience can be precious, real, and profound. They can have important meaning for us individually, for those with whom we work, and for our organizations. Ultimately, what we stand for can make for a better world—and we deeply know that this is what keeps us going.

References

1. McGREGOR, Douglas, M. *The Professional Manager.* N.Y.: McGraw-Hill, 1967, p. 244.
2. BENNIS, Warren G. *Changing Organizations.* N.Y.: McGraw-Hill, 1966, p. 4.

PART TWO: Focus on methods
and phases of development

As I mentioned in the Introduction, it is not really possible to communicate a really personal experience through the medium of words. A description can never be the same as the thing itself. There have been attempts at telling others what T-Group Training is all about (sometimes called 'group dynamics', 'sensitivity training', 'group relations training'). In chapter 3, Rein van der Vegt and Raymond Caldwell present a clear picture of what a manager might expect to find of value. Obviously there is no such thing as a standard training experience. Every group, every course must be different because the people who attend are different and the content of discussion turns on the personal relations that are built up. This membership theme and learning how to learn is discussed more fully in chapter 4. Lee Bradford, one of the founders of T-Group Training in 1947, has done much to develop this powerful tool of inductive learning and learning from one's own immediately felt experiences. In his article, he stresses four learning goals—learning how to learn, learning how to give help, becoming more sensitive to what goes on in the group, and being a more effective contributor in a work group.

Yet, while no two groups are ever alike, when trainers have run many groups they begin to discover common patterns and stages of development in the activities of different groups. Warren Bennis and Herbert Shepard, two skilled trainers, as early as 1956 wrote a paper entitled 'A Theory of Group Development', and which is reproduced as chapter 5. In this they describe the central issues that get discussed in one way or another by every group—power, affection, authority, and intimacy. If these words seem strange to those who have not yet attended such a course—perhaps with the thought 'What have feelings and attitudes got to do with WORK'—all one can say is that these *are* the topics normal hardworking managers want to discuss and want to resolve to their own satisfaction.

Twenty years ago the focus of human relations training was on helping individuals to build more effective working relationships with their peers and subordinates. Gradually, those who designed those courses saw the need to use their expertise to help create organization climates that would allow those interpersonal skills to flourish. This is the theme of chapter 6 in which Howard Baumgartel shows how new styles of managing and new personal attitudes are being called for if organizations are to remain effective in rapidly changing environments.

3. The laboratory method of human relations training for managers

Rein van der Vegt and Raymond B. Caldwell

We conceive a manager as being a person who is seeking to control and regulate a whole range of technical, economic, political, and social processes within the organization in which he is working. He is also in continuous interaction with the environment, which is primarily made up of other organizations, social and political institutions, and of individuals in their roles as consumers, members of the public and members of other organizations and institutions.

The foregoing appears to be a broad definition of the role of the manager and seems a little too vague a definition, upon which to design a graduate course in administration.

A quick perusal of the content of many courses provided for the students of management gives the impression of a growing but, as yet, disconnected discipline. Both students, staff, and other interested parties still express dissatisfaction with the design of such courses, usually on the grounds that many of the inputs are irrelevant to the manager's needs. This dissatisfaction is in part due to the fact that people have no clear idea of the nature of the manager's role.

A precise statement of the role requirements and needs of managers is a difficult task which would require a great deal of research. However, the fact that human relations training forms an integral part of many management courses reveals a few of the assumptions about how the role of the manager is perceived.

Assumptions and objectives

Before describing the method of human relations training, we would like to make explicit some of the assumptions on which the educational objectives are based:

1 An important aspect of a manager's work is concerned with working in and with groups. These groups carry out a variety of activities, such as making decisions,

• Reproduced with permission from *Management*, Journal of the Irish Management Institute, Vol. XV, June, 1968.

developing plans, gathering data or performing a concrete task. Groups, it would appear, are important vehicles for the manager in carrying out many of his tasks and he generally finds that a great deal of his time is spent in planning committees, board meetings and staff discussions, etc.

It would appear that the effectiveness and productivity of groups in business and other organizations is related to the specific characteristics of these groups, and therefore it is important for the manager to know something about the dynamics of small group life. Such knowledge is especially important for the managers who are compelled to rely on groups for the carrying out of tasks which are instrumental in achieving organizational goals. Therefore, our first educational objective could be formulated as *increasing one's understanding of group phenomena and of the dynamics of groups at work.* This implies increasing one's ability to diagnose the nature of those interpersonal and group reactions which sometimes hamper a working group's progress, i.e., productivity and efficiency in dealing with various tasks.

2 In these groups, however, one participates in several roles: as leading managers, as subordinates, as consultants, but basically as the person one happens to be. Each person has his own specific input to make to the group: his capacities, his feelings, his needs and wishes, his personal goals. The processes which help or hinder a group in the achievement of its tasks are greatly influenced by these personal factors. If a manager is using a particular group in order to accomplish some task, then it would seem important for him to know both what impact he makes on the group and on other individuals in the group. The manager will want answers to such questions as: How do the other members perceive me? Are there any discrepancies between my intentions and the way people perceive my intentions? Why do people resist my proposals? Why do they accept my points of view so easily, too easily? etc.

On that basis, the second objective could be formulated as: *increasing the awareness of one's own functioning in small groups.* A greater awareness and understanding of both group processes and one's own functioning under a varying set of conditions in a small group are important for managerial activities.

3 There is a third related aspect. Every person tends to hold more or less consciously a sort of philosophy with respect to human nature, which usually implies a set of assumptions about the motivation behind other people's actions, and these assumptions tend to influence the way a manager relates to his subordinates. Thus, a manager who holds that employees are not to be trusted, will be influenced by this assumption in his leadership style, his freedom to delegate, his policy-making, etc. But we seldom check these implicit notions or assumptions; What they are and whether they are valid. Yet to answer this complex question is particularly important because the manager, in formulating his policy and in taking actions, will be guided by them, valid or not, with respect to individual and group behaviour.

Thus, the third educational objective should be: *testing one's general assumptions with regard to human behaviour in groups and one's own behaviour in particular.*

32

4 Whatever definition (and there are many) seems appropriate to managerial activities, ours would include the *problem-solving* or *conflict-management* aspect. In the context of this article, this implies dealing with interpersonal or intergroup problems and conflicts.

In problem-solving, the eventual solution tends to depend largely on a manager's perception and formulation of the initial problem. His formulation usually includes some of the characteristics of the situation which he perceives as the main determinants of the problem. A common reaction to problem-solving in human conflict situations is a blaming approach, which tends to localize the causes of the conflict in the individual by blaming his particular personality make-up. Thus, one often hears managers make such statements as 'He is just plain obstinate', or 'Smith is far too conservative, as long as he is around we will never finish the job'.

Such statements lead to a formulation of the problem in terms of stable, almost unchangeable, personality factors, and are usually a pretty sound rationalization for leaving the conflict unresolved. Naturally, this is not to imply that personality factors at a more or less deeper level do not play a part in business organizations; they definitely do. However, there is ample social psychological research evidence which proves that individual and group behaviours are also highly influenced by the social and psychological *conditions* under which these behaviours are being displayed. A search for these conditions, as an essential part of the manager's problem-solving activity, implies a different approach from the former one. It means looking for 'determining conditions' more than for 'single causes among personality traits'. (For example, obstinacy or uncooperativeness could then be defined as a symptom of a still unresolved interpersonal conflict and not as a more or less stable, unmodifiable trait of a person or a total group.)

The reason for stressing this is simple. The former approach leaves the manager relatively powerless, as he defined the problem in terms of almost stable traits or factors. The latter one provides him with the opportunity to change things, that is, to work on changing the conditions, especially as he is in a position at least to initiate the process of changing the conditions under his control. Of course, it needs more than having formal authority; it requires both an awareness of the characteristics of the problem as well as skill in working with individuals and groups.

Within the context of an educational setting, it seems important to us to start the development of this problem-solving approach, which then implies: *learning to define (inter-)personal problems in terms of the dynamics of social and psychological conditions.*

The method: A short description

Objectives can be reached in a variety of ways. The educational method being used in our course resembles basically the so-called 'laboratory method of learning'. Although there are many variations in the objectives and design of human relations training laboratories, the method can be described as follows:

Emphasizing inductive learning

Many know the method whereby the student is first offered a rule, a principle, or a concept, which is then explained by the teacher. This is then followed by carefully selected examples to illustrate the principle or concept, after which the student is given material for practising, for the purpose of familiarizing himself with the principle or concept. This 'rule-example' sequence is known to us from many didactic situations. However, we also know the reverse: the student is asked to select certain examples or experiences from a range of concrete observations. Thus, by inductive reasoning, the student can create out of experience and observations a principle or concept which can be verified by further experience or by comparison with accepted theories. Consequently, the starting point of such a learning process is not so much a carefully presented concept or theory, but rather a learning situation which enables one to make concrete observations and to discover by induction, principles and concepts which underlie the observations.

This inductive or experimental method of learning is an essential aspect of the laboratory method of learning in human relations. The method is experience-centred, hence the term 'laboratory method'. The group members focus their attention almost exclusively on the actual here and now phenomena in their group. By doing so, they are using actual observations, perceptions and experiences with respect to ongoing processes in their own group. The basic idea is simple: in order to learn about group dynamics each person uses his own group as a field of study. So the members are both producers and consumers of the phenomena under study. The actual experiences, observations, etc., shared by all members constitute the data upon which generalizations with regard to interpersonal and group processes are based. The group, by studying its own development, provides itself with the necessary data for gaining insight into group dynamics. Staff members help to install the conditions in the group which will facilitate such an inductive type of learning, and they also provide theoretical information to help the group members integrate their group experiences on an intellectual level. The theory behind this is that meaningful and integrated learning will take place when participants have first hand experience of group processes. It also makes it possible for theories of group dynamics to be presented on the spot and illustrated with behaviour which participants have created themselves.

Thus, the approach to learning is one in which participants collect data, test its accuracy, and generalize it on a theoretical level, the method is therefore basically inductive and experimental.

Emphasizing the here and now

It will be clear from the above that, guided by the training staff, the group members focus exclusively on the actual here and now processes in their T-(=training) Group. This means that the members not only originate their own data for study, but also that they pay an exclusive attention to perceptions, feelings, etc., arising out of interactions within their own group. Negatively put, they usually do not study topics stemming from the outside world, i.e., outside the context of their group.

34

(This holds true for the T-Group sessions; in other programme-activities within the laboratory these topics may be relevant, and thus can be discussed at length in order to integrate T-Group learnings with there and then, that is: back-home problems.) Issues directly related to people's more inner, personal realms and specific personality structure are also not discussed. The legitimate—legitimized by the training staff—fields of study are present interrelational aspects. Within this domain, people can share mutual reactions and feelings with respect to current phenomena in their group. It is not the whys, but, basically, the hows of group behaviour which are the primary focus of attention (the impact one has on others, and vice versa). Of course, inner motivations are at stake, as they are in everyday life situations; the very nature of the course can emphasize this inner, more personal area. So, it is possible that the individual member may discover for himself, out of the group's here and now study, some inner reasons for his behaviour, his hitherto blind spot. The T-group, however, is not the place for him to work out all the intricacies of his personal discoveries. 'It is the place for him to gain insight into his social self—to see how his behaviours impinge on others' (Miles, 1959).

It is the responsibility of the training staff to install this basic rule of the here and now process. Furthermore, both members and staff must be involved in setting up conditions appropriate to thorough study of these phenomena.

Emphasizing process on a group and individual level

Managers who use groups as a means of accomplishing an organizational task should recognize that the nature of the particular task will result in the group becoming structured in a certain way. Depending on the task, an appropriate division of labour will be created, together with procedures for efficient information flow. Certain rules concerning the type of behavior allowed will be tacitly accepted and adhered to in varying degrees. There will also be a power structure, usually consisting of one or a number of positions in the group, from which some individuals can exert influence.

These structures tend to become fairly rigid in time, and often tend to be applied indiscriminately to new and more complex tasks. In the training laboratory, participants should be given the opportunity to build a group structure from scratch and, as their group develops, to institute new structures to suit changing circumstances. In this way, participants can gain insight into the various characteristics of group structure and learn new skills in redesigning such structures to meet new needs.

Groups and individuals not only occupy themselves with tasks, they also have to find a set of solutions for their preoccupations. By preoccupations are meant socio-emotional concerns which group members have in relation to each other; these are basic to each human encounter, and any group of persons has to find a solution for these common interpersonal issues. For example, a predominant preoccupation which members of a new group experience is the issue of acceptance or rejection: some members will argue their own point of view *ad infinitum* because

35

they unconsciously feel that rejection of their ideas implies rejection of themselves as people. Another preoccupation is the issue around control and leadership: What are the criteria for leadership behaviour? How can I influence and whom can I influence? How can I relate to authority figures? Under what conditions am I myself willing to be influenced?

As we indicated, we assume that it is important to know more about these processes in order to find answers to obvious questions like, why it is that sometimes a group of highly competent persons is not able to work creatively on a task. It could quite well be that, although technically competent, these persons are hampered by still unresolved socio-emotional issues, and, consequently, they may find it difficult to relate to each other in a resourceful way. It is in the T-Group that the members explicitly study these common undercurrents, these group processes. As such they occupy themselves with pre-occupations. But, at the same time, by studying the development of their own group, they are actively engaged in the birth of a small social system.

Developing conditions to facilitate feedback on the person's group behaviour

A central theme of human relations training based on the laboratory method principles is, besides learning about group processes, increasing individual insight into functioning within the group: How do I react in situations of conflict, of power exertion, of being accepted or rejected? The method explicitly tries to install those conditions which will enable the group members to give and receive feedback on each other's behaviour in the group, that is, conditions which make it possible to exchange here and now information on how a person reacted on certain group issues.

A general condition is the psychological safety in the group: a supportive climate where it is safe to receive information from others as to the effect our own behaviour has on them. Sometimes such information can highlight discrepancies between intentions and how others actually perceive the intentions. Participants who discover such discrepancies can then construct and experiment with new ways of behaving which are more efficient in communicating their ideas.

Emphasis on integrating intellectual, emotional and behavioural aspects of learning

Basically, learning is a problem-solving activity. The laboratory training method, as an educational method, holds the conception of learning as a *process of change*, involving the person's cognitions, feelings, attitudes and behavioural skills. So, the training design should—within the limits of the objectives—focus on these aspects in an integrated way. The assumption is that an integrated approach increases the likelihood of change on all relevant levels of functioning, while making newly acquired knowledge and understanding more meaningful for personal life. This characteristic of the laboratory training method closely relates to the first one, which stressed inductive learning principles (learning by experience). We can illustrate the relationship by drawing upon Lewin (Lewin, 1948), a social psychologist whose contributions to theory and practice are highly important.

Learning by experience is seen as a central principle of the laboratory training method. But 'even extensive firsthand experience does not automatically create correct concepts (knowledge)' (Lewin, 1948). And we agree. Thus, more needs to be done, among other things, helping the person to clarify on an intellectual level his actual group experiences, so that things fall into place, i.e., will become part of his cognitive structure. But on the other hand: 'as a rule, the possession of correct knowledge does not suffice to rectify false perception'. This implies that transmitting information and knowledge—though important—does not necessarily lead to changes in values, attitudes, or behaviour. There is ample research evidence to support this point of view.

The conception of learning as a process of change is, though simple and by no means new, essential. It provides, however, the educator with a still broadening range of educational techniques, based on principles and strategies of change as developed in the behavioral sciences.

The laboratory training method has been labelled as a major innovation in education (Bradford *et al.*). This seems partly due to the fact that in this method newly developed learning principles became operationalized in a more or less integrated way. Yet, there remains a lot to be done.

The group as a vehicle for effecting change

One point which Lewin and his coworkers made was that behavioral attitudes, opinions, etc., are not only formed in groups, but are also supported by the groups to which the individual belongs. This means, in practice, that, when trying to change the attitudes and opinions of the individual, his actual group relations have to be taken into consideration as well, since his attitudes and opinions tend to be supported by these group relations.

This way of thinking, which over the years has become common intellectual property, has consequences for putting a strategy of change into practice. It implies, among other things, that the group is seen as a vehicle for effecting individual and organizational changes, and, therefore, in many aspects of the laboratory method we see a group-oriented approach. An extreme consequence is that changes on an individual level imply a reorientation towards the groups to which the individual belongs. To see or do something in a different way, the individual has to adapt himself to groups of which he is a part or of which he would like to become a part. This means that a process of change has social or group implications, and that the latter can serve as a strategic leverage point for an attempt to change attitudes and behaviour.

The above six items are a few essential characteristics of the laboratory training method, and it is obvious that training staffs will give different interpretations of them, partly due to differences in professional background and personal styles. Thus, some emphasize integrating emotional and cognitive learnings; others the 'experiencing' aspect. Staff members also differ in focus: some operate predominantly on the level of group processes, while others prefer a more personal level. Moreover, training courses differ in their specific objectives, population characteristics, and practical arrangements like duration, location, etc. Consequently, several factors lead to variations in the actual training design. We will turn now to a brief description of the most important components of the training design.

Design of the course: Some components

An educational programme can be considered as an operationalization of educational objectives. Designing a programme and devising the subparts means basically 'translating' objectives into learning experiences serving as vehicles for reaching educational goals. Furthermore, ideally speaking, a programme should not be conceived of as a series of separate or disconnected activities, but as an integrated set. This is especially important for the course we are describing here, as one of the basic principles listed above stresses integrating intellectual, emotional and behavioural aspects of learning. So, when mentioning some of the components, it should be borne in mind that, in practice, deliberate attempts are made to relate these as much as possible.

The *T-(= training) Group* is the central component of the programme. It is the vital vehicle in bringing about learnings about group processes, and about oneself as a member by studying the here and now data. The T-Group usually consists of about 12 persons and one or two trainers. The group starts its life in a somewhat unorthodox way: without formal rules, without an agenda, without a given formal structure, and without stated or fixed procedures. Even the trainer does not exert leadership or chairmanship in the traditional sense. Of course, there are some basic rules. The core of these basic rules implies the here and now and the group process focus, and it is the trainer who attempts to install these rules right from the start of the T-Group sessions. And, of course, there is an explicit task, namely, studying interpersonal processes in one's own group. However, it is obvious that in the beginning stage of the group's life this is not an easy task to accomplish. So, the group members find themselves in a relatively unstructured situation. The rationale for this is that an initial lack of group structure confronts the members with the problem of developing a structure of relationships which meets task and personal needs. For instance: How to organize for work, how to relate to each other and to the trainers as authority figures, and what and how to contribute to the group discussion. And other questions like these. In other words, this initial lack of structure creates a series of dilemmas for the group and will consequently lead to searching or problem-solving activities on the part of the group members. The group will have to discover how to establish its structure, its rules and norms, its mutual relationships, as answers to, or solutions for, its dilemmas. But, paradoxically speaking, this very activity is at the same time working on the (educational) task, i.e., learning how a group organizes itself. This is, in our opinion, an important aspect. As has been said before, in daily life one tends to perceive these structural and normative provisions as almost 'impersonal givens'.

In the here and now of their T-Group, the members are in a position to see that structures and norms are products of group life, fulfilling a function in relating the group to the task and in regulating their interactions and relationships. Over time, conditions in the T-Group change, due to changes in the task and in the perceptions and needs of the persons involved. Former solutions become no longer functional and have to be modified. So, the life of the T-Group is essentially a process of change. Being involved in this continuous group developmental process, provides the members with opportunities to study these phenomena. For instance, having solved at some point in the life of the group the issue of leadership and power exertion, later on the members will find themselves in a position to reexamine this issue, due to changed needs and requirements in their own group.

Thus, on a socio-emotional level, a group which is working on its own identity problems may allow the leadership roles to be distributed to the few members who are most articulate and fluent in describing their experiences in the group. If the group then moves on to deal with the problems of openness and trust, leadership roles may have to be redistributed to those members who have high trust levels coupled with a relatively high emotional investment in the learning experience of the laboratory. In many cases, then, a leadership struggle can develop between two subgroups, namely a highly articulate, low trust, subgroup and a not so articulate, high trust, high investment, subgroup.

All the phenomena which are studied explicitly in the T-Group occur in one form or another in ordinary everyday family and work groups. Phenomena like leadership struggles, issues of trust and openness, different reactions to problems of change, decision-making, the problem of expressing warm or antagonistic feelings, are issues of our everyday lives, and it is in the T-Group that we have a chance to experience and study these things directly, explicitly and legitimately.

But being involved in this process of learning implies also a personal confrontation. That is, in and through working on actual group issues, the person will be provided an opportunity to experience and to clarify how he personally tends to feel and to react in typical group situations of power exertion, of conformity pressures, of acceptance and rejection. Under conditions of trust and supportiveness—conditions the group will have to establish gradually—the other members can provide him feedback on his group behaviour by giving him here and now information on the way they reacted to his actions in the group.

It is the role of the trainer to facilitate the group members in studying their own group. Each trainer has a different set of objectives as well as different ways of achieving them. Some trainers intervene quite a lot, others may say very little and, generally, the functions which the trainer performs are taken over gradually by the members themselves.

Given the necessary conditions, life in the T-Group is involving and potentially learningful. However, other programme activities are essential in order to further intellectual clarification and to facilitate transfer of T-Group learnings. In the T-Group, and in the other programme components, there are ample opportunities to practice one's skills in diagnosing and in intervening. For example, observational exercises whereby one subgroup provides the other with information on how they carried out a task. Or an exercise in which one person acts as a consultant to another group member, who is engaged in a problem-solving meeting. Or sessions whereby each individual of one subgroup can take any initiative in helping the task subgroup in such a way that their work will be facilitated. All these exercises give the student opportunities to take an active intervening or consultant role, while being in the position to apply the knowledge he gained during later T-Group sessions. The consulting aspect can also be highlighted in an extended, special exercise. The individual, participating in a group of three persons, is asked to present a real human relations problem in which he is personally involved. One of the other two group members acts as a consultant to him, and the other as an observer of the consulting process. After having discussed this problem for a certain time, they change roles. This finally leads to a summarizing discussion on problems with respect to giving and receiving help, problem-solving dimensions, and (role-) relational aspects of these types of exercises.

Lectures or lecturettes are essential for clarifying intellectually the T-Group processes in which the participants are engaged. The timing of theoretical inputs is important, as the (inductive) learning theory holds that information will be more readily assimilated and integrated on a cognitive level when issues have actually been experienced and worked through in the T-Group and then followed up with a theoretical presentation.

Furthermore, it is important to introduce concrete tasks, be they simple case studies or a planning group who designs part of the programme of the laboratory. This latter type of activity is most useful for giving participants the opportunity to apply knowledge gained to a real life type of situation.

In practice, most programmes based on the principle indicated above, are highly flexible in nature. 'Planning educational activities' means here constantly taking into account the needs of the group members, and the overall objectives of the course. The final programme, however, is the product of a dynamic interplay between learning needs, objectives and (staff and student) resources. This implies that the realization of the programme results from a collaborative effort of both students and staff members, both of which are involved in an experimental fact-finding situation which in essence characterizes a laboratory.

So far we have described the assumptions, objectives and methods of the laboratory method of human relations training. We have also described some of the programme components which are used in the design of such training courses. Our basic thesis was that management consists largely of working with groups, and therefore we try to increase managers' awareness of the following areas:

1 Group processes.
2 The manager's own functioning in groups.
3 The manager's assumptions about human behaviour in general.
4 Techniques of conflict resolution.

In describing the method of laboratory training we emphasized the inductive approach to learning, whereby managers actually experience the phenomena under study. We also mentioned that laboratory groups do not study outside topics, but collect data on the functioning of their own groups, and with the help of the training staff, use this data to test for themselves current theories on group dynamics.

References

MILES, MATTHEW B. *Learning to Work in Groups.* New York: Teachers College Press, 1959.
BRADFORD, LELAND P., GIBB, JACK R., and BENNE, KENNETH D. *T-Group Theory and Laboratory Method.* New York: Wiley, 1964.

4. Membership and the learning process*

Leland P. Bradford

Experience in social creativity provided by the T-Group has learning values difficult to secure elsewhere. Seldom in life does one share in the creation of a segment of society. Individuals are born into families where a structure and organization are already present. They enter school, go to a church, become part of a community. In each instance, they confront and accept (or resist) rules, customs, and laws set down for them. Even marriage, where a new family group is created, has relatively established role expectations and cultural traditions; and even when one is a founding member of a new organization, the pattern of organization is largely set through precedent and tradition.

Few people have the opportunity to be tossed, figuratively, from the sky to face the necessity of hacking their way collaboratively out of a social jungle. Given such an opportunity, they might come to understand, on cognitive, feeling, and behavioral levels, the great need for both order and change and the delicate relationship and balance that must lie between them. If in the process they have to re-earn position through present accomplishments rather than to rely on previously secure status symbols, they might become more innovative and creative in other social situations. If through this same process they learn to test assumptions about social organizations, they might refuse to perpetuate archaic organizational models. If they have to create a new kind of organization, they might develop more of the wide range of skills required for responsible membership.

If they examine the interpersonal difficulties encountered in their collaborative struggle out of the social jungle, they might learn important truths about themselves and their relations with others. Each person exists in a network of

● Reproduced with permission from *T-Group Theory and Laboratory Method, 1964*, pp. 190-215, New York: Wiley.

* The author has been helped by a number of individuals in thinking through the materials in this chapter. He particularly wishes to acknowledge the contributions of Chris Argyris, Kenneth Benne, Warren Bennis, Douglas Bunker, Jack Gibb, Edgar Schein, and Ronald Lippitt. Dorothy Mial helped greatly in its final expression.

human interrelationships and a mixture of cultural forces which place conflicting strains on his ability to adjust, to utilize his potential resources, and to grow. As a result, people adjust only partially to their worlds. They allow abilities to atrophy. They secure less than adequate understanding of themselves. Fearful of upsetting the precarious balance of internal-external relationships, they find little opportunity to become more aware of themselves, to find greater meaning in living.

The unstructured nature of the T-Group provides opportunity for these kinds of learnings. Methods of observation and data collection on the complex processes involved in the development of a group help to make sense of these processes. Norms that support an experimental approach to individual and group problems help to give range to what can be learned. The intense personal nature of involvement in the T-Group provides the energy—the motivation—for learning of considerable depth.

Learning may be focused on a number of emphases: on the development of cultural norms in the group; on the process of social organization; on the dynamics of group behavior; on interpersonal relationships; on individual perceptions and motivations; or on individual and group values. Data about all of these aspects of human behavior—far more than can be utilized—are generated in the T-group.

The very fact that so many interrelated learnings are available makes some order and organization of learning goals essential if the trainer is to develop and hold to a set of consistent premises guiding his behavior.

A first goal: Learning how to learn

A first purpose of the T-Group is to help individuals to learn how to learn from their continuing experience in the areas of self-awareness, sensitivity to phenomena of interpersonal behavior, and understanding of the consequences of behavior—one's own and others'. Learning in these areas requires willingness to explore openly one's motivations and one's feelings; to utilize the reactions of others as feedback about the consequences of one's behavior; and to experiment with new ways of behaving. Since each of these steps requires emotional support, the T-group faces the dual task of creating a supportive climate and of developing situations in which members can learn through examining their own experience.

The essence of this learning experience is a transactional process in which the members negotiate as each attempts to influence or control the stream of events and to satisfy his personal needs. Individuals learn to the extent that they expose their needs, values, and behavior patterns so that perceptions and reactions can be exchanged. Behavior thus becomes the currency for transaction. The amount each invests helps to determine the return.

Through this negotiating, the individual can validate or correct his assumptions. He can learn to recognize and use feelings, and he can evaluate his behavior and learn to make it more consistent with his intentions. As individual members grow in these directions, the group itself grows in its capacity to encourage still further individual learning. Through a very genuine experience the group learns that barriers to learning—defensiveness, withdrawal, fear, distrust—can be reduced so

43

that problems of interrelationships can be dealt with on deeper and more realistic levels.

In the process of learning how to learn, the concept of interdependence takes on new meaning. Learning as a transactional process implies *active* negotiation among peers rather than dependence on superiors. It implies mutual help in coping with problems that cannot be solved by 'teacher'. The trainer is himself a party to the transaction. He, too, must be willing to receive reactions as well as to give—to be taught as well as to teach. Indeed, this is one part of the trainer's reward.

In helping individuals to learn how to learn, usually certain attitudes about learning must be changed. Typically, learning is assumed to take place only in formal learning situations. Individuals seek to repeat previous behavior, even if only moderately satisfying, rather than deliberately to seek to change. Most individuals seem unaware that they themselves can engage in a deliberate process of learning from everyday events.

A second goal: Learning how to give help

The transactional nature of the learning process is illustrated by the fact that individuals can most effectively seek and use feedback about their own behavior as they help others in the same process. Resistance to learning may be more clearly seen in others than in oneself. The individual does not feel so alone if others are involved with him in learning. Observing others who are working on problems similar to one's own stimulates ideas for improving one's own behavior. Finally, joint collaboration lessens the possibility that an offer of help will be interpreted as an attack. As these discoveries are made, individuals learn that giving help and receiving help are extremely difficult—but that they can help one another more than they had thought possible.

A third goal: Developing effective membership

A successful transaction requires an association, however temporary, of those persons involved. The more difficult and delicate the transaction, the more carefully developed the association must be, and the more open, stable, and trusting it must become. To build and maintain such an association requires membership skills. Members must develop diagnostic sensitivity to difficulties facing the group, increase their ability to communicate so that diagnostic suggestions will be heard, and learn to behave in ways that will help the group move forward. These membership skills are not easily acquired. Their acquisition is a major goal of the T-Group: in fact, a key to the accomplishment of the other goals.

There are also other reasons why the development of membership ability is important. Each individual needs the satisfaction of participating with others and of being accepted by them. Each discovers part of his own identity as he relates to others. Each should both influence others and be influenced by them if, together, they are to solve problems collaboratively. All of these needs call for the ability to carry out membership functions effectively.

44

In any association, each member brings many differences: different past experiences and present problems; different fears and anxieties about possible consequences of membership; different pressures to learn and to change; different degrees of pain in the process; different assumptions, values, and perceptual screens; different self-concepts; different patterns of relationships to others and to authority; and different approaches to learning. All of these differences must somehow be accommodated by the members if a learning association is to be created.

Maintaining the association is also a membership responsibility. Barriers to openness and trust must be located and reduced; differences in premises about goals and methods discovered and resolved; motivations of individual members understood; normative structures for communication and problem solving developed.

The T-Group provides opportunity for developing insights and skills, at successively deeper levels, necessary for carrying out these membership responsibilities. Participants learn through experience that apathetic, irresponsible, or ineffective membership reduces the effectiveness of the group; that silent or withdrawing members withhold from the group the resources needed for individual and group growth; that irresponsible members distort the group to serve their own purposes. Participants learn that full membership necessitates continuing questioning of assumptions and values underlying behavior and continuing validation of perceptions and diagnoses.

The T-Group process

The T-Group, then, is a crucible in which personal interactions are so fused that learning results. The members provide the data for their own learning as they interact and construct a learning group. In a sense, members write their own textbook as they read it. The trainer faces the task of encouraging and occasionally helping the group members to supply sufficient relevant data, to learn *how* to read the book they are writing, and to utilize the results of the reading in experimenting with new ways of behaving.

The T-Group process accomplishes a substantive goal as well as the methodological goal of developing sensitivity and skill. Learnings about group process, group behavior, and group development are gained from analyzing the dynamics of the T-Group. Thus, the process of group development, with all of the attendant problems of individual change, is itself a part of the content of learning.

The goals of learning to learn and to help others to learn, of developing membership skills, and of increasing sensitivity, are gradually approached as individuals gain more self-awareness, sensitivity to others, diagnostic and problem-solving abilities in group development, and the ability to seek and to accept realistic and responsible membership functions. They are learned in the heat of the transactional process of the T-Group.

This, then, is the T-Group: a group formed for individual learning purposes where the data are created and analyzed by the work of the group and not fed in from outside and interpreted by a teacher, where learning is a group task entered into jointly, where the trainer does not deny the group members the experience of creating and maintaining their own group even though this experience will be difficult and may produce anxiety, and where the motivation for learning comes from the high degree of emotional involvement of the members.

These characteristics suggest dimensions for examining the T-group more thoroughly. They deal with eight central learning factors, around which the remainder of this chapter is built: (1) the ambiguous situation; (2) the identity stress; (3) self-investment or participation; (4) collaboration and learning from peers; (5) motivation for learning; (6) experienced behavior and feedback; (7) group growth and development; (8) trainer-intervention.

Factors of the ambiguous situation and the identity stress

Anyone who has observed or participated in a T-Group has been struck by the extraordinary amount of emotional involvement and energy expenditure. After a two hour session, people frequently feel drained but still eager to continue. Extra sessions often are held. Small clusters of T-Group members continue to talk about the group during meals and recreation periods. Various members sit through long evening hours, playing back the tape-recording of the previous session to squeeze out further meaning. This degree of involvement seems to continue throughout the life of the group. What are the causes of such involvement? Does involvement result in learning or does it inhibit learning? Or both?

One source of emotional involvement, particularly in the early days of the T-Group, lies in the ambiguous situation created by the unstructured beginning. This ambiguity seems to produce stresses related to individual identity and group survival. The question as to whether one wants to be a member of the group, the uncertainty as to how to proceed, the very unpredictability of the situation, cause people to forget much of their learning purposes and to become deeply concerned, first about their own identity and position in the group and then about the survival of the group itself.

The group opens with ambiguity and uncertainty about power and leadership, about goals and pathways to goals, about norms to guide behavior, about which status symbols or efforts will secure a place in the group, about rewards and punishments, and about what will happen to each individual. This situation mobilizes individual defense systems to operate until greater predictability is secured. To some degree, an identity stress is created for each individual. People gain identity partially in relationship to other people, in differentiation from them, and in relationship to position and function in the social organization. In a situation with few boundaries and very little structure and direction, each person is uncertain as to what he is supposed to do and, consequently, who he is to be. Frequently, the identity stress generated in the T-Group motivates individuals to examine many more areas of their lives than the ones involved in the immediate situation.

Each individual is not only uncertain as to how he should behave, as he would be if he were entering an extremely foreign but already formed culture; he is also unable to find, in the beginning T-Group, any obvious pattern of membership through which to discover what is expected of him. The group has not yet established ways to evaluate or utilize contributions. It has developed no way to confer membership. It has not even determined what constitutes membership. What appears to be a rejection to an individual making a suggestion may be merely inability to do anything because no conscious group goal or pattern of procedure is present (in reality, the basic goal of the group in the beginning is the survival of the members). Contributions 'die on the table' for lack of a procedure for testing or accepting. Perceived rejection of what the individual sees as a logical suggestion increases his uncertainty. He interprets the rejection as a reflection upon his ability or as an indication that he is not liked. Increased individual anxiety causes him to listen more to his 'internal noises' than to what others are actually feeling and saying.

The uncertainty with which individuals enter any new situation is thus compounded in the T-Group. Individuals react in a variety of ways. Some deny that there is an uncomfortable and unpredictable situation. Members will say, with hands clenched, that they are relaxed and comfortable. Others seek to handle the situation by withdrawing into the role of an observer. They are here, they say, to learn by watching others behave. Others attempt to work out their own survival by trying to force the group to become a traditional and predictable group. Still others try to coerce the trainer into saving them. When this fails, they may punish him.

An early basic problem facing the T-Group, therefore, is how to handle individual anxiety. The early hours of a T-Group are spent in trying to place other people in relation to self; in discovering their motives, their power or superiority, and their ability to hurt; in endeavoring to find comfortable and familiar situations; in finding out whether one is liked; or in trying to win power or approval. Some of the dependent and counterdependent reactions to the trainer grow out of the desire that he should, as the one known power figure, reduce the discomfort.

Essentially, then, the individual is trying to bring order and security out of chaos. When his first move to get help from the trainer fails, he usually tries to relate the situation to know familar patterns. He may, for instance, suggest that a leader be appointed. The fact that he does not perceive that his suggestion is seen as a desire to take leadership himself reflects the poor perceptual communication in the beginning hours of the group.

Since members differ in their perceptions of what is desirable and what is uncomfortable, early efforts to lead the group around the shoals of discomfort generally result in a clash over leadership. The individual contender may seek out one or more other members who appear to feel the way he does. By attempting to form relationships with them, he seeks support and some validation of his own perceptions. The group forms or takes shape as these efforts to look for support and to confirm perceptions succeed and continue.

In the early days of the T-Group, members are concerned almost exclusively, but not consciously, about individual anxiety. Can I survive? What will happen to me? What will be demanded of me? Can I accept feedback from others? Dare I give it? Yet discussion usually wanders in apparent aimlessness from descriptions of events back home to discussions of abstract or harmless topics and thence to suggestions for immediate group actions without adequate diagnosis. Discussion, interestingly, centres on group procedures or events not overtly related to individual concerns and anxieties.

There are many reasons why this is true. Even under stress over identity there seems to be awareness, or at least hope, that individual anxiety may be reduced by group formation. There are many suggestions for group development—from having formal introductions to electing a leader, developing a formal agenda, or imposing rigid procedures—but little effort to diagnose group problems. If the trainer suggests that diagnosis would be helpful, the group does not hear him—or heed him. This may be because members have had little experience in examining group actions, and there has been little cultural legitimacy for doing so; or it may be because diagnosis, if it means digging into interpersonal relations, could open up areas of personal anxiety.

Yet even in the early hours there is desire to communicate with other people about oneself—but it has to be done in safe ways, and it must not reveal too much. Members tend to discuss themselves in terms of their organizations or events back home. Only much later does it come out how little of this early effort to communicate is really heard.

There is a paradox in the history of the T-Group. When individuals are feeling their own anxieties and fears most keenly, they seem to conspire to keep the discussion centered on group action or on events unrelated to the present anxiety. Later, when some predictability has developed, some norms for sharing feelings and perceptions have been constructed, and greater understanding of one another has been established, concern centers on the group and its developmental problems. But now there is much more discussion of individual feelings, perceptions, and needs. Indeed, group problems are resolved through open discussion of individual reactions. A problem of group movement is examined not only in terms of suggestions for group action, but also in terms of individual perceptions and individual needs.

The stress over problems of individual identity and of group survival is never relieved once and for all, because new events present new threats. Gradually, however, individuals learn that they need to alert their defenses less frequently. Gradually, they see that openness in sharing feelings and motives and willingness to give and receive feedback are not only less dangerous than imagined, but can be extremely helpful if one's goal is to improve interpersonal behavior and to discover more fully one's own identity.

Factor of self-investment or participation

People generally approach learning and change with ambivalence. They would like to improve—provided change is not too threatening. But any learning situation does imply a threat to the individual's perception of himself and to the perception others have of him. The potentiality of failure, the unpredictability of what the future may be like if change is undertaken produce ambivalence. Therefore, people approach learning and change with positive motivation but also with a considerable defense against going too far. This ambivalence toward personal investment is heightened in the T-Group because its ambiguity creates anxiety, and the involvement demanded is not clear.

Here, each individual faces, in heightened form, his own personal problems of membership in a group. As in any other group, he is asking: How important is this group to me? What will its consequences be for me? What gain—at what pain—may I expect? How close do I want to be to these people? How much am I willing to invest? He is concerned, too, about whether he will be accepted and whether he can measure up to expectations. He is uncertain what to contribute or how to measure its effectiveness. His defenses against correction are high.

Learning and improvement follow in large part from the individual's struggle to find membership which both satisfies him and contributes to the group. Satisfying membership implies more than acceptance. It also implies caring behavior. Membership entails the opportunity for growth through contributing out of one's own resources and through concern that others also have an opportunity to grow. When this is achieved, there is less need for individual defenses. The needs and resources of all can be used freely.

In struggling to achieve such membership, individuals acquire new insights into self, into others, and into the group itself. They gain new skills of cooperative action and new ways of learning. They discover, in clearer terms, the problems blocking learning and growth. Gradually, individuals find that they can open themselves up to learn and to help others in learning. A group for learning—that is to say, a group whose members are willing to consider the possibility of personal change—gradually emerges. It takes shape as members learn that they can both influence others and be influenced by them in collaborative problem-solving.

This movement, however, is not easily achieved. Entering an interchange of influence can be extremely threatening; hence the necessity, first, for personal security that the individual's integrity and identity will be maintained, and second, for willingness to invest self—to take out membership, even if this involves risk of exposure and of change.

Effective membership means that the individual has achieved a healthy balance between investment of self and withholding of self. With help from others, he has reduced his anxieties so that he can determine the investment he will make on the basis of relevancy to group concern and to his own interest. He invests himself sufficiently to assume his share (but not more than his share) of responsibility for group movement. He accords others the same opportunity

Investment of self requires considerable awareness of one's own motivations and personal defenses. It also requires awareness of personal identity and sufficient ego strength to relate to others interdependently rather than dependently or counter-dependently. Finally, to invest himself constructively, the individual has to be able to diagnose what is happening in the group. As these learnings take place in the T-Group, members come to see that membership is something to be worked at and earned. They begin to see that through experimentation they may learn how to become more effective members.

Many events in the life of the T-Group can be understood in the light of membership problems. If, for example, the group can be formed into a familiar pattern, and if the individual member can control the group so that it does not go off in threatening directions, then he can feel safe. It is for this reason that the groups often struggle vehemently over issues seemingly of little importance. The struggle is not over the expressed issues, but over the larger issue of group direction and its implications for the personal safety and comfort of the members involved.

The classic split which first separates most T-Groups into those members who wish more imposed structure of goal and procedures and those who are willing to venture down uncharted pathways is part of the battle over membership and group direction; the struggle over this split sometimes takes on epic proportions. The struggle between group and trainer is also in large measure an aspect of the struggle over membership. The push and pull on the trainer may be efforts to resolve the problems of membership by utilizing the trainer as a surrogate for unresolved power struggles among members.

Each individual works on the problem of how much he will invest of himself throughout most of the T-Group. The group forms and re-forms as each individual makes his initial resolution of this question—some dramatically through a major conflict, others quietly as they slip into more active membership. No two individuals make it in the same way or to the same extent. Even after initial decisions by individuals to invest, there are continuous changes in the membership contract for each individual. Premature joining may cause persons to draw back from the group, to seek membership more thoughtfully later. As the group proves to be less threatening and more supportive, and as satisfactions and learning accrue, most individuals are able gradually to invest more. In turn, greater membership investment means greater resources for group development and individual learning. As learning increases, membership becomes easier to accept. And so a cycle of growth continues.

In the beginning, T-Group members are generally operating under the assumption that the group will move without much investment on their part. They find it difficult to believe that the trainer does not have it all arranged and that at the proper time he will resolve their problems for them. In one group, an individual summed up the group wish with a colorful analogy. 'Don't worry,' he said, 'when my children are watching Lassie on television and are biting their fingernails as they see her surrounded by fire on all sides, I don't worry. I know that the advertising agency has too much money invested in Lassie to let her burn.'

Only gradually do the members recognize that the show is not rigged, that the group will move and individuals will learn only from their own efforts and that without these efforts 'Lassie *could* burn'.

Factor of collaboration and learning from peers

The T-Group is perhaps unique in the extent to which learning influences come from peer members rather than from a teacher. There are many reasons why peer influence can be effective in learning. Because the individual is seeking a place in the group, peer efforts to influence him may be more clearly heard than efforts from 'outside'. Because the peer is perceived to be 'in the same boat', defensiveness resulting from fear of exposure is reduced. A group of peers has more sources of data, more refractory mirrors for feedback, more possibilities for identification than has the trainer. Peers do not raise the authority problems that frequently distort or inhibit learning in a superior-subordinate relationship. Finally, since behavioral change must be carried out with peers in the outside world, learning through the influence of peers has the advantage of setting in motion processes likely to continue.

One of the basic purposes of the T-group is to enable people to communicate with one another in more areas of thought and feeling than are usually attempted. The underlying assumption is that people can come to know one another better through such communication and that, with knowledge, they will reduce the distrust separating them, increase their desire to give help, and feel freer in giving it. With less fear of being misinterpreted, less fear that they will hurt or be hurt, they are able to listen to one another better. With better communication, collaboration increases. Energy often used in inhibiting feelings is released for joint problem-solving.

Factor of motivation for learning

The identity stress and the group survival stress growing out of the unstructured nature of the T-Group and the resultant ambiguities have been seen as motivating considerable emotional involvement (not necessarily immediately satisfying) and the release of considerable emotional energy for the defense of the individual. As members gradually identify their common problems, learn to express and utilize observational and feeling data, and build a group organization, individual anxieties reduce somewhat and the individual moves toward less defensive behavior.

Closely intertwined with identity stress is concern with group survival and organization. Indeed, the development of some kind of organization to hold the members together and the emergence of a supportive group climate are seen as means of reducing anxiety. In the early stages of the T-Group, motivation directed toward group survival leads toward the development of rigid controls. Deviancy is met by punishment, efforts to enforce conformity, or rejection. In later stages of maturity, group defensive behavior is reduced. Instead of strong pressures for conformity, there is acceptance of deviancy. The group is more secure, and efforts are directed toward improving conditions conducive to individual growth, group achievement, and individual freedom and belonging.

As the T-Group continues, the energy generated from early defensive motivations is increasingly expended in identifying basic individual and group problems, collecting and using relevant data about present behavior in the problem area, trying out new ways of perceiving and behaving, and generalizing from this process. This is a formula for learning.

As a learning group is constructed with a high level of trust, individuals are able to lower their defenses and develop satisfying relationships with others. They become freer in expressing and accepting caring feelings. Because it satisfies and

51

rewards the individual, each venture towards accepting the reaction of others and expressing helpful feelings towards others reinforces the next venture. As the group grows in its capacity to support experimentation, risk-taking becomes easier.

As defensive motivation is reduced, other driving forces lead toward continued high expenditure of emotion and behavior. Increasing trust in the group and in other members and the desire to grow as an individual and to help others, serve as driving forces that encourage openness, acceptance of feedback, acceptance of feelings, and readiness to experiment with new ways of behaving.

Like waves on a beach one set of motives follows on the reduction of others. One crests early and then breaks, making way for the others to increase in force. And the same pattern recurs at changing height and depth. The following model may help depict the order of these interrelated motivational learning waves.

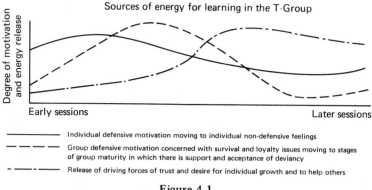

Figure 4.1
Sources of energy for learning in the T-Group

Factor of experienced behaviour and feedback

The mature and effective group needs to build into its structure and process a school for members as well as a clinic for group difficulties. A school for members implies the development by the group of a norm that legitimizes and a process that encourages open, experimental behavior and feedback of data about the consequence of behavior. The individual widens his repertoire of member skills through participation and feedback. In the process, he collaborates with others to create a group which will encourage still further individual learning.

As the T-Group progresses through its early concerns over survival, changes gradually occur in individual behavior. Increasingly, individuals bring out for consensual validation their perceptions of what is happening. They test whether what they see is what others see, and they begin to collect data about the discrepancies between their own perceptions and the perceptions of others. With anxiety about their own identity reduced, they find they can listen to other people with less interference of personal 'static'. They begin to compare observational data reported by others with the data of their own feelings. They develop some willingness to explore the behavior of the group as well as their own behavior and

52

attitudes. They gradually look at what they do and its consequences for the group and for individual members. They develop a willingness to receive feedback from the group. They learn to check what other people say about them against their own self-perception. They come to see that feelings and perceptions represent information important to improvement of individual and group performance. They see that improvement can occur only if information is reported, listened to, and tested.

As the group accepts the need for a clinic for group difficulties, it develops a norm for analyzing and diagnosing problems blocking group progress. An experimental approach—the 'provisional try'—becomes an accepted norm for the group when confronted with problems. The group learns to generalize from present experiences to future events. As this occurs, individuals also can learn much about the behavior and development of groups.

The value of the T-group lies in the fact that the process by which individuals develop a group in which they can participate effectively is the process of learning. The conditions include exposure of problem areas, collection of data, analysis, experimentation, generalization, and application to other situations. Its genius lies in the deep involvement and expenditure of energy called forth by its unstructured nature coupled with a process of inquiry, action, and evaluation.

Factor of group growth and development[1]

The T-Group's function is to construct itself into a mechanism for learning in which the process of group development and the process of individual learning are intertwined, and in which the method of inquiry serves both processes.

Because the T-Group does not start with a fully formed structure and accepted procedures for learning, these must be developed by the learners to conform with their readiness for learning. The T-Group can develop only as the individual members learn. It must be sufficiently flexible so that it changes as their readiness and abilities to learn change. With a minimum assistance from the trainer, the learners are themselves creating the group through which learning takes place. The content of their learning comprises the methods and processes they employ, the feelings produced, and the results achieved.

Group growth does not occur in a straight line. One way of looking at the T-Group is to see it as a cyclic process in which learning recurs in increasing depth. The T-Group approaches and reapproaches the same basic problems of relationships to authority, of interpersonal distance and relationships, of goal formation, of decision-making, of norm-setting, of communication. Growth lies not in ultimate solution, but in the readiness to face up to basic problems and in the improvement of methods by which the group approaches them.

Part of the problem of group growth lies in the fact that, while the group must proceed from dissatisfaction to satisfaction to dissatisfaction to satisfaction, it is very easy to become frozen at some point of satisfaction. The impetus for growth comes from dissatisfaction with an organization previously effective, but now impeding action. Difficulties arise when past successes serve to perpetuate a structure that does not fit changing goals and competencies. A T-Group which has won in a planned competition with another T-Group in producing a specific product, for example, usually considers its organization validated and resists examination of its continuing effectiveness. The problem facing the T-group, therefore, is that of learning how to study its structure so that it can recognize, change, or discard previously useful parts.

No two T-Groups grow at identical rates, nor does any T-Group grow at a constant rate. Variation in ability to solve problems arises in part from the fact that the T-Group, probably more than other groups, re-forms and is a different group each time it meets. This is not to say that its history does not have impact upon it. Rather, in its new formation the group deliberately utilizes the consequences of previous activities, but its unstructured nature means that events from the previous day are not forced on the next session. The group task shifts each day as different individuals take focal positions, and the group re-forms to meet the new task. Efforts to control the group come from various people and in different guises, each presenting different problems. Efforts to work out authority problems with the trainer also continue in different forms because the trainer's role shifts with the change and growth of the group. The significant development through this shifting situation is the accomplishment of a difficult task—that of bringing more and more reactions to the surface of group awareness and of learning better ways of handling these reactions.

The T-Group rather quickly develops some structure (often arbitrarily imposed by an individual or a small subgroup), some tentatively accepted norms about what constitutes areas of discussion and acceptable levels of communication, some efforts to encompass or control a few members perceived as deviants. Once the group has organized itself sufficiently to tackle a problem successfully, a greater sense of cohesion develops. Members often compare the group favorably with other groups that are perceived as not being so 'good'.

Somewhere in the relatively early life of the T-Group, however, the group generally encounters a major barrier that tests the strength of this cohesiveness. The group faces an unexpected situation and is unable to react to it adequately. The federation of members, precariously built despite lack of understanding of one another, gaps in communication, and false assumptions about group behavior, crumbles and falls apart. The group must reconstruct itself on a firmer basis.

A variety of problems and events may precipitate the first major barrier. Sometimes, it is an apparently minor problem for which the group is unprepared. Sometimes, it is the emergence of a problem the group has tried to keep covered or a behavioral consequence of a decision reached in an earlier meeting (e.g., a plan to rotate leaders every hour or to impose time limits on participation). Sometimes, it is a result of overconfidence; the group attempts a problem beyond its present competence. Sometimes, it is an imposed task in competition with another group in which the first group is the loser.

Frequently, a barrier results from some interpersonal event. This may be a severe attack by some member on the trainer, threatening previously established norms of how one reacts to authority and creating fear among dependent members as to what will happen if a member can destroy the leader. Part of the group may be immobilized by anxiety, while others join the attack or grapple with the attacker.

Sometimes, a member who has been inhibiting or controlling the group is spoken to sharply. If he leaves the room, becomes overnice, or gives other evidence of feeling punished, the group may be badly disrupted. Feelings of guilt, fear of a situation in which anyone can attack anyone, and feelings that the punished member deserved the treatment he received may be mixed together. Some may turn on the punishing member, who very probably did everyone a good turn, if somewhat ineptly, and attack him. Others may move to establish group boundaries, strait-jacketing the group and preventing reactions from member to member.

Sometimes, a conflict between two members who are competing for leadership spills over in an overt clash. The group may be immobilized by the fight. Peaceful members, afraid to seek peace by working on the conflict itself, would like to pretend that nothing has happened. The group has no methods to control fight, it is possessed by fears of the consequences of widespread fight.

At times, a manipulative situation occurs. Overnight, two or three members gang up to direct or control the group. If the manipulation is carried out by relatively dominant individuals, the group may have no way to control or prevent private experimentation at group expense. Sometimes, a dominant individual, fearful that feedback might reach him, may succeed in preventing the group from any but the most innocuous there and then discussion.

Sometimes, the cleavage between those who seek structure and dependency and those who can tolerate greater ambiguity splits the group. The two sides polarize, and without adequate group problem-solving methods, each issue or topic is treated as a battlefield.

At times, the group is disrupted by the speed with which it moves into new and uncharted areas. The border zone in which learning goes on represents continual oscillation between fantasy and actual daring. As movement takes place, newly found skill and insight make yesterday's daring today's commonplace, but seeing other people jump into real or fancied danger may arouse anxiety in those not ready for such daring. Thus, in meeting a major problem the group may be disrupted by those who wish to move ahead aggressively and those who fear the consequences.[2]

In the face of such barriers, hard-won effectiveness may disintegrate. Like pioneers who have gained some distance on their trek only to face what looks like an insurmountable mountain, the group now faces a major task of reorganization.

At this point of 'failure shock', group members begin to look for causes or targets for blame. After hopelessness, 'scapegoating' appears, generally focused on the behavior of an individual—whether member or trainer. The permissiveness of the trainer has 'allowed' the group to get into a mess—or he has been too directive and has led the group into trouble. If a member is blamed, it may be for leading the group farther than it wanted to go, for punishing weaker members or for being unconcerned about the welfare of the group. Punishment is liberally distributed.

A second pattern of behavior at the point of group disintegration is to regress to far more structured standards of behavior with reduced learning goals, more formalized procedures, more autocratic use of power. The group may set rules that no one may say anything even remotely critical of others, that discussion shall deal with outside the group topics, that formal leadership shall be rotated, that each person may have so many seconds to talk, that a leader shall be appointed and given authority. In one group, under shock from the attack of one member, it was almost unanimously agreed to select a leader by lot and give him authority to make *all* decisions concerning the areas and procedures of discussion and the behavior of members. This classic picture of abdication of all power and control to a single leader as a result of fear does not always appear so clearly. However, the ingredients are usually present.

Whatever the pattern of reaction to the barrier, it generates a great deal of behavior. There may be violent disagreement about past events and about decisions made. Past decisions are distorted. There may be compulsive doubting that the group can make any decision whatsoever. The members may defer abjectly to authority. Argument, persuasion, manipulation, creation of false data, emotional appeals, and coercive social pressure take the place of other methods of problem-solving. Communication decreases. The purposes of others are misperceived. Undisclosed personal agendas increase. Discrepancies between individual perceptions and reality multiply. Subgroups tend to form to a greater extent than formerly. There is flight from the group problem.

This is a critical period—one in which group members learn, almost for the first time, that structure and organization will not come miraculously or easily. As they work through their initial needs to 'scape-goat', to fight, or to run away, they come to learn that the group will develop only as it utilizes scientific methods of inquiry and problem solving. This means collecting relevant data, evaluating and analyzing these data, establishing and testing hypotheses, and planning and taking joint action. At this point, members may realize that group development and their own growth will come only through facing and surmounting a series of major barriers and through continuously reorganizing available forces. The further realization may come that there is no final group organization which will be discovered and bring peace forever after.

Yesterday's problems do not appear to be problems today. The group faces new problems with increasing courage and security, and with increasing ability.

Looking back, the members often see the period in which they faced their first major crisis as a dark valley of despair and frequently wonder how they came through it. This crisis, the regression that followed, and the slow, painful process of re-forming and repair may, however, be seen as the major event in their learning.

Factor of trainer-intervention

Through this complex process of discovery, failure, reorganization, and achievement, the position of the T-Group trainer is a difficult one involving a seeming contradiction. His interventions, or lack of interventions, have much to do with the process of the group, the problems analyzed, and the learning that results, yet the trainer is neither a teacher, in the usual sense, nor a discussion leader. He does not pre-determine the specific learnings or direct the work of the group, but neither is he passive and without responsibility for helping learning to take place. He does not hold the clear-cut authority of the teacher or leader; neither does he become a complete member of the group, although he usually approaches full membership more closely than does the teacher or leader.

The trainer does not have the easy security of knowing what the curriculum content will be, because this must emerge each day from the problems of the group. The trainer who enters a given meeting of the T-Group with assurance that he can predict what will happen that day will probably find himself blocking group movement as he tries to force what he has predicted, or he will be unable to 'read' the group process and to determine which, among the many issues and problems before the group, is presently focal.

In the T-Group, it is not the trainer who controls process and gives direction to interaction, rather, it is the method of inquiry itself. The trainer's concern is to help the group to develop adequate methods of inquiry. He is himself involved in interaction in the group, and he needs to work on the emergence of his role just as do other members. For trainer as for group member, roles must grow out of what the group requires and out of the perception, abilities, and behavior patterns within the group.

The trainer, however, should and does have certain advantages in the emergence of his role. He may not know more about the individual needs and problems than do other members, but he has the security of knowing better how to discover them. He should have a clearer image of the functions and process flow of the T-Group and thus be more constantly aware of the basic purposes. Through work with other T-Groups, he may anticipate some aspects of the general experience, the broad problems groups face, even though he cannot predict specific interactions or prevent himself (nor should he) from receiving feedback about his own behavior. He cannot escape involvement in new situations from which he must learn either to extricate himself or to use creatively. One of his rewards is his own learning.

The trainer does not predetermine group goals, but it is highly important that he have a general sense of direction to aid the group as it moves towards its goals. Otherwise he tends to be immobilized and to rationalize his immobility to the point of shirking his responsibility for the training. Or, uncertain of ultimate purposes, he intervenes under different assumptions each day and ends up by becoming a major group problem himself.

The trainer's purposes might be summarized as follows:

1 To help to develop a group whose purpose is to learn about the sensitivities, understandings, and skills necessary for membership in social situations—To accomplish this, the trainer needs to help members break off continuity with the outside or back-home world. By helping to establish a cultural island, as opposed to a mainland culture, he helps the group to examine new facets of behavior in new ways.

The ambivalence with which most individuals approach learning has already been discussed. In the T-Group, where heightened ambiguity creates initial tension, members tend to subordinate the learning purposes they brought with them to the perceived need to survive. At this point probably only the trainer is holding onto learning purposes. If he, like the others, allows himself to be swept into the struggle for survival, of which the first moves are toward tradition and safety, he may lose sight of the real problem facing the group.

Members and trainer probably see different needs in the beginning of the T-Group:

Group needs as participants see them	*Group needs as the trainer sees them*
For structure	For exposure of member-behavior
For predictability	For permissiveness to reduce defensive-
For security	ness
For measurable progress	For sanction and support to explore
For safe position	feelings and behavior
	For methods of data collection, feed-back, study, and experimentation

This difference in perceived needs means that the trainer should help to develop a learning group that will be unlike customary groups on the mainland. In his initial contract with the group, his assumption that a different group will emerge and his belief that members can learn from their experiences if they will study these experiences, help to keep present the task of developing a group as a way to learn.

2 To help to remove blocks to learning about self, about others, and about the group—Most individuals have barriers to learning that need to be overcome. They may have to remove self-imposed restrictions on participation in learning experiences. They may have to reduce anxiety about revealing their assumptions and feelings. They may have to overcome their resistance to observing their own behavior or to become more diagnostic about their own and others' behavior. They may have to become more willing to consider feedback.

In the early stages of the T-Group, the trainer should take certain definite steps to help group members to develop learning processes. He should first legitimize the expression and analysis of feeling. If members are not encouraged to express their real reactions, important information may be withheld and no patterns of collecting data established. The trainer can help by showing calmness rather than tension as feeling begins to be expressed in conflicting behavior. He can accept an explosion of feeling as normal. He can use such words as 'feeling' and 'emotion' in the same tone of voice as when speaking of other phenomena. He can keep himself from exerting control when a conflict breaks out. He can resist punishing individuals or the group. He can feel free to express his own feelings as objective data, if he does not endeavor to impose his feelings on others. He can speak of diagnosis and analysis of group barriers. ('What is happening in the group now?' 'How are we feeling now?') In his efforts to help the group to face its feeling problems, he may himself react to a group event by expressing his own reactions as a part of the group.

Second, he can model a participant-observer behavior as he reports observation of the consequence of his behavior or of the behavior of the group. Again, he can accept reactions to his behavior from the group in a manner which invites such reactions, and after considering and testing their validity and the possibility of change, he can mend his behavior.

3 To help to develop a group climate in which learning can take place—There must be a norm of permissiveness that makes it easy to express feelings and reactions without fear of punishment or rejection. There must be emotional support for members who undergo sometimes painful reassessment of attitudes and behavior. There must be standards that encourage members to invest themselves in learning situations and foster willingness to explore new attitudes and behavior. There must be sufficient interpersonal trust, acceptance and care, and group cohesiveness so that individuals can give and accept influence.

The trainer can help to build such a climate in many ways, but he cannot alone build climate. If he could, he would control the group and thus prevent learning.

He can make explicit, from time to time, evidences of climate building, and he may wish to raise to the level of discussion the consequences of an inadequate climate. He can help to bring about mutual understanding by testing for misunderstanding. He can try to keep issues open between persons and within the group until they are worked through so that mutual trust can grow as members learn that problems can be faced and dealt with rather than concealed.

4 To help the group to discover and utilize methods of inquiry—action, observation, feedback, analysis, experimentation—as ways of group development and individual growth—The trainer should encourage the group to focus on here and now experience during the early part of the T-Group. He should indicate dimensions of behavior for observations. He may want to support courage in each member to assess and diagnose his own behavior and to experiment with new approaches. He may feel it desirable to support and model various methods of self-inquiry and inquiry into group behavior. He may wish to encourage and support collaborative problem-solving efforts and methods. Unless the group can develop and use methods of inquiry, experiences may be filled with feeling, whether comforting or threatening, but little learning will result.

5 To help the group to learn how to internalize, to generalize, and to apply learnings to other situations—An insight is not used until it results in change in the way events are perceived and in the way the individual responds. The role of the trainer includes responsibility for encouraging individuals to explore and test new perceptions until they become part of the pattern of the thinking and behavior of the group. Equally, he should help in the process of generalization so that learning can be utilized in other situations. Otherwise the group may pass from experience to experience, gaining understandings about the specific experiences without enlarging the understandings to apply to other situations. With no planned curriculum events in the T-Group and no set times for generalizing from immediate learnings, it becomes important that the trainer recognize opportunities when the group may profitably, and with the least interruption to the flow of experiences, discuss their learnings in relation to other situations. With practice and encouragement, the group itself learns to generalize its learnings.

The trainer must be systematically understanding and aware of the problems of effective learning that the learning group faces. He must be aware of the points at which the group needs help. He must be aware of the seduction of resolving current difficulties without learning from these difficulties. Perhaps most important of all, he must endeavor to help group members become equally sensitive to their problems so that they grow in ability to direct their own continuing learning. Otherwise he subtly maintains the reins in his own hands.

The questions continuously facing the trainer are whether or not he should intervene at any given point and, if so, in what role and for what purpose. His intervention should aid the group and not do work that the group itself is ready to do.

The trainer has three roles in which he may make interventions. As an observer and, occasionally, as an interpreter it may be appropriate for him to ask the group to report their observations of a given event or to report his own observations to stimulate further thought and discussion. He may think it appropriate to give his interpretation concerning some of the possible causes and consequences of the event and to invite others' interpretation also.

In his member role, the trainer may occasionally intervene by contributing his own feelings as part of the needed data when the group is dealing with their relations to him, or to work with the group on other events in which his behavior is involved. To be unwilling to participate in a releasing way when group members discuss his behavior would be to inhibit their effective dealing with his presence and behavior.

As a source of resources for the group, the trainer may feel it appropriate to suggest or to model ways of data collection or study so that the group interactions may be effectively utilized for learning.

Behind trainer decisions about interventions should lie a personal theory of learning and change and a set of values concerning his relations to other individuals. Hopefully, these values would include the desirability of being empathic as well as discerning and the willingness to be open as to his own motives and purposes to the extent that individuals and the group need these perceptions and have the ability to utilize them.

Purposes reviewed

Having followed the T-Group through the intricacies of its intensive life, it may be helpful to review the purposes of this invention for learning.

The first major purpose of the T-Group is to help individuals to learn how to learn in the areas of self-understanding and relationship with others. The T-Group builds on the concept that learning about self and about others comes best from experiences with others and the analysis of these experiences. Analysis of experience, however, requires access to the data about the experience, much of which lies in feelings and perceptions which the individual should recognize and understand. Some of these data, however, are in the possession of others—their perceptions and feelings about a given situation. Learning how to make these data available so that the individuals and the group can learn from them is a major task of the T-Group. Each individual in the group should invite and utilize help from others and give help in return.

Thus, the first two T-Group goals of learning better how to learn from continuing experiences and learning how to give help to others in their learning and growth experiences are interactive and reciprocal. The relationship may be expressed thus:

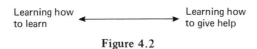

Learning how to learn   ⟷   Learning how to give help

Figure 4.2

The third purpose of the T-Group is to develop skills of effective membership. The raw data for learning these skills are the actions the group takes toward its goals. As the individual invests himself in group membership, he learns better how to give and accept influence and how to work with others in creating a climate that encourages collaborative problem-solving and a process by which it can take place. In so doing, he creates conditions for learning about himself and about others, about the processes of continued learning, and about ways of helping others to learn and grow. He is learning how to become a more effective member. Thus, a third dimension is added to the model:

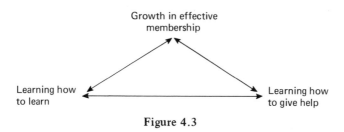

Growth in effective membership

Learning how to learn   Learning how to give help

Figure 4.3

The unstructured T-Group is the crucible in which learning goals can be realized. Through a living and very real experience in earning and bestowing membership and through analyzing this experience, individuals develop sensitivity to group processes and to individual behavior. In so doing they are developing skill for continued learning and for continuing help to others. And they are learning about membership behavior and group process. Thus, the purposes of the T-Group interact in the following manner:

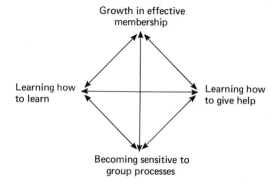

Figure 4.4

The integration of these purposes and their interactive influence on one another comprise some of the major purposes of the T-Group.

References

1. Much of this section has been developed from a paper by BRADFORD, LELAND P., and MALLINSON, THOMAS, 'Group Formation and Development'. 1951. Reprinted in *Dynamics of Group Life*. Washington, D.C.: National Training Laboratories, N.E.A., 1958.
2. *Ibid.*, p. 78.

5. A theory of group development*

Warren G. Bennis and Herbert A. Shepard

If attention is focused on the organic properties of groups, criteria can be established by which phenomena of development, learning, or movement toward maturity can be identified. From this point of view, maturity for the group means something analogous to maturity for the person: a mature group knows very well what it is doing. The group can resolve its internal conflicts, mobilize its resources, and take intelligent action only if it has means for consensually validating its experience. The person can resolve his internal conflicts, mobilize his resources, and take intelligent action only if anxiety does not interfere with his ability to profit from his experience, to analyze, discriminate, and foresee. Anxiety prevents the person's internal communication system from functioning appropriately, and improvements in his ability to profit from experience hinge upon overcoming anxiety as a source of distortion. Similarly, group development involves the overcoming of obstacles to valid communication among the members, or the development of methods for achieving and testing consensus. Extrapolating from Sullivan's definition of personal maturity, we can say a group has reached a state of valid communication when its members are armed with '... referential tools for analyzing interpersonal experience, so that its significant differences from, as well as its resemblances to, past experience, are discriminable, and the foresight of relatively near future events will be adequate and appropriate to maintaining one's security and securing one's satisfactions without useless or ultimately troublesome disturbance of self-esteem' (Sullivan,[1] page 111.)

Relatively few investigations of the phenomena of group development have been undertaken. This paper outlines a theory of development in groups that have as their explicit goal improvement of their internal communication systems.

● Reproduced with permission of the authors from *Human Relations,* Volume 9, No. 4, 1956, pp. 415-457.
* This theory is based for the most part on observations made over a five-year period of teaching graduate students 'group dynamics'. The main function of the seminar, as it was set forth by the instructors, was to improve the internal communication system of the group, hence, a self-study group.

A group of strangers, meeting for the first time, has within it many obstacles to valid communication. The more heterogeneous the membership, the more accurately does the group become, for each member, a microcosm of the rest of his interpersonal experience. The problems of understanding, the relationships, that develop in any given group are from one aspect a unique product of the particular constellation of personalities assembled. But to construct a broadly useful theory of group development, it is necessary to identify major areas of internal uncertainty, or obstacles to valid communication, which are common to and important in all groups meeting under a given set of environmental conditions. These areas must be strategic in the sense that until the group has developed methods for reducing uncertainty in them, it cannot reduce uncertainty in other areas, and in its external relations.

The two major areas of internal uncertainty: Dependence (authority relations) and interdependence (personal relations)

Two major areas of uncertainty can be identified by induction from common experience, at least within our own culture. The first of these is the area of group members' orientations toward authority, or more generally toward the handling and distribution of power in the group. The second is the area of members' orientations towards one another. These areas are not independent of each other: a particular set of intermember orientations will be associated with a particular authority structure. But the two sets of orientations are as distinct from each other as are the concepts of power and love. A number of authorities have used them as a starting-point for the analysis of group behavior.

Freud noted[2] that 'each member is bound by libidinal ties on the one hand to the leader . . . and on the other hand to the other members of the group' (page 45). Although he described both ties as libidinal, he was uncertain 'how these two ties are related to each other, whether they are of the same kind and the same value, and how they are to be described psychologically.' Without resolving this question, he noted that (for the Church and the Army) 'one of these, the tie with the leader, seems . . . to be more of a ruling factor than the other, which holds between members of the group' (page 52).

More recently, Schutz[3] has made these two dimensions central to his theory of group compatibility. For him, the strategic determinant of compatibility is the particular blend of orientations toward authority and orientations toward personal intimacy. Bion[4,5] conceptualizes the major dimensions of the group somewhat differently. His 'dependency' and 'pairing' modalities correspond to our 'dependence' and 'interdependence' areas; to them he adds a 'fight-flight' modality. For him these modalities are simply alternative modes of behavior, for us, the fight-flight categorization has been useful for characterizing the means used by the group for maintaining a stereotyped orientation during a given subphase.

The core of the theory of group development is that the principal obstacles to the development of valid communication are to be found in the orientations toward

64

authority and intimacy that members bring to the group. Rebelliousness, submissiveness, or withdrawal as the characteristic response to authority figures, destructive competitiveness, emotional exploitiveness, or withdrawal as the characteristic response to peers prevent consensual validation of experience. The behaviors determined by these orientations are directed toward enslavement of the other in the service of the self, enslavement of the self in the service of the other, or disintegration of the situation. Hence, they prevent the setting, clarification of, and movement toward group-shared goals.

In accord with Freud's observation, the orientations toward authority are regarded as being prior to, or partially determining of, orientations toward other members. In its development, the group moves from preoccupation with authority relations to preoccupation with personal relations. This movement defines the two major phases of group development. Within each phase are three subphases, determined by the ambivalence of orientations in each area. That is, during the authority (dependence) phase, the group moves from preoccupation with submission to preoccupation with rebellion, to resolution of the dependence problem. Within the personal (or interdependence) phase, the group moves from a preoccupation with intermember identification to a preoccupation with individual identity to a resolution of the interdependence problem.

The relevant aspects of personality in group development

The aspects of member personality most heavily involved in group development are called, following Schutz, the dependence and personal aspects.

The dependence aspect is comprised by the member's characteristic patterns related to a leader or to a structure of rules. Members who find comfort in rules of procedure, an agenda, an expert, etc., are called 'dependent'. Members who are discomfited by authoritative structures are called 'counterdependent'.

The personal aspect is comprised of the member's characteristic patterns with respect to interpersonal intimacy. Members who cannot rest until they have stabilized a relatively high degree of intimacy with all the others are called 'overpersonal'. Members who tend to avoid intimacy with any of the others are called 'counterpersonal'.

Psychodynamically, members who evidence some compulsiveness in the adoption of highly dependent, highly counterdependent, highly personal, or highly counterpersonal roles are regarded as 'conflicted'. Thus, the person who persists in being dependent upon any and all authorities thereby provides himself with ample evidence that authorities should not be so trustingly relied upon; yet he cannot profit from this experience in governing his future action. Hence, a deep, but unrecognized, distrust is likely to accompany the manifestly submissive behavior, and the highly dependent or highly counterdependent person is thus a person in conflict. The existence of the conflict accounts for the sometimes dramatic movement from extreme dependence to extreme rebelliousness. In this way counterdependence and dependence, while logically the extremes of a scale, are psychologically very close together.

The 'unconflicted' person or 'independent', who is better able to profit from his experience and assess the present situation more adequately, may, of course, act at times in rebellious or submissive ways. Psychodynamically, the difference between him and the conflicted is easy to understand. In terms of observable behavior, he lacks the compulsiveness and, significantly, does not create the communicative confusion so characteristic of, say, the conflicted dependent, who manifests submission in that part of his communication of which he is aware, and distrust or rebellion in that part of his communication of which he is unaware.

Persons who are unconflicted with respect to the dependence or personal aspect are considered to be responsible for the major movements of the group toward valid communication. That is, the actions of members unconflicted with respect to the problems of a given phase of group development move the group to the next phase. Such actions are called barometric events, and the initiators are called catalysts. This part of the theory of group development is based on Redl's thesis concerning the 'infectiousness of the unconflicted on the conflicted personality constellation'. The catalysts (Redl calls them 'central persons') are the persons capable of reducing the uncertainty characterizing a given phase. 'Leadership', from the standpoint of group development, can be defined in terms of catalysts responsible for group movement from one phase to the next. This consideration provides a basis for determining what membership roles are needed for group development. For example, it is expected that a group will have great difficulty in resolving problems of power and authority if it lacks members who are unconflicted with respect to dependence.

Phase movements

The foregoing summary has introduced the major propositions in the theory of group development. While it is not possible to reproduce the concrete group experience from which the theory is drawn, we can take a step in this direction by discussing in more detail what seem to us to be the dominant features of each phase. The description given below is highly interpretive, and we emphasize what seem to us to be the major themes of each phase, even though many minor themes are present. In the process of abstracting, stereotyping, and interpreting, certain obvious facts about group process are lost. For example, each group meeting is to some extent a recapitulation of its past and a forecast of its future. This means that behavior that is 'regressive' or 'advanced' often appears.

Phase 1: Dependence

Subphase 1: Dependence-flight—The first days of group life are filled with behavior whose remote, as well as immediate, aim is to ward off anxiety. Much of the discussion content consists of fruitless searching for a common goal. Some of the security-seeking behavior is group-shared—for example, members may reassure one another by providing interesting and harmless facts about themselves. Some is idiosyncratic—for example, doodling, yawning, intellectualizing.

The search for a common goal is aimed at reducing the cause of anxiety, thus going beyond the satisfaction of immediate security needs. But just as evidencing boredom in this situation is a method of warding off anxiety by denying its proximity, so group goal-seeking is not quite what it is claimed to be. It can best be understood as a dependence plea. The trainer, not the lack of a goal, is the cause of insecurity. This interpretation is likely to be vigorously contested by the group, but it is probably valid. The characteristic expectations of group members are that the trainer will establish rules of the game and distribute rewards. He is presumed to know what the goals are or ought to be. Hence his behavior is regarded as a 'technique'; he is merely playing hard to get. The pretense of a fruitless search for goals is a plea for him to tell the group what to do, by simultaneously demonstrating its helplessness without him, and its willingness to work under his direction for his approval and protection.

We are here talking about the dominant theme in group life. Many minor themes are present, and even in connection with the major theme there are differences among members. For some, testing the power of the trainer to affect their futures is the major concern. In others, anxiety may be aroused through a sense of helplessness in a situation made threatening by the protector's desertion. These alternatives can be seen as the beginnings of the counterdependent and dependent adaptations. Those with a dependent orientation look vainly for cues from the trainer for procedure and direction, sometimes paradoxically they infer that the leader must want it that way. Those with a counterdependent orientation strive to detect in the trainer's action elements that would offer ground for rebellion, and may even paradoxically demand rules and leadership from him because he is failing to provide them.

The ambiguity of the situation at this stage quickly becomes intolerable for some, and a variety of ultimately unserviceable resolutions may be invented, many of them idiosyncratic. Alarm at the prospect of future meetings is likely to be group-shared, and at least a gesture may be made in the direction of formulating an agenda for subsequent meetings.

This phase is characterized by behavior that has gained approval from authorities in the past. Since the meetings are to be concerned with groups or with human relations, members offer information on these topics, to satisfy the presumed expectations of the trainer and to indicate expertise, interest, or achievement in these topics (ex-officers from the armed services, from fraternities, etc., have the floor). Topics such as business or political leadership, discrimination, and desegregation, are likely to be discussed. During this phase, the contributions made by members are designed to gain approval from the trainer, whose reaction to each comment is surreptitiously watched. If the trainer comments that this seems to be the case, or if he notes that the subject under discussion (say, discrimination) may be related to some concerns about membership in this group, he fails again to satisfy the needs of members. Not that the validity of this interpretation is held in much doubt. No one is misled by the 'flight' behavior involved in discussing

67

problems external to the group, least of all the group members. Discussion of these matters if filled with perilous uncertainties, however, and so the trainer's observation is politely ignored, as one would ignore a *faux pas* at a teaparty. The attempts to gain approval based on implicit hypotheses about the potential power of the trainer for good and evil are continued until the active members have run through the repertoire of behaviours that have gained them favor in the past.

Subphase 2: Counterdependence-flight—As the trainer continues to fail miserably in satisfying the needs of the group, discussion takes on a different tone, and counterdependent expressions begin to replace overt dependency phase. In many ways, this subphase is the most stressful and unpleasant in the life of the group. It is marked by a paradoxical development of the trainer's role into one of omnipotence and powerlessness, and by division of the group into two warring subgroups. In subphase 1, feelings of hostility were strongly defended; if a slip were made that suggested hostility, particularly toward the trainer, the group members were embarrassed. Now expressions of hostility are more frequent, and are more likely to be supported by other members, or to be met with equally hostile responses. Power is much more overtly the concern of group members in this subphase. A topic such as leadership may again be discussed, but the undertones of the discussion are no longer dependence pleas. Discussion of leadership in subphase 2 is in part a vehicle for making explicit the trainer's failure as a leader. In part, it is perceived by other members as a bid for leadership on the part of any member who participates in it.

The major themes of this subphase are as follows:

1 Two opposed subgroups emerge, together incorporating most of the group members. Characteristically, the subgroups are in disagreement about the group's need for leadership or 'structure'. One subgroup attempts to elect a chairman, nominate working committees, establish agenda, or otherwise 'structure' the meetings; the other subgroup opposes all such efforts. At first, this appears to be merely an intellectual disagreement concerning the future organization of group activity. But soon it becomes the basis for destroying any semblance of group unity. Fragmentation is expressed and brought about in many ways: voting is a favorite way of dramatizing the schism; suggestions that the group is too large and should be divided into subgroups for the meetings are frequent; a chairman may be elected and then ignored as a demonstration of the group's ineffectiveness. Although control mechanisms are sorely needed and desired, no one is willing to relinquish the rights of leadership and control to anyone else. The trainer's abdication has created a power gap, but no one is allowed to fill it.

2 Disenthrallment with the trainer proceeds rapidly. Group members see him as at best ineffectual, at worst damaging to group progress. He is ignored and bullied almost simultaneously. His interventions are perceived by the counterdependents as an attempt to interrupt group progress, by the dependents, as weak and incorrect statements. His silences are regarded by the dependents as desertion, by the counterdependents as manipulation. Much of the group activity is to be understood as punishment of the trainer for his failure to meet needs and expectations, for

getting the group into an unpleasant situation, for being the worst kind of authority figure—a weak and incompetent one, or a manipulative, insincere one. Misunderstanding or ignoring his comments, implying that his observations are paranoid fantasies, demonstrations that the group is cracking up, references to him in the past tense as though he were no longer present—these are the punishments for his failure.

As, in the first subphase, the trainer's wisdom, power, and competence were overtly unquestioned, but secretely suspected; so, in the second subphase, the conviction that he is incompetent and helpless is clearly dramatized, but secretly doubted. Out of this secret doubt arises the belief in the trainer's omnipotence. None of the punishments meted out to the trainer are recognized as such by the group members; in fact, if the trainer suggests that the members feel a need to punish him, they are most likely to respond in injured tones or in tones of contempt that what is going on has nothing to do with him and that he had best stay out of it. The trainer is still too imposing and threatening to challenge directly. There is a secret hope that the chaos in the group is in fact part of the master plan, that he is really leading them in the direction they should be going. That he may really be helpless as they imply, or that the failure may be theirs rather than his, are frightening possibilities. For this reason subphase 2 differs very little in its fundamental dynamics from subphase 1. There is still the secret wish that the trainer will stop all the bedlam which has replaced polite uncertainty, by taking his proper role (so that dependent members can cooperate with him and counter-dependent can rebel in the usual ways).

Subphase 2 thus brings the group to the brink of catastrophe. The trainer has consistently failed to meet the group's needs. Not daring to turn directly on him, the group members engage in mutually destructive behavior: in fact, the group threatens suicide as the most extreme expression of dependence. The need to punish the trainer is so strong, however, that his act of salvation would have to be magical indeed.

Subphase 3: Resolution-catharsis—No such magic is available to the trainer. Resolution of the group's difficulties at this point depends upon the presence in the group of other forces, which have until this time been inoperative, or ineffective. Only the degenerative aspects of the chain of events in subphases 1 and 2 have been presented up to this point and they are in fact the salient ones. But there has been a simultaneous, though less obvious, mobilization of constructive forces. First, within each of the warring subgroups bonds of mutual support have grown. The group member no longer feels helpless and isolated. Second, the trainer's role, seen as weak or manipulative in the dependence orientation, can also be perceived as permissive. Third, his interpretations, though openly ignored, have been secretly attended to. And, as the second and third points imply, some members of the group are less the prisoners of the dependence-counterdependence dilemma than others. These members, called the independents, have been relatively ineffective in the group for two reasons. First, they have not developed firm bonds with other members in either of the warring subgroups, because they have not identified with either cause. Typically, they have devoted their energies to an unsuccessful search for a compromise settlement of the disagreements in the group. Since their attitudes toward authority are less ambivalent than those of other members, they have accepted the alleged reason for disagreement in the group—for example, whether a chairman should be elected—at face value, and tried to mediate. Similarly, they have tended to accept the trainer's role and interpretations more nearly at face value. However, his interpretations have seemed inaccurate to them, since, in fact, the interpretations have applied much less to them than to the rest of the group.

Subphase 3 is the most crucial and fragile in group life up to this point. What occurs is a sudden shift in the whole basis of group action. It is truly a bridging phase; if it occurs at all, it is so rapid and mercurial that the end of subphase 2 appears to give way directly to the first subphase of phase 2. If it does not occur thus rapidly and dramatically, a halting and arduous process of vacillation between phases 1 and 2 is likely to persist for a long period, the total group movement being very gradual.

To summarize the state of affairs at the beginning of subphase 3: First, the group is polarized into two competing groups, each unable to gain or relinquish power. Second, those group members who are uncommitted to either subgroup are ineffective in their attempts to resolve the conflict. Third, the trainer's contributions only serve to deepen the cleavage in the group.

As the group enters subphase 3, it is moving rapidly toward extinction: that is, splintering into two or three subgroups. The independents, who have until now been passive or ineffectual, become the only hope for survival, since they have thus far avoided polarization and stereotypic behavior. The imminence of dissolution forces them to recognize the fruitlessness of their attempts at mediation. For this reason, the trainer's hypothesis that fighting one another is off-target behavior is likely to be acted upon at this point. A group member may openly express the opinion that the trainer's presence and comments are holding the group back, suggest that 'as an experiment' the trainer leaves the group 'to see how things go without him'. When the trainer is thus directly challenged, the whole atmosphere of the meeting changes. There is a sudden increase in alertness and tension. Previously, there had been much acting out of the wish that the trainer were absent, but at the same time a conviction that he was the *raison d'être* of the group's existence—that it would fall apart without him. Previously, absence of the trainer would have constituted desertion, or defeat, fulfilment of the members' worst fears as to their own inadequacy or the trainer's. But now leaving the group can have a different meaning. General agreement that the trainer should leave is rarely achieved. However, after a little further discussion, it becomes clear that he is at liberty to leave, with the understanding that he wishes to be a member of the group, and will return if and when the group is willing to accept him.

The principal function of the symbolic removal of the trainer is in its effect of freeing the group, to bring into awareness the hitherto carefully ignored feelings towards him as an authority figure, and towards the group activity as an off-target dramatization of the ambivalence towards authority. The leadership provided by

70

the independents (whom the group sees as having no vested interest in power) leads to a new orientation toward membership in the group. In the discussion that follows the exit of the trainer, the dependents' assertion that the trainer deserted and the counterdependents' assertion that he was kicked out are soon replaced by consideration of whether his behavior was 'responsible' or 'irresponsible'. The power problem is resolved by being defined in terms of member responsibilities, and the terms of the trainer's return to the group are settled by the requirement that he behave as 'just another member of the group'. This phrase is then explained as meaning that he should take neither more nor less responsibility for what happens in the group than any other member.

The above description of the process does not do justice to the excitement and involvement characteristic of this period. How much transferable insight ambivalent members acquire from it is difficult to assess. At least within the life of the group, later activity is rarely perceived in terms of submission and rebellion.

An interesting parallel, which throws light on the order of events in group development, is given in Freud's discussion of the myth of the primal horde. In his version: 'These many individuals eventually banded themselves together, killed [the father], and cut him in pieces. . . . They then formed the totemistic community of brothers all with equal rights and united by the totem prohibitions which were to preserve and to expiate the memory of the murder.' (Freud,[2] page 112.)

The horde's act, according to Freud, was soon distorted into an heroic myth: instead of murder by the group, the myth held that the father had been overthrown single-handed by one person, usually the youngest son. In this attribution of the group act to one individual (the hero) Freud saw the 'emergence of the individual from group psychology'. His definition of a hero is '. . . a man who stands up manfully against his father and in the end victoriously overthrows him.' (Freud,[6] page 9.) (The heroic myth of Freud thus shares much in common with Sullivan's 'delusion of unique individuality'.)

In the training group, the member who initiates the events leading to the trainer's exit is sometimes referred to as a 'hero' by the other members. Responsibility for the act is felt to be shared by the group, however, and out of their experience comes the first strong sense of group solidarity and involvement—a reversal of the original version, where the individual emerges from the group. This turn of events clarifies Freud's remark concerning the libidinal ties to the leader and to the other group members. Libidinal ties toward the other group members cannot be adequately developed until there is a resolution of the ties with the leader. In our terms, those components of group life having to do with intimacy and interdependence cannot be dealt with until those components having to do with authority and dependence have been resolved.

Other aspects of subphase 3 may be understood by investigating the dramatic significance of the revolt. The event is always marked in group history as 'a turning-point', 'the time we became a group', 'when I first got involved', etc. The mounting tension, followed by sometimes uproarious euphoria, cannot be entirely explained by the surface events. It may be that the revolt represents a realization of important fantasies individuals hold in all organizations, that the emotions involved

71

are undercurrents wherever rebellious and submissive tendencies towards existing authorities must be controlled. These are the themes of some of our great dramas—*Antigone, Billy Budd, Hamlet,* and our most recent folk-tale, *The Caine Mutiny.* But the event is more than the presentation of a drama, or an acting-out of fantasies. For it can be argued that the moments of stress and catharsis, when emotions are labile and intense, are the times in the group life when there is readiness for change. Leighton's analysis of a minor revolution at a Japanese relocation camp is worth quoting in full on this point:

> While this [cathartic] situation is fraught with danger because of trends which may make the stress become worse before it gets better, there is also an opportunity for administrative action that is not likely to be found in more secure times. It is fairly well recognized in psychology that at periods of great emotional stir the individual human being can undergo far-reaching and permanent changes in his personality. It is as if the bone structure of his systems of belief and of his habitual patterns of behavior becomes soft, is fused into new shapes and hardens there when the period of tension is over. . . . Possibly the same can be true of whole groups of people, and there are historical examples of social changes and movements occurring when there was widespread emotional tension, usually some form of anxiety. The Crusades, parts of the Reformation, the French Revolution, the change in Zulu life in the reign of Chaca, the Meiji Restoration, the Mormon movement, the Russian Revolution, the rise of Fascism, and alterations in the social sentiments of the United States going on at present are all to some extent examples. (Leighton,[7] page 360.)

Observers of industrial relations have made similar observations. When strikes result from hostile labor-management relations (as contrasted to straight wage demands), there is a fluidity of relationships and a wide repertoire of structural changes during this period not available before the strike act.[8]

So it is, we believe, with the training group. But what are the new values and behavior patterns that emerge out of the emotional experience of Phase 1? Principally, they are acceptance by each member of his full share of responsibility for what happens in the group. The outcome is autonomy for the group. After the events of subphase 3, there is no more attribution of magical powers to the trainer—either the dependent fantasy that he sees farther, knows better, is mysteriously guiding the group and protecting it from evil, or the very similar counterdependent fantasy that he is manipulating the group. exploiting it in his own interests, that the experience is one of 'brain-washing'. The criterion for evaluating a contribution is no longer who said it, but what is said. Thereafter, such power fantasies as the trainer himself may have present no different problem from the power fantasies of any other group member. At the same time, the illusion that there is a struggle for power in the group is suddenly dissipated, and the contributions of other members are evaluated in terms of their relevance to shared group goals.

Summary of phase 1—The very word development implies not only movement through time, but also a definite order of progression. The group must traverse subphase 1 to reach subphase 2, and subphase 3 before it can move into phase 2. At the same time, lower levels of development coexist with more advanced levels.

Blocking and regression occur frequently, and the group may be stuck at a certain phase of development. It would, of course, be difficult to imagine a group remaining long in subphase 3—the situation is too tense to be permanent. But the group may founder for some time in subphase 2. In short, groups do not inevitably develop through the resolution of the dependence phase to phase 2. This movement may be retarded indefinitely. Obviously, much depends upon the trainer's role. In fact, the whole dependence modality may be submerged by certain styles of trainer behavior. The trainer has a certain range of choice as to whether dependency as a source of communication distortion is to be highlighted and made the subject of special experiential and conceptual consideration. The personality and training philosophy of the trainer determine his interest in introducing or avoiding explicit consideration of dependency.

There are other important forces in the group besides the trainer, and these may serve to facilitate or block the development that has been described as typical of phase 1. Occasionally there may be no strong independents capable of bringing about the barometric events that precipitate movement. Or the leaders of opposing subgroups may be the most assertive members of the group. In such cases the group may founder permanently in subphase 2. If a group has the misfortune to experience a traumatic event early in its existence—exceedingly schizoid behavior by some member during the first few meetings, for example—anxieties of other members may be aroused to such an extent that all culturally suspect behavior, particularly open expression of feelings, is strongly inhibited in subsequent meetings.

Figure 5.1 summarizes the major events of phase 1, as it typically proceeds. This phase has dealt primarily with the resolution of dependence needs. It ends with acceptance of mutual responsibility for the fate of the group and a sense of solidarity, but the implications of shared responsibility have yet to be explored. This exploration is reserved for phase 2, which we have chosen to call the 'Interdependence Phase'.

Phase 2: Interdependence

The resolution of dependence problems marks the transfer of group attention (and inattention) to the problems of shared responsibility.

Sullivan's description of the change from childhood to the juvenile era seems pertinent here:

> The juvenile era is marked off from childhood by the appearance of an urgent need for compeers with whom to have one's existence. By 'compeers' I mean people who are on our level, and have generically similar attitudes toward authoritative figures, activities and the like. This marks the beginning of the juvenile era, the great developments in which are the talents for cooperation, competition and compromise (Sullivan,[12] pages 17, 18. Emphasis ours.)

The remaining barriers to valid communication are those associated with orientations toward independence: i.e., intimacy, friendship, identification. While the distribution of power was the cardinal issue during phase 1, the distribution of affection occupies the group during phase 2.

73

	Subphase 1 *Dependence-Submission*	Subphase 2 *counterdependence*	Subphase 3 *Resolution*
1 Emotional modality	Dependence—Flight	Counterdependence—Fight. Off-target fighting among members. Distrust of staff member. Ambivalence.	Pairing. Intense involvement in group task.
2 Content themes	Discussion of interpersonal problems external to training groups.	Discussion of group organization; i.e. what degree of structuring devices is needed for 'effective' group behavior?	Discussion and definition of trainer role.
3 Dominant roles (central persons)	Assertive, aggressive members with rich previous organizational or social science experience.	Most assertive counterdependent and dependent members. Withdrawal of *less* assertive independents and dependents.	Assertive independents.
4 Group structure	Organized mainly into multi-subgroups based on members' past experiences.	Two tight subcliques consisting of leaders and members, of counterdependents and dependents.	Group unifies in pursuit of goal and develops internal authority system.
5 Group activity	Self-oriented behavior reminiscent of most new social gatherings.	Search for consensus mechanism: Voting, setting up chairmen, search for 'valid' content subjects.	Group members take over leadership roles formerly perceived as held by trainer.
6 Group movement facilitated by:	Staff member abnegation of traditional role of structuring situation, setting up rules of fair play, regulation of participation.	Disenthrallment with staff member coupled with absorption of uncertainty by most assertive counterdependent and dependent individuals. Subgroups form to ward off anxiety.	Revolt by assertive independents (catalysts) who fuse subgroups into unity by initiating and engineering trainer exit (barometric event).
7 Main defenses	Projection Denigration of authority		Group moves into phase 2

Figure 5.1
Phase 1: Dependence—power relations*

*Course terminates at the end of 17 weeks. It is not uncommon for groups to remain through out the course in this phase.

74

Subphase 4: Enchantment-flight—At the outset of subphase 4, the group is happy, cohesive, relaxed. The atmosphere is one of 'sweetness and light'. Any slight increase in tension is instantly dissipated by joking and laughter. The fighting of phase 1 is still fresh in the memory of the group, and the group's efforts are devoted to patching up differences, healing wounds, and maintaining a harmonious atmosphere. Typically, this is a time of merrymaking and group minstrelsy. Coffee and cake may be served at the meetings. Hours may be passed in organizing a group party. Poetry or songs commemorating the important events and persons in the group's history may be composed by individuals or, more commonly, as a group project. All decisions must be unanimous during this period, since everyone must be happy, but the issues on which decisions are made are mostly ones about which group members have no strong feelings. At first the cathartic, healing function of these activities is clear; there is much spontaneity, playfulness, and pleasure. Soon the pleasures begin to wear thin.

The myth of mutual acceptance and universal harmony must eventually be recognized for what it is. From the beginning of this phase there are frequent evidences of underlying hostilities, unresolved issues in the group. But they are quickly, nervously smoothed over by laughter or misinterpretation. Subphase 4 begins with catharsis, but that is followed by the development of a rigid norm to which all members are forced to conform: 'Nothing must be allowed to disturb our harmony in the future; we must avoid the mistakes of the painful past.' Not that members have forgotten that the painful past was a necessary preliminary to the autonomous and (it is said) delightful present, though that fact is carefully overlooked. Rather, there is a dim realization that all members must have an experience somewhat analogous to the trainer's in subphase 3, before a mutually understood, accepted, and realistic definition of their own roles in the group can be arrived at.

Resistance of members to the requirement that harmony be maintained at all costs appears in subtle ways. In open group discussion the requirement is imperative: either the member does not dare to endanger harmony with the group or to disturb the *status quo* by denying that all problems have been solved. Much as members may dislike the tedious work of maintaining the appearance of harmony, the alternative is worse. The house of cards would come tumbling down, and the painful and exacting work of building something more substantial would have to begin. The flight from these problems takes a number of forms. Group members may say, 'We've had our fighting and are now a group. Thus, further self-study is unnecessary.' Very commonly, the possibility of any change may be prevented by not coming together as a total group at all. Thus, the members may subgroup through an entire meeting. Those who would disturb the friendly subgroups are accused of 'rocking the boat'.

The solidarity and harmony become more and more illusory, but the group still clings to the illusion. This perseveration is in a way a consequence of the deprivation that members have experienced in maintaining the atmosphere of harmony. Maintaining it forces members to behave in ways alien to their own feelings; to go still further in group involvement would mean a complete loss of self.

The group is therefore torn by a new ambivalence, which might be verbalized as follows: First, 'We all love one another and therefore we must maintain the solidarity of the group and give up whatever is necessary of our selfish desires.' Second, 'The group demands that I sacrifice my identity as a person, but the group is an evil mechanism which satisfies no dominant needs.' As this subphase comes to a close, the happiness that marked its beginning is maintained only as a mask. The 'innocent' splitting of the group into subgroups has gone so far that members will even walk around the meeting table to join in the conversation of a subgroup rather than speak across the table at the risk of bringing the whole group together. There is a certain uneasiness about the group; there is a feeling that 'we should work together, but cannot'. There may be a tendency to regress to the orientation of subphase 1: group members would like the trainer to take over.

To recapitulate: subphase 4 begins with a happy sense of group belongingness. Individual identity is eclipsed by a 'the group is bigger than all of us' sentiment. But this integration is shortlived: it soon becomes perceived as a fake attempt to resolve interpersonal problems by denying their reality. In the later stages of this subphase, enchantment with the total group is replaced by enchantment with one's subgroup, and out of this breakdown of the group emerges a new organization based on the anxieties aroused out of this first, suffocating, involvement.

Subphase 5: Disenchantment-fight—This subphase is marked by a division into two subgroups—paralleling the experience of subphase 2—but this time based upon orientations towards the degree of intimacy required by group membership. Membership in the two subgroups is not necessarily the same as in subphase 2: for now the fragmentation occurs as a result of opposite and extreme attitudes toward the degree of intimacy desired in interpersonal relations. The counterpersonal members band together to resist further involvement. The overpersonal members band together in a demand for unconditional love. While these subgroups appear as divergent as possible, a common theme underlies them. For the one group, the only means seen for maintaining self-esteem is to avoid any real commitment to others; for the other group, the only way to maintain self-esteem is to obtain a commitment from others to forgive everything. The subgroups share in common the fear that intimacy breeds contempt.

This anxiety is reflected in many ways during subphase 6. For the first time openly disparaging remarks are made about the group. Invidious comparisons are made between it and other groups. Similarly, psychology and social science may be attacked. The inadequacy of the group as a basis for self-esteem is dramatized in many ways—from stating, 'I don't care what you think,' to boredom, to absenteeism. The overpersonals insist that they are happy and comfortable, while the counterpersonals complain about the lack of group morale. Intellectualization by the overpersonals frequently takes on religious overtones concerning Christian love, consideration for others, etc. In explanations of member behavior, the counterpersonal members account for all in terms of motives having nothing to do with the present group; the overpersonals explain all in terms of acceptance and rejection in the present group.

Subphase 5 belongs to the counterpersonals as subphase 4 belonged to the overpersonals. Subphase 4 might be caricatured as hiding in the womb of the group; subphase 5 as hiding out of sight of the group. It seems probable that both of these modalities serve to ward off anxieties associated with intimate interpersonal relations. A theme that links them together can be verbalized as follows: 'If others really knew me, they would reject me.' The overpersonal's formula for avoiding this rejection seems to be accepting all others so as to be protected by the others' guilt; the counterpersonal's way is by rejecting all others before they have a chance to reject him. Another way of characterizing the counterpersonal orientation is in the phrase, 'I would lose my identity as a member of the group.' The corresponding overpersonal orientation reads, 'I have nothing to lose by identifying with the group.' We can now look back on the past two subphases as countermeasures against loss of self-esteem; what Sullivan once referred to as the greatest inhibition to the understanding of what is distinctly human, 'the overwhelming conviction of self-hood—this amounts to a delusion of unique individuality'. The sharp swings and fluctuations that occurred between the enchantment and euphoria of subphase 4 and the disenchantment of subphase 5 can be seen as a struggle between the 'institutionalization of complacency' on the one hand and anxiety associated with fantasy speculations about intimacy and involvement on the other. This dissociative behavior serves a purpose of its own: a generalized denial of the group and its meaning for individuals. For if the group is important and valid, then it has to be taken seriously. If it can wallow in the enchantment of subphase 4, it is safe; if it can continually vilify the goals and objectives of the group, it is also safe. The disenchantment theme in subphase 5 is perhaps a less skilful and more desperate security provision with its elaborate wall of defenses than the 'group mind' theme of subphase 4. What should be stressed is that both subphase defenses were created almost entirely on fantastic expectations about the consequences of group involvement. These defenses are homologous to anxiety as it is experienced by the individual; i.e., the state of 'anxiety arises as a response to a situation of danger and which will be reproduced thenceforward whenever such a situation recurs.' (Freud,[13] page 72.) In sum, the past two subphases were marked by a conviction that further group involvement would be injurious to members' self-esteem.

Subphase 6: Consensual validation—In the groups of which we write, two forces combine to press the group toward a resolution of the interdependency problem. These are the approaching end of the training course, and the need to establish a method of evaluation (including course grades).

There are, of course, ways of denying or avoiding these realities. The group can agree to continue to meet after the course ends. It can extricate itself from evaluation activities by asking the trainer to perform the task, or by awarding a blanket grade. But turning this job over to the trainer is a regression to dependence; and refusal to discriminate and reward is a failure to resolve the problems of interdependence. If the group has developed in general as we have described, the reality of termination and evaluation cannot be denied, and these regressive modes of adaptation cannot be tolerated.

The characteristic defenses of the two subgroups at first fuse to prevent any movement toward the accomplishment of the evaluation and grading task. The counterpersonals resist evaluation as an invasion of privacy: they foresee catastrophe if members begin to say what they think of one another. The overpersonals resist grading since it involves discriminating among the group members. At the same time, all members have a stake in the outcome of evaluation and grading. In avoiding the task, members of each subgroup are perceived by members of the other as 'rationalizing', and the group becomes involved in a vicious circle of mutual disparagement. In this process, the fear of loss of self-esteem through group involvement is near to being realized. As in subphase 3, it is the independents—in this case those whose self-esteem is not threatened by the prospect of intimacy—who restore members' confidence in the group. Sometimes all that is required to reverse the vicious circle quite dramatically is a request by an independent for assessment of his own role. Or it may be an expression of confidence in the group's ability to accomplish the task.

The activity that follows group commitment to the evaluation task does not conform to the expectations of the overpersonal or counterpersonal members. Its chief characteristic is the willingness and ability of group members to validate their self-concepts with other members. The fear of rejection fades when tested against reality. The tensions that developed as a result of these fears diminish in the light of actual discussion of member roles. At the same time, there is revulsion against 'capsule evaluations' and 'curbstone psychoanalysis'. Instead, what ensues is a serious attempt by each group member to verbalize his private conceptual scheme for understanding human behavior—his own and that of others. Bringing these assumptions into explicit communication is the main work of subphase 6. This activity demands a high level of work and of communicative skill. Some of the values that appear to underlie the group's work during this subphase are as follows:

1 Members can accept one another's differences without associating 'good' and 'bad' with the differences.

2 Conflict exists but is over substantive issues rather than emotional issues.

3 Consensus is reached as a result of rational discussion rather than through a compulsive attempt at unanimity.

4 Members are aware of their own involvement, and of other aspects of group process, without being overwhelmed or alarmed.

5 Through the evaluation process, members take on greater personal meaning to each other. This facilitates communication and creates a deeper understanding of how the other person thinks, feels, behaves; it creates a series of personal expectations, as distinguished from the previous, more stereotyped, role expectations.

The above values, and some concomitant values, are, of course, very close to the authors' conception of a 'good group'. In actuality, they are not always achieved by the end of the group life. The prospect of the death of the group, after much procrastination in the secret hope that it will be over before anything can be done, is likely to force the group into strenuous last minute efforts to overcome the

78

obstacles that have blocked its progress. As a result, the sixth subphase is too often hurried and incomplete. If the hurdles are not overcome in time, grading is likely to be an exercise that confirms members' worst suspicions about the group. And if role evaluation is attempted, either the initial evaluations contain so much hostile material as to block further efforts, or evaluations are so flowery and vacuous that no one, least of all the recipient, believes them.

In the resolution of interdependence problems, member-personalities count for even more than they do in the resolution of dependence problems. The trainer's behavior is crucial in determining the group's ability to resolve the dependence issue, but in the interdependence issue the group is, so to speak, only as strong as its weakest link. The exceedingly dependent group member can ride through phase 1 with a fixed belief in the existence of a private relationship between himself and the trainer; but the person whose anxieties are intense under the threats associated with intimacy can immobilize the group. (Figure 5.2 summarizes the major events of phase 2.)

Conclusions

Dependence and interdependence—power and love, authority and intimacy—are regarded as the central problems of group life. In most organizations and societies, the rules governing the distribution of authority and the degree of intimacy among members are prescribed. In the human relations training group, they are major areas of uncertainty. While the choice of these matters as the focus of group attention and experience rests to some extent with the trainer, his choice is predicated on the belief that they are the core of interpersonal experience. As such, the principal obstacles to valid interpersonal communication lie in rigidities of interpretation and response carried over from the anxious experiences with particular love or power figures into new situations in which they are inappropriate. The existence of such autisms complicates all discussion unduly and in some instances makes an exchange of meanings impossible.

Stating the training goal as the establishment of valid communication means that the relevance of the autistic response to authority and intimacy on the part of any member can be explicitly examined, and at least a provisional alternative formulated by him. Whether this makes a lasting change in the member's flexibility, or whether he will return to his more restricted formula when confronted with a new situation, we do not know, but we expect that it varies with the success of his group experience—particularly his success in understanding it.

We have attempted to portray what we believe to be the typical pattern of group development, and to show the relationship of member orientations and changes in member orientations to the major movements of the group. In this connection, we have emphasized the catalytic role of persons unconflicted with respect to one or the other of the dependence and interdependence areas. This power to move the group lies mainly in his freedom from anxiety-based reactions to problems of authority (or intimacy): he has the freedom to be creative in searching for a way to reduce tension.

	Subphase 4—Enchantment	Subphase 5—Disenchantment	Subphase 6—Consensual validation
Emotional modality	Pairing-Flight. Group becomes a respected icon beyond further analysis.	Fight-Flight. Anxiety reactions. Distrust and suspicion of various group members.	Pairing, understanding, acceptance.
Content themes	Discussion of 'group history', and generally salutary aspects of course, group, and membership.	Revival of content themes used in Subphase 1: What is a group? What are we doing here? What are the goals of the group? What do I have to give up—personally—to belong to this group? (How much intimacy and affection is required?) Invasion of privacy vs. 'group giving'. Setting up proper codes of social behavior.	Course grading system. Discussion and assessment of member roles.
Dominant roles (central persons)	General distribution of participation for first time. Overpersonals have salience.	Most assertive counterpersonal and overpersonal individuals, with counterpersonals especially salient.	Assertive independents.
Group structure	Solidarity, fusion. High degree of camaraderie and suggestibility. Le Bon's description of 'group mind' would apply here.	Restructuring of membership into two competing predominant subgroups made up of individuals who share similar attitudes concerning degree of intimacy required in social interaction, i.e., the counterpersonal and overpersonal groups. The personal individuals remain uncommitted but act according to needs of situation.	Diminishing of ties based on personal orientation. Group structure now presumably appropriate to needs of situation based on predominantly substantive rather than emotional orientations. Consensus significantly easier on important issues.
Group activity	Laughter, joking, humor. Planning out-of-class activities such as parties. The institutionalization of happiness to be accomplished by 'fun' activities. High rate of interaction and participation.	Disparagement of group in a variety of ways: high rate of absenteeism, tardiness, balkiness in initiating total group interaction, frequent statements concerning worthlessness of group, denial of importance of group. Occasional member asking for individual help finally rejected by the group.	Communication to others of self-system of interpersonal relations; i.e., making conscious to self, and others aware of, conceptual system one uses to predict consequences of personal behavior. Acceptance of group on reality terms.
Group movement facilitated by:	Independence and achievement attained by trainer-rejection and its concomitant, deriving consensually some effective means for authority and control. (Subphase 3 rebellion bridges gap between Subphases 2 and 4.)	Disenchantment of group as a result of *fantasied expectations of group life*. The perceived threat to self-esteem that further group involvement signifies creates schism of group according to amount of affection and intimacy desired. The counterpersonal and overpersonal assertive individuals alleviate source of anxiety by disparaging or abnegating further group involvement. Subgroups form to ward off anxiety.	The external realities, group termination and the prescribed need for a course grading system, comprise the barometric event. Led by the personal individuals, the group tests reality and reduces autistic convictions concerning group involvement.
Main defences	Denial, isolation, intellectualization, and alienation.		

Figure 5.2

Phase 2. Interdependence—Personal Relations

We have also emphasized the 'barometric event' or event capable of moving the group from one phase to the next. The major events of this kind are the removal of the trainer as part of the resolution of the dependence problem; and the evaluation-grading requirements at the termination of the course. Both these barometric events require a catalytic agent in the group to bring them about. That is to say, the trainer-exit can take place only at the moment when it is capable of symbolizing the attainment of group autonomy, and it requires a catalytic agent in the group to give it this meaning. And the grading assignment can move the group forward only if the catalytic agent can reverse the vicious circle of disparagement that precedes it.

Whether the incorporation of these barometric events into the training design merely makes our picture of group development a self-fulfilling prophecy, or whether, as we wish to believe, these elements make dramatically clear the major forward movements of the group, and open the gate for a flood of new understanding and communication, can only be decided on the basis of more, and more varied, experience.

The evolution from phase 1 to phase 2 represents not only a change in emphasis from power to affection, but also from role to personality. Phase 1 activity generally centres on broad role distinctions, such as class, ethnic background, professional interests, etc.; Phase 2 activity involves a deeper concern with personality modalities, such as reaction to failure, warmth, retaliation, anxiety, etc. This development presents an interesting paradox. For the group in phase 1 emerged out of a heterogeneous collectivity of individuals; the individual in phase 2 emerged out of the group. This suggests that group therapy, where attention is focused on individual movement, begins at the least enabling time. It is possible that, before group members are able to help each other, the barriers to communication must be partially understood.

References

1. SULLIVAN, H. S. 'Tensions, Interpersonal and International.' In Cantril, Hadley (ed.), *Tensions that Cause Wars.* Urbana, Ill.: Univ. of Illinois Press, 1950.
2. FREUD, SIGMUND. *Group Psychology and the Analysis of the Ego.* Translated by J. Strachey. London: International Psycho-Analytical Press, 1922; N.Y.: Liveright, 1949.
3. SCHUTZ, W. C. 'What Makes Groups Productive?' *Hum. Relat.*, Vol. VIII, No. 4, 1955, p. 429.
4. BION, W. R. 'Experiences in Groups: I.' *Hum. Relat.*, Vol. I, No. 3, 1948, pp. 314-20.
5. BION, W. R. 'Experiences in Groups: II.' *Hum. Relat.*, Vol. I, No. 4, 1948, pp. 487-96.
6. FREUD, SIGMUND. *Moses and Monotheism.* London: Hogarth Press, 1939; N.Y.: Vintage Books, 1955.
7. LEIGHTON, A. H. *The Governing of Men.* Princeton: Princeton UP, 1946.
8. See GOULDNER, ALVIN[9] and WHYTE, W. F., Jr.[10] PARK, ROBERT E.,[11] writing in 1928, had considerable weight on some functions of revolution and change.
9. GOULDNER, ALVIN. *Wildcat Strike.* Yellow Springs. Ohio: Antioch Press, 1954; London: Routledge & Kegan Paul, 1955
10. WHYTE, W. F., Jr. *Patterns for Industrial Peace.* N.Y.: Harper, 1951.
11. PARK, ROBERT E. 'The Strike.' *Society.* N.Y.: Free Press of Glencoe, 1955.
12. SULLIVAN, H. S. *Conceptions of Modern Psychiatry.* Washington, DC: William Alanson White Psychiatric Foundation, 1940, 1945; London: Tavistock publications, 1955.
13. FREUD, SIGMUND. *The Problem of Anxiety.* Translated by H. A. Bunker. N.Y.: Psychoanalytic Quarterly Press and W. W. Norton, 1936.

6. Changing goals of human relations training

Howard Baumgartel

Fifteen to twenty years ago, the central goal of the human relations training movement was to teach people the kinds of skills and attitudes that would be useful in reducing *dissatisfaction* and *grievance* among the manager's employees. In some ways, the movement had negative objective—the elimination of sources of discontent and unrest. On the positive side there was, however, interest in discovering the sources of employee satisfactions and training supervisors and managers in the kinds of skills leading to greater employee satisfaction. Either way, satisfaction and dissatisfaction were the focal concern of such management training courses.

If one surveys the contemporary human relations training movement, one finds quite a different set of concerns. There seem to be two central foci: one is an interest in training managers in more *effective* ways of building working relationships with *colleagues:* the second central goal of contemporary training is the development of skill in *creating organizational climates* conducive to high rates of technological innovation and organizational effectiveness.[1] These new training goals, thus, are of a positive sort. What are some of the reasons for these changes in emphasis?

Research in industrial human relations in the 'fifties demonstrated again and again that there is no simple correlation between worker satisfaction and productivity. Satisfied workers are not necessarily higher producers and, conversely, dissatisfied workers are not necessarily low producers.[2] Factors other than satisfaction seem to determine productivity. The reason why satisfaction and productivity are uncorrelated is, of course, because people with low motivation and high reward may be very satisfied, while people with high motivation will be less satisfied, etc.[3] It should be pointed out, however, that satisfaction *is* related to

• Reprinted with permission from *Management Bulletin*, Vol. 4, No. 4, Oct./Dec. 1967, Journal of the Department of Business Management and Industrial Administration, University of Delhi, India.

turnover and absenteeism.[4] People who are dissatisfied tend to leave the situation. And, of course, labor unrest produced by dissatisfaction continues to be a realistic problem for many industries. Organized labor unrest is apparently much more linked with general economic and social conditions and with problems in union management relations than it is with the human relations skills of supervisors. Solution to these problems lies at a different level of analysis than that of the leadership skills of supervisors and managers.

The development of the human relations training movement led, in the 'fifties, to a series of major research studies aimed at assessing or measuring the effectiveness of such training. The results of these studies raised serious questions about the whole philosophy of the movement. Findings of several studies showed that foreman and management training courses had little or no effect.[5] These studies showed further that whether or not training was effective was greatly dependent on the *organizational climate*. Where there was a progressive organization characterized by (a) problem-solving attitudes, (b) widespread participation in decision-making processes, and (c) considerate as opposed to distant and impersonal management, then the training of supervisors and managers seemed to have beneficial results. Otherwise, no benefit was *measurable*. Furthermore, training effects were shown to be greatest in companies which were engaged in self-conscious programs of organizational development concurrent with their managers' participation in formal programs of management training.

This new focus on organizational climate led to an awareness that the problems of how managers get along with each other—how the management team functions—were much more relevant to organizational effectiveness than were the more restricted problems of worker-management relations. With this new insight, human relations training has tended to focus much more on how the manager can build effective work relationships with his own colleagues[6]. Dynamic, complex organizations require extensive interpersonal skills within the managerial group itself. It is somewhat assumed that, if effective work relationships are established within the management team, some of the other human problems will solve themselves. This trend has resulted in a changed goal of training from how to 'handle' subordinates to how to 'handle' *oneself*—a much closer look at the personal behavior patterns of the manager himself.

Another factor accounting for this change in the goals of human relations training stems from the increased understanding of the role of technological innovations in both national economic development and in the growth and success of individual firms and enterprises. Economists and developmental analysts have demonstrated that in any nation there can be no significant improvement in *per capita* income without an accelerating rate of technological innovation.[7] Even optimum levels of capital formation will not produce real economic gains unless there is continuous technological innovation. This identification of the key role of technology in economic development has led organization specialists to look to the human-organizational factors conducive to high rates of innovation and change.[8] Human relations specialists realize that getting a little more work out of factory supervisors and workers is a small problem compared to that of creating the climate

83

where major technical 'break-through' can double worker and plant productivity overnight—without, so to speak, anybody working any 'harder'. The public realization of these basic realities has, then, been another factor in the shift in goals of the human relations training movement.

Given these new directions in human relations training for managers, we can begin to specify more concretely some of the specific goals of this new movement. A fundamental problem has been the discovery through research of what are the organizational forms and personal skills most conducive to high rates of technological innovation.[9] Elton Mayo conceptualized the problem many years ago as the change from 'traditional' organizational forms to what he called the 'adaptive' form.[10] Perhaps the required changes in organizational patterns can be shown as follows:

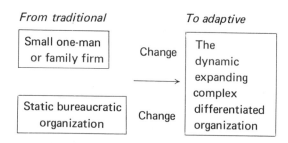

It is the main postulate of this paper that entirely new styles of management and new personal attributes are required for effective functioning in the new adaptive organizations as compared with traditional organizational forms. The task of human relations training, specifically, and management education, more generally, is to develop and prepare the supply of 'new men' needed for the optimal functioning of new organizational forms. Preparing oneself for a managerial role in an expanding, innovative enterprise not only involves acquiring skill in the new technologies, but also fundamental changes in personal outlook, patterns of interpersonal relationship and organizational role-taking.[11] What are some of these latter types of changes required of individual managers?

Let us think of these changes as occurring potentially at several levels of human functioning. Four levels seem appropriate for analytical purposes—cognitive, motivational emotional, interpersonal, and organizational. When we speak of the *cognitive level* we refer to the manner in which the individual thinks about, believes in, and perceives the world about himself. For example, social anthropologists have observed that some people do not have cause-effect concepts in their thought processes. Or some people 'see' human life as being determined entirely by fate or impersonal, unknowable forces.[12] These basic thought processes structure and influence the behavior of people in organizational life as well as in ordinary social affairs.

The second level of analysis is the *motivational emotional*. This concept refers to the dynamics of feelings and sentiments within the individual's personality structure. Some individuals and indeed some groups of people can be characterized, for example, as having basic feelings of security or insecurity, or they may be full of hatreds or resentments, or whatever. These psychodynamic or basic personality factors may be appropriate for some social structures and inappropriate for others.[13]

The third level of analysis we have called the *interpersonal level*. Obviously, the various levels of analysis are clearly interdependent—interpersonal patterns are closely tied to emotional dynamics. Particularly with regard to the management process. It is important to separate the two levels for analytical purposes. The concept of interpersonal level refers to the prevalent and persistent styles and forms of face to face interaction. To what extent people communicate with each other and how much people trust each other, and so on, are interpersonal phenomena. A leader's 'interpersonal style' may have a great influence on his organizational unit.[14] We can discuss interpersonal patterns independently of personality concepts.

Finally, there is the *organizational level* of analysis. By this concept we mean the structural and dynamic properties of the relationship among persons and groups of persons in larger social units. Just as there are many structural differences among different chemical compounds, so there are differences among social organizations and these differences can be abstractly analyzed. The development of general systems theory in modern science generally has resulted in major breakthroughs in organizational analysis.[15]

Dimensions of change

The basic thesis of this paper is that, as organizations change from traditional forms to the new forms adapted for accelerated technological change, entirely new skills, attitudes, and outlooks are required of the manager. As a matter of emphasis, we can hypothesize that these newer organizations can only come into being where these new skills and personal characteristics are already present or coming into being. Furthermore, we propose that the goal of human relations training and, for that matter, all management education should be, at its center the creation of the new manager for the new organizations. These training goals can be conceptualized in terms of four levels of analysis.

At the *cognitive level* the fundamental requirement is that the new type of manager take a problem-solving attitude toward all aspects of the working environment. This means that, first, he must give up custom, for example, and become *experimental*. New ideas must be given a try, a climate of experimentation should be encouraged. Second, traditional practices will need to be subjected to careful rational analysis. By rationality we refer to the logical analysis of means-ends relationships. The modern scientific management movement, as evidenced by the field of operations research, is the elaboration and extension of the principle of scientific rationality. Along with this change and closely associated with it are two others. Instead of relying on beliefs (things held to be true by 'nature')—he will want to be habitually testing beliefs against the hard data and facts of industrial life.[16] As we have mentioned earlier, for many years workers in personnel management 'believed' that happy workers were good workers. Recent empirical research has demonstrated this to be a myth.[17] Finally, the new manager will be required to be more *relativistic* and less absolutistic in his outlook toward the world. He will need to regularly understand that there are different ways of viewing things and that there is no correct way of viewing some things.[18] To illustrate, empirical approaches to the classic problem of 'span of control' have indicated that there is no one right way to formulate organizations.[19]

The attributes of emotional makeup required for functioning effectively in the new organization are more difficult to conceptualize and achieve through education. One fundamental requirement is that the individual become less impulsive and more *controlled* in his character structure. The high degree of differentiation and interdependence in a complex, expanding organization requires people to give up impulsivity. The manager of a family firm can suddenly leave for a vacation on a personal whim; a manager of a complex, highly integrated organization cannot. A corollary of this principle is that the new man must be characterized by more highly developed *internal controls* on his own behavior and less dependent on external controls. Several other personality changes are required for effective functioning in complex organizations.[20] The new manager must be able to have more *tolerance for frustration*—complexity brings frustration—and he must be able to postpone gratification—years are required for the fulfillment of complex schemes.[21] He also must give up seeking perfect clarity and lack of *ambiguity* in organizational affairs. He must be able to live *with ambiguity* and lack of clarity. For example, no one will be able to state perfectly his duties and responsibilities. Finally, the new manager's motivations will need to be oriented toward the positive goals of *achievement* and *self-actualization* and away from the negative or defensive goals of status-preservation and security.[22]

New patterns of *interpersonal relations* are required in developing, growing, innovative organizations. More *openness* is required. Organizational effectiveness requires an adequate flow of information on both ideas and feelings. Less of distrust and more of *trust* is also an interpersonal requirement. Dynamic organizations are too complex, skills are too specialized for a climate of distrust to be functional. Concurrently, people with skill in *interdependence*—collaborative working patterns among peers—will be more important than people with skill in building interpersonal relationships on the basis of who is 'above' or 'below' the individual.[23] The traditional hierarchical patterns may function effectively in organizations with routine tasks, but they can hamper the effectiveness of growing, innovative organizations. Finally, the effective member of an adaptive organization will be more *close* and considerate in his interpersonal relations and less distant and unconcerned about others.[24]

We have stated earlier that managers can learn new attitudes and behavior patterns but unless the organizational climate is supportive of these new patterns no benefit will derive. To the extent that the managerial team creates this climate, we can identify the dimensions of change to be sought at the *organizational level*. Organizational patterns will change from paternal-authoritarian to *participative-consensual*. One simple fact makes this change imperative and inevitable. The mere size, complexity and specialization of the new organization means that one man or a small *élite* group can no longer manage everything, review all decisions, and so forth. Furthermore, managerial and staff specialists can only perform their functions optimally when they can effectively influence decisions and when they are themselves consensually and not acquiescently in agreement with the decision. Attitudes of self-reliance and achievement cannot thrive in the father-son patterns of paternal structures. As alluded to earlier, the complex adaptive organization must, of necessity, rely more on *internal controls*—self-created through identification and other socialization processes—and less on a system of external controls. Rigid external controls may be required in military and paramilitary organizations, but they are dysfunctional (harmful) in innovative work organizations. *Long-term organizational* growth and development will become the driving dynamic force in the creative organization[25] rather than short-terms personal goals of key people—as in some family enterprises. Problem-solving and achieving goals will be paramount functions and power-struggles and status preoccupation will be less salient in the new organizational structures.

One thing may not be fully recognized: great skill and effort are required to build and maintain complex-innovative organizations. The demands of the management role are greater than the demands in the traditional family business or static organizations.[26]

No one has a right to say to another what the other should want. One of the greatest defects in various 'helping' programs, such as the US foreign aid programme, is the tendency to try to tell the client party what he should have for his goal, what he should want, instead of trying to help him achieve what he wants to achieve. But one can indicate some guidelines for achieving goals once they are determined. In this paper, we have indicated that if a people *want* to have a rising standard of living, then there must be accelerating rates of technological innovation. Some of the hypothesized dimensions of personal and organizational change have been outlined. While this is not the place to explore in depth the implications of this thesis for management education and human relations training, we do propose that a changed emphasis and a changed technology in management education are already in evidence. Human relations training, for example, has become less oriented to problems of workers morale and more oriented toward helping managers become more skilful and effective in their daily contact with other managerial colleagues. New techniques in management training and management consultation are consistent in utilizing increased involvement and participation of the trainees or clients in the process itself. New training methods create live situations, where people learn by doing and learn from feedback on experience. And, finally, since we are hypothesizing that the training of managers involve some basic reeducation and reorientation of attitude and outlook, we find that management trainers are turning increasingly to social psychologists and psychotherapists for insights and skills indicating how to facilitate the processes of personal growth and change. Dynamic learning experience on the part of the learner appears to be essential. Change and the facilitation of change have thus become the central focus of the management training movement. Beyond that, training efforts are increasingly coordinated with planned programmes of organizational change *within* organizations concurrent with general training activities.[27] The developing man requires a developing organization for effective fulfillment and action.

References

1. See, for example, SCHEIN, E. H. and BENNIS, WARREN, G., *Personal and Organizational Change Through Group Methods: The Laboratory Approach.* N.Y.: Wiley, 1965.
2. The Classic reference on this point is BRAYFIELD, A. H. and CROKETT, W. H., 'Employee Attitudes and Employee Performance.' *Psychol. Bull.,* 1955, 52 pp., 377-95. See also LIKERT, RENSIS, 'Measuring Business Performance.' *Harvard Bsns. Rev.,* 1958, pp. 41-50. A major industrial experiment was conducted where, among other things, productivity was increased while worker satisfaction declined. See also BAUMGARTEL, HOWARD and GOLDSTEIN, G., 'Some Human Consequences of Technical Change.' *Pers. Admin.,* Vol. 24, 1961, pp. 32-40.
3. MORSE, NANCY, *Satisfaction and the White Collar Worker*, Ann Arbor, Mich.: Survey Research Center, University of Michigan, 1953.
4. See, for example, MANN, FLOYD, and BAUMGARTEL, *Absences and Employee Attitudes.* Ann Arbor, Mich.: Institute for Social Research, 1952. See also ROSS, I. C. and ZANDER, A. F., *'Need Satisfaction and Employee Turnover.' Pers. Psychol.,* Vol. 10, 1957, pp. 327-38.
5. Two influential studies were: HARITON, T., *Conditions Influencing the Effects of Training Foremen in New Human Principles.* University of Michigan: Doctoral Dissertations, 1951; FLEISHMAN, E. A., 'Leadership Climate: Human Relations Training and Supervisory Behavior.' *Pers. Psychol.,* Vol. 6, 1953, pp. 205-22.
6. ARGYRIS, C., *Interpersonal Competence and Organizational Effectiveness.* Homewood, Ill.: Dorsey-Irwin, 1962.
7. For this point, the author has relied on the clear lectures on the economics of development by Prof. ASHOK MITRA, formerly with the Indian Institute of Management, Calcutta.
8. STEINER, GARY, *The Creative Organization.* Chicago: The University of Chicago Press, 1965.
9. *Comparative Theories of Social Change* (A symposium). Ann Arbor, Mich.: Foundation for Research on Human Behavior, 1967. See also, ROGERS, EVERETT M., *The Diffusion of Innovation.* N.Y.: Free Press of Glencoe, 1962.
10. MAYO, ELTON, *The Social Problems of an Industrial Civilization.* Boston: Harvard Graduate School of Business Administration, 1945.
11. See *The World Food Problem.* New Delhi: The United States Information Service, 1967, p. 12. 'The scarcest and most needed resource in the developing countries is the scientific, technical, and *managerial skill* needed for systematic, orderly decision-making and implementation.'
12. KLUCKHOHN, CLYDE, 'Values and Value Orientations in the Theory of Action.' In *Toward a General Theory of Action.* PARSONS, T. and SHILS, E. eds. Cambridge, Mass.; Harvard U.P., 1951, pp. 388-433.
13. GERTH, H. and MILLS, C. W., *Character and Social Structure.* N.Y.: Harcourt, Brace, 1953.
14. BAUMGARTEL, HOWARD, 'Leadership as a Variable in Research Administration.' *Admin. Sci. Quart.,* Vol. 2, 1957, pp. 334-60.
15. KATZ, D. and KAHN, R. L., *The Social Psychology Organizations.* N.Y.: Wiley, 1967.
16. See News Release (UNI) reporting speech by SARABHAI, VIKRAM Dr, dated 25 August 1967.
17. See reference 2 above.
18. TUMIN, M., 'Obstacles to Creativity.' *ETC*, Summer 1964, pp. 11 ff.
19. See James Worthy's article and others in PORTER, D. E. and APPLEWHITE, P. B., *Studies in Organizational Behavior and Management.* Scranton: International Textbooks, 1964.
20. One of the most stimulating discussions of this point is in HAGEN, EVERETT E., *On the Theory of Social Change.* Homewood, Ill.: Dorsey, 1962.

21. JAQUES, ELLIOT, *The Measurement of Responsibility*. London: Tavistock Publications, 1958.
22. McCLELLAND, DAVID, *The Achieving Society*. N.Y.: Van Nostrand, 1961.
23. PAREEK UDAI, Lecture. The University of Kansas, Committee on International Development, 1967.
24. LIKERT, RENSIS, *New Patterns in Management*. N.Y.: McGraw-Hill, 1950. (See also Pareek's concept of the need for empathy.)
25. SRIVASTVA, SURESH, 'Process and Management of Change.' In *Readings in Group Development for Managers and Trainers*, Baumgartel, H., Bennis, W. G. and De, N. R.
26. 'Participation' managers spend more hours per week at work and spend more hours per week working with colleagues than do 'directive' or *laissez-faire* managers. See reference 14 above.
27. See, for example, BAUMGARTEL, H., 'Using Employee Questionaires Results for Improving Organization.' In *Readings in Group Development for Managers and Trainers*, Baumgartel, Bennis, and De, N. R.

89

PART THREE: Focus on systematic task performance

The next four chapters indicate a distinct shift in emphasis. While still concerned with here and now issues, there is a determination to use this inductive way of thinking in a more systematic fashion. There is another difference. The emphasis is turned towards performance rather than current feelings and activities.

Furthermore, all four authors, especially Ralph Coverdale and Peter Honey, believe that people learn best when they practise new ways instead of just talking about practising new ways.

Matthew Miles was probably the first American in the NTL network to emphasize the cyclical nature of problem-solving. The quotation from his book *Learning to Work in Groups*, which has the US school and educational system as its backcloth, emphasizes the need for psychologically safe skill practice sessions, if improved behaviours are to be won and maintained. But quite independently, two British psychologists, who are not members of that NTL network, pioneered a fresh approach to the development of individuals that has been well received in many British companies. First, Ralph Coverdale in the late 'fifties formulated a set of ideas aimed at improving the practice of management. He was concerned with achievement; his emphasis is on individuals and groups of individuals being more effective in action. As Seamus Roche points out in chapter 8, intimate revelations of self need not and do not occur because the training group only considers those behaviours and forces that help or hinder the accomplishment of the task.

More recently, Peter Honey has developed this manner of training a stage further. He so rightly says in chapter 9 that organizations want learning not learned managers, i.e., people who can improve their own performance and that of their subordinates; head knowledge of itself is of little use. Since there is a world of difference between saying and doing, he, like Coverdale, sees that the way to reduce that gap is through simple exercises that men can perform in a climate supportive of new behaviours. He goes a stage further. In the design of a course for particular individuals, he sees the need for precourse research to establish those behaviours that senior managers in the employing organization perceive to be both effective and ineffective.

The fourth author in this group, Hugh Marlow, in chapter 10, has struck out in a new way. He, like Peter Honey, shows the value of understanding the environment in which individual executives are embedded. From this, he develops the need for fashioning a simulation exercise. At the end of his article, there is the outline of a systems model composed of four loops. This is perhaps a pointer to ways in which behavioural scientists and computer specialists may both be drawn closer to the line manager. It may lead to a conceptual ability to look at organizations as on-going systems rather than as a series of interpersonal and intergroup relationships. This, in turn, may lead to the creation of real-time educational experiences. Later, in chapter 21, Alistair Mant develops this point further.

7. How does a training group differ from other groups?

Matthew B. Miles

For a variety of reasons, training for better group behavior takes place best in a *training group*. Such groups differ in certain respects from work groups, from classroom groups, and from psychotherapy groups. A description of these differences may help to clarify the nature of training further.

Focus on member change

A training group differs most centrally from a *work group* on the job in placing less emphasis on the accomplishment of a specific external task and more emphasis on improvement of its members' skills. For example, a work group that had great difficulty in reaching decisions would be a flop on the job. When a training group has decision-making difficulties, however, they are grist for the mill. The members can analyze the difficulties, try again, and learn from the experience. This is the essential nature of the laboratory approach.

Since a training group's objective is *change* in its members' ways of doing things, their procedures, their practices, most training groups do not also try to accomplish 'work' tasks. Their work, in effect, is to cause themselves to learn to be better group participants. Since a training group does *not* have to make up new curriculum guides, agree on playground policy, or clarify bond issue proposals, the members are freer to experiment and learn about group behavior. This idea is often puzzling to people who have not attended training groups. 'What on earth do you talk about?' The answer—it is perhaps a maddeningly vague one—is that a training group talks about any and all group process problems that appear in the course of its work.

Most training groups, then, have a limited life span. They remain together for a specified period of time. It is assumed that their members, as they move back to

• Reprinted with the permission of the publisher from Matthew B. Miles, *Learning to Work in Groups*. New York: Teachers College Press. Copyright © 1959.

their work groups, will keep on behaving in the new, more effective ways they have learned in the training group.*

Focus on the here and now

How does a training group differ from the usual *classroom group*? Both are concerned with changes in their members' behavior, yet these changes are of somewhat different sorts.

In a classroom, the content discussed and the skills learned are ordinarily drawn from the surrounding culture. Thus, children are to learn to read, to write, to handle numbers, to be familiar with certain facts and generalizations essential to adequate functioning in the adult world. Most of this content is externally given, originating outside the classroom in time and space. The teacher's task, in a sense, is to help the child relate his here and now experience to this body of content.

In a training group, on the other hand, the here and now is the major source of content. What is discussed originates almost completely within the group. The members of a training group are actively motivated to discuss group process difficulties of a sort which a teacher may well choose to ignore, handle without mentioning, punish, or only analyze wearily in the teachers' room with friends. In some classrooms (for example, core classes, homerooms), a large fraction of time may be spent in discussing here and now behavior, and nearly all teachers encourage such discussion occasionally (as in evaluation of committee work). But it is unusual to see a class situation where almost exclusive attention is paid to the analysis of what is happening between people, right now, as a means to learning. This is as it should be. The classroom group is not primarily a training group.

Focus on the social self

It may be asked, finally, what the difference is between a training group and a *group for psychotherapy*. Both groups are concerned with changes in their members' behavior, and both use here and now content.

Although all positive change in people has therapeutic aspects, there are some important differences between training and therapy. In a therapy group, the participants are patients. They are ill. Illness implies that something in the person has gone wrong, that the person is troubled or suffering and needs cure.

In a training group, on the other hand, the members are healthy, are not suffering, but do have dissatisfactions about their own *skills*. They would like to be able to do something better, to cope with everyday problems in an improved manner.

Finally, in a training group, as the distinctions above imply, there is less emphasis on a person's inner workings and much more emphasis on his 'outer

---

* Some recent experiences with training groups which were actually job groups suggests that good learning is possible, but rather difficult unless added freedom to experiment is built in. This can be done by meeting for longer periods of time than usual (1-2 days), working in a physically isolated setting, encouraging informal dress, etc.

workings'—the way he relates to people. A training group is usually less concerned with the inner reasons for *why* someone does something, and more concerned with *how* he does it, what the impact is on others, and how he can improve what he does to become more skillful.

A member of a training group may discover for himself how his inner problems are hindering his effectiveness with other people, but the training group is not the place for him to work out all the intricacies of these problems. It is the place for him to gain more insight into his social self—to see how his behaviors impinge on others. This distinction cannot, of course, be sharply made, but the emphasis is as stated.

In summary, then, a training group is a group designed to help its members make constructive changes in their social selves, by means of analysis of here and now experiences.

It might be added here, incidentally, that the relatively impersonal account above probably communicates little of the specific sense of excitement and involvement that is a part of most training group sessions.

How people learn through training

Given the background comments above on the nature of training, it may be helpful to present here a description of the process of learning better group behavior. What is the experience of a person like, as he grows and learns during one or several training activities? Figure 7.1 shows a general outline of the psychological steps in the training process, expressed in graphic form. The process of learning is here shown as cyclical. After going from step A_1 through step E_1, the learner returns to step A_2, which is then followed by B_2, C_2, and so on. Over a period of time, the

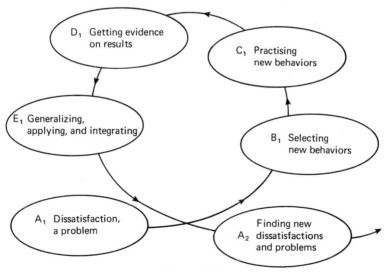

Figure 7.1
Steps in the training process

95

learning cycle would be repeated many times as shown in Fig. 7.2. If training is effective, this spiral moves, over time, in the direction of better and better behavior in groups.

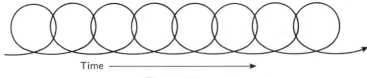

Time ————————————————→

Figure 7.2

It should immediately be said that learning is more than a rational process. At each of the stages above, the person faces emotional problems and stresses, since what is involved is change—*change in me.* For this reason, learning during training is not the neat, stepwise progression implied; but it is useful to look at a simplified model as a means of understanding the living, exciting process of learning more clearly. Here again, the reader is invited to turn to his own model of learning for comparison. The ideas presented below have roots in more general conceptions of learning (compare John Dewey's treatment in *How we think,* for example), but are focused on the special case of learning to work more effectively in groups.

Below, each of several stages in learning is discussed in turn, and the basic feelings involved are explored. The problem of training, in effect, is to provide conditions to help this learning process go forward effectively.

Dissatisfaction, a problem

Why *would* a person want to change and learn? Before there is likely to be much significant improvement in a person's group behavior, the person himself must first believe that effective group work is an important matter for him; and, second, be dissatisfied to some extent with his own attitudes, understandings, and behaviors as a participant in working groups. Initially, this may be a vague, unfocused feeling of discomfort, but as learning proceeds, it becomes more defined ('How can I explain my ideas more clearly to others?'). The learner must, in effect, come to feel some more or less specific *inadequacy* in relation to his own role in groups, or learning

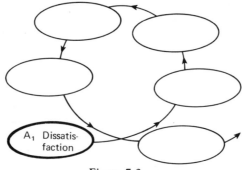

Figure 7.3

96

cannot go forward. This inadequacy is a relative matter; even a very capable group participant may wish to improve what he does, even though he feels his behavior is fairly effective already.

Immediately, emotional problems are involved; frequently the natural desire is to protect the self by believing that all human relations problems are somehow due to the inadequacies of others. And old fears of punishment and failure are at work; so it is hard for the individual to feel—let alone openly express—inadequacy. If all this is so, how do feelings of dissatisfaction and perceived inadequacy come to increase before and during a training program?

If an 'outsider', such as a consultant, a supervisor, or a status leader, points out some of the person's limitations to him, the person's dissatisfaction with his own group behavior may increase. This is psychologically hazardous—and usually fails to work. If the outsider is seen as having power over the individual, what often results is resentment, covering-up of real dissatisfactions and inadequacies, and various types of attempts 'to please the boss'.

Another source of desire for change is a situational difficulty in the person's work in the school. A sensitive person is constantly made aware, in one way or another, of the successes and failures of his work. ('Why are the committee members so apathetic?' 'Did I handle the situation all right when Mary kept going off on a tangent?' 'Why don't the principals carry through on decisions they seemed to agree to?') Most school people want strongly to do better what they are already doing, and this is a basic source of creative dissatisfaction.

Finally, if the person has become dissatisfied enough with his own behavior to enter a training activity (which he hopes will reduce the dissatisfaction), additional desires for change may appear. In a supportive training group, he may learn that 'I'm not the hot-shot I thought I was', as one principal ruefully remarked. He may be able to shift from blaming others to looking at what he himself is contributing to make group work ineffective. Until such a shift can be made—and it is difficult—he may feel frustrated or angry that he is not getting the answers he had hoped for.

Practical experience in training programs suggests this generalization: When the primary motivation for improvement comes from an individual's concern about what 'outsiders' want him to do, the changes in his behavior are apt to be confused, transitory, unintegrated, and irrelevant to the real demands of the job. When the primary motivation for improvement comes from the strong desires of the person—aided by 'insiders' who are members of the same training group—to improve his own ways of working with others, then the changes in his behavior can become increasingly systematic, permanent, integrated, and job-related.

Even when there is intrinsic motivation for changing, however, there are still emotional problems of resistance, loss of status, and fear of failure. An atmosphere must be developed in which people can safely talk about the tensions, dissatisfactions, and difficulties they personally are experiencing. Such expressions serve as a basis for training. But dissatisfaction with one's effectiveness in work is not likely to be voiced in an atmosphere that involves hazards of threat, punishment, or criticism. It is important to use off the job meetings, role-playing, and other methods to increase psychological safety.

97

Selecting new behaviors

Given dissatisfaction and the willingness to attend a training activity to reduce that dissatisfaction, there is a next important step.

The person in training must become aware of, and consider trying out, new actions which promise to help him solve the problem(s) he faces in his work with groups. That is, the learner needs to think creatively of different practices that might reduce his dissatisfactions with his present behavior. ('Maybe I don't have to hold the reins so tightly when I am the chairman,' or 'Perhaps I should try to listen more carefully instead of thinking of what I'm going to say next.')

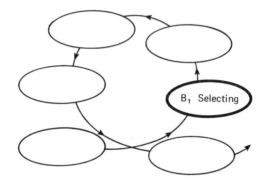

Figure 7.4

These pictures in the mind, or models of better behavior in groups, stem from many different sources. They may come from books or materials on group work, from the observed behavior of other members of the group (including, quite frequently, the trainer), and from the comments and suggestions of other associates.

In effect, the learner is now framing an action hypothesis which might read: *'If* I try this new behavior (for example, "Shut up in meetings for a change"), *then* some desirable consequences will result ("Other people will take more responsibility and be less apathetic").'

At first, people do not usually consider a very wide range of different behavioral possibilities. In early meetings of training groups, members may not think of ideas much more challenging than 'talking more' and 'talking less'. This restriction on possibilities for changed behavior is not unusual. Most people have specialized in certain ways of behaving for so long (being the aggressive deflater, the smooth harmonizer, the non-listener) that freely and frankly considering the idea that one could behave differently is quite difficult. And the idea that problems in groups are really *someone else's* fault is a very durable one. For these reasons, the creative non-judging atmosphere of the good training group is important. It can help to widen the range of new possible behaviors from which to select. Furthermore, if the group members hold the expectation that everyone is in the process of changing and learning—and that this is to be desired—then visualizing new and improved behaviors is really aided.

Practicing new behaviors

Given the felt need to learn, and some new ideas about what might work, the person must have numerous opportunities to practise, with reasonable safety, some of the behaviors that he and others consider to be promising. This practice can be thought of as a provisional try, taking place under circumstances that involve a minimum of threat and risk. In effective training programs, considerable energy

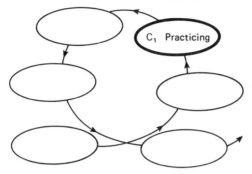

C_1 Practicing

Figure 7.5

usually goes into the planning of methods that permit behavioral experimentation with little risk. Role-playing, for example, can be used to practice skills and behaviors under semireal conditions before thay are tried out in job situations.

Role-playing is not the only way to practice new behavior. In a training group, where people have supported each other through initial phases of frustration and hesitancy in admitting inadequacy, a person who has been extremely vigorous and articulate, even interruptive, may decide to keep quiet for a meeting to 'see how the other half feels'. Or someone who wants chairmanship skills may volunteer to serve as chairman while the next agenda item is discussed.

In a good training program, group members also carry on considerable experimentation of the job. Successful experience with new behaviors in the training group gives them courage to try out these new behaviors in their work situations. Intense discussions of 'how it worked' follow. And when concrete and realistic job problems are brought into the training group, there is considerable promise for improved job-functioning.

During this tryout stage of learning, the primary emotional need is for *support*. The individual has, in effect, unfrozen some of his old ideas about the way to work with people, wants to try out some new ones, but is unsure what the consequences of the new departure are likely to be. He is defenseless and awkward at this point. If others in the training group accept and admit their own uncertainty as they try out changes, this can supply much support to all.

Getting evidence on results

The person who is experimenting with his behavior in a training situation must be able to get *evidence* as to the effectiveness of what he does. Learning by doing is not enough. The learner must, in addition, see the actual effect of his new behavior on others. What happened when, ever so gently, he invited non-participant Jane to comment? If in spite of all his attempted tact Jane says she felt put on the spot, then this information is important evidence for the learner to have as a basis of generalizing and applying his learning further.

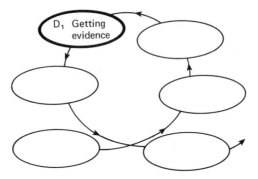

Figure 7.6

One of the limitations most of us struggle under on the job is our inability to get honest appraisals of our impact on others. We have to rely on fleeting facial expressions and official protestations, and we do not learn how we are doing in groups very often, or very accurately.

In the language of training, the term for a report to the learner of how his behavior is affecting others is 'feedback'. This technical term comes originally from the field of automation (ex: thermostat gives feedback to a furnace on how well the furnace is doing at heating the house), but seems clearly applicable to training as well. To be most helpful for learning, feedback must: (a) be clear and undistorted; (b) come from a trusted, non-threatening source; (c) follow as closely as possible the behavior to which it is a reaction. With quick, accurate, trusted evidence, the learner can proceed to correct his behavior effectively.

Much of the power of human relations training seems to stem from building in regular feedback procedures as a part of the training setup. Evaluation at the end of meetings, analysis of role-playing, use of a process observer who reports what he sees to the group, playback of tape recordings—all these can serve as a mirror, and give the learner more and better information about 'what behavior leads to what' than he has ever had before. And it's exciting.

Generalizing, applying, and integrating

Now that the learner knows what works (or perhaps more frequently, what does not work), he must tie this new knowledge into his picture of himself, relate it to his job situation, and in general make it part of the way he sees group life. Concrete action implications need to be drawn: 'Do not call on anyone unless he clearly wants to get into the discussion and can't.' The learner needs to see links between the training experience and his job situation: ('Here in the training group, we found

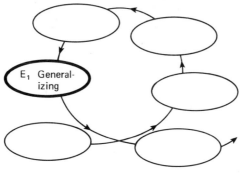

Figure 7.7

we had all these hidden feelings about the decision to meet Thursday night, and that's why we didn't carry it out. I think that same kind of thing may account for the poor attendance at my grade level meetings. What can I do about that?').

During this stage, careful, sober thinking is needed—but even here the person needs support and positive emotional reinforcement from other learners in the group, as he considers new learnings that are hard for him to accept, deep down. Otherwise the learnings stay at the 'talk' level and never really become a part of his normal ways of behaving.

Finding new dissatisfactions and problems

Finally, the learner almost inevitably emerges from a process like that described above with *new* dissatisfactions and problems, in addition to new insights and ways of behaving. ('All right, apathy may mean that the goal of the group is not clear to some people, but what can you do to make it clear, then?' or 'Bringing out the gripes did seem to clear the air in this group, but I'm not sure I'd know how to encourage it—or whether I would want to—in the principals' meeting.')

New ways of behaving lead to new problems (which might never have occurred under the old ways of behaving), and the training cycle continues. In other words, after the feedback of evidence which helps him see the consequences of his own

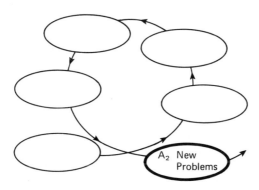

Figure 7.8

101

group behavior, the individual realizes that his behavior is still inadequate, or is inadequate in some new respect. He then repeats the process of getting creative ideas regarding further change, trying them out in both contrived and real situations, seeing what works, and generalizing about the results. It is through steady repetitions of this experimental learning process that he becomes more sensitive to what is going on in groups, has clearer diagnostic ideas as to what is needed and why, and can act more effectively.

Getting this conception of learning built into the person is even more important than his learning specific skills of 'handling conflict', 'stimulating participation', or whatever. If the learner has *learned how to grow and learn*, how to take an experimental approach to the problems of group life he encounters, then he will grow and learn on the job.

The training group as a place to learn

It may serve as a useful review of the process of learning better group behavior if the special usefulness of the training group, as such, is discussed. The training group has been repeatedly mentioned above, and the question might be raised: 'Why can't an interested person improve his behavior in groups independently?'

Clearly, much individual reflection, analysis, and experimentation may be necessary before a person comes to the realization, as did one teacher, that '*I* am really the only person whose behavior I can do much of anything about.' Experience with many different training programs, however, suggests that individual growth and learning about group behavior takes place best in a group setting. There seem to be reasons for this.

Shared support

In the first place, change in one's own group-relevant behavior, like any change, inevitably involves risk. If behavior changes are attempted by members of a group, the support they can give each other is extremely helpful. The training group is a collection of persons all dissatisfied to some degree with their group behavior. All are trying to get help in improving this behavior, and are willing to be vulnerable, in a sense—open to learning. This makes for shared support within the training group. There is often the sense of having 'lived together a lot in a short time', as one person said, with a resultant feeling of warmth.

Furthermore, in a successful training group, standards or norms are developed which encourage and support experimental change.[1] These norms can be quite strong.

After the training group has disbanded and members are attempting innovations on the job, each individual also receives support—and sometimes concrete help—from the fact that colleagues are trying similar things as they go about their work. Often recollection of what went on in the training group seems to serve as a kind of conscience for the member, continuing to encourage him at difficult points. Attitudes or values learned in the training group often have considerable carryover, for this reason.

Added resources

Training goes well in a group setting because different individuals can provide widely varied resources for intelligent behavior change by any particular learner. Many different ideas about job innovations can emerge. Ingenious procedures for learning can be devised more quickly. There is a greater possibility of penetrating, mistake-correcting analysis. In addition, because of group support, each person can hear and respond to group suggestions about his behavior which he might ignore if they were the suggestions of an outside expert or status figure.

The group as laboratory

A third reason for the effectiveness of the group situation is that it provides a learning laboratory which helps the individual observe himself in relation to others. Not only can he see the effect that his behavior has on other people but he can get frank, objective statements from them—their reports of the effects of his behavior. The group provides the individual with a testing ground where he can experiment with promising new behaviors. In a real sense, trying to study and improve one's own group-functioning without being in a group is something like trying to learn to swim without going into the water.

Immediacy

Another advantage of the group situation is its immediacy. New behaviors are practised *where* they are needed (in the group) and *when* they are needed (just following feelings of difficulty or dissatisfaction). Learnings are not postponed to another place or time, but are worked on here and now.

Realistic success

Finally, the group situation helps insure that learning goes on within realistic limits. (This, of course, assumes that the group makes its own decisions instead of having them made for it by the trainer.) Group members are not likely to attempt new behaviors that look extremely difficult. But the group can and does support innovations that are both challenging and feasible. During training, positive success experiences with new behaviors are essential—otherwise they will never be tried out on the job.

Reference

1. CARTWRIGHT D. has identified some very useful ideas which help explain why groups are so powerful in bringing about change in their members. See 'Achieving change in people: some applications of group dynamics theory.' *Human Relations*, Vol. 4, 1951, pp. 381-92.

8. Coverdale Training

Seamus Roche

Coverdale Training is a comparatively new approach to self-development of managers and organizations, devised by Ralph Coverdale, an English industrial psychologist and management consultant, in collaboration with Bernard Babington Smith of the Department of Psychology at Oxford University.

Coverdale developed his methods during the 'fifties and early 'sixties when he was working with the Steel Company of Wales and the Esso Petroleum Company Limited. The Irish Refining Company Limited, at its oil refinery at Whitegate, Co. Cork, was the first company to embark on a full-scale project of management development and organization development using Coverdale's method. Subsequently, Esso Petroleum Company Limited has initiated large-scale projects in its Marine Department and in its oil refinery at Fawley, Southampton. Many other companies, the largest being ICI, are now developing the use of Coverdale Training, and at the Civil Service Department and the British Transport Staff College, Coverdale Training is being used as a block exercise at the beginning of longer management development programmes.

Background

To understand the Coverdale approach, it is necessary to see it in the perspective of recent trends in management theory. Joan Woodward,[1] distinguishes four separate approaches to organization theory and problems which have emerged since 1950. These she calls:

1 The sociological approach—of which she says: 'basic to this approach is the concept of the social system, and the sociologist approaches the industrial firm as he would any other institution; in his analysis he attempts to identify the parts of the system and study their interdependence.'
2 The approach of individual psychology. 'In this setting, organization is evaluated

• This Chapter is based on material drawn from the publications listed in the bibliography, page 113.

in terms of its ability to achieve its goals while simultaneously providing means for individual self-realization.'

3 The decision theory approach. This approach 'concentrates on the rational approach to decisions and analyses the decision process.'

4 The mathematical approach, which 'sees organizations as a system of mathematical processes.'

The proponents of each of the above approaches have a tendency to denigrate the others and to infer that all the answers are provided by their particular system, but, as Miss Woodward points out, each of these approaches can contribute to our understanding of managerial and organizational problems, and one should look towards the building of a unified body of knowledge rather than a mutually exclusive approach.

Briefly, the approaches described above arise from the emergence in this century of psychology and sociology as branches of science rather than areas of theoretical speculation. These new sciences, when turned to the study of organizational problems in industry and business, revealed the fact that the classical theories of management were inadequate and at best could cater for only limited aspects of a very complex situation. Classical management theory can be useful as a means of showing the formal distribution of authority and of indicating channels and methods of control which, in theory, lead to efficient technical functioning. Scientific study showed that complex social and psychological factors operate in industrial and business situations which are not recognized or catered for in classical theory, and that these can have a considerable influence on what happens. The findings of such studies are summarized as follows by Selznick:[2]

> All formal organizations are moulded by forces tangential to their rationally ordered structures and stated goals. Every formal organization, trade union, political party, army, corporation, etc., attempts to mobilize human and technical resources as means for the achievement of its ends. However, the individuals within the system tend to resist being treated as means. They interact as wholes, bringing to bear their own special problems and purposes. ... It follows that there will develop an informal structure within the organization which will reflect the spontaneous efforts of individuals and subgroups to control the conditions of their existence ...

These findings highlighted the hitherto unsuspected importance of the influence of social or psychological processes on the workings of business organizations. The fact that people were being controlled to an important extent by pressures in the social environment of which they were unaware was obviously a discovery of vital significance to management. It indicated that many of the things which happen in industry or business are under the control of hidden or irrational forces.

As Miss Woodward points out, the problem of bringing this situation within the scope of rational control is being tackled in different ways by sociologists, psychologists, those who emphasize the rational aspect of the decision process, and those who favour a quantitative approach. None of these has yet come up with anything like a definite solution or set of laws, nor are they likely to in the foreseeable future, but each has a great deal to contribute to the way of research findings and techniques to help the manager cope with his problems.

The approach of individual psychology

The Coverdale system has its roots in what Miss Woodward calls the 'individual psychology' approach, in which the achievement of goals of the organization and the self-realization of individual employees who contribute to them are seen as indivisible. Not surprisingly, considering the common subject matter, it impinges here and there on the adjoining fields of sociology, and of 'rational decision-making'.

The type of questions which the 'psychological' approach tries to answer are:

How can people in an organization become conscious of the social processes which influence their behaviour?

How can people disentangle themselves from these pressures in order to get work done more effectively and rationally?

Can the tables be turned—can these irrational forces be harnessed and used in the pursuit of rationally decided objectives?

What are the implications of the discovery of these social processes for the organization structure?

There are two basic concepts common to all attempts to approach organizational problems from the psychological standpoint:

1 **Skills**—People can learn to control social and psychological processes and turn them to positive use, by means of appropriate social skills which can be learned.

2 **Personal resources**—Understanding and effective control of social processes frees the individual from the meshes of the environment enabling him to be more himself and less a member of a herd, enabling his unique personal strengths to develop to the benefit of both himself and of the social organization (e.g., company) of which he is a member.

Commonly, one form or another of small group training or 'laboratory education' is used to enable people to learn these skills and discover personal strengths suppressed by pressures in the social environment. Several variations of this small group training exist under intriguing and obscure titles, e.g., T-Group Training, sensitivity training, group dynamics, Managerial Grid. The concept of social skills as the key to controlling social pressures, is expounded by Matthew B. Miles. Speaking of difficulties encountered in educational groups, he says:

> There is considerable evidence that the problem is one of *skill*, broadly conceived; we really do not know how to work well with others. For most adults today, the abilities required to work effectively as a leader, or member of a co-operative group do not come naturally, perhaps because our traditional educational system has generally ignored or discouraged shared effort. (Miles,[3] page 1.)

106

He then goes on to talk about some of the social processes that take place whenever people work together:

> All that is meant here are the actual, concrete behaviours in the group—*how* things are happening, rather than *what* is being talked about. Whether the members of a group are discussing merit-rating, textbooks, or the difference between jet and piston engines, certain processes—basic to all groups—are taking place. For example, the goal or task of a group must be agreed on; this is a process which takes time. Members must exchange ideas through the process of communication. A process of systematic problem-solving and decision-making must take place, or the group discussion will waste time. Group members must develop reasonably harmonious relationships with each other through the processes of getting acquainted and developing mutual support. Group processes are thus going on all the time. . . .
> The skilled person can help carry on such processes effectively in all the groups of which he is a member or leader. (Miles,[3] page 3.)

The second basic concept which we referred to, i.e., human resources which are suppressed by pressures in the social environment, is expressed in the following paragraphs from an article by Raymond E. Miles:

> In addition to sharing common needs for belonging and respect, most people in our culture desire to contribute effectively and creatively to the accomplishment of worthwhile objectives.
> The majority of our work force is capable of exercising far more initiative, responsibility and creativity than their present jobs require or allow. These capabilities represent untapped resources which are presently being wasted.
> The manager's basic task is to create an environment in which his subordinates can contribute their full range of talents to the accomplishment of organizational goals.
> He must attempt to uncover and tap the creative resources of his subordinates. The overall quality of decision-making and performance will improve as the manager makes use of the full range of experience, insight, creative ability in his department. Subordinate satisfaction will increase as a by-product of improved performance and the opportunity to contribute creatively to this improvement.[4]

Group training

It has already been stated that small-group training is the medium used to introduce managers to these ideas, and there are several reasons why it is suited for this purpose.

First, the society in which we live emphasizes the formal pyramidal structure, virtually to the exclusion of all other factors. This is true in school, in church matters, legal matters, and in local and national administration. We tend to carry with us into our business life strong assumptions which are by no means always valid in business situations about how things should be ordered and how they should be done. Thus, a process of reeducation is necessary. We must learn to challenge our assumptions—a process which Argyris refers to as 'the unfreezing of old values'. In an article in the *Harvard Business Review,* he explains this process:

> In order to begin the unfreezing processes, the executives must experience the true uneffectiveness of old values. This means they must have a 'gut' experience of how incomplete the old values are. One way to achieve this is to give them a task to accomplish in situations where their power, control and educational influences are minimized. The ineffectiveness of the old values, if our analysis is correct, should then become apparent.[5]

By having to work in a group without a formal structure, managers discover that many of their assumptions about how things should be managed are inadequate. They are forced to look for alternative ways to work, and this leads them to discover that 'good' or 'bad' management means something different from what they had assumed.

Second, the group is a kind of laboratory in which the members can study the social processes at work within their own small society—the relationships which build up, the interactions between different personalities, the way in which the skills and characteristics of individuals complement each other. They discover that certain social processes occur in the group when it works effectively, and that these vary according to the nature of the task being done, according to the people in the group, according to the size of the group, etc.

Third, the training group provides a medium for testing and practising new ways of working and managing, in a situation where mistakes can be made without serious consequences.

As has been pointed out, there are many different forms of group training in existence. At one end of the scale are the 'unstructured' courses—people sit around a table and are given virtually no instructions. They have no agenda or task, they receive no formal instruction—it is simply a matter of seeing what happens and gaining knowledge from these events with the aid of a consultant. At the other end of the scale is the production-centred work situation where difficulties of human interaction are suppressed or disregarded. Between these extremes come a variety of structured and codified courses, such as Blake's 'Managerial Grid'. Blake's course is based on T-Group work, but has a strong element of formal instruction, making use of textbooks, case studies, diagrams, and questionnaires.

While group training can be enormously illuminating and valuable, it also had drawbacks. In certain circumstances, it can place people under considerable tension and strain, particularly when men remain in analysis. It can lead people to an undesirable degree of self-revelation and intimate discussion of each other. It can lead to a feeling of comfort and safety within the group which makes people reluctant to face outside realities. The insights which people get in groups can produce over-enthusiasm which may lead to rash behaviour on return to the work situation.

The Coverdale approach

In formulating their approach to group work, Coverdale and Babington Smith were acutely aware of the possible snags as well as the advantages of group work. In analysing the potential of group work as a medium for training managers, they came to the following conclusions:

1 Only those social and emotional processes which arise when people work together at a task are the proper concern of management training. It is not legitimate to put a businessman into a situation where he may be forced to do things which he may later regret.

Intimate self-revelations are not legitimate topics for public consumption at a management course, in contrast to discovering a man's skills and strengths.

2 Frustration, brought about by excessive analysis, which can arise when people face the need to change their assumptions, or to clarify their meaning, verbally, should not be allowed to build up or to continue unrelieved.

3 The ultimate purpose of any group of managers is to get men to accomplish certain tasks effectively. Attention should be kept focused on the objectives, so that while managers take all necessary measures to ensure effective group working, the well-being of the group does not take precedence over the accomplishments of the task.

4 Insight is not synonymous with skill. The insights which people obtain in group work will not of themselves necessarily lead to improved performance. It is necessary that insight be coupled with the acquisition of skills and techniques if it is to be converted into practice.

As a result of these conclusions, Coverdale designed a training experience which is unique in many respects:

1 The experience is built around short tasks. The tasks are in themselves insignificant, e.g., 'Change the wheel of a car' or 'Carry out a survey to find what course members think of the catering of this hotel'. However, they are real tasks, quite distinct from role-playing or case studies, in the sense that they must be carried out rather than discussed. It can subsequently be clearly established whether the group has succeeded in carrying out its task, and whether it has done well or badly. People are concerned with the part they took in doing this task, rather than playing assumed roles.

2 After each task, team members analyse their own *task performance* and the *social processes* which occurred, and use their experience to plan to improve *both* in future tasks.

3 The team learns to use a framework called the 'systematic approach' as an aid to keeping the balance between thought and action, both while working on their allotted task and while dealing with social processes.

The inclusion in the course of tasks which have to be physically carried out serves several purposes:

It keeps before peoples' minds at all times the realities of the management situation—getting the job done is the real purpose of any group of managers, and the 'sensitivity' aspects are a means to this end.

The fact that the team is working on tasks acts as a control on the type of processes which arise. Only the type of social issues which spring naturally from doing a task together arise. Amateur psychoanalysis is out.

Frequent activity stages relieve frustration and tension, and provide a safety valve which keeps the emotional situation under control.

The systematic approach to achieving objectives provides a framework and serves the following purposes:

It acts as a reminder to the team not to omit any of the basic stages necessary for successfully dealing with either a task or a problem of social process.

It helps the team to identify how far they have progressed on an objective, and helps them to avoid getting at cross-purposes as to what needs to be done next.

It focuses the team's attention on what they have to achieve, and helps to forestall needless discussion.

It acts as a framework within which members' contributions can be placed together into a coherent whole.

The systematic approach framework is applied to social processes as well as to the task. By practice and experiment, members develop skills and techniques which they carry back with them into the work situation. Observations made at work can then be dealt with systematically, plans can be formulated for taking advantage of the social skills of employees, and the processes taking place within groups.

About six months after attending the course described above, which lasts five days, managers may attend a second course. This deals with the problem of the individual who has to operate in a series of different groups, or in groups of frequently changing composition. This is the situation in which busy managers find themselves in real life. Permanent 'teams' of fixed membership are rare in management.

Further advanced courses help delegates to develop greater flexibility in the use of the techniques and skills introduced on the first course. It places them in situations which are pyramidal or hierarchical in character, and gives them an opportunity to study the issues which arise when the lessons of group work are applied in a management hierarchy.

The distinctive features of the Coverdale method can be summarized as 'the application of a systematic approach to carrying out the *task* and to the control and effective use of *social processes*'.

Coverdale distinguishes his approach from that of other exponents of group work by saying that his training is not primarily concerned with such questions as 'How do I feel about myself in the group?', or 'How do I feel about the group?'. The question which he believes to be the relevant one for team members to keep in mind is 'What should be done next in order to achieve our objectives?' His method places greater emphasis on the objective and rational, the task and the systematic approach, than is generally the case in group training. He is concerned that the group must not become an end in itself, but merely the medium for practice of leadership and management skills.

110

Organization development

Inevitably, managers who receive this training will reach a stage of development where they will begin to question the relevance and the adequacy of the existing company organization. It is at this point that the transition is made from 'manager self-development' to 'team self-development'. The raising of the level of management skill and insight results in a questioning and probing as distinct from a passive acceptance of the *status quo*, and managers then set about changes they see to be desirable.

Here again, Coverdale advocates an approach of systematic experimentation rather than a theory of organization. Using the basic Coverdale techniques, managers test and improve their organizational ideas in controlled limited-risk situation, gradually introducing changes to the organization by a series of tested steps. The development of systems for adapting the organization to changing circumstances is emphasized, rather than any particular organizational system. Coverdale's reasons for advocating this experimental and adaptive method approach to organization development are twofold. First, each organization is unique. The balace of interactions between personalities, technology, and economic factors is never the same in any two organizations. Second, every organization is, to a greater or lesser extent, in a state of perpetual change. Changes in personnel, in technology, and in markets are continually occurring, and the balance between the various factors in the organization is changing accordingly. Further, it is a matter of observation that the rate of technological advance and social change has accelerated in this century to an extent never before experienced. This has obvious implications for management—as the following extract from the British Petroleum Company staff magazine illustrates: 'The job content of someone described five years ago as an assistant chemist has changed since then and will change even more. Saying that X number of assistant chemists will be needed in 1980 is totally meaningless. . . B.P. reckons that the refinery of 1980 will theoretically need nobody to operate it.'

Managers are becoming increasingly aware of the influence of change on their work. At a recent conference of senior managers in Britain, managers were described as 'agents for change'.

If these assumptions are correct regarding the increasing part played by change in organizations, then Coverdale's approach may well prove of considerable value. Burns and Stalker,[6] report conclusions which they reached after studying organization in a large number of firms; i.e. that whereas in stable conditions a 'mechanistic' (i.e., formal) type of organization is appropriate, in changing conditions an 'organic' (i.e., informal and adaptive) organization is more appropriate. It follows that managers must get practice in the skills of dealing with change.

Basic to Coverdale's approach is the concept that the increasing pace of change and the increasing complexity of technological and social development can only be coped with by the fullest use of personal skills and resources, the development of greater insight and skill in social behaviour, and the continuous sytematic application of these to the changing situation.

It is difficult to separate out the influence of training on a firm's profitability from all the other influences. However, there is no doubt that, in the conduct of such experiments as the Coverdale projects, a great deal is being discovered about an important field of human activity which has previously been the province of assumption and guesswork. As the *Financial Times* points out in an article on the Coverdale project at the Fawley refinery:

> The study of human motivation, how people's behaviour and attitudes interact with each other, the relationship between the individual and the organization in which he works—all this has a very important bearing on the profitability of the enterprise. Hence, it is natural that progressive firms should want to analyse these problems with just the same scientific rigour which they apply, for example, to a study of capital spending opportunities.[7]

Responses to formal training

After completing only four and a half days' initial training, participants claim a range of insights, and indicate, by their attempts to learn or improve their performance, an increasing curiosity. Fifty-five out of seventy-nine respondents to a written inquiry claimed a range of 30 different benefits, which varied from 'better judgement of personal qualities' through a 'more questioning and curious approach' to 'getting action more quickly', 'tolerance', and 'initiating change by questioning assumptions'. Out of another sample, 80 per cent claimed advantages. Strangely, even when delegates are not themselves aware of any personal changes, their superiors or contemporaries may be; the nominating managers are often more than satisfied with the effects of training, although students themselves may not be aware of any benefits. A third sample of 145 delegates, who had eight days of training, showed 97 per cent favourably disposed to the experience, and 88 per cent reported one or more practical applications of what they had learned. On average, this sample claimed some seven benefits each (ranging from one to twenty-seven).

When men are practised in the complex skills of cooperation, inevitably they find cooperation to be easier. There follows a favourable response in terms of attitude, but the really significant feature is the change in the way men work or behave. When behaviour changes and people cooperate with greater effect, the organization may begin to reap a reward in terms of an improvement in the achievement of commercial objectives. Obviously examples prove nothing more than temporal coincidence and effects are not casual but may be worth recording.

Unit cost reduced by 18 per cent and 14 per cent.
Industrial injuries reduced by 87 per cent.
Sales volume increased by 14 per cent, 7 per cent, and 42 per cent.
Major reduction in waste.

No one could claim that training led directly to these commercial results; such a mechanistic assumption about cause and effect would be quite inappropriate to an organic system like a commercial or industrial concern. The point is that managers know themselves to be more self-confident, and other people see them to be managing well. The managers who claim more self-confidence and who are seen to be managing well improve the commercial results that they set out to achieve.

The final test of the effectiveness of Coverdale Training is to apply the methods advocated by self-confident and successful trained managers, who are seen to be managing well, in a variety of different situations with managers who have not yet received this training and to watch for improving commercial results which occur simultaneously with the training. If the results are rewarding and the men themselves are well pleased, one may be onto something good.

References

1. WOODWARD, J., 'Industrial Organization–Theory and Practice.' London: Oxford U.P., 1965, p. 250.
2. SELZNICK, P., 'TVA and the Grass Roots.' University of California Press, 1949, pp. 280-1.
3. MILES, MATTHEW B., 'Learning to Work in Groups.' Teachers College, Columbia University, 1959.
4. MILES, R. E., 'Human Relations or Human Resources.' *Harvard Bsns. Rev.,* July/August 1965.
5. ARGYRIS, C., 'T-Groups for Organizational Effectiveness.' *Harvard Bsns Rev.,* March/April 1964.
6. BURNS, T. and STALKER, G. M., *Management of Innovation.* London: Tavistock Publications, 1961, pp. 119-25.
7. OWEN, G., 'How much democracy in running a business?' *Financial Times,* 4 August 1960.

Bibliography

1. ROCHE, SEAMUS, 'Coverdale Training–A Method for Developing Managers and the Organization.' *Manpower and Applied Psychology,* Vol. 1, No. 1. Spring 1967, Ergon Press, Cork, Ireland; and *Management,* June 1967. Irish Management Institute.
2. COVERDALE, R. and ROCHE, SEAMUS. In *Coverdale Training for Development,* Hinton, I., ed. London: Training Partnerships, 1967.
3. COVERDALE, R. *Thought–A Frame for Teamwork.* London: Coverdale Training Limited, 1968.

9. Organic Skill Training described

Peter Honey

A few years ago, the text for the day on my desk calendar read 'when all is said and done far more is said than done'. Since then I have ruined its pithiness by adding '. . . especially when it comes to talk about managing people.'

There seems to be a staggeringly wide gap between what people say they will do or, indeed, say they do and what they actually do. Managers frequently claim that human resources are the most valuable asset they possess, but behave as if this were not so. Most managers agree that people need to have clear, precise, measurable objectives to which they are committed, but they behave as if the thought never entered their heads. They readily agree that people who are interested in their work do rather better than those who are not and that effective communications are important, but behave as if this were not the case. Managers will agree with one breath that situations involving people are infinitely variable and that there cannot be panacea-like right answers, yet with the next breath ask for just such a thing.

But, of course, the point I am making is a well known phenomenon. The gap between, say, a politician's words and his actions is frequently remarked upon. Newspaper leaders solve the world's problems again and again—in words. If words and actions were synonymous, then our accomplishments would be indeed remarkable. It is almost as if man's ability to use words provides him with an effective means of dodging reality. Certainly actions speak louder than words. Just think how many more actions there would have to be if man was suddenly robbed of his chief means of gaining credibility (albeit temporarily), that powerful ally of procrastination, words.

Still, in the absence of any indications that mankind is about to lose his faculty of speech, we must look to other ways of closing the gap between what is said and what is done. And this seems to be a particularly difficult thing to do, and management training activities all too often fail to help. Indeed, since the bulk of management training and education traffics in words and has aims to do with increasing management knowledge and dispensing information, leaving it to the learner to struggle with the problems of application, it is more likely to widen the gap between saying and doing than close it. Pump a manager full of behaviour science knowledge, and the most likely behaviour change will be at the verbal level—he will use words he did not use before and he will talk about concepts that he did not talk about before. Unhappily, neither of these activities is anything like a guarantee that he will do things that he did not do before.

Organic skill training is a way of helping managers to behave more effectively— particularly in situations in which they are dealing with people—be they subordinates, peers, colleagues, bosses, or customers. As such, it is pretty unusual in that it concentrates massive attention on the *doing* side of the gap and puts relatively little emphasis on the business of giving information. While being unusual in this respect, it is far from unique; there are a number of close relatives in the management training field, in which Coverdale Training, Blake's Grid, and various versions of structured sensitivity training are perhaps the best known.

It is my intention here to give some of the operating assumptions upon which Organic Skill Training is based, and then go on to describe the main activities that are undertaken under its banner. My colleagues and I have been developing this training over a four year period. The early development work took place in British Overseas Airways Corporation. However, International Computers Ltd has provided the enthusiastic home for all the recent developments—some of them resulting in enormous strides forward. ICL has established a management training team which spends virtually all its time engaged on the organic skill training activities which we intend to describe. In a twelve month period, the ICL team has nearly completed the first cycle of Organic Skill Training activities in its UK sales organization, and is just embarking on the cycle in the servicing and manufacturing parts of the company. So far as courses are concerned, we have run something approaching one hundred, the majority in BOAC and ICL, but with some experience in British Steel, Fison's, and with the Atomic Energy Research Establishment.

Organic Skill Training is based on a number of fundamental beliefs. First, we believe that managing *people* is different from managing *things*. Things are less complex and more predictable and, consequently, stand still long enough to have techniques evolved for coping with them. People are more complex and less predictable and, despite frequent and gallant attempts, seem to keep techniques for dealing with them at a good arm's length. The closest we seem to be able to get is to the 'general principles' level. And that is not near enough for most of us. Second, and as I have already indicated, we believe that, especially when it comes to managing people, there is a great difference between knowing what to do and actually doing it. If knowing were sufficient prerequisite for doing, then we would all do a lot better. Finally, we believe that it is possible for people to learn to get better at managing other people. The suitable learning process is not so much a question of knowing what to do, it is rather a question of learning from the experience of practising. This way, what you finish up knowing is how to do so and so, and what sort of knowledge is not at odds with reality.

These three closely related beliefs have far reaching implications for the whole field of management training and profoundly affect the way we tackle organic skill training. They have led me to suggest that the management trainer's sphere of activities can be broken down into a simple classification system as shown in Fig. 9.1. These distinctions would seem to be important because different training methods are appropriate for different areas. For example, lectures, programmed instruction, and other information transmitting media are suitable in the mechanistic knowledge area; in the organic knowledge area, lectures, in combination with case study work and other participative discursive methods, are more suitable; in the mechanistic skill area, demonstrations, practice under guidance, and simulation techniques are appropriate; in the organic skill area, no one really knows what to do, but practising under guidance and inductive learning processes, at our present state of knowledge, seem the most appropriate.

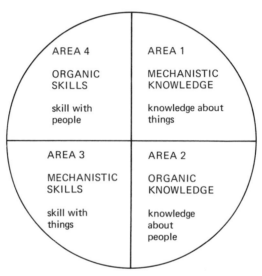

Figure 9.1

The implications of all this for management training activities, which aim to help improve performance in the managing people area, are considerable. In this crucial area, it looks as though informational knowledge is not anything like a sufficient prerequisite for action. And yet, management trainers continue to churn out informational knowledge giving courses, either hoping for a miracle, or content to pander to the expectations of their audiences. It is not that information has not got a role to play, but rather that it is strange to pour so much energy into increasing a manager's knowledge, when all the time we know that it is what he *does* with what he *knows* that is important. An answer might be to strike a healthier balance between *giving information* and helping managers to develop the skills involved in *using information* and knowledge appropriately. The case for pursuing this line is strengthened when it is remembered how short of valid informational type knowledge we are in the organic field in any case. If there can be no specific rules of supervision which will work well in all situations, then the information we can pass on is bound to be pretty anaemic. All behavioural scientists would agree that

116

supervision is always a relative process. To be effective, a leader must always adapt his behaviour to take into account the expectations, values, and interpersonal skills of those with whom he is interacting. Accordingly, it seems suitable to encourage the growth of learning by doing approaches in management training. The way to master any skill, be it mechanistic or organic, is by practice coupled with an appropriate system of performance feedback. What needs to be done, therefore, is to put managers into a series of carefully designed situations where they have the opportunity to practice learning from experience. Later, I shall try to describe how organic skill training sets about doing this. Three more brief beliefs first.

We believe that any organization is dependent for its results on the activities of people. People are the means to the organization's ends, in fact. We know that people find it difficult to cooperate and coordinate together, but we believe that it is possible to achieve more because of, rather than in spite of, people. Further, we believe that interactive competence increases to the extent that the interactors are willing and able to

1 make interactive issues appropriately explicit, and
2 make and action 'people' plans.

It is interactively less competent to leave people issues at an implicit level. This 'management by explicitness' philosophy is an interesting one and seems to be the common thread pulling together so many current approaches and developments. Management by objectives, for example, clearly has much to owe to the basic idea that making people's objectives explicit is a worthwhile thing to do. The Glacier Metal experiments, productivity bargaining (when done properly), Blake's Grid 'candour', and many other approaches, are all based on the assumption that making people issues suitably explicit, rather than leaving them at an implicit level, aids the processes of agreement between people. Explicitness seems to be the stuff of which trust is made.

Finally, we believe that if a manager is going to learn to behave more effectively, then:

1 he must be capable of learning from his experiences;
2 he must know the difference between effective and ineffective behaviour in a particular situation;
3 he must recognize that it is possible for him to do even better than at present;
4 he must want to do even better;
5 he must have the opportunity to try out different ways of behaving and doing things;
6 he must have worthwhile feedback from others.

That concludes a brief look at the philosophical considerations inherent in, and so important to, Organic Skill Training. I shall now go on to describe the training activities which have evolved and are continuing to develop from these beliefs. Table 9.1 summarizes these activities under the three headings of 'Investigating and motivating', 'Changing', and 'Reinforcing', and shows how these relate to precourse work undertaken in the managerial work situation, the course itself, and postcourse work again undertaken in the work situation. It is important to grasp that the word

	Activities undertaken in the managerial work situation	*Activities undertaken in the course situation*
Investigating and motivating	Survey to discover what inter-personal behaviours dis-tinguish effective from less effective managers. Exercise linking commercial objectives and managerial be-haviour. Exercise to set objectives for courses to achieve and to de-vise practical monitoring and evaluation procedure. Face to face precourse interviews with prospective course mem-bers and also with their bosses.	
Changing		Course members progress through a highly structured learning by doing experience. They under-take group tasks and projects which are the vehicles they use to travel towards achieving learning ends to do with im-proving their interpersonal behaviour. Trainers help them to do this by observing the group at work and categorizing the inter-active behaviours. At suitable stages in the structure they give either group or individual feedback.
Reinforcing	Nothing is forced on people, but if the changing process has been worth its salt then these sorts of activities start to happen: The formation of short-lived project teams to crack problems and come up with action-able proposals. Managers making time to consciously and deliber-ately plan interpersonal behaviour and, after the plan has been actioned, to evaluate what has happened in order to make plans for im-proved future perfor-mance. Organizing follow-up days where managers can exchange plans and support one another. Inviting management trainers to observe and behaviour analyse formal and informal meetings and setting aside time for feedback and performance im-provement planning, etc.	

'training' in the title organic skill training is used to describe all these activities and not just the course activities alone.

The process begins with a survey which is conducted in order to find out about the behaviour of managers when tackling the managing people aspect of their jobs. The idea is to ensure that any behavioural changes brought about during an off the job course situation are suitable ones in terms of the on the job working situation. Clearly, the more influential and effective the change methods, then the more it matters that changes are in the required direction. The survey is undertaken to achieve the following purposes:

1 to provide a basis of information in terms of the behaviours, if any, which significantly distinguish effective from less effective managers;

2 to involve the managers in a company or organizational subpart in such a way that they are interested in the survey findings and committed to the activities which follow closely in the survey's wake. This is why I describe these precourse steps as investigating *and* motivating in the same breath. The survey starts from scratch in the sense that the questionnaire itself is compiled as a result of a participative process involving as many managers from each level as possible. This is done by gathering groups together and, after some initial discussion about the proposed survey, inviting them to fix their thoughts on the most effective manager who reports to them and, having done that, to start describing the managerial behaviour typical of the person they have in mind. They are not asked to identify the person, nor are they asked to justify anything they come up with. Pressure is only applied by the interviewer when they produce global, descriptive statements, such as, 'He is a good leader', 'He is interested in people', 'He has confidence', and so on. In such cases, contributors are asked 'What does he do which leads you to conclude that (he is a good leader, interested in people, has confidence)? What is it about his behaviour which causes you to make this inference?' In this way, it is possible to break down some of the descriptive statements into more precise behavioural elements. Later in the proceedings, attention is switched to the behaviour of less effective managers.

The material generated by these sessions is assembled, with practically no editorial work, into an unvalidated questionnaire of one hundred items, or more. The questionnaire can take many forms, but here are some typical items:

Lets his people get on with their work in their own way						Interferes with his people's work
Delegates tasks in such a way that his people know precisely what is expected of them						Delegates tasks in such a way that people are confused about what is expected of them
Cuts people off in mid-sentence						Listens to what other people say
Covers up for his people's mistakes						Exposes his people's mistakes

Works out how a task is to be tackled and then tells his people						Asks his people for their opinions about how to tackle a given task
Remembers people's names						Forgets people's names
Makes encouraging noises like 'Good thinking', 'Well done', 'I'll buy that', 'I wish I'd thought of that'						Does not say such things
Trusts his people to do a good job						Checks up on his people's work
Tears strips off his people						Gets his people to appraise their own performance
Says one thing and means another						Says what he means
Lets his people know what he thinks about them						Keeps his opinions to himself
Knocks people's ideas						Develops people's ideas

Once a questionnaire exists, the actual conduct of the survey can begin. Briefly what happens is that each manager is visited on two occasions separated by two days or more. On the first occasion, he might complete a questionnaire with the behaviour of his most effective subordinate manager in mind, and, on the second, with his least effective subordinate manager's behaviour as the benchmark. When all the participating managers have completed two questionnaires in this way, statistical analysis on each item is done, in order to determine whether the item is a significant distinguisher between effective and less effective managers. This whittles the number of items down considerably; some fail to show significance because they were poor items in the first place, but, more usually, they fail because the behaviour they described was shared by both effective and less effective managers. Depending on the size of the area being surveyed, the results can be broken down into subsets, either hierarchically or functionally.

A number of alternatives present themselves once the survey results have been studied by all the participating managers. At the very least, a meeting of the appropriate top management is held, where the implications of the survey results are spelled out, and where the significant questionnaire items are fashioned into clear, precise, measurable objectives for the courses to achieve. Better still, an exercise, complementary to the survey into managerial behaviour, may be undertaken with the aim of explicitly linking the commercial objectives with interpersonal behaviour. This is done by taking each manager's objectives and key tasks (if these do not already exist, then, of course, the first step is to help them set and

120

120

120

state their objectives) and breaking them down into a number of key interpersonal behaviours. Here is an example:

Objective (for, say, a regional sales manager):

To operate within the agreed budget in order to help ensure that the sales division productivity plan is achieved, spending money in such a way as to close the financial year with a sales income/cost ratio of not less than 11:1. Established Divisional policy and procedural constraints will be observed and communicated to regional staff in a manner that will result in both understanding and validation of such constraints.

Key tasks:

Investigate current financial controls exercised in each area.
Etc.

Key interpersonal behaviours

Communicating the purpose of investigation in such a way that it will lead to acceptance, support, and development.
Supporting existing organizational constraints when in contact with his staff.

When this identification of key interpersonal behaviours is tackled, then these, together with the survey results, combine to form the basis for setting sensible relevant objectives for the courses to achieve.

The final item in the investigating and motivating phase of the training concerns a personal interview, conducted by the trainer, with each prospective course member and their respective bosses. The aim of these interviews is to help people to have reasonably accurate expectations of the course and to sort out what each person wants to be able to do better.

Relating back to the six 'musts' listed on page 117, which combine to determine whether or not managers learn to behave more effectively, it can be seen that three of them have been catered for by the precourse activities I have just described. The survey and the identification of key interpersonal behaviours helps those who are now coming on the course and their managers who will come later, to know the difference between effective and ineffective behaviour in particular situations. Their participation in all these events and the precourse interview helps them to recognize that it is possible to do even better than at present and to *want* to do even better. It falls to the course itself to meet the other two 'musts'—the opportunity to try out different ways of behaving and doing things, and having worthwhile feedback from others. All the managers in the company or organizational subpart have been involved in most of these precourse activities, and they are all destined to come on the course itself, usually starting with the top manager and working, layer by layer, down to include first line management.

The course is difficult to describe because each one is designed in the light of the survey findings in conjunction with the precourse interview information, and so on. Our aim is to structure a series of situations which give the manager an opportunity to learn from his shared experiences. Therefore, rather than attempt to give a blow by blow account of a typical course, which would be misleading, I will attempt to

121

show what sort of a learning experience they can give by highlighting five important elements. These are learning by doing, the structural framework, people-planning, behavioural analysis and feedback, and, finally, the trainer's behaviour.

Learning by doing

The first thing to grasp is that an Organic Skill Training course is essentially a learning by doing situation. Readers who followed my introductory remarks will understand why. The course is concerned with helping managers to improve their organic skills. The implication of 'organic' is that there is nothing meaningful to teach and the implication of 'skills' that, even if there were, it would not do much good, since skills have to be learned by practising, preferably with the luxury of helpful guidance and counselling. So, formal lectures are non-existant and the few information-giving sessions that there are are participative, designed merely to push the learner into trying something that he might not otherwise have tried, either at all or so quickly. Now, since organic skill training is concentrated on improving managers' interpersonal behaviour, we are able to cash in on the presence of managers in the course situation. All we need do is set about structuring events so that the managers are thrown into purposeful interaction, one with another, and the interactive issues that inevitably arise and start hampering their progress become, in a very real sense, the learning material of the course. The sorts of interactive issues I have in mind are:

people being at cross-purposes and not realizing it, either at all or, at best, until they have gone round in circles for most of the available time,
people misunderstanding, or failing to hear, points and suggestions from others,
people disagreeing with one another to the extent that proceedings are either greatly delayed or brought to a deadlock;
people falling victims to the interactive climate and failing to participate as competently as they might.

There is also a 'two birds with one stone' point to be made about learning by doing as a method. Not only is this sort of approach sensible in terms of helping a manager to improve his interpersonal performance, but there is a direct pay-off in the sense that one of the frequent outcomes of a concentrated dose is that managers learn to get better at learning from experience. This is a useful thing to achieve since, most of the time, managers are on their own and there are strong arguments in favour of producing learning managers rather than learned ones.

The structural framework

An Organic Skill Training course is very carefully structured. Since we know exactly what we want to achieve from the survey into managerial behaviour and from the precourse interviews, events are structured in such a way as to increase the probability of managers learning what we want them to learn. Indeed, specific day by day measures are set to determine the success of both the course structure and our behaviour as trainers. The structuring takes the form of a series of tasks which are given to groups of managers. Initially, the tasks are fairly trivial by comparison with the tasks managers normally have to tackle. This is deliberate, since it is essential that course members realize the relationship between the tasks they are asked to tackle and their need to improve their interactive performance. The intrinsic interest of a task that is too absorbing seems to interfere with learning to improve interpersonal competence. Not only are they trivial, but they are set within specific and fairly tough time-limits. Tasks to do with sorting things, making things, reporting on things, deciding things, are all characteristic of the first couple of days, and they are all interactive and—very importantly—they all have a clearly identifiable action stage rather than just being talking all the way affairs. This emphasis on action is a vital design feature of this training, for it is when people are in action that cross-purposes evidence themselves, that previously apparent agreement turns to obvious disagreement, and that apparently well-constructed plans fall apart and show their inadequacies. Also, action generates the information needed to compare results against the objectives set by the group at an early stage in their preparatory work. This way, the results of their labours are inescapable and talk is about what *will* be done rather than hypothetical talk about what would be done if... ('we were really doing it').

After a couple of days, the tasks get tougher. This is done in a number of ways. First, the concrete, action-type tasks I have referred to above start to decrease in number, and tasks explicitly concerned with studying and coping with interactive issues which are cropping up in the group begin to increase. Second, the time-limits for tasks get longer. This may sound an easing in restrictions rather than a toughening, but, in practice, we find that managers tend to wallow for even longer in interactive snarl-ups. Third, the ambiguity of the task is stepped up, thus putting increased onus on the managers to make their differing interpretations explicit and work the task into a clear, precise, and measurable form.

People-planning

This is fundamental to the success of the course as a change agent. It seems that learning from experience and improving interactive performance do not grow on trees. Nor can it be left at the level of mere intentions, however good these intentions might be. The key to improving performance, if there is a key, lies in planning. Now the odd thing is that every manager knows that a plan is *always* a detailed statement of what has to be done, spelling out how it will be done, who will do what, and when and where they will do it, and yet fails to realize the significance of the word 'always'.

Most managers are relatively good at making plans with all these ingredients when those plans are about things (planning the summer schedule, planning the maintenance rota, planning the budget allocation for next year), but this is not so in the case of people-planning (so-called manpower plans are not, in fact, plans at all). This is because it is assumed that people and planning are incompatible: it is sad and extraordinary how defeatist most people are about human behaviour. The outward signs of hopelessness are the frequent shoulder-shrugging references to 'human nature' which is, it seems, an undesirable but unchanging variable, which is beyond the bounds of human comprehension, let alone human planning. Certainly, people-planning is tougher than thing-planning, since people are far more complex and more unpredictable in their behaviour. If it is true that human behaviour is unpredictable, then at least that much is known, and what is known is available information, for which plans can deliberately be made. Accordingly, on an Organic Skill Training course, people set about making interactive issues explicit in order to plan improvements. They might start off on this people-planning by drawing up a scheme wherein they agree their overall procedures, or working framework, and the behavioural codes of conduct within it. If they decide to have a group leader, then part and parcel of their people-planning is to draw up his terms of reference in some detail. Later in the course, as pointed out in the next section, they progress to setting behavioural targets and planning how to maximize the probability of achieving them. People cannot learn from their experience as usefully as they might unless they collect up information about mistakes and successes in order to *plan* to avoid them in the future and to increase the chances of success. Consequently, performance improvement planning tasks are explicitly built in to the structure of an Organic Skill Training course.

Behavioural analysis and feedback

I now want to describe the method we use to collect information about the interactive behaviours and the use to which we put this information. Remember that the aim of the course is to help managers improve their organic or interpersonal skills. I have already described how, before a course is even designed, a survey is conducted in order to establish what behaviours distinguish between effective and ineffective managers in a particular company or organizational subpart. Once this is established, we set about creating situations into which to put the managers in order that they have the opportunity to practise improving the behaviours which have been associated with effectiveness in each particular case. So, for example, we have found that in one particular part of an organization a highly significant behaviour is concerned with what managers do when the going is tough. More effective managers come to their bosses with proposals for overcoming difficulties. Less effective managers come to their bosses with the problems and difficulties. Once this behaviour pattern has been discovered, we set about devising ways to encourage the development of 'proposing behaviour' and the reduction of 'stating difficulties behaviour' in managers operating in that part of the organization.

In this way, we arrive at a list of interpersonal behaviours that we are primarily interested in with a given group of managers. The list is not intended to be exhaustive, since it would be an unwieldy length if it were. Currently, for example, one set of behaviour categories, stemming directly from a particular set of survey findings, has only twelve categories. A copy of the behaviour analysis form is shown in Fig. 9.2. The form is designed to allow for the collection of behavioural data for

Task No: 26	Description: Undertake an activity that the group agrees will serve a useful purpose.	
Start time: 14.50	Finish time: 15.35	Any time absent: None

	DON	PETER	JOHN	DAVID	JIM	BILL	MIKE
SEEKING SUGGESTIONS (ideas and proposals)	HHT HHT II I		II	IIII	II		I
CAUGHT PROPOSALS	III	HHT III	HHT HHT	HHT	IIII	HHT HHT HHT II	HHT HHT HHT IIII
ESCAPED PROPOSALS	I	I	I	IIII	HHT III	II	I
BUILDING	I	I			III		
DISAGREEING and CRITICIZING	III	HHT II	HHT HHT II	IIII	II	HHT I	III
SEEKING CONFIRMATION (agreement and support)	HHT HHT HHT I	III	HHT HHT I	III	II	III	HHT HHT II
SUPPORTING	II	II		HHT HHT HHT I	HHT IIII	III	HHT HHT
SEEKING CLARIFICATION, EXPLANATION, AND INFORMATION	HHT HHT HHT I	HHT HHT HHT	HHT HHT I	HHT II	HHT HHT	III	III
OTHER BEHAVIOUR (including providing information and explanations in response to requests)	HHT IIII	HHT HHT II	HHT HHT II	HHT HHT HHT	HHT HHT II	HHT I	HHT HHT HHT HHT
OFFERING (uninvited) EXPLANATIONS, REASONS, and DIFFICULTIES	II	HHT HHT I	HHT HHT HHT HHT I	HHT	III	HHT I	HHT II
UNSTRUCTURED CONTRIBUTIONS (thinking aloud, rambling on, and contradicting oneself, etc.)	II	HHT	I	I	HHT	III	IIII
MULTISPEAK (talking over and interrupting)	HHT HHT HHT I	HHT II	HHT HHT HHT	HHT IIII	II	II	HHT HHT HHT HHT II

Figure 9.2

each individual group member. It is a very simple information-gathering device, being an on-the-spot tallying system; each piece of behaviour, whether discursive or brief, gets just one tally mark somewhere on the form.

There are four reasons for undertaking the behaviour analysis in this way. In the first place, it provides an observational structure for the trainer, so that he can make sense of the interactive complexities and survive the tidal wave of information generated by these interactive situations. Second, it provides some of the information necessary for giving behavioural feedback to the working group and to individual group members. This feedback is usually given in two ways. (a) For the group-oriented feedback, it often takes the form of a simple histogram: an actual example from a recent Organic Skill Training course is shown in Fig. 9.3. This can be presented to the group, with interpretative guidance from their trainer, on, say, the third day. By then, the interactive trends characteristic of the group have started to show themselves and, far more importantly, the group may have learned enough about how to process this sort of information into actionable plans, and, using this sort of behavioural feedback, groups of managers can do remarkable things to improve their interactive effectiveness. (b) For individually oriented feedback, which is less dramatic, but more detailed, course members each get a computer printout, giving them a detailed analysis task by task of their own behaviour. For each behaviour category, they get three figures; the total number of their behaviours that were categorized during the session, this number expressed as a percentage of their own behaviour and as a percentage of the group's behaviour. The trainers give help and guidance on an individual basis as course members draw up their own aims and plans for behavioural change. After an hour's individual work of this kind, the first task when the group reassembles is, typically, to agree plans for supporting each other in achieving individual behavioural aims.

The third purpose in behaviour analysing is to provide some of the information required as a basis for deciding the constitution of the working groups. At some stage during the course, the groups are usually mixed in order to provide better learning situations. The basis for the mix varies, depending on the course objectives and on the picture of individual performances, but, for example, low contributors can be put together to force up the contribution rate, high proposers can be put together to teach them a lesson, and so on.

The fourth purpose is to provide some of the information needed in validating the course design. One of the joys of this sort of training is that the trainers are not dependent on what managers *say* they have learned; the evidence is inescapable— observable behaviour changes.

The trainer's behaviour

It must already be apparent from the last three sections that the trainer does not behave as a 'Listen to me, I know all the answers' type teacher. Of course, if the group asks him a question, he answers it as helpfully as he can. He may, on occasion, as he judges necessary, intervene with a suggestion or query of some kind, but for the most part he observes the group at work and categorizes the behaviours as they occur. It is his job to help managers to learn usefully from their experience, and since the sort of interactive issues they are struggling with fall squarely into the 'easier said than done' category, he knows that the more he says, the more he becomes instrumental in creating a situation where 'when all is said and done, far more is said than done'. And that is unforgivable in an organic skill trainer.

In conclusion, we must consider the evaluation of the activities which have been described. The term 'evaluation' here refers to measures of the worthwhileness of training in terms of its contribution to achieving commercial objectives. This

126

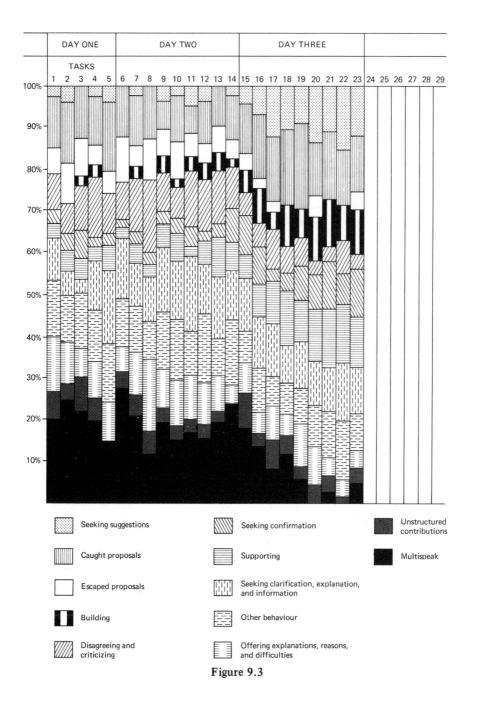

	DAY ONE	DAY TWO	DAY THREE	
TASKS	1 2 3 4 5	6 7 8 9 10 11 12 13 14	15 16 17 18 19 20 21 22 23	24 25 26 27 28 29

Seeking suggestions

Caught proposals

Escaped proposals

Building

Disagreeing and criticizing

Seeking confirmation

Supporting

Seeking clarification, explanation, and information

Other behaviour

Offering explanations, reasons, and difficulties

Unstructured contributions

Multispeak

Figure 9.3

127

reserves the term validation for use in describing the measures of effectiveness taken during the course itself, together with measures taken after the course, but which are purely course-related. Thus, measuring an increase in, say, supporting behaviour during a course is validation; as is checking on the survival of that behaviour in the postcourse situation. Measuring the effects of supporting behaviour in contributing to the achievement of commercial objectives is evaluation. The distinction is not, therefore, temporal, as it is often taken to be. It involves what is measured rather than when the measuring is done. Now, of course, the learning by doing approach generates lots of data to compare with the validatory measures, and we know very well that organic skill training is extraordinarily effective in the sense that significant behaviour changes take place, in the required direction, and with sufficient frequency. At a verbal level, we also know the sorts of things that managers claim they are doing after the training, but this is cold comfort to trainers who believe that there is a gap between what managers say and what they actually do.

The problem of how to evaluate the training is a considerable one, but we have recently made something of a breakthrough by realizing that it is impossible to evaluate training activities which have not got any work-related objectives. Further, we now see that the user-management should set these objectives and apply the measures after the training. Accordingly, we now help them to do this rather than assuming that it is all our business. The first full-blooded experiment embodying these ideas is still in progress in ICL, and so it is too early to be more definitive about the success of Organic Skill Training in achieving the evaluatory, as distinct from the validatory, measures which have been set.

10. Behavioural science contributions to improved performance and task achievement

Hugh B. Marlow

One of the most remarkable features of the last 10 years has been the increasing number of contributions from the behavioural sciences directly related to an understanding of many aspects of managerial performance and organizational effectiveness.

However, despite these contributions and their relevance, the practising manager has by and large not taken account of these findings. This may be due to faults on both sides; the behavioural scientist tends to speak in a language with which the manager is not familiar, while on the other hand, the operating manager may focus his interest too narrowly on immediate considerations.

The aim here is to draw together a number of contributions with which the writer has been concerned in the past years and to try to relate them to the actions of the experienced manager.

The failure to achieve results in major systems changes

Every manager is directly concerned with introducing changes, new systems, new methods of working, and yet, in 1969, at the Datafair Conference in Manchester the figure of 70 per cent was quoted[1] as the percentage of EDP systems failing to meet their performance requirements after installation. To every manager, this means three things: a failure to meet objectives, costs in excess of estimates, and the inability to utilize one of the most powerful aids to more effective decision-making.

The behavioural sciences have clearly shown and identified the reasons why many management projects fail to achieve the expected results.

129

The pattern of effective change

Change does not take place by accident; but many managers behave as if this was the case. One of the most important single factors in the failure to achieve results is the lack of the required forward planning and control to make implementation effective. The use of network or gant charts to control projects or production processes is well accepted, yet a similar use of network charts to monitor and control the attitudes associated with the acceptance of change is limited to the social scientist or the researcher.

In practice, this kind of network chart shows that effective change takes place in four characteristic phases. It also indicates the relationship between the formal and informal managing system, how they interact and their significance in a period of major change.

The patterns of change associated with the introduction of EDP systems are characteristic of all major method changes. The four phases associated with one particular EDP project from 1962 to 1965, and logged on a network chart showed the following characteristics:

Phase 1 was associated with the systems team gaining acceptance for themselves as:

(a) individuals who could speak the language of operating managers;

(b) persons coming from one group in the organization, namely, the data processing department, whose role within the organization was acceptable to operating managers;

(c) persons able to make an acceptable contribution to the resolution of the technical problem being examined.

In phase 1, the systems analyst member of the team did not gain access, at first, to the real problem of the user department. However, the difficulties that were discussed were used to facilitate the process of personal acceptance. This is why the systems analyst usually found after a few weeks in the user department that he was dealing with a very different problem from the one he was initially called in to examine.

Phase 2 was concerned with underlying attitudes to change, particularly the feelings of managers and others towards the objectives of the proposed new systems. In general terms, no matter how much information was given about the intended changes, the information given was not accepted at its face value. Each manager at this stage was asking, 'How is this change likely to affect me?'

At this point, the informal system came to life. Underlying feelings of hostility, suspicion, and anxiety concerning the proposed changes expressed themselves through the informal system. This was a critical point in managing change; if not correctly handled, resistance to change could at this stage have hardened into open opposition.

Phase 3 was the point in time when the first practical steps were taken by operating managers to further the proposed objectives of the new system by initiating systems investigations into areas under their control.

Phase 4 was building into the organization a facility for constantly reappraising the effects of change on organization structure, tasks, and roles. Change, at this stage, was seen as a continuous process and not as something that happened at infrequent intervals. If the ability to achieve continuous adaptation to new needs was not built into systems procedures, within a relatively short time the currently effective managing system would have become gradually less and less relevant. The formal system would then have been gradually placed on one side and allowed to fall into disrepute.

Many practising managers will recognize from their own experience the validity of the four phases associated with the introduction of major changes. While the network chart cannot yet be used accurately to predict the timespans associated with specific projects, it can be used to evaluate the effectiveness with which change is being introduced in a variety of situations.

The simulation exercise, task achievement, and the effective working group

In many major projects, it is the technological aspects which first appear to be of overriding importance. The human, organizational, and communication problems tend to be overlooked, with the result that inadequate resources are allocated to their identification and resolution.

The simulation exercise is one of a number of training techniques which can be used to demonstrate the importance of resolving these related problem areas, if management or technical objectives are to be achieved. When the simulation exercise is used as part of an ongoing project, the technical and managerial objectives of the proposed systems changes can be used as the medium for examining the underlying problems of organization, communications, and human relations. The attitude of mind which limited the speed of the first steam locomotives to that of a man walking in front with a red flag is still a powerful influence today.

The simulation exercise was developed from the Tavistock Institute intergroup exercise, and bridged the gap between a conference devoted solely to learning about organizational behaviour, and the need to construct a learning situation which could be seen by managers to a direct replica of the work situation. It retains the objective of the intergroup exercise: it provides opportunities for learning about attitudes to authority and inter- and intra-group processes, but is, in addition, designed to demonstrate the following propositions:

1 that the technological problems within an organization are relatively easily capable of solution with existing skills, knowledge, and experience;

2 that these technical problems may appear, in practice, to be insoluble, because they are used to disguise underlying attitudes to organization structure, communications, and human relationships;

3 that the use of specialized training techniques can assist in the resolution of these underlying difficulties, thus making possible technical advances which would not otherwise be achieved.

The tasks of an effective working group

The role of the group advisers in the simulation exercise has been widened to take account of the demands made on the working group in real-life situations. The group consultants are now concerned, in addition, with identifying the behavioural style of the group that has requested their assistance.

A working group in real life, to be effective, must take account of changes in the external environment, the action of competitors, new markets, and products. At the same time as adapting to changes in the external environment, the working group must be able to use its own internal resources effectively, whether physical, financial, human, or technical. While these factors are being taken into account, the manager must ensure that the energies of the group are directed towards achieving maximum effectiveness in terms of business performance.

The simulation exercise as part of its contribution to more effective performance throws light on one of the difficulties faced by top management in achieving effective relationships between the functions of sales and marketing, design and production. It is noticeable that, on the breakup of a plenary session, the groups that form usually display characteristics of behaviour that exist in organizations where there is a high level of interdepartmental conflict. The patterns of behaviour typical of the different groups may be described as:

1 An externally oriented group that considers the resolution and examination of the technical or management task to be the primary objective of the exercise. In pursuit of this objective, consideration of feelings, organizational constraints and the need to communicate with other groups are felt to be unimportant. It is also noticeable that this group has a limited capacity to examine its own motivation and behaviour, and that the technical solution it proposes is likely to take inadequate account of human, organizational, or similar constraints.

2 An internally oriented group that argues that the real task is the examination of its own internal behaviour. The members of this group fail to appreciate that their commitment to the examination of internal behaviour is a way of avoiding the external task and the pressures of the environment.

3 The third group appears to have less well-defined characteristics. Its major task appears to be one of setting up communication systems with the other groups and the staff group. The concentration on setting up communication systems appears to be accomplished at the expense of an effective technical solution to the problem under consideration.

These three types of groups appear to form through some kind of psychological process in which persons of similar characteristics group together for their own defence. These groupings create barriers to achieving effective task performance. The processes seen at work in the simulation exercise may influence the selection of personnel in everyday life and reinforce the barriers between functions, which may in the extreme case cause the sales representative to see the production function as 'the enemy'.

The benefits of the simulation exercise to improving task performance can be appreciated if the externally oriented group is seen as representing the sales function, the internally oriented group the production function, and the communication group in the position of the design activity.

Management style and work task performance

The simulation exercise provides learning opportunities in its own right, but it is also a bridge between the 'human relations' school of thought and the more recent exponents of the importance of management style, for example, Blake's Grid and Reddin's 3-D Managerial Effectiveness. The learning from the simulation exercise suggests that a management style which takes account of task requirements, the use of the internal capabilities (human resources) of the working group, and the need to relate the resources of the group to the total environment, is the most effective. This concept of managerial effectiveness comes very close to that of Reddin's more effective 'styles'.

The simulation exercise can be used in two main types of situation:

1 Where the participants are drawn from a variety of organizations with differing levels of seniority.

2 Where the participants are drawn from a particular organization faced with a major systems change. The technical task which is used in this instance is the managerial objectives associated with the introduction of new systems.

The benefits resulting from the simulation exercise when managers return back to their jobs appear to be:

1 Improved communications and relationships *within* departments and functions.

2 Improved communications and relationships *between* departments and functions.

3 An improvement in the quality of management decisions, leading to the more effective achievement of the objectives of the new systems.

Limitations of the external course

The use of external courses as part of a manager's development has enjoyed very considerable popularity, in spite of certain limitations. The limitations of the external course tend to be:

1 Only part of the course syllabus can be relevant to the current needs of each individual participant. Those elements of the course which cannot be immediately applied lose a large part of their value.

2 The development of the individual is isolated from the management team of which he is an integral part.

3 Even though use may be made of group discussions and syndicate exercises, the application of the principles discussed in the training environment cannot be applied directly to improving business performance in the home situation during the period of the development programme.

4 The transfer of learning from the course situation to the work situation is in many cases limited through inadequate debriefing procedures. In practice, few managers make direct changes in their departments as a result of attending an external course. The comments, 'That would not work here', or 'That doesn't meet our needs', are familiar responses to the suggestions of the returning course members.

Developments in in-company training

The recent emphasis away from the external course to in-company training has undoubtedly been influenced by the behavioural sciences. The main element in this trend has been the increasing recognition that effective change means the development, not of part, but of the whole management team in relation to the achievement of business objectives. A number of different influences can be detected in this trend. First, the management by objectives approach, second, that of Blake's Grid, emphasizing the search for an ideal management style, and, third, Reddin's 3-D Managerial Effectiveness Programmes which stress the output requirements of a manager's job.

These approaches emphasize business objectives, the importance of identifying the end product of a manager's activity, and the recognition that the introduction of change demands a full understanding of the human factors involved in making such programmes effective.

The Mant report[2] drew attention to the importance of in-company training for the experienced executive who had not had the opportunity of obtaining formal professional qualification. The future trend is likely to be a combination of the management style approach, with an in-company development programme of the kind used by Associated Industrial Consultants under the name of 'Accelerated Individual and Company Development'. This is described as a method of improving company performance through the development and training of individual managers.

1 It uses the actual objectives and problems within the organization as the basis for the training and development programme.

2 It shows that business results are dependent on:

(a) The level of functional skills, since these determine the efficiency of such activities as marketing, research, and production.

(b) The disciplines of forecasting, planning, and controlling since these indicate the extent to which business plans are being achieved.

(c) The effectiveness of decision-making, which shows how far a manager possesses the will to manage and the ability to shape events.

3 The essence of the approach is to bring together these three activities into the overall managing system, so that no part of the organization's activities remain untouched. This objective is achieved by using a wide range of training methods, such as information, application, and review sessions, together with tutorials and projects, to achieve the maximum impact.

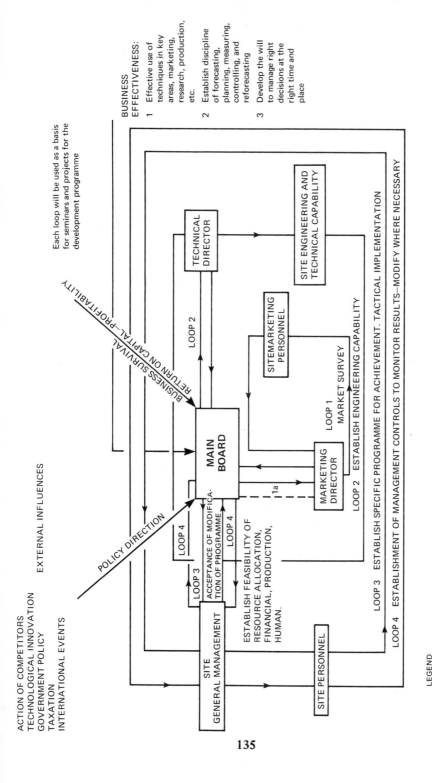

ACTION OF COMPETITORS
TECHNOLOGICAL INNOVATION   EXTERNAL INFLUENCES
GOVERNMENT POLICY
TAXATION
INTERNATIONAL EVENTS

BUSINESS
EFFECTIVENESS:

1 Effective use of
   techniques in key
   areas, marketing,
   research, production,
   etc.

2 Establish discipline
   of forecasting,
   planning, measuring,
   controlling, and
   reforecasting

3 Develop the will
   to manage right
   decisions at the
   right time and
   place

Each loop will be used as a basis
for seminars and projects for the
development programme

BUSINESS SURVIVAL—RETURN ON CAPITAL—PROFITABILITY

POLICY DIRECTION

MAIN BOARD

TECHNICAL DIRECTOR

LOOP 2

SITE ENGINEERING AND
TECHNICAL CAPABILITY

SITE MARKETING
PERSONNEL

LOOP 1   MARKET SURVEY

MARKETING DIRECTOR

LOOP 2   ESTABLISH ENGINEERING CAPABILITY

1a

LOOP 4

LOOP 3

LOOP 4

ACCEPTANCE OF MODIFICA-
TION OF PROGRAMME

ESTABLISH FEASIBILITY OF
RESOURCE ALLOCATION,
FINANCIAL, PRODUCTION,
HUMAN.

SITE
GENERAL MANAGEMENT

SITE PERSONNEL

LOOP 3   ESTABLISH SPECIFIC PROGRAMME FOR ACHIEVEMENT. TACTICAL IMPLEMENTATION

LOOP 4   ESTABLISHMENT OF MANAGEMENT CONTROLS TO MONITOR RESULTS—MODIFY WHERE NECESSARY

LEGEND

Loop 1   Establish nature of market and product range
Loop 2   Establish development and engineering feasibility of proposed product
          range in terms of performance specification

Loop 3   Establish feasibility of resources required to achieve production of
          proposed product range
Loop 4   Establish management controls to monitor agreed programme

Figure 10.1

Schematic diagram showing the series of management loops designed to monitor and control effective performance

135

4 Since the purpose of these activities is associated with making changes designed to improve performance, there is explicit recognition that the human factors associated with the introduction of change must be fully taken into account.

5 When appropriate, to enhance an understanding of the extent of the human, organizational, and communication problems, simulation exercises may be used. These can provide direct experience and learning about the difficulties of coordinating activities and the changes required between and within departments if new methods and approaches are to be effectively utilized.

6 It is also recognized that change is a continuous process and so people in an organization are trained in the methods and skills required to build a system of continuous critical reappraisal within that organization. This ensures that indicators are constantly available as to the direction in which adaptation and change should take place.

7 The use of a project appraisal panel consisting of consultants and directors of the user organization enables the findings of the project teams to be taken into account in assessing current business decisions. This method of appraisal is also used to test out the ability of a manager to manage in the next step up, prior to actual promotion, thus avoiding the danger of promoting a man beyond the level of his ability or capacity.

This type of programme has all the advantages of the external course with none of its disadvantages. The timespan over which an in-company programme takes place ensures that the results of improved performance can be seen by all the participants.

Figure 10.1 shows the business model on which a typical in-company development programme is based. The seminars, review sessions, and projects are based on improving the total effectiveness of the management team and company performance by upgrading management skills, disciplines, and decision-making. These activities are, in turn, related to the four major loops associated with the strategy and tactics of successful business performance.

In-company development programmes are likely to become an established feature of the 'seventies, in the same way that the Staff Colleges and Business Schools dominated the 'sixties, which were a period of experimentation as far as the behavioural sciences were concerned. In the 'seventies, by contrast, the practising manager will be applying the findings of the behavioural sciences in order to achieve improved individual and company performance.

References

1. *The impact of human and organizational problems on the introduction of computer systems.* Booklet prepared by International Computers Ltd with the assistance of Associated Industrial Consultants.
2. MANT, ALISTAIR, *The Experienced Manager: A Major Resource,* London: British Institute of Management, 1969.

PART FOUR: Focus on applications in organizations

Chapter 11, 'Command Group Training', is concerned with application in the work context. Geoffrey Holroyde has developed a means of bringing training to the workplace rather than taking the managers to a training location. His method is a blend of group training and individual training. Since the manager of the work group himself takes part in the group learning experience with his own men, there is much more chance of the learning being transferred to the workplace. Furthermore, it is seen as a work improvement session not as an inflicted training exercise. Why? Because the boss is in the chair and the so-called trainer is in the background as a kind of catalyst and helper.

The NICB survey referred to in chapter 1, page 4, described the Managerial Grid as a variant of sensitivity training. (It is material-intensive not tutor-intensive as most other experiential courses are.) As such it has stimulated widely differing reactions—from high praise to swingeing criticism (see 'Grid on the Grill.' *Management Today*, September, 1970). Chapter 12 by Colin Hutchinson documents very fully the kinds of improvements accruing to one company that has made extensive uses of the specific phases in this form of training. His use of the term 'organization development' draws attention to a most important issue which will be taken up later in this book. It is that the unit to be changed may be the organization itself rather than one of its members. When the organization, and not an individual in it, becomes the target of change maybe new methods of learning have to be deployed.

11. Command Group Training

Geoffrey Holroyde

This is a well-tried way of improving the performance of a business or any organized unit, by training together all the people who actually manage it, round their current opportunities and problems.

Individual training may have little pay-off

Many firms have spent a lot of money on training their managers. In some cases, managers have been selected almost at random to be anointed by the sacred oil of management education, and it is hardly surprising that the results have been disappointing. Sometimes, however, managers have been carefully chosen to attend well-run courses, which are ideally suited to their current needs, but the results have still been disappointing.

After investing large sums in the training of many managers and supervisors over five years, a senior executive told me that there was not a shadow of evidence to show improvement in the total managerial or supervisory performance of the business.

This failure is explained by three remarks which are frequently made by delegates to management training courses:

1 I cannot put any of this into practice when I get back because I am one among so many.

2 The boss would not subscribe to this kind of thinking or practice, so it would be more than my life is worth to try.

3 It does not apply to my current situation, so is interesting but of no immediate use to me.

I have heard all these remarks, even in circumstances when quite a number of the delegates' colleagues have already been through a similar course, but at different times; and when his boss has also been exposed to, and agreed with, similar ideas. It would seem that we are not very good at relating what we learn on courses to the workaday managing situation, or telling those we work with about what we have learnt.

Putting teeth into training

These three arguments for doing nothing can be bowled out if we build a training situation as follows:

1 Train all the people who manage in the unit, at the same time and in each other's presence.
2 Have the boss of the unit as a permanent member of the selected group while the training is going on.
3 Design the training syllabus to be totally appropriate for the current opportunities and problems facing the unit, and then follow each training session with an application session, in which the group decides how it proposes to apply what it has learnt in its everyday management situation.

Command Group Training does pay off

The purpose of Command Group Training is to make an early and significant improvement in the results that a unit is getting, and to equip the managers of the unit with a technique which they can go on using to make continuing improvements. It achieves this in the following ways:

1 It works on the team of managers (and others) who between them exert the greatest leverage on the results that the unit achieves.
2 It develops their knowledge and skill, and makes the changes in their perceptions and assumptions that the current situation makes necessary.
3 It makes the necessary changes in any part of the organization which surrounds them, and which may be inhibiting their current performance.
4 It gets them to develop plans which improve not only their individual performance, but also their combined operations.

In order to plan the training experience, the senior manager of the unit must have a clear objective in mind. He must be able to say what sort of improvement he is looking for, or what kind of changes, and in which team of cooperating managers (and others). If he is unable to do this, then the team must get together with him and study their current situation and then decide in what specific activities or areas they need to get better results.

There are two approaches to Command Group Training which can be used, and both will be explained and illustrated by examples in this paper.

1 The open-ended approach—The senior manager determines the objectives of the Command Group Training, and which people should be in the group. A rough outline of a training programme is designed, but the group is allowed and encouraged to

modify and add to this programme as it proceeds, and as its own needs become clearer. Therefore, it is not possible to say at the start how long this project will last. But it is a mature approach, in which the seniors have tacitly conceded that they do not have a monopoly of solutions to the groups' problems, or of useful ideas about how it may develop itself.

2 **The restricted approach**—Where time and resources are short, or where large numbers of people are going to be developed, a more planned approach may be necessary. A few seniors, perhaps in consultation with a sample of juniors, will determine the purpose of the training, and design a syllabus to that end, and lay down membership of groups.

Training application to the job

In both cases, all training sessions must be followed by application sessions. The group must decide what it is going to do, and by when, as a result of what happened in the training sessions. Training, with no application plan will achieve nothing. The senior manager must be party to the application, and that is why he must be a group member. If this is done something will actually happen as a result of the training.

The group should first concentrate on making some improvements which will happen fairly quickly so that confidence in the exercise is built up, and a determination to continue is established.

An example of open-ended Command Group Training

A new manager joined an established unit. He found a long tradition of authoritarianism and an unwillingness of junior managers to accept delegated responsibility and authority, together with a rather defensive and departmental attitude.

He decided to use CGT to achieve the objective of being able to delegate more responsibility and authority, and increase interdepartmental cooperation. It was obvious that if there was to be greater delegation of decision-making the juniors would need a much greater understanding of the business as a whole, and the role of their own and other departments in the business. Their current understanding was very blinkered by departmental horizons. They would also need to be educated in up to date methods of control and technology, and have access to more control information than at present. A sketchy programme was put together on these lines, and the actual programme evolved as follows. Meetings lasted half a day and were held at fortnightly intervals.

Part 1—After the purpose of the exercise was explained, the group had to identify the objectives of the business and the major opportunities and problems facing it and, thus, themselves. They needed to call in specialists for help and information, and they took quite a long time to get this done. Some brief tuition was needed to help them to ask the right questions, but the group was not spoonfed; it had to plan its own progress. The members found this an unusual and rather alarming experience, and, at this stage, probably doubted the validity of this kind of training.

Part 2—The results of part 1 were then translated into objectives, problems and opportunities at departmental level and analysed by the whole group.

Part 3—Each group member outlined the purpose of his job, the limits of his authority, and identified the major objectives and problems he would have if the business was to seize the opportunities agreed upon in Part 1. He emphasized the service he gave to, and expected from, other members present, and the boss. He modified his proposals in the light of constructive comment from the others.

Part 4—Each group member was allowed to choose the one or two most important things he needed to help him to be more effective in achieving his objectives, and overcoming the problems identified in part 3, under each of these headings.

(a) Information: To help him make plans.
                To help him control operations.
(b) Resources, services, or authority.
(c) Knowledge: Technical updating
             of the environment;
             of systems and techniques.
(d) Skills

A training programme to meet group and individual needs was established.

Part 5—The group redesigned the inadequate control system, with specialist assistance which they called for when needed.

Part 6—Group members suggested ways of using currently under-utilized strengths or resources to seize opportunities or overcome difficulties.

Part 7—Group members identified what they would like to do next to help them improve their managerial performance. They went on to study:

(a) Delegation of responsibility, authority and accountability.
(b) Communication—attitude, skill, media.
(c) Finance—getting, allocating, controlling.
(d) New technology—impact, changes needed, skill.

The field was limitless. But they now knew enough about themselves to decide what they needed to study, or to work on, and they went on doing this, without outside stimulus.

After six months, the manager was able to delegate considerably more responsibility and authority, was delighted with the level of interdepartmental cooperation, and the willingness of people to spot problems and solve them, not just sweep them under the carpet. He also carried out a reorganization, in which three people who had shown themselves able and willing to have better jobs, got them.

Conclusions

Where training of operating groups of managers has been carried out in this way, the results have been most encouraging. Normally, the professional trainer is the catalyst who gets it all going. Frequently, however, long after the basic agreed programme is completed, and the trainer has disappeared, one finds the group continuing to hold regular development sessions—sometimes entirely on their own—and sometimes inviting specialists in to stimulate them. The managers have found this to be a thoroughly practical way of continually improving their managerial effectiveness as a team, and it has become a part of their management process. Compare this with the attitude that management training is something managers do when they can spare the time.

There is another side to this coin. After the process is outlined to the senior manager, he will perceive that he is putting himself into a situation where he will hear criticism of himself, and the organization that he has set up, and that he will have to make changes, and may have to execute unpleasant decisions as a result of what emerges. Only a manager who is secure and adaptable will put himself in this situation, one who is insecure and unwilling to change will avoid such a sharp training tool. Many effective tools are dangerous, and this is no exception, but completely safe tools are often ineffective.

Command group training gets results because

1 The boss takes part in the exercise. He is the one who can initiate and authorize the changes needed. He directs the learning and learns himself. No member of the team can make flippant suggestions or outrageous promises and subsequently duck out of them.

2 The team members learn together. They cannot make the others an excuse for not doing anything. They agree publicly and in the boss's presence, to cooperate on certain issues. Their mutual understanding increases, by working together as a team, on problems, in a learning situation. They build on each other's strengths and recognize the need for combined operations, rather than individual showmanship.

3 The real training requirements for individuals emerge and the boss sees that they are met.

The mechanics of setting up Command Group Training

Forming the group

The group must consist of the people, who, in the opinion of the senior manager, make considerable impact on the results which the business is achieving; the group will contain more people than those with the title 'manager'. Any person who influences the use of resources to create results is playing a part in the management team. Theoretically the more people who are brought in, the better, but, in practice, a group should be less than 12 people. Although the training tool is designed for a business or independent autonomous unit, it can be applied in a subunit provided the unit is fairly autonomous and has clearly defined objectives.

Examples of groups might be:

1 General manager, his heads of departments, and a few people from junior positions selected because of their impact on total performance.

2 Production manager, works manager, planning engineer, production controller, quality controller, materials controller, and production superintendents.

3 A superintendent and his foremen.

4 The chief engineer, his laboratory manager, chief metallurgist, stress engineer, project leaders, and drawing office superintendent.

In a large unit, the exercise may have to be carried out in stages, starting with the senior people (group 1) and working down through the organization (Group 2a, 2b, 2c), etc. Particular communication problems which come to light may demand some meetings of people across normal departmental boundaries, i.e., mixed (a), (b), and (c).

At each stage, the senior manager in the group is totally and intimately concerned with the exercise.

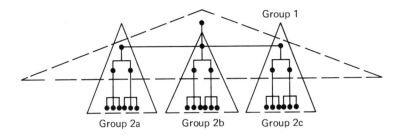

Figure 11.1

Where organizational structures are loose, the first problem facing the senior manager is who shall belong to which groups. People will want to belong to a group which they think is sufficiently senior for them. Where a man is leaving, retiring, or being promoted shortly after the exercise, it may be desirable to include his successor, thereby disclosing who the successor is going to be. It is essential that much thought is given to group membership, or more harm than good may be done by the exercise.

Ideally, the senior manager of the group carries out the training himself, bringing in specialists where necessary; experience has shown that a practised outsider can make a vital contribution:

1 To get the exercise successfully launched.

2 To chair the meetings impartially.

3 To give opinions from his unique position of being a non-member, not emotionally implicated in the discussions or relationships.

4 To bring distilled experience from previous, but similar, Command Group exercises.

Location and timing

The meetings may be held anywhere; the essential feature must be freedom from interruption. Experience shows that it works best if meetings are a little distance away from the workplace.

Command Group Training gets a flying start if members see some need for holding it, for example:

Following a reorganization.

Upon introduction of a new product or process.

When there are many staff changes.

When problems and opportunities look large.

The total time cannot be determined till the objective of the exercise has been identified. In the open-ended exercise, the magnitude of the training problem will only emerge after the third or fourth meeting.

The first few meetings should be short, particularly if the participants are not used to this kind of situation. Later, when confidence in the exercise and enthusiasm for it has emerged, times may be lengthened. The meetings may be either in or out of working hours. Holding them in working hours convinces the juniors that the senior manager believes in the importance of the exercise.

Subsequent meetings may be held on selected half days spread over several weeks, or the manager may elect to take his group right away for a few days' continuous training. Here are some points to consider.

1 Senior managers should not normally be dealing with routine daily problems and can thus get away for a few days. It is more difficult to release firstline supervisors who deal with current minute by minute problems.

2 Attitudes are only changed in a fairly lengthy residential climate. If the need is to shift attitudes, training must be residential.

3 Preparation work between sessions can be done thoroughly if several days elapse between them. If there is need for accurate investigations and detailed suggestions, gaps in the programme are essential.

4 Interruptions are minimized and creative thinking is improved when people are removed from site for a considerable period and start to forget current crises.

5 Removal of senior people for a period forces them to delegate, and is good for their juniors. (After the senior people were removed from a certain business for three days, they rushed back to see how their superintendents and section leaders were getting on without them. 'How did you get on while we were away?' 'Have you been away?' was the reply—leaving the senior people aghast.)

The sequence

1 The senior manager (perhaps with one or two of his immediate juniors) identifies the results wanted from Command Group Training. See Appendix I for some recent examples of Command Group Training objectives.

2 The senior manager must decide who are the people who influence the results—who should belong to the group or groups.

3 Either the senior managers—or in some cases the whole group, at the first meeting, then determine the topics the group needs to work on.

4 The programme is established:
   (a) Timing.
   (b) Location.
   (c) Stimulants and inputs required, and from whom, to get the group thinking around the problems that need solution, or the skills they need to acquire, are determined.

5 Preparation work, and exercises are designed, if appropriate.

6 The group is told what is going to happen and why.

Note—1 Members need plenty of preparation time between meetings if they are to come up with sensible answers. They may also need help.

2 Effective chairing of the meetings is vital, to control discussion, to distil the crucial issues, and summarize findings.

3 The presence of the senior manager is vital to answer queries, agree and approve objectives, take action where needed, resolve conflict, and place requirements on group members.

4 Issues requiring the attention of a minority of the group can be reserved for small sub-meetings (time and place fixed by chairman) to save time of the whole group.

The meetings must be constructive, and it is the duty of the chairman to keep them so.

Experience shows that frequently the group likes to start with an outsider as chairman—someone impartial—someone not in authority. Very soon they will get so used to working constructively together that they get along with their own informally selected chairman, the outsider may thus become redundant. Inhibitions having their origin in the pecking order will soon disappear, and really constructive debate will ensue.

There is, of course, an infinite variety of topics to study. Command Group Training encourages the senior manager to think through his own situation in deciding what topics his group should work on and who should be in the group.

Probable outcomes

Experience shows that, even after four or so meetings, the following are likely to be achieved:

1 The members develop a far greater feeling of belonging to a team, and a wish to cooperate, and an understanding of the other man's point of view.

2 Managers concentrate on what needs to be done, rather than on just being busy. People start to develop sensible plans for getting needed results.

3 People discover unused strengths and resources, and also acquire a willingness to take on an extra load rather than find reasons why other people should have it.

4 The senior manager may have to carry out some reorganization, and establish more information flow, or reallocate resources.

5 A training programme will emerge
   (a) for the whole group;
   (b) for particular individuals.
It will be tailor-made to requirements, and it must be followed up.

6 The group asks for regular continuing meetings to update their understanding of opportunities and problems, and to make plans for combined operations.

7 The group requests meetings with other groups with whom members interact, and discussions with senior managers from other departments.

The group wants to play a more effective role in making the business a success.
New ideas for improving performance will be welling up from within the group.
This method of working becomes a part of their management life—and ceases to be an inflicted training exercise. They will want to go on doing it. This is the measure of its success. It is part of the natural process of creative management.

Subsequent action

The senior manager must:

1 Make the changes he promised to make at the meetings.
2 Set up and publish the training programme for the group or for individuals.
3 Establish and programme such further meetings as were agreed to be desirable.

The group members should be encouraged to carry out a similar exercise with their own subordinates (where appropriate) and may require:

1 Training in discussion group leading.
2 Help with setting up a programme.
3 Facilities for meetings.

147

The restricted approach to Command Group Training

The senior manager of a unit, perhaps after consultation with junior managers or other people, may identify some areas in which improved performance by his team is needed.

He would then set up a programme of training sessions to cover these areas, inviting specialists from within or from outside the company to conduct the sessions. The tighter he defines the requirement, the more tailormade will be the session. Alternatively, he may deliberately leave the 'tutor' broad terms of reference, to increase the catchment of new ideas. Case studies and problems could be drawn from their own business or similar ones (see examples, Appendix 3).

Each training session must be followed by an application session, where the team members pick out from the training the things which they could use in their own situation. They must decide on action, and what they intend to change, and who does it, etc.

The training sessions need not be formal lectures. They could be exercises, discussions, provocative questions, reports of research projects, etc. The training sessions could be made up of management people from different command groups, with the deliberate idea of cross-fertilizing ideas, as long as they are reconstituted in management groups, with their own boss, for the application sessions.

Follow-up meetings to assess progress should be established, so that people know they must do that which they promised to do.

Each member of the training group should keep a notebook, a specimen page of which is shown in Appendix 2. The top of the page outlines briefly the intended coverage of the session. Most of the page is left blank, so the member has space to note what for him are the really significant matters which arise in the session. At the foot of the page he writes:

1 What he intends to do—to change—acting on his own permitted authority, to improve the managerial output of himself or his management group.

2 What he should raise at the subsequent application sessions, where he wants to see action or change which can only be brought about by several members of the group in combined operation.

Thus, every member takes away from the training sessions his personal action plan. The agenda for subsequent application sessions is the sum total of what all the group members bring from the bottom righthand corners of the pages of their notebooks. (This notebook does not replace any handouts that the tutor may give out, it is in addition to them, and has this important 'follow up action' purpose.)

An example

This exercise was carried out in a large organization in which about 170 people were identified as having managerial roles for part of their time. The top few senior managers were convinced of the need to make changes if the business was to survive. They suspected that the desired change in managerial output would only be achieved by a change in attitude, and an injection of knowledge, in all 170

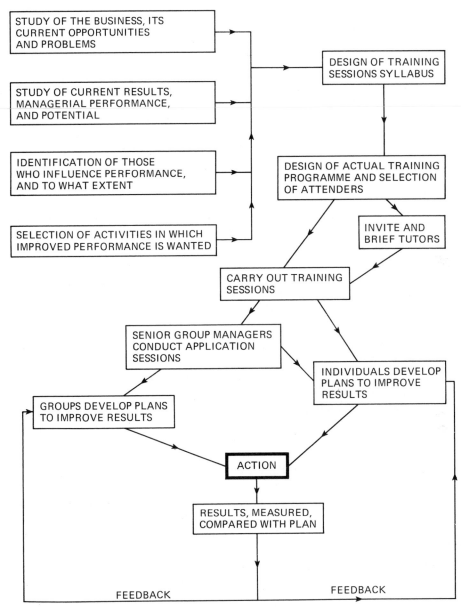

Figure 11.2
The sequence for the restricted approach

managers. They recognized that the change was most likely to occur if the injection happened to everyone in a short timespan.

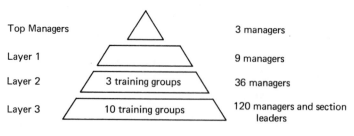

Top Managers		3 managers
Layer 1		9 managers
Layer 2	3 training groups	36 managers
Layer 3	10 training groups	120 managers and section leaders

Figure 11.3

Stages

Month 1. Top 3 discussed the problem and agreed to broad plan with the trainers.

Month 1. Top 3 and layer 1 met for about six hours with the trainers to agree the changes needed and hammer out the training syllabus and agree the plan.

They agreed to let layer 2 experience and modify the syllabus before it went to layer 3. At least one member of layer 1 would be present at all training session of layer 2, and often at training sessions of layer 3. The syllabus contained about 20 hours training (talk and discussion) and was based on:

  (a) the changing business environment;
  (b) the cost and control of money,
  (c) the planning and control of operations;
  (d) getting results from people, and managing change;
  (e) building communication networks;
  (f) improving communication skills.

Note that by designing the syllabus, layer 1 had put itself through a mini-training course.

Month 2. Layer 2, in three mixed-department groups, was exposed to the training material, in the presence of layer 1 representatives. They were invited to add to or modify the syllabus in the light of their experience and their perception of the problem. (The syllabus was put across in about 12 hours for the people at this level.) Layer 2 modified the training syllabus slightly, with layer 1 approval, and also agreed to have at least one representative at every layer 3 training session.

Month 3. Each member of layer 3, in 10 mixed department groups, was exposed to 20 hours training material, in the presence of layer 2 representatives, and frequently also layer 1 representatives. Mixing of departments did much to spread understanding of the roles of other departments, and increase the desire to cooperate across functions.

Month 4. Layers 1, 2, and 3 were reformed in eight command groups, each with its own boss in the chair. The bosses were mainly from layer 1, with a few from layer 2. These groups examined the action proposals of their individual members, and their suggestions for group action, and made plans to achieve specific results and changes.

Each group made recommendations for subsequent study at a final meeting of layer 1 and top 3, on issues which were outside the scope of their normal authority.

Layer 1 and top 3 met to examine the recommendations of the command groups, to take action where necessary, to appraise the entire exercise, and to recognize the next step.

Conclusion—The shift in attitude was achieved, and many managers saw more clearly what was required of them, and made plans to achieve results. Much distrust and suspicion got washed away. A major reorganization of a substantial department took place.

The effect subsequently wore off in some areas, but in other areas these management groups went on having development or training meetings for many months after the completion of the exercise. In these groups, improvement continued and interest was maintained. The practice of participation and of group problem-solving had become established as a way of managing.

Appendix 1

Some recent examples of Command Group Training

Before attempting Command Group Training, the senior manager must determine what he wants to get out of it.

1 To change the attitude of many managers in a highly technical company when trading moved from government customer to commercial market place, with competition and cash shortage.

2 To determine the management style and organization most suited to the technology of the business, and plan to make the changes found necessary, and design the control systems needed for that particular style.

3 To design and introduce a new system of control in a company recently taken over, and reform the corporate spirit after the disruption of takeover and the imposition of new managers on remaining ones.

4 To create teamwork in a company where hitherto departmental loyalty and interdepartmental distrust had inhibited total performance.

5 To get managers to think and grow, and want more authority delegated to them, and to use it, in a department with a tradition of little delegation and authoritarian style. This was needed as a result of a change of manager who wished to delegate more.

6 Following a major reorganization, to teach a new management team:

(a) Five-year planning, and the significance of the plan for each departmental head.

(b) Budgetary control, and how to use the financial information to control operations.

(c) To understand the mutually supporting roles of departments.

7 To improve the productivity of an enterprise by getting many different people involved in designing and creating the changes needed to improve the productivity of the total system—not just the shopfloor productivity.

8 For a large recently formed company of small companies, to design the personnel policy and the procedure for corporate planning and control.

9 Establish meaningful financial ratios as measurements of the health of a business. Show middle managers how what they do influences the ratios. Develop new objectives to improve the ratios, and meaningful control information at lower levels of management.

10 In a business which had gradually got slack over a long period, to raise the morale, and heighten the determination to act and get results.

Appendix 2

Specimen page of notebook for member in a Command Group Training session

In this part of the page will be a short summary of what the meeting expects to cover, or expects to hear in a tutorial session, or cover in a discussion.

○

(Most of the page is left blank for their own notes. The vital bit is at the bottom—where they commit themselves to doing something.)

○

Individual action:	To raise with others:
(Things he can do to improve his own performance, acting on his own initiative.)	(Things he would like to see done which are outside his control, and which must be raised at application session.)

DON'T FORGET — TELL THE BOSS WHAT HE NEEDS TO KNOW

Examples of Command Group Training material

There is no limit to the range of topics which a training group may study. The choice depends entirely on the current business situation, and the strengths and weaknesses of the management team.

A useful approach is to take the group through a range of ideas, possibly using a visiting speaker. Ideally, he should know the situation well enough to put his finger on where it hurts. Then, the group answers a set of questions about themselves, from which an action plan for improvement can be built.

Two examples follow, as a guide for design of material:

A. Organization and management style

Brief synopsis of talk—The kind of organization which will enable the best results to be achieved is probably determined by the complexity of the technology of the product. It is important that the shape of the organization and the communication channels are designed by the managers and not just allowed to evolve.

The organization exists to produce corporate results from individual efforts. There must be allocation of responsibility and authority, and a means of establishing targets and measuring results. Decision-making must be invested in the people best equipped and sited to make the decisions (and those people must have access to all the information needed to make good decisions).

Information must flow freely to where it is needed, so that understanding is created in people's minds of what needs to be done, and so that senior managers are told things they need to know to retain control and reset objectives, without becoming immersed in detail.

The organization must encourage the sensible use of staff services and management emphasis might best be centred round function, project, or product, depending on the type of business.

People will be highly motivated when they have helped to develop the plans for the business and for their department, and when they are working for meaningful targets with as much authority and freedom of action as they can cope with, and when they have enough information to measure their progress. People want to be trusted by their superiors, and to be able to earn the respect of their colleagues, and of themselves, by the effective use of their talents and their ideas.

The questions which follow will help you, in discussion, to formulate how organic or mechanistic your organization[1] should be, and how X or Y[2] your style of management. As a group, you can then devise a strategy for changing your organization or style if you need to.[3]

154

1 Do you believe that managers and people in controlling roles should have their responsibility and authority defined in writing? If so:
   (a) What are the advantages and disadvantages of doing this?
   (b) How detailed should it be?
   (c) Who should write it and how often should it be updated?

2 What does you organization chart tell you about:
   (a) People's responsibility and authority and accountability?
   (b) Communication networks and relationships?
   (c) Management succession?

3 Discuss the relative size and importance of staff and service departments to line departments. Are there any difficulties to be ironed out? Do line managers make the most effective use of staff officers? Should there be more, or less, emphasis placed on:
   (a) functional management?
   (b) project management?
   (c) product management?

4 Are many letters copied to people other than the recipient? What are the advantages and disadvantages of this practice?

5 Are important administrative or technical decisions made at relatively junior levels? Do your salary distribution curves merit placing more or less decision-making at these levels?

6 Have you examined the reasons why people have left the firm during the last few years? What do their reasons tell you about the organization?

7 How much do people in middle management know and need to know about business opportunities and strategy?

8 How much emphasis is placed on obedience to seniors, conformity to established practice, and departmental loyalty?

9 How are people prepared for increased responsibility?

10 Would you say that the present environment:
   (a) Encourages change—technical or administrative?
   (b) Encourages cost and profit awareness?
   (c) Encourages juniors to accept responsibility?
   (d) Encourages commitment to company objectives?
   (e) Encourages risk-taking?
   (f) Fosters combined operations?
   (g) Makes individuals ambitious?

11 What sort of hours do people at various levels work? How busy are they while they are there? What are they busy doing?

12 How do we measure the contribution of an individual to the business?

Productivity

Brief synopsis of talk—Productivity is a measure of the effective use an enterprise makes of the resources invested in it—that is plant, materials, ideas, people, services, goodwill, etc. A basic skill of management is the way the resources are combined and used to make the maximum wanted and valuable output for the minimum input of resources.

Nowadays, more people are thinking than doing: that is, there are more researchers, planners, maintainers and controllers, and fewer operators. Productivity is concerned with the output of all these activities, and their balanced integration into a business plan. It is wasteful to measure with great precision the use of one resource while another more costly one is running away unchecked.

The management must identify measurements they need to make to assess the productivity of the business, or of a department, or of a scarce resource, etc. (Examples of suitable ratios for this kind of operation should be given.)

Some activities nearly defy quantitative measurement, or the cost of measurement would outweigh the saving. Perhaps the answer lies in the attitude of all the people concerned—in people's understanding of what needs doing, and why, and their commitment to doing it—in management's ability to provide the resources and services as and when they are wanted—in the belief that all the people in the organization are there for their mutual good—that survival is based on corporate success.

The following questions and statements may help you to start thinking about your organization and recognizing some of the problems which the group needs to solve. (It may help to quote some of the most significant productivity performance measurements which are available, together with trends, and comparisons with other firms.)

QUESTIONS FOR DISCUSSION

1 Which are the most expensive resources used in your activity where an increased efficiency would exert the greatest leverage on productivity? How are resources allocated?

2 How do you measure productivity? What ratios would be meaningful? What information would you need to produce the ratios?

3 In what order of priority do your customers list the following features of your output?

   Cost, quality, technical supremacy, programme.

4 Outline the business opportunities that await you, provided improvements can be made in which particular products or production activities. How widely is this understood and believed throughout your organization?

5 To what extent do your systems of reward in various departments encourage or inhibit productivity, either on an individual, or on a group basis? How could matters be improved?

6 What is the level of cooperation and understanding between departments? A rough guide may be:
  (a) Time spent by seniors resolving conflict.
  (b) People changing jobs across departmental boundaries.
  (c) Geographical or status discrimination.
  (d) Paperwork to justify action taken by department.
  (e) Distrust of, or unwillingness to follow instructions of, or take work from, another department.

7 What proportion of the people make good suggestions for improving productivity? How many concern improved production methods, or technical features, or administrative procedures? How many are made in one department, concerning the work of another? How many are adopted?

8 How do you determine the correct balance of effort and expenditure between production departments, and backing-up service and planning departments?

9 How often are junior people held up by shortage of work, facilities or resources where, rightly or wrongly, the blame appears to them to be a management failure?

10 How often are programmes behind, and planning ignored, and how much emergency progress chasing is done by senior people? Why is this so?

11 Do the supervisors supervise? How much training have they received in how to supervise? From whom? How much time is devoted to telling people about the business, and what is going on?

12 Do you feel most improvement in productivity can arise from:
  (a) More use of modern techniques of production, control, and communication?
  (b) Reorganization, interdepartmental understanding?
  (c) Scientific work measurement in works and office?
  (d) Change in attitude of people?

13 For which heading you have chosen in 11, how much time are you prepared to invest in making the changes? Outline a strategy to be followed.

Other subjects frequently studied during CGT are:
  Management information and control.
  Planning of operations.
  Personnel policy and use of people.
  Quality control and customer satisfaction.
  Finance; project appraisal; profit centres; budgets; overheads.
  Stock control; production control; work in progress.

References

1. BURNS, T. and STALKER, G. M., *The Management of Innovation*. London: Tavistock Publications, 1961.
2. McGREGOR, DOUGLAS M., *The Human Side of Enterprise*. N.Y.: McGraw-Hill, 1960.
3. WOODWARD, JOAN, *Industrial Organization: Theory and Practice*. London: Oxford U.P., 1965.

12. Organization development in British-American Tobacco Company Limited

Colin Hutchinson

Many people recognize that most, if not all, organizations could be more effective, and that the same applies to most managers. Typically, it is the integrated effort of several people which produces results; consequently, the effectiveness of the organization, as well as individual competence, needs to be developed.

Many organizations consciously strive to improve their effectiveness, but their efforts are not always successful, and do not always cover all important areas. Before implementing a systematic development programme, the top team of the organization needs to answer the following questions:

1 What development activities are used at present, and with what results?
2 What development programme do we intend to implement?
3 How long will it take?
4 What will it cost?
5 Who will be responsible for coordination? . . . and for implementation?
6 What results do we expect?

Since the focus is on organization development, it is necessary to define what is meant by 'an organization' and what development means. An organization is defined as a group of people working together to achieve a common purpose, and, as such, can be applied to a company, a branch, or a department. Development means undertaking systematic activities which lead to increased effectiveness.

An organization can improve its effectiveness in many ways:

By a *commercial* decision which affects the nature or purpose of the organization, or the manner in which it is financed, or by the methods used for measuring its economic performance.

By developing the concept of *customer orientation* throughout the company, so that market opportunities can be identified better and exploited more effectively.

Through *operations research* leading to better or cheaper ways of acquiring raw materials, of designing production processes, of marketing and selling, of distributing manufactured goods.

From *technological* developments which result in the creation of new products and processes.

By developing the quality of the *human organization* and increasing the ability of people to integrate their efforts more effectively.

Changes in the first four areas are always dependent on the reactions and attitudes of people in the organization both individually and collectively, the integration of effort they can achieve, and the quality of decisions that they make. Development of the human organization has widespread and long-term impact on results, because it increases the capacity of the organization to deal effectively with all kinds of problems and opportunities.

The problem we faced

Although general agreement had developed during the period 1958-65 that the ideas of Drucker, McGregor, and Herzberg described a management philosophy that was appropriate to BAT, we were not satisfied with the depth of understanding and, hence, the application that was being achieved. In one division, which is used later in this paper as an example, results were poor, and had not responded to various different approaches. We believed that the Managerial Grid[1] was entirely compatible with the management philosophy we were trying to apply, and that the Grid approach would lead to better comprehension and application of this philosophy.

The belief in the Grid approach developed after a number of managers at various levels had taken part in Managerial Grid seminars. The decision to go ahead followed some months after Drs Blake and Mouton had run a seminar for 20 senior managers, including 1 deputy chairman and 5 directors of BAT's main board, in July 1965.

What is grid organization development?

Discussions with senior managers both within BAT and in other organizations reveal widely differing views on the meaning and value of organization development. The literature on management also indicates that there is no general understanding at the present time.

The meaning that is associated with this article is largely based on the work of Scientific Methods Inc., the organization established in Austin, Texas, USA by Drs Blake and Mouton. Their approach starts with the Managerial Grid seminar and leads into grid organization development. This is not the only approach to improving organizational effectiveness that has been used in BAT, but it is the focus of attention in this article.

Grid organization development[2] is a six phase approach which begins with individual learning, works through teamwork development to defining the

159

objectives and goals of the organization, and applies these principles throughout the organization. A description of the phases follows in order to give understanding of how this works in practice.

The Managerial Grid (phase 1)

Understanding one's own style of management and the style which is likely to be most effective, aided by the managerial grid, can be compared with making a journey with the aid of a map. In both cases, it is very desirable to know where one is and where one is going. During the journey, it is necessary to check that progress

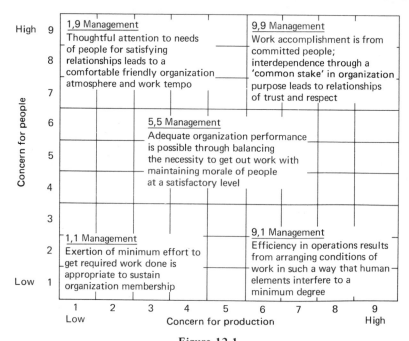

Figure 12.1
The Managerial Grid (From *The Managerial Grid* by Dr Robert R. Blake and Dr Jane S. Mouton. Copyright 1964 by Gulf Publishing Company, Houston, Texas. Used with permission)

is being made, and while some may prefer to rely on instinct and guesswork others find that the use of landmarks and cross-checking with the map is helpful. The Managerial Grid is probably the most effective map that has so far been developed as an aid to improving managerial effectiveness (see Fig. 12.1).

Prior to attending the Grid seminar, each participant is required to do some preparatory work which is concerned with identifying one's own style of management and learning the variations that the Grid offers. The exercises all present a choice of statements depicting alternative managerial values and the task is to arrange them in order of personal preference.

160

At the seminar, the tasks dealing with comprehension of Grid styles are tackled in teams of six to eight with a time limit for each task. Each individual and each team scores its own answers and the achievement of the team is measured by the improvement on both the average and the highest individual score. Each team task is followed by an assessment of effectiveness where the team evaluate their performance and identify for themselves how their team action might be improved. The tasks become more difficult and progress from a written case history to a film in which the managerial style of six jurors is identified. Each task is followed by a critique session in which positive steps for improving team action are identified.

The penultimate task, which is concerned with individual styles, is to aid each person to identify his own managerial style. This is done by describing each member's approach to such things as conflict, conviction, expression of ideas, and readiness to change one's mind. Verbal descriptions are developed of each team member's managerial style, aided by the learning that has already taken place. Most people find that this is a rewarding experience, and although some weaknesses are identified, it often draws attention to strengths that the individual did not know he possessed.

The final task is concerned with organization culture, or defining the ideal and actual operating practices within the firm, and identifying the barriers which impede progress.

Key items of learning from the Grid seminar include the management of conflict, the use of critique and the significance of organization culture. Each is discussed below.

Managing conflict—Attendance at the seminar leads to worthwhile learning about the management of conflict and disagreement. When different views are expressed in the early stages of the seminar, they are often not pursued very forcefully. However, when the scoring of individual and team results reveals correct answers which were not included in the team solution, or incorrect answers which were included because of the forcefulness of argument rather than reason, then all team members are stimulated to probe more deeply the alternative approaches to managing conflict. There is also the opportunity to see how the dominating personalities can cause the quiet ones to remain silent, irrespective of the quality of their contribution. Resorting to a show of hands to resolve disagreement can still lead to the team recording a wrong answer, because the minority can still be right. Some teams go out of their way to give all a fair hearing, irrespective of what has been said before, and time runs out. By the end of the seminar the need to probe for causes and reasons to support points of view with succinct argument and good examples, is more clearly seen as the path to obtaining the best solutions, with all working with commitment to team results.

Critique—Critique as used here describes the practice by a group of monitoring its own problem-solving discussions in order to ensure that progress and results are achieved within the appropriate time.

At the conclusion of each task, teams assess their effectiveness against criteria

161

which are provided. These include direction of effort, decision-making, communication, atmosphere, and use of on-going critique. The inclusion of the last item as one criterion leads to the realization that the use of critique to monitor progress and performance, while working, can be a valuable technique. It contributes significantly to the quality of contributions, the management of time, and to the results which are obtained.

Organization culture—All organizations develop their own unique culture, or said another way, they create their pattern of working practices. These include past traditions, established practices, and habits. This organization culture or climate exerts a profound influence on the working practices of individuals, in many silent ways. Organizations in which people are genuinely stimulated and encouraged to express their thinking are fortunate. The open discussion of disagreement becomes a valuable source of creative ideas, and is likely to contribute to increased effectiveness. Too often, the culture and working practices that exist grew in an unplanned way, and exert a rather negative influence.

The reality often places emphasis on established practices from the past, or on maintaining peace and harmony, or on strict adherence to the authority of the hierarchy. The relative merits of these alternatives are fully discussed.

Examination of organization culture is in two parts. The first deals with describing the ideal that would support the best management practices. Here participants are asked to consider not only the best working approach, but what back-up would be used in descending order of preference, should the best fail for any reason. Often, it is not difficult to make the first choice the one which describes the thoroughly discussed, universally agreed solution. It is much harder to decide what would be the next best if this failed. Following agreement of the ideal culture the same questions are reviewed a second time to determine the culture that actually exists, and where there is a discrepancy what prevents the ideal from being achieved.

This clarification of the gap between sound and actual working practices constitute a clear objective for organization development efforts.

The organization development seminar (OD)—When a few managers in a company have attended a Managerial Grid seminar, interest in this approach often develops. The organization development seminar provides an opportunity to learn the full scope of the phases of Grid organization development and how they might be applied in a particular situation. Ideally, this seminar is attended by teams of two to four people, from the same company, and led by the chief executive. The pre-work study for this seminar requires 40-50 hours. During the seminar much of the work is carried out in company teams, so that understanding of each phase of Grid OD can immediately be related to the circumstances and development needs of the participant's own organization. The basic seminar design is the simulated application of each phase of Grid OD, thereby understanding what it aims to achieve, and often learning much about one's own organization in the process.

Attendance at an OD seminar is recommended before the first pilot grid seminar is run, but it is still relevant after the pilot Grid seminar, and before proceeding further with Grid organization development.

Instructors for Grid seminars (ID)—Line managers make good instructors for Grid seminars because they are best able to relate the learning that is taking place to actual work experience, and because as instructors their leadership and involvement in Grid OD is seen by all participants. Another significant benefit is that attendance at the instructor development programme and the role of instructor both provide much deeper insight into the concepts contained in Grid OD, than can be obtained in one week's participation in the Managerial Grid seminar. This learning has much direct significance to the work of line managers, many of whom find the ID experience of value even if they do not go on to run a seminar.

Teamwork development (phase 2)

Experience and a limited amount of research[3] seem to show that participants in Grid seminars can and do apply the concepts to their work, and some improvement in effectiveness is noticeable. Without adequate follow-up, the benefits to the organization can be limited, even insignificant in time, because phase 1 on its own often has little impact on the organization culture. For this reason, teamwork development is provided as the means for transferring Grid learning into practice within actual work teams.

Teamwork development should start with the top team of the organization, however this has been defined. For instance, the organization may be the parent company, it may be an associated company, or a branch, or a division. The criterion should be that the organization has responsibility for its own development and, ideally, is a profit centre. Selecting the top team can present problems, and the organization chart is not always the best guide to the real work team. The prework for phase 2 takes 10-12 hours, and the new materials (SMI's 1969 version) provide a preliminary step which requires less than a half-day and tests that the team composition (normally 5 to 10 people) is sound, and that teamwork development is needed.

Five days are needed for effective completion of teamwork development, and these are divided into five basic activities, interspersed with critique. The first activity is concerned with assessing the ideal and actual work team culture, or, said another way, establishing the working procedures for the real work team, and identifying the development needed in working practices. The second activity is to aid each team member to identify his managerial style and to be specific about improvements that he can make to his performance. This differs from phase 1 in that the style now defined is the style used at work, as seen by work colleagues.

The third activity shifts the focus away from methods and styles of working to the work itself. This step is called 'management by objectives', and establishes the principal work results for which the team is responsible. A demonstration project on one specific problem aims to show how teamwork can be used to solve real work problems, some of which may have been around unrecognized or unsolved for a long time.

The fourth activity explores the possibility of extending teamwork development, since top team members (except the Chief Executive) are all also leaders of their own teams. If teamwork development has been successful, the desire to extend can be strong, but firm plans should still be made before breaking up, to ensure that good intentions do get translated into practice.

The fifth activity takes place two to six months later, and is provided for a review of progress.

Typically teamwork development results in improvement to objectivity, candour, the use of critique, and clarification of team objectives. The more successful the occasion, the greater the improvement to the team's problem-solving ability, and hence its overall performance.

Achieving intergroup coordination (phase 3)

Since teamwork development tends to occur most frequently with departmental teams (after the top team activity is completed), it does not always overcome intergroup or interdepartmental problems which may exist. A separate activity is sometimes needed to come to terms with this kind of problem if it exists between departments, between different levels within an organization, or between management and union. As yet we have no experience of this intergroup linking activity within BAT.

In outline, however, the first step of this phase is jointly to define the aim. The two parties then separately develop their own description of the ideal relationship that is required, and meet to compare results. There is usually agreement over 80 per cent of the issues. Next, the parties separately develop their own description of the actual relationship that does exist. A comparison between these is the next step, and from here work is done to close the gap that has now been more clearly identified.

Designing an ideal strategic corporate model (phase 4)

In the same way as the emphasis in the middle of teamwork development shifted from methods of working to the work itself, so, too, this occurs for the organization as soon as work begins on the corporate model. Designing an ideal strategic corporate model involves a thorough and penetrating analysis of the business logic on which an organization is founded, and the creation of the model which will be applied in the future. It is not only a difficult thing to do, but it is a rigorous critique of the manner in which the business is managed. Phase 4 is a top team activity, which should begin as soon as the top team have completed their teamwork development.

As part of the standard prework, *My Years with General Motors* by A. P. Sloan[4] is studied, and provides the means for understanding the conceptual model of another firm. Unlike the earlier phases, there is now an opportunity to create sentence descriptions of each element of the business wherever those that are provided do not adequately convey the correct meaning. Work on developing the model itself begins with identifying the constraints within which it is necessary to work. These constraints are then tested to ensure that they really are fixed restrictions, and typically a great many disappear during the process. Usually only governmental restrictions are left, and at this stage the model itself is created by examining and writing answers to six issues:

Financial objectives.
The nature of the business.
The nature of the market.
The organization structure.
Policies.
Development of both products and people.

At the conclusion of phase 4, the equivalent of an artist's sketch of the business model has been prepared, which then needs to be tested and refined by discussion with others in the organization, until the blueprint for the business is ready.

Implementing the model (phase 5)

The completed model next needs to be put into practice. At this stage, the details of exactly how and where, for instance, production should take place, stocks should be stored and dispatched, and distribution should be effected, are worked out. Management techniques, especially network analysis and operations research are particularly valuable for this purpose, as is the detailed application of management by objectives.

Evaluation and critique (phase 6)

The evaluation and critique of an organization and its performance can be introduced at any stage of Grid OD. This is an activity which has many varied applications, but it may be particularly apt to introduce this at the year end, when the balance sheet is finalized and a review of performance will be taking place. *Corporate Excellence Diagnosis*[5] was designed for this purpose and it consists of 200 searching questions about every aspect of the business. The main divisions of the text are:

Human resources.
Financial management.
Operations.
Marketing.
Research and development.
Corporate.

The questions offer descriptions of the best and worst situation that might exist, but invite a written description of the actual standards as they are. Application can be on a departmental or corporate basis, and can use all questions or be selective. Those who have used this, and so far its use in BAT is limited, have found that it leads to a penetrating and worthwhile diagnosis of organizational effectiveness, from which development plans can be made.

Progress in associated companies

To trace evolution in BAT,[6] it is necessary to go back at least 10 years, because the 'sixties have seen the beginnings of application of management by objectives, the use of the work of Drucker, McGregor and Herzberg, among others, and the introduction of budgetary accounting, as well as the use of Grid OD. Some examples of what has been done in BAT's associated companies are given below:

Example 1—In one company after a period of adverse circumstances, when sales and profits suffered a sharp decline, it was necessary to undertake a systematic review of how the company's performance could be improved. Many things were investigated and a wide variety of decisions affected the slow and steady recovery. Among these was the use of the profession of management programme, developed by the Louis Allen organization. The chief executive and some of his colleagues took part in this programme, believed it had merit and was relevant. They led its introduction throughout management.

Example 2—In another associated company, after two or three senior managers, including the chief executive, had attended grid seminars, the decision was taken to adopt this approach. Two pilot seminars were organized to cover all management and supervisory staff. Concurrently teamwork development was undertaken by the top management team. The introduction of the seminars and teamwork development was undertaken by a man from the parent company, who had had prior experience of both these phases of grid OD.

Example 3—In a third company, several managers had experience of the Managerial Grid seminar and believed it to be valuable for their own organization. This persuaded the company to run a pilot seminar which would be attended by the chief executive, two company directors, and several senior and middle managers. Another director with prior experience of the grid seminar, took part in an instructor development programme, and he and a man from London together ran this seminar. Later, teamwork development was installed for the top management team, and extended to several other departmental teams. The current development activity focuses on management by objectives.

Example 4—In another associated company, management by objectives was introduced in 1960 and later supported by systematic budgetary accounting procedures. Interest is now being shown in Grid OD, but more understanding and experience of this approach will be obtained before deciding on any major application.

Example 5—One division within BAT which had suffered adverse profit and sales performance provides a fifth example. After lack of success from other approaches the Grid was introduced and virtually all staff attended seminars over a three-year period. Effective use was made of teamwork development in several main teams operating within or from the parent company. The building of a strategic corporate model (phase 4) was also undertaken successfully and proved beneficial. A satisfactory profit and sales growth has occurred over the last five years, and team spirit and morale are greatly improved.

The remainder of these notes describe approaches that have been used to try to evaluate the benefits derived from Grid organization development, since this is the approach that has been used most extensively within BAT.

How many people have been involved?

Since January 1965, when the first Managerial Grid seminar took place in England, nearly 1500 managers have taken part in these seminars. Considerable use has also been made of other elements of Grid organization and details are given in Table 12.1.

	Total no. of management staff	Number of people taking part ‡					
		MGS	ID	Inst	BAT OD	SMI OD	PHASE 2
UK	305	669*	52	44	56	18	146§
North America	1114	73	1		4	12	
Central America	65	51			2	14	
South America	495	93	5	1	1	5	
Caribbean	63	88*				2	8
North and West Africa	268	64				2	
East and Central Africa	113	58			1	2	
South Africa	132	10				1	
Europe	172	193*	10	8	2	4	32
Far East	1100	128	4	1		8	
Australasia	424	13			1	1	
Miscellaneous†		33	1				
	4251	1473	73	54	67	69	186

Notes:
* In the UK, Caribbean, and Europe the use of the grid seminar has been extended beyond management.
† The figure for miscellaneous is made up of people outside BAT's tobacco interests, who have attended seminars organized by BAT.
‡ MGS   = Managerial Grid seminar
 ID   = Instructor development programme
 Inst   = Those who have been Grid instructors
 BATOD= BAT's version of the organization development seminar
 SMIOD = Scientific Methods Inc.'s OD seminar
 Phase 2 = Teamwork development
§ One division has done Phase 4—Building an ideal strategic corporate model.

Table 12.1
Use in BAT of the phases of Grid. organization development January 1965 to December 1969

167

Reactions of managers

Reactions to the Managerial Grid seminars and to teamwork development have been predominantly favourable. On several occasions, participants' reactions have been systematically collected both at the conclusion of a seminar and at varying time intervals thereafter.

April 1967: A circular was sent to a majority of directors and senior staff in the UK, some months after their participation in a grid seminar to test their reaction and to ascertain their willingness to act as an instructor. Sixty-four letters were sent out and forty-nine replies were received:

General Reaction

Favourable	40
Qualified approval	5
Question not answered	3
Not in favour	1
No reply	15
	64

Willingness to act as instructor

Willing to be instructor	22
Willing, but no time available	11
Not available	1
Agreeable, but hope not required	2
Unwilling, with reasons given	8
Unwilling, no reasons given	5
No reply	15
	64

January 1967 to August 1969: The seminar provided an opportunity to discuss organization culture and to identify the barriers which prevent the organization from becoming more effective. Data from 34 seminars representing 138 teams is available, and reveals the consistency with which certain barriers were mentioned:

Communication	mentioned by	92%	of all teams
Planning	,,	73%	,,
Critique	,,	67%	,,
Creativity	,,	62%	,,
Commitment	,,	61%	,,
Expense (cost) consciousness	,,	41%	,,
Coordination	,,	40%	,,

October 1967: It was apparent that communication was most frequently stressed as the main barrier to organizational effectiveness, and a survey was carried out among UK Grid participants. Over 300 replies (from 371 letters) were received, and these revealed that 91.7 per cent of respondents believed that communication could be improved. Weaknesses in communication were seen by respondents to be more severe from the top downwards than laterally. Since many bosses and their subordinates were answering the same questionnaire, it is clear that often the boss thought he was communicating effectively, but the subordinate did not agree:

Upwards from themselves	34%
Upwards to themselves	19%
Downwards from themselves	22%
Downwards to themselves	83%
Sideways	73%

168

Improvement in communication was felt to be required in some quite specific areas:

	All those replying %	Yes important %	Yes, but not important %	No improvement required %
Between groups and individuals	100	77	11	12
Company objectives	100	67	15	18
Company plans	100	67	17	16
Company policy	100	66	17	17
Own job	100	42	14	44
Factual company news	100	34	24	42
Conditions of service	100	27	19	54
Special company news	100	17	39	44

Many people now report improvement in communication and believe that efforts made in the past two years have had considerable effect. BAT have embarked on a major application of management by objectives, and forward planning is receiving increased attention within the associated companies.

November 1967: Two Grid seminars were held in Teresopolis in Brazil in June 1967, attended by 64 directors and senior managers from 17 associated companies throughout Latin America and the Caribbean. Six weeks afterwards, reactions were obtained by the completion of a questionnaire (49 people), or from a letter (15 people), with the following reactions:

(a) Are you keen to take this matter further?

Positively enthusiastic	37
Reasonably enthusiastic	16
Undecided	7
Not keen, but would not oppose	2
Opposed	2
	64

(b) Did you find the seminar:

Interesting?	Stimulating?	Beneficial?	Enjoyable?	Response
45	40	26	33	Extremely
8	9	22	19	Moderately
7	8	9	8	Other affirmative
—	3	3	—	Slightly
1	1	1	1	Not very
—	—	—	—	Not at all
—	—	—	—	Other negative

Three replies did not describe personal reactions of any kind. The 'not very' response was a different person in each case.

February 1968: A full report from 14 seminars involving 371 people (330 from the UK and 41 from overseas) which were held at the BAT's Management Training

Centre from January to April 1967, was finalized and circulated to the board of BAT. The main conclusions were summarized as:

1 Understanding of what is required for effective managerial behaviour is markedly increased.

2 Individuals gain a clearer understanding of their own managerial behaviour, and a high proportion see the need to set themselves improved standards of behaviour.

3 Generalizing, BAT is seen on average as predominantly 5.5, with the back-up seen as being either 9.9 or 1.9 in roughly equal proportions, although there are interesting departmental differences.

The assessment of organization culture involved ranking five alternatives (representing the five Grid styles) for each of 20 questions. Five points were awarded to the alternative that was most preferred, four to the next, down to one for the least preferred alternative. In the event of the same Grid style being selected in first place for each question, a score of 100 would be obtained. Conversely, a Grid style always ranked in fifth place would obtain a score of 20. By deducting the scores for ideal and actual organization culture, the extent to which a change is desired can be expressed numerically:

	9.9	9.1	5.5	1.9	1.1
Ideal culture	99	62	66	48	25
Actual culture	62	51	86	63	38
Shift required	+37	+11	−20	−15	−13

In the pre-work and at the end of the seminar, each individual assesses his own managerial values, by indicating a preference for one statement in each of 40 paired statements, and by distributing three points between the pair. Each statement is identifiable with a Grid style, and if it is awarded three points each time it occurs, the maximum any Grid style would obtain would be 48, the minimum 0. During the seminar, managerial values of participants shifted:

	9.9	9.1	5.5	1.9	1.1
Prework score	35	24	33	21	7
Score at end of grid	41	24	31	18	6
Shift which occurred	+6	−	−2	−3	−1

The shift in personal managerial values in aggregate, corresponds with the manner in which managers seek to change the organization culture, except for the absence of a shift towards 9.1 values. This, however, tends to develop later, especially after teamwork development, when this kind of question is closely examined in its application to a working team.

170

All participants assess their own managerial style before and after the grid seminar. The dominant style of 371 people, completed on a self-assessment basis is:

	Before	After
9.9	61%	31%
9.1	10%	25%
5.5	23%	33%
1.9	6%	8%
1.1	—	3%

Whereas values focus on the assumptions and beliefs about effective management, styles focus on how people assess their current managerial behaviour. A more realistic assessment of existing style of management, coupled with an endorsement of the elements of effectiveness, act as a strong magnet for increasing personal effectiveness.

April 1968 to August 1969: In April 1968 we began using a Grid critique form developed by SMI. This is completed by delegates on the last day of the Grid week, and seeks answers to two key questions. A nine-point scale is used, where 9 represents a very favourable reaction and 1 a very unfavourable reaction. Responses are available from 12 seminars representing 282 people:

	Average assessment on a nine-point scale
How rewarding was the week as a learning experience?	8.2
How applicable was the content learned for increasing managerial effectiveness?	7.7

Team performance v. individual achievement

The tasks contained in the Grid seminar provide an opportunity to measure the results that individuals can obtain when working alone, and their ability (or otherwise) to improve on the average of the individual performances when working together as a team. The data from BAT teams has not been collected, but SMI have studied this in public seminars[8]:

Team performance results	Percent of experiments by nations							
	USA	S. Africa	Canada	England	Australia	Middle East	S. America	Japan
Team results better than average of individual scores	97	97	94	100	92	100	81	100
Team results better than highest scoring individual	41	39	38	50	29	42	6	30
Team results poorer than average of individual scores	2	3	6	0	7	0	19	0
Team results poorer than lowest scoring individual	0	0	0	0	0	0	0	0

Observation of many seminars suggest that BAT results fall within this range.

Reactions to OD seminar (SMI's version)

The objectives of an organization development seminar are:

1 Learn and understand the rationale for the ideal model of grid organization development.
2 Test the applicability of Grid OD to your company.
3 Become familiar with all six phases of Grid OD.
4 Develop convictions with all six phases of Grid OD.
5 Gain insight into your own organization.

At the conclusion of the seminar, delegates are asked to assess their experience. The results from one seminar attended by 31 senior managers from BAT companies, including 8 chief executives, are:

	Average rating out of 9	Range	Per cent recording 7, 8, or 9
Achievement of seminar goals	7.3	4 to 9	87
Achievement of personal goals	7.4	5 to 9	83

Comparative rating—Grid v. others

We have used the Grid seminar as part of the management training courses run each year for junior and middle managers. In 1968, we asked for detailed assessment of all main subjects. Four points were awarded for the most favourable reaction, one for the least favourable, and an average score obtained. Some months (three to nine) after return to work, delegates were again asked for their views, but this time on the practical value they had obtained from each main subject:

	End of course reaction	3-9 months later —practical value
Managerial grid seminar	3.82	3.83
Management by objectives project	3.46	3.73
An objective setting project	3.28	3.51
A management & motivation project	3.40	3.46
A purpose of business project	3.15	3.10
An environment of business presentation	3.13	3.07
A management services presentation	3.34	2.95
An accounting & finance presentation and project	3.02	2.78
A personal work project	3.32	2.76
A marketing presentation & project	2.29	2.13
A technology of tobacco presentation	2.47	2.11
A personnel presentation	2.53	2.03

Reactions to teamwork development (phase 2 of Grid OD)

After taking part in teamwork development, the reactions to this phase of grid OD has also been recorded. In the judgement of participants, teamwork development is a worthwhile activity for improving relationships between team members, and for clarifying work problems, but the degree of success varies. Recorded reactions are available from 23 teams (out of a total of 41):

	Effect on relationships	Understanding of work problems	Enthusiasm for tackling work problems
Much improved	10	14	4
Improved	11	9	19
No change	2	–	–
Worse	–	–	–

The remaining 18 teams have not recorded their reactions formally, or this record is not now available, but informal discussions have clearly indicated that 12 of these were successful. Little or no information is available on the other six, two of which departed from the design. It is now known that five days, rather than three, is needed for the work to be done thoroughly, and that each occasion teamwork development takes place this should be undertaken with a qualified person to ensure that the work to be done is understood correctly. SMI have redesigned the materials since these activities took place, and a clearer distinction is now made between methods or styles of working and the work for which a team has responsibility. Much of the early teamwork development in BAT concentrated much more on methods of working and left little time for adequate discussion of the work to be done, work priorities, and follow-up, and this was aggravated by the belief that three days was sufficient time and that it could be self-administered by the team leader. Current phase 2 applications are being installed by people who are familiar with the design, and five days are being allocated.

Management by objectives

The introduction in 1968 of the management by objectives project on Management Development Programmes at all levels, provides additional supportive material. A questionnaire was used prior to participation in the Management Grid seminar. Respondents were asked to select the statement which they would regard as the soundest way for themselves to work, and which best described their own work situation. There was little difficulty in identifying the soundest, but many fewer were able to select this as descriptive of their own situation:

	Selected as soundest %	Selected as descripitive of actual situation %
1 Responsibilities have been agreed and are clear	98	29
2 Important areas where results matter are systematically discussed, agreed, and reviewed periodically	96	24
3 My boss and I work out my objectives together	83	39
4 Nearly all my work is forward-looking, and I work systematically towards planned objectives	96	20
5 I carry out a systematic and regular analysis of how I use my time to plan its use in future	91	13
6 My subordinates and I work effectively as a team and produce desired results	90	28
7 Standards of performance and/or a budget which my boss and I agree, form the basis for systematic valuation and review of work results	89	29

For questions 1, 3, 4, and 7 used in 1968 and 1969, there were 242 respondents, and for questions 2, 5, and 6 there were 91 respondents. The number differs because questions 2, 5, and 6 were added in 1969.

Evaluation of results

The data given so far has concentrated on the reactions of managers and is largely based on opinion. Two studies have been undertaken to try to evaluate the results more objectively. The first of these was in a division which had had longer and more consistent experience of Grid OD than any other within BAT. Here, the approach was to identify the results obtained by the division over the period October 1964 to September 1969, and then to look at the factors which could have affected these results, and to try to assess their impact. The second study, undertaken by Dr A. P. O. Williams of City University, London, involved interviewing people at a UK branch of BAT, before and after participation in the Grid Seminar. A similar approach was used for the top team of the branch in relation to their teamwork development.

One division

During the period 1963-64, dissatisfaction with the division's performance prevailed. Performance figures were incorporated in BAT's consolidated accounts, and the division and its components had difficulty in assessing the situation correctly. Many briefing notes were produced by the three members of the top team, and much of what they contained can now be traced in working practices. It is significant to look back and see the extent to which the recommendations about what should be done tended to be a one-way communication from the top. This

174

was seen to be correct and sound throughout the organization, but a significant change began with a conference in 1965, incorporating the Managerial Grid seminar.

A two week conference was held in Brighton in January 1965, attended by 25 people. The Grid in the first week was followed by a week's task in which four teams prepared reports on the future role and organization of the division. This was the first time that the members of management of the division had been asked their views in a formal way, and was most favourably received.

In 1966, more people took part in Grid seminars, and some attended other courses. In October 1966, the top team undertook teamwork development, guided by Mr R. L. Sloma of SMI and Mr J. MacKenzie of BAT. Later, it was found that the omission of area managers meant that much of the work had to be discussed in full with a larger team, including the area managers, and this was done in December 1966. During this year, a start was made to establish a planning cycle system.

1967 was a period of consolidation and further training, with many more people attending grid seminars, and 15 people attending marketing courses. During the year standard costing was introduced to the UK production branches from which the division obtained many of its supplies. In October, teamwork development without a phase 4 link was repeated for the top team of four people, this time led by the BAT director responsible for the division. All four had personal experience of running grid seminars, and considerable understanding of organization development, and this contributed to a particularly satisfying occasion.

In 1968 and 1969, teamwork development was extended to several teams in the division and much work was done to improve the planning cycle aided by the application of management by objectives.

During the period 1965 to 1969, divisional results have shown considerable improvement, even after deducting the improvements caused by known factors, such as the devaluation of sterling and price changes. After making deductions like these, there is still a 73 per cent increase in profits and a 45 per cent increase in sales:

	1965 (base)	Performance in one division			
		1966	1967	1968	1969
Profits	100	110	124	159	173
Sales	100	112	125	139	145

Regrettably, comparable figures prior to 1965 cannot be given because of a different accounting procedure. Budgeted performance for 1970 suggests a continuation of the trend with figures of 192 and 152 respectively for profits and sales, taking the base for each as 100 in 1965. The number of people employed in the division throughout the period has not changed significantly, although there has been considerable movement of management staff in and out. Money spent on training of all kinds (Grid, plus management and marketing training) amounted to £59 750.

175

	1965	1966	1967	1968
Total number employed in London	75 (est)	77	80	76
Total manweeks spent in training	72	27	66	74
Total costs incurred on all training @ £250 per manweek	£18 000	£6750	£16 500	£18 500

The principal training and development activities have been:
   Managerial Grid seminar (Grid OD—Phase 1—104 people).
   Teamwork development (Grid OD—Phase 2—10 teams involving 30 different people).
   Intermediate and junior management courses (12 people).
   Ashridge and BAT marketing management courses (17 people).
   Designing an ideal strategic corporate model (Grid OD—Phase 4 by the top team).

Training costs have been generously estimated at £250 per manweek to include salary earned during training, course fees, accommodation and expenses, and travel to and from each course. Calculated in this way, the total costs of all training and development activities, during the period 1965-69, represent 2.2 per cent of the overall profit improvement, or 4.3 per cent of the adjusted figure.

The dilemma is to decide the extent to which the improved performance should be attributed to different causes, such as new people, new markets, product improvements, or organization development.

No one in the division believes that these results could have been obtained without their organization development activity, but modesty may preclude some from claiming a degree of personal credit.

The main focus of attention in organization development is on improving the quality and effectiveness of the human organization. This is the area in which practice and performance has very often fallen behind, and where improvements can have the most far reaching effects. So often, a new idea or new technique is killed before it has really been understood or tested. It is much easier to smother new thinking than harness it for effective action that will produce results. If the quality and performance of the human organization can be improved, the impact will be felt throughout the organization, since it is the insight and ideas of people that produce improvements in technology, marketing, production, accounting, and all other functions of the business. Measuring the extent to which this has been achieved is clearly very difficult.

Independent research studies

Dr Williams undertook some research on our behalf into the effects on attitudes and performance of the Managerial Grid seminar and teamwork development (i.e., phases 1 and 2 and Grid OD). The studies were carried out with small samples, and were aimed at testing the research approach as well as the effects of OD. However, the conclusions were wholly supportive of our other data, and the impressions of our managers. They can be summarized as follows:

1 The perception of needed changes is altered by participation in the managerial grid seminar.

2 The trend of altered perception is towards recognizing greater importance of changes to managerial style and organization culture.

3 The need for change and improvement is recognized in such things as communications, control, and decision-making practices of self and others.

4 The seminar brings about a more participative approach to management.

5 Grid-learning tends to weaken and fade with the passing of time, especially if follow-up within working groups is long delayed or not provided.

6 Teamwork development communications, motivation, teamwork and organization structure, improve more than policy or technical matters, but the last two also show improvement, and this is the real test.

Integration of development activities

The concept of organization development is becoming better understood and accepted as more evidence accumulates to demonstrate its value. Manager training was usually the starting point, but this led to recognition of the importance of management development. The latter still focuses on the individual manager as the key unit for change, but recognizes the need to be concerned with the whole management group, often including supervisors and foremen. At this stage, much attention is paid to such things as appraisal, selection, succession planning, and individual career planning. With organization development, the focus shifts from the individual to the organization as the unit of change. This leads to examination of the role or purpose of the organization, to the whole range of interacting forces between groups and individuals, and to the effectiveness with which aims and intentions are carried out. This is a results-oriented concept, which concentrates on the quality of achievements of the organization, the sub-groups or departments of which it is comprised, and the individuals working within the whole. Development is concerned with all these and, with their inter-relationship.

The starting point for organization development can vary, and there is no general rule that would suit all circumstances. In the case of Grid OD, the starting point is often the attendance by a few managers at a Grid seminar. If this experience is positive, it is wise for a few top executives to gain deeper comprehension of the scope of, and approach adopted in, the whole of Grid OD. This can be done without any obligation to use any element of Grid OD, but is very valuable as a basis for decision-making and planning. Another valuable step is for key executives to carry out a diagnosis of the development needs of the organization. However, in some cases where communications are poor, and where people do not feel they can speak freely, this diagnosis can be a shallow and rather worthless exercise. In these circumstances, it is preferable to have an independent study carried out by an outsider, or to undertake some individual and team development before undertaking the detailed diagnosis.

When development has started, it is important to maintain the impetus, and this requires detailed planning. For instance, if a large number of managers take part in the managerial grid seminar before a plan is made for the implementation of teamwork development, many people will experience a considerable time gap between these two steps. Fade-out occurs and frustration due to inability to apply concepts that have been learned is often the result. At best, the organization obtains very small benefits; at worst, there can be negative consequences.

A second stage of integrated planning is to recognize that the top team of an organization can move quickly through the individual and team development phases. They can then move straight on to diagnose development needs or to develop the corporate strategic model; there is no need to wait for the remainder of the organization to conclude the individual and team development.

Integration is again needed, with carefully prepared plans, when the strategic model is ready for translating into action plans. At this stage, the top team, and the remainder of the organization, need to come to terms with dividing their time and resources between the existing activities and those that are emerging from the new strategic model. An organization that has learned to work effectively, with sound communication and planning, can tackle this stage with success, even though it is difficult. Others might not be so fortunate.

The starting point

There is a basic problem of choice of the focus of development strategy which is not easily resolved. Development activities which aim to improve behaviour through changes to organization culture and managerial style are different from those which aim to change the purpose, policies, and objectives of a business. Often, both changes are needed and a choice has to be made to select one as the starting point, or to tackle both together. Although they are different concepts, they relate to the same organization, and have to be undertaken by the same people. Often, there is a great temptation to start first on the purpose, policies, and objectives, but if the prevailing organization culture is ineffective, with limited trust and frankness in managerial discussions, then the quality of redefined objectives may be poor or commitment to conclusions may be lacking. If the start is made on the development of behaviour, there is a risk that preoccupation with style of management and organization culture will tend to become an end in itself. Both are needed. They are different, and if one has a priority over the other it is likely to be the behavioural development, unless the business is in dire trouble needing immediate profit improvements. A simultaneous start on both can occupy too much managerial time with an adverse effect on current results.

Evaluation

Finally, all this needs to be evaluated through the use of systematic assessment at all stages. Evaluation is difficult to accomplish to a standard that leaves no doubts about the relationship between cause and effect, but continued efforts to strive for this are needed. Much greater objectivity can be achieved by establishing the criteria and installing the method before the programme begins. This requires considerable effort because the main preoccupation is inevitably with getting on with the programme. One approach to evaluation has four facets:[9]

What was the *reaction* of participants to the programme?
What was *learned* from taking part?
How was *behaviour* influenced?
What *results* were achieved?

In BAT's use of grid OD, and especially within the division that made extensive use of this approach, these four criteria can be used as the basis for discussion, even though this approach was not installed when the programme began.

Reaction

The repeated reaction to all phases of Grid OD is overwhelmingly favourable, but it is not a unanimous view as has been shown in some of the tables in this chapter.

Learning

Since managers change their perception of their own managerial style, this must stem from something that is learned. Furthermore, the values and beliefs about effective management also alter as a result of Grid experience. The values of 9.9 management are endorsed by individuals, and this augurs well for increased effectiveness on return to work.

Behaviour

There is widespread endorsement among BAT managers that many improvements have been obtained since we started using the Grid. For example, communications have improved, better planning and objective setting is now being achieved, with individual responsibilities more clearly defined. In the division quoted here, there is more imagination and creativity in the solution of work problems, and commitment and morale are greatly improved. In this division, there has also developed an effective planning cycle linked to a budgetary system, and there is more cost consciousness.

Obviously, other changes have also been taking place, but there is an element of doubt about the extent to which cause and effect can be related.

Results

The divisional results continue to improve, and the costs involved in these development activities are a small proportion (less than 5 per cent) of the improvement in performance. It is not possible to say specifically how much of the improvement is attributable to Grid OD—the variables are too numerous to isolate. However, we do believe that the Grid is a valuable approach to organization development, and can be effectively linked with management by objectives which is the next major development effort in BAT.

References

1. BLAKE R. R. and MOUTON J. S., *The Managerial Grid.* Houston, Texas: Gulf Publishing, 1964.
2. BLAKE R. R. and MOUTON J. S., *Building a Dynamic Organization through Grid Organization Development*, Reading, Mass.: Addison Wesley, 1969.
3a. BLAKE, MOUTON, BARNES and GREINER, 'Breakthrough in Organization Development'. *Harvard Bsns Rev.,* November/December, 1964
3b. SMITH P. B. and HONOUR T. F., 'The Impact of Phase 1 Managerial Grid Training.' *Journal of Management Studies,* Vol. 6, No. 3, October 1969.
4. SLOAN A. P., *My Years with General Motors,* N.Y.: Doubleday, 1963.
5. BLAKE R. R. and MOUTON J. S. *Corporate Excellence Diagnosis.* Austin, Texas: Scientific Methods, 1968.
6. McCORMICK A. D., 'Management Development at British-American Tobacco Co. Ltd.' *Management Today,* June 1967, pp. 126-8.
7. BROLLY M. H., 'The Managerial Grid.' *Occup. Psychol.* London, 1967.
8. BLAKE R. R. and MOUTON J. S., 'Organization Development in the Free World.' *Pers. Admin.,* July 1969.
9. CATALANELLO R. F. and KIRKPATRICK D. L., 'Evaluating Training Programmes—The State of the Art.' *Training and Development Journal,* May 1968.

PART FIVE: Focus on the inner man

It is the secret wish of many a manager to be able to organize the powers and talents of men around them without intrigue. Somehow, the politics of other managers as well as their own selfish desires get in the way of that ideal and they become as calculative (or realistic) as those around them. Field-Marshal Lord Slim, speaking in another context, once said:

> There is a difference between leadership and management. The leader and the men who follow him represent one of the oldest, most natural and most effective of all human relationships. The manager and those he manages are a later product, with neither so romantic nor so inspiring a history. Leadership is of the spirit, compounded of personality and vision; its practice is an art. Management is of the mind, more a matter of accurate calculation, of statistics, of methods, time-tables and routine; its practice is a science. Managers are necessary; leaders are essential.

A leader in a democratic community is one who wins the respect, the willing support, and even, possibly, the affection of those who follow him. Such a response comes only when they see the leader to be genuine; they may not like him—but they trust him.

When a manager aims to improve his personal approach to others, he should try not to be too calculative about the outcome. Indeed, the motive behind his quest is crucial and he should remember: 'But thou hast only the right to work; but none to the fruit thereof. Let not then the fruit of thy action be thy motive; nor yet be thou enamoured of inaction.' (*The Geeta, The Gospel of the Lord Shri Krishna*, chapter 2, verse 47.)

Such a person will gain most from others when they learn to give him descriptive non-evaluative feedback about his own behaviour and the impact it has on them. These comments are like holding a mirror up for him to look into if he wishes. Samuel Culbert says in chapter 13, 'It takes two to see one'. This chapter opens up the topic of self-disclosure (information about oneself that others do not have, but which the person now feels free to disclose because of the supportive climate). What he makes of their subsequent comments may play an important part in any reassessment of himself as a person; this kind of feedback is essential to a man's search for identity.

Such reassessments are unlikely to be dramatic or permanent unless the manager is able to practise new behaviours and see the benefits from so doing. As Evans-Pritchard wrote about the Nuer, an African tribe:

> Each bit of belief fits in with every other bit in a general mosaic of mystical thought. If, in such a closed system of thought, a belief is contradicted by a particular experience, this

merely shows that the experience was mistaken, or inadequate, or the contradiction is accounted for by secondary elaborations of belief which provide satisfactory explanations of the apparent inconsistency.

For those who wonder why they cannot use or do not use the information that they gain on a training course, this extract from *The Wind in the Willows* may not come amiss. For 'smoking-room' substitute 'training course' and the story may be all too apt:

'There's only one thing more to be done,' continued the gratified Badger. 'Toad, I want you solemnly to repeat, before your friends here, what you fully admitted to me in the smoking-room just now. First, you are sorry for what you've done, and you see the folly of it all?'

There was a long, long pause. Toad looked desperately this way and that, while the other animals waited in grave silence. At last he spoke.

'No!' he said a little sullenly, but stoutly; 'I'm not sorry. And it wasn't folly at all! It was all simply glorious!'

'What?' cried the Badger, greatly scandalized. 'You back-sliding animal, didn't you tell me just now, in there—'

'O, yes, yes, in there,' said Toad impatiently. 'I'd have said anything in there. You're so eloquent, dear Badger, and so moving, and so convincing, and put all your points so frightfully well—you can do what you like with me in there, and you know it. But I've been searching my mind since, and going over things in it, and I find that I'm not a bit sorry or repentant really, so it's no earthly good saying I am; now is it?'*

There is something essentially honest about Toad's reply even if it is not what was expected or hoped for. At least they and he now knew where he stood.

'Know the truth; the truth shall set you free.' With that knowledge may come a greater or lesser desire to be a leader. One thing is sure, a man with such an outlook is likely to be more at peace with himself. Effective organizations need such men who may appreciate chapter 14, 'Desiderata', which I found in a shop in Buffalo, New York State.

13. The interpersonal process of self-disclosure: It takes two to see one

Samuel A. Culbert

Although philosophers, theologians, social scientists, and mental health professionals have for many years dealt with self-disclosure, little accumulation of theory has taken place. The little that has taken place is attributable to the variety of issues studied rather than to one theorist's building on what has come before. This lack of continuity seems to stem from the sparsity of discussions that either (a) spell out, in a given context, exactly what is meant by self-disclosure or (b) deal with the intra- and interpersonal factors that differentially characterize any given self-disclosure. For the most part, theorists have tended to skip over these tasks, devoting their attention instead to the specific effects on and outcomes for the individual who self-discloses. Unfortunately, experimentation in this area has also frequently occurred without adequate definition of self-disclosure or careful delineation of the dimensions that characterize it.

The purpose of this paper is to take steps toward developing a comprehensive theory of the interpersonal processes in self-disclosure. Hopefully, such a theory will lead to theorizing about and experimentation with the dynamics of self-disclosure in a variety of contexts.

What is meant by self-disclosure?

This paper offers the following definition of self-disclosure:

> Self-disclosure refers to an individual's explicitly communicating to one or more people some personal information that he believes these others would be unlikely to acquire unless

● This paper is a reprint, with modifications, of a manuscript written originally for the book, *New Directions in Client-centered Therapy*, edited by J. T. Hart and T. M. Tomlinson and published by Houghton Mifflin, Boston, Massachusetts. The paper is reprinted with the permission of the author, the Houghton Mifflin Company, and *The Journal of Applied Behavioral Science*. Copyright © 1968 by Samuel A. Culbert.

he himself disclosed it. Moreover, this information must be 'personally private', that is, it must be of such a nature that it is not something the individual would disclose to everyone who might inquire about it.

By this definition self-disclosure is different from 'self-description'. Self-description designates self-data that an individual is likely to feel comfortable in revealing to most others. Additionally, self-description includes information that an individual knows about himself, that is readily perceivable by most others, and by which he agrees to be known. Self-description is likely to include an individual's physical characteristics, his occupation, marital status, and so on. However, both self-disclosure and self-description, as defined here, contain many *relative* aspects. Self-information that is 'personally private' for one individual may not, for whatever reason, be personally private for another. Self-information that one individual believes most others have about him may be the guarded secret of another. Self-information that one individual acknowledges others have, and thus faces up to, may be vigorously denied by another, lest he be flooded by feelings of embarrassment.

Self-disclosure requires the presence of others and is preceded by disclosure to one's own self; that is, an individual must first become explicitly aware of some self-information before he can disclose it to others. This is not to say that all we know about another is the self-information of which he has explicitly made us aware. We do, in fact, know much more. We know, for example, factual aspects of the other which we can readily perceive. We make assumptions about others by extrapolating both from the information we have about them and from our knowledge of others with the same or similar characteristics. We get information (true or false) about the other from mutual acquaintances. We get information by viewing the words and actions of the other and by making our own inferences about what is going on inside him. Indeed, we may know even more about some aspects of the other than he knows about himself. Nevertheless, this information does not necessarily involve self-disclosure.

A framework for conceptualizing self-disclosure

This issue is self-disclosure of the communicator's *willingness to be known* finds a useful perspective in the 'Johari Window'.[1] This schema is hypothesized to be an instantaneous representation of a person's self-data at a given point in time. It portrays a person's self-data in a two by two matrix—known and unknown to self and known and unknown to others. Cell I, *known to self and known to others*, is what Luft call the 'area of free activity'. In self-disclosure terms, it is frequently called the *'public self'*. At first glance, self-information in this area appears to fit the category, self-description, however, this is not necessarily the case. An individual has the option of deciding for himself whether he wants to be publicly known by cell I data. If not, he may exercise numerous behavior options, at some subsequent moment in time, to change the location of the data. There are two mechanisms for these options: (a) he may act on others, with anger, threat, guilt, and the like, so that they no longer behave as if these data existed; or (b) he may establish barriers

	Known to self	Not known to self
Known to others	I Area of free activity	II Blind area
Not known to others	III Avoided or hidden area	IV Area of unknown activity

Figure 13.1
The Johari Window

within himself, by such means as repression, projection, or denial, so that he himself no longer behaves as if the data existed. The first mechanism could serve to move the self-data from cell I to cell III, *known to self but unknown to others.* The second mechanism could move the data from cell I to cell II, *unknown to self but known to others.*

Given these behavior options, we can now specify when self-disclosure takes place in cell I. *This happens when an individual agrees to be known either by generally accessible data through which he has not previously agreed to be known or through non-generally accessible data which he acknowledges with some 'knowers' and continues to keep unknown from 'non-knowers'.*

Cell III, *known to self but unknown to others*, contains self-data that most clearly have relevance for self-disclosure. Luft calls this cell the 'avoided or hidden area'. By definition, *self-disclosure takes place when self-data which have been knowingly concealed from at least some others are later revealed.* Frequently, after the passage of time, an individual decides that some self-information no longer requires even selective concealment. This information then becomes part of cell I. Sometimes, an individual rejects his own private knowledge of a particular bit of self-data, and it then becomes reclassified in cell IV, *unknown to self and to others.*

Cell II, *unknown to self but known to others*, may be considered a somewhat equivocal area relative to self-disclosure. Does self-disclosure involve only data of which the discloser is conscious? Does the disclosure have to be intentional? In the absence of criteria to distinguish conscious from unconscious and intentional from unintentional, it has seemed parsimonious to limit the definition of self-disclosure to those data which are explicitly perceived or known by the disclosing individual and intentionally disclosed by him. The criterion *explicitly* known, because it excludes marginal states of awareness, is more exclusive than *consciously* known. Moreover, it does not differentiate for intention. Thus, an accidental slip of some self-data would be self-disclosure only if the speaker himself also realized the meaning and agreed, after the fact, to be known by this newly disclosed information. This *after the fact acknowledgment* is the self-disclosure and, since it is now known to the discloser, it takes place either in cell I or cell III.

While self-disclosure *per se* does not take place either in cell II or in cell IV (both unknown to self), it does have some general attitudinal relevance in these situations. In cell II it becomes relevant once an individual admits that someone else has some information about him that he does not know about himself. The individual's willingness and ability to receive self-data from another person usually entails a mutual expectation that the one individual agree to explicitly acknowledge newly learned data in the presence of the other. In a similar way, cell IV has attitudinal implications for self-disclosure. Here, a self-disclosing attitude makes no assumption about another's knowledge of unknown self-data. It merely connotes a willingness to *explore* unknown self-material while in his presence. This type of exploration also implies an unspoken agreement to explicitly acknowledge newly accepted data.

The context of self-disclosure

The Johari schema has been used here to focus on the various types of self-data that may be disclosed and thus to clarify our definition of self-disclosure. The complex of issues addressed shifts now to the context in which the self-disclosures occur. Context will be shown to be a critical factor in making a *desirability judgement* for a given self-disclosure.

Most expositions on self-disclosure have argued that self-disclosure is good, positively valued, growth-facilitating, or that in some way it adds meaning to a person's life. While such expositions usually specify contexts which seem to justify these claims, a more comprehensive position is that 'it depends'; for self-disclosure may also result in bad, negatively valued, growth-inhibiting outcomes. In taking an it-depends position, one becomes cognizant of the defining specification that self-disclosure always involves at least two persons. Hence, an understanding of the role played by the receiver as well as that played by the communicator is essential to the study of any given disclosure.

The receiver's involvement—A first step in understanding the role played by a receiver of a self-disclosure is to look at his involvement. Is he directly and closely involved, in that he asked a specific question which prompted the disclosure? Is he somewhat less involved, in that he is taking part in a dialogue with the communicator, and the disclosure is relevant to their interaction, to a mutual task, or to their ongoing relationship? Is he rather uninvolved, in that no specific communication is taking place, and the disclosure represents something of the order of a getting-to-know-you process? Or is the receiver quite uninvolved, receiving a disclosure for which he has made no solicitation whatsoever? The receiver's involvement will, among other factors, contribute to the personal impact the disclosure has for him. Moreover, what the receiver decides to do about this impact will be related to how his involvement took place.

The receiver's obligations—Another way of thinking about the relationship between how the involvement came about and the impact on the receiver is to consider the *response obligations* engendered in the receiver. Depending upon how he became involved, all other things being equal, the receiver is likely to experience himself as charged with differential amounts of responsibility and/or obligations. For example, someone may disclose that he is troubled because he is delinquent in paying his bills. A receiver who is 'directly and closely involved'—one who perhaps may ask about the discloser's finances or is a close friend—may feel obliged to help the discloser look for possible solutions, and may even go so far as to lend money to the discloser. On the other hand, a receiver who is 'quite uninvolved'— one who is approached by a stranger on the street or by a recent acquaintance at a cocktail party—is not likely to feel obliged to react with much concern. Of course, there are numerous other factors which enter in and discussion of these follows.

The receiver's behavior—Having made the connection between the way the disclosure comes about and the implications it holds for the receiver, two elements remain in this line of reasoning: (a) the receiver's subsequent behavior and (b) the discloser's reaction to the receiver's response. Assuming for the moment that the receiver's response is an accurate reflection of his inner reaction and that it is perceived that way by the discloser, the receiver is now in an excellent position to exercise controls over the discloser. The receiver's response structurally parallels what information theorists call 'feedback'. One might visualize receiver responses on a continuum: at one end, the receiver intends them as rewarding and serving to encourage the communicator to make self-disclosures; in the middle, he intends them to be neutral—neither rewarding nor punishing, encouraging or discouraging; and at the other end, he intends them as punitive and to discourage the communicator from making additional self-disclosures. While a more complete discussion of the receiver's power is forthcoming, the *intensity*, or subjective importance, attributed by a receiver to the self-disclosing statement is central in determining the range of the continuum. Disclosures which the receiver perceives as low intensity, or unimportant, will probably evoke receiver reactions near the neutral point, while high intensity or important ones will be likely to evoke stronger reactions.

Discloser reaction—In encountering feedback, the discloser is faced with the immediate explicit consequences of his disclosure. He is behaviorally confronted with the fact that his self-disclosures affect others. Assuming that the discloser is open to perceiving these receiver reactions and that he accurately does so, he may or may not interpret them as consistent with his intentions for being open. Moreover, these reactions may or may not be within his predisclosure set of expectations. Even with the most predictable receiver, the discloser is always less than certain that the receiver will hear him as he intended to be heard or react as he expected him to react. A quality of *risk* emerges which is inherent in every disclosure. Risk is also closely tied to the *intensity* attributed to the self-disclosure by the communicator. It can be speculated that the risk in self-disclosing corresponds with the following equation:

$$\text{Risk} = f\left[\frac{\text{Intensity}}{Pr\,(\text{Intention}) \times Pr\,(\text{Expected reactions})}\right]$$

187

That is, the risk in self-disclosure is a function of the intensity or importance the communicator places on the disclosure divided by the product of the probabilities that the receiver will hear the disclosure as the communicator intended and that the receiver will react as the communicator expected. The greater the risk, the more the communicator is thought to be vulnerable with respect to the disclosure.

Regardless of the discloser's precommunication expectations (including no conscious expectations at all), he must in some way deal with the receiver's reaction. There is a good probability that he will counter with an explicit response, but whether his response will be in the direction of another self-disclosure is a complex issue involving many more variables. For example, if the original receiver's response contains a self-disclosing statement, the original discloser's comments will be comprised partly of his reaction to feedback on his disclosure and partly of his reaction to the receiver's disclosure. The original receiver is now a discloser and takes on the risks and vulnerabilities that accrue from this position.

As a further illustration of some of the pressures operating in a relationship where at least one participant has a propensity towards self-disclosure, consider the following. An individual's self-information is stratified along a dimension of *intensity* which, as will be described, subsumes intimacy, vulnerability, and emotional charging. Obligations to be fulfilled by the receiver become progressively more demanding as the communicator perceives himself to be making higher intensity self-disclosures. Depending upon the specific interpersonal relationship, these obligations may include communicator demands that the receiver himself reciprocate with self-disclosures. Besides self-disclosure, obligations take many forms. They include demands such as acknowledgement of one's interest and concern, comments to reaffirm the relationship, promises of confidentiality, and non-reprisal pacts.

Discloser vulnerability—A key factor underlying the discloser's need to make demands upon his receivers is his vulnerability. The more intense a disclosure, the more likely an individual is to perceive himself as vulnerable. At high levels of vulnerability, the discloser has a greater need to trust his receiver. He has given this other person access to private information which if misused, that is, not used exclusively in the service of the project for which he intended it, may lead to personal hurt. The placing of obligations upon one's receiver, in particular the seeking out of personal information from the receiver, is an attempt to protect one's vulnerability. Receiver self-disclosure serves as a deterrent, for it gives one a means of reprisal should his self-information be misused.

Vulnerability does not arise solely out of one's fear that someone will misuse the self-data disclosed. It also arises out of situations in which one individual is substantially dependent on a second to take some course of action. The failure of this second individual to respond as desired may become a source of imposition or irritation. The disclosure of those needs, which specifically involve the receiver or over which the receiver has some controls, makes explicit the receiver's option to either service or frustrate them. Vulnerability under this condition, then, is a two-step process. The first step is the investment one makes in the other person, this other now having the potential to satisfy or frustrate the needs of the first. The second step entails the communication of the investment, possibly by the explicit means of self-disclosure, the other thus coming to understand his position and potential leverage. As with the misuse of self-data, an individual who has leverage with his receiver (he knows the receiver is vulnerable with respect to him), takes less risk by disclosing his complement vulnerability than an individual without such leverage.

Again, looking at a conventional relationship in which at least one participant has a propensity toward self-disclosure, a conservative strategy emerges, conservative in that it involves minimal risk. The communicator may begin by making low intensity disclosures. He correspondingly imposes low-level demands upon his receiver, for if he were to impose high-level demands for a low-level disclosure he would run the risk that his receiver would leave the relationship. Progressively he increases the intensity of his disclosures, each time checking the extent to which the receiver fulfills his obligations. By fulfilling the obligations, the receiver, in turn, is also becoming vulnerable. Some examples of receiver vulnerability are interest and concern for the relationship, increasing regard for the discloser, or perhaps self-disclosure on his own part.

The discloser who fails to evaluate his receiver responses and/or is not able to adjust his behavior accordingly is likely to become quite vulnerable. A state of disequilibrium arises whenever one participant is significantly more vulnerable than the other. To the extent that the less vulnerable participant chooses to exercise his leverage (that is, his power to take some action that will have important implications for the other participant without the other's having the reciprocal power to equally affect him), he is able to create a 'crisis' for the more vulnerable one. The more vulnerable participant is likely to experience negative outcomes, at least until he can either recognize what is happening to him or take steps to improve his situation. Frequently, however, these negative outcomes persist even after the individual has taken some corrective action. Such is the case when ex-friends reveal to a third person material that previously had been privy between them.

A disclosing individual instead may create a crisis for his receiver. This happens when he skips up the scale of intensity and makes a disclosure that is far more intense than any yet experienced in the relationship. At this point, the discloser has gone against conventional norms and placed a strain on the relationship. To the extent that the receiver desires outcomes from the relationship and to the extent that he would like to remain in the relationship, he will be in a crisis. He can resolve the crisis either by deciding to fulfill the obligations demanded by the disclosure, by fulfilling part of them and hoping the discloser will lower his demands, or by deciding that the relationship does not justify such an expenditure on his part. This last alternative—not fulfilling the obligations established by the discloser—may switch the crisis from the receiver to the discloser. At this point, the discloser is overextended, and he is potentially highly vulnerable; for the relationship is now in disequilibrium.

189

Why self-disclose?

With this background on what is meant by self-disclosure and the demands it places on the receiver, the next question that might be asked is: Self-disclosure for what purpose? Since self-disclosure always involves at least one other person, a readily apparent answer is: for the accomplishment of projects which involve others. Of course, there are self-disclosures which do not literally involve others, at least in the sense that they involve *any* other. Examples of these are found under the heading of 'catharsis' or 'getting something off one's chest'. In such instances, self-disclosures seem to be end points in and of themselves. However, it is a moot issue as to whether the same catharsis would be experienced with just any type of receiver or without the presence of the specific receiver involved.

Most typically, self-disclosures involve *specific* others and function as a means to furthering some greater project. Thus, in referring to communicator-initiated disclosures, the dual qualifications of *relationship to receiver* and *project serviced* are essential; that is, given the self-disclosure, we can begin to answer the question as to why by first filling in the communicator's relationship to his receiver at the time of the disclosure and then identifying the interpersonal project the disclosure was meant to service. For example, consider an individual's private concern that he does not possess the technical skills to perform his job adequately. He will expect different behavioral comsequences for such a disclosure depending upon whether he makes it to his wife or to his boss. Likewise, the personal project being serviced (for example, of gaining support or seeking censure) will influence his decision to disclose such self-data.

Relationship to receiver

The Johari window (Fig. 12.1) has been used here to illustrate the kinds of self-data possessed by an individual. One can also think of this schema as a picture, at a given moment, of one individual's self-data in relation to a specific other; that is, the relative areas of the four cells will differ in relation to a specific other. In the strictest sense, one individual possesses as many Johari windows as there are specific others who populate his lifespace at a given time. However, there is a more economical way of looking at this.

Rickers-Ovsiankina[2] and Jourard and Lasakow[3] have postulated that amount and kind of self-disclosure would be dependent upon the formal relationship between the communicator and the receiver. Rickers-Ovsiankina looked into differential disclosure patterns which are set up for receivers who were labeled strangers, acquaintances, and close friends; Jourard and Lasakow looked into the patterns for same and different sex parents. Bugental, Tannenbaum, and Bobele[4] made a similar prediction about the self-disclosure determinant of *situational context.* They predicted and found differential disclosure patterns depending on whether receivers were work associates or social acquaintances. The experimenters in each case concluded that the receiver's relationship to the communicator is a major variable in determining patterns of self-disclosure.

Certain relationships between communicators and their receivers are sufficiently formalized so that neither participant has much doubt about how the receiver will handle most self-disclosures. Clergymen, psychotherapists, and, perhaps, bartenders are examples of receivers who, by the nature of their role-relationship to the discloser, are expected not only to keep the discloser's confidence, but to make their responses consistent with the best interests of the discloser. Competitors and salesmen are examples of receivers who are likely to treat self-disclosure in ways which are consistent with their own interests, rather than with those of the communicator.

The greater number of communicator-receiver relationships is not so formalized. In the absence of formalization, the communicator must make a judgement about how his receiver will treat his self-information. As the discussion of vulnerability has suggested, a communicator's *risk* varies with his receiver. Goffman[5] has made a similar point in emphasizing the importance of concealing data that one believes inconsistent with the self-image one is attempting to advance. For example, while a student may disclose to some peers that he receives good grades through the use of short cuts, he is likely to conceal this fact from teachers and parents.

Perhaps the most crucial aspect of 'relationship to receiver' is illustrated by considering Thibaut and Kelly's[6] notions of *fate control* and *behavioral control*. *Fate control* refers to one participant's ability to control the outcomes of a second, regardless of what the second does, and *behavior control* refers to one participant's ability to make it desirable for a second to vary his behavior according to the choice of the first. Both these types of interpersonal power may be a function of any number of factors. French and Raven,[7] for example, have discussed five highly relevant sources of power. To the extent that the communicator has such power, and to the extent that the receiver desires to stay in the relationship, the communicator can self-disclose with minimal risks for doing so; and he can be said to be utilizing his advantage in power in the service of self-disclosure. Should his self-disclosures make him too vulnerable, he runs the risk of losing this power advantage. If the power advantage belongs to the *receiver*, it is likely that the communicator will be more judicious in his decisions to self-disclose, lest he make himself any more vulnerable than he already is.

Many self-disclosures may be classified as either 'receiver-relevant' or 'receiver-irrelevant'. Relevance depends upon whether a given self-disclosure is perceived by the communicator as likely to make a difference in his relationship with his prospective receiver. For example, a woman's disclosure that she is using cosmetics to improve her appearance is likely to be relevant to receivers of the opposite sex and irrelevant to those of the same sex. Moreover, depending upon such individual considerations as her marital status, her individual needs to be seen as attractive, and so on, differing numbers of receivers of the opposite sex will be seen as relevant.

Receiver expectations of which the communicator is aware are another variable of prime importance in self-disclosure: they serve either to promote or inhibit disclosure. Some expectations automatically accrue as a relationship develops. Such is the case in dating relationships, where greater familiarity is expected with each successive date. Other expectations take place as a function of the more formalized roles accepted in the relationship. For instance, a particular employer may see himself as having the right to inquire into details of an employee's family life. Many expectations are a result of societal norms to which the participants adhere. An example in the United States might be the widespread taboo against mixed-company discussion of personal sexual practices. Still other expectations arise as a result of the receiver's desire to satisfy the many idiosyncratic needs and curiosities he experiences in himself or observe in his communicator. Regardless of the source that underlies receiver expectations, the communicator has the responsibility for balancing expectations with his own needs to disclose or conceal. Unless a balance is maintained, the relationship may become increasingly uncomfortable and unproductive for both participants.

It is important not to overlook the possible consequences for a communicator who neglects his 'relationship to receivers'. Such neglect might result in the communicator's needlessly passing up situations where disclosure would be to his best interest, or disclosing in situations where disclosure unnecessarily places his projects in jeopardy. Also of consideration is the secondary project of *emotional comfort*, whichi almost always is at stake. Failure to consider the specific receiver relationship may result in an erroneous decision either to seek immediate comfort or forfeit longer-range comfort or to bind immediate discomfort in favor of hoped-for, longer-range comfort. In conclusion, there is little question but that selective disclosure is a more difficult task than maintaining a consistent level of disclosure, regardless of receiver or circumstance. Among other things, a consistent discloser is not faced with the pressure of remembering who knows what about him. But while selective disclosure entails added tensions and risks, it also contains possibilities for more positive outcomes than are otherwise available. To repeat, the choice is that of the communicator, and he errs by not accepting it.

Project serviced

Self-disclosure is usually performed in the service of some greater goal. This is readily apparent when one considers the risks, objective as well as subjective, that accompany nearly all disclosures. (We have not talked about objective risks. They are quite analogous to subjective risks, with the addition that material possessions or gains desired by the discloser are controlled by the receiver.) The utility of self-disclosure is questionable unless one can identify some discloser goal, either subjective or objective, whose benefits are of equivalent magnitude to the risk of the disclosure. Unfortunately, this line of reasoning leads immediately to complexity, if not confusion, for no scales are available for comparing gains and costs of self-disclosure.

It is difficult to identify a limited number of projects a disclosure may be intended to service, largely because of the multiple levels on which projects occur. Illustrative is the seemingly uncomplicated self-disclosure, 'I like you'. In its most literal context, the disclosure may be servicing any number of specific projects—for one example, the bringing of warmth to a relationship. At the level of interpersonal dynamics, this disclosure suggests other types of relevant projects, perhaps the one of evoking a similar disclosure from the receiver. Next, conceptualizing this disclosure within the broader context of what precedes and follows it, the disclosure may serve to bring about a change of pace to the discussion, for instance, by changing the topic or level of emotionality. And, finally, projects of the deepest meaning, of the kind often hypothesized to be at the core of man's existence—such as self-acceptance—may be serviced by this self-disclosure.

Little is gained, however, by taking the first of the last-mentioned project levels and addressing the question. 'Why self-disclose?' on a very specific or literal basis. Such analysis would undoubtedly yield as many, if not more, specific reasons for self-disclosing as there are specific needs or projects. Moreover, at present, we lack systems of categorization which would be needed to put this level of analysis to practical use.

The level of interpersonal dynamics offers a more immediate contribution to the question, 'Why disclose?' Self-disclosure's function here already has been implied somewhat in the earlier discussion on vulnerability. Perhaps its most unique function in this context derives from instances when the most salient interpersonal project being serviced by a disclosure is kept hidden from the receiver. Specific examples of such usage have been documented under the heading of interpersonal 'games', currently an issue of wide speculation and interest (e.g., Berne[8]). The receiver's inability to be aware of or to understand all the interpersonal consequences of the communicator's disclosure makes him susceptible to being controlled by the communicator. Whether or not the communicator is himself aware of the important dynamics underlying his communication, he is now in a position to regulate or influence the behavior and/or attitudes of his unknowing receiver.

Also within the context of interpersonal dynamics are some projects serviced by self-disclosure about which the communicator knows the receiver is aware. There are many such projects. Among them, some serve as implicit trades on the order of 'You tell me this and I'll tell you that'; others, as Goffman[5] (page 142) explains with his term 'inside secret', service group needs for cohesiveness; and still others serve to bolster relationship- relevant attitudes mutually held by the participants.

Most writers who have endorsed self-disclosure as a positively valued activity have done so in the context of rather molar projects. For example, self-disclosure has been cited as an essential means by which man may find his philosophical and theological value in the world. Buber[9] has written that the goals of greater self-experience and greater relationship with God derive out of the progressively intimate and deeper experiences one individual has with others. Given this goal, the implications for self-disclosure are quite clear. Tillich[10] has argued that man must necessarily experience his lack of value in the world before he is able to experience in the world value. Tillich postulates religious symbolism as the means by which man may transcend his lack of value. Although this is epitomized by the symbol of Christ on the cross, Tillich acknowledges its everyday value in an individual's 'courage to be' his real-self in the presence of others. Thus, for this theologian, it is the act of disclosing that carries primary meaning, rather than the specific content of the disclosure itself.

Self-disclosure has been mentioned as the means by which man may decrease his alienation from self as well as from others. Fromm[11] has written of the societal forces which contribute to man's alienated condition and the relationship of this alienation with man's ability to disclose his self. Rogers[12] has focused quite centrally on man's need to accept his own self and on the critical role that acceptance by others plays in this process. To this end, self-disclosure must precede real-self-acceptance by others.

Mental health experts have written that self-disclosure is important to an individual's quest for better psychological adjustment. Jourard[13] has been a formidable spokesman for this viewpoint, in particular postulating that 'real-self-being' is a necessary but not sufficient condition for a healthy personality. Moreover, Jourard[13] (page 15) has specified that self-disclosure bears a curvilinear relationship to mental health, with either too little or too much disclosure being inconsistent with an individual's goal of greater health. Mowrer[14] has formulated a theory of behavior pathology in which guilt from *not* self-disclosing is the underlying causal factor. He states that guilt emanates *not* from one's 'sins' or errors that have been internalized as moral wrongs, but from 'the fear of being found out and punished' for these wrongs, regardless of whether they were accidentally or intentionally committed. Mowrer goes on to explain that it is only by confessing, self-disclosing, these sins that the neurotic conflicts so engendered may be dissolved.

Given these molar projects which self-disclosure seemingly services, the converse reasoning is now relevant. That is, what are the consequences that befall an individual who fails to self-disclose? There are many, and a number of them could be listed merely by inverting some of the reasons which have already been listed in this 'why' section. However, one general consequence does stand out. It is the added difficulty a non-self-disclosing person faces in obtaining information about the reality or objective aspects of relationships in which he participates. To use psychological terminology, insufficient self-disclosure is accompanied by insufficient reality testing. This point has been made theoretically by Jourard[13] (page 3) and it has been demonstrated experimentally by Bugental *et al.*[4] Failure to disclose one's self to others with whom one is having relationships forfeits important opportunities for feedback. Moreover, as was recently concluded in a study by Vosen,[15] a self-perceived lack of personal disclosure results in reduced self-esteem.

It is of interest to speculate about the differential coping behavior of individuals who are at opposite poles on the dimension of self-disclosure, one termed a *concealer* and the other a *revealer*. With the presentation of new interpersonal contexts, the concealer typically reacts by hiding his feelings and other relevant self-reactions. He conceals these personal data until he inwardly feels he has mastered either the interpersonal problem or his reaction to it. The revealer, on the other hand, is likely to react by immediately disclosing any self-information to which he has access. The revealer, too, is attempting to master the problem, but for

194

him mastery seems to be attained by explicitly acknowledging and labeling all the relevant elements comprising the situation. While a concealer runs the risk of having insufficient external feedback, a revealer runs the risk of overlabeling the limited number of objective elements present or of labeling them so early that their usefulness in the relationship is nullified. Here, as in Jourard's[13] discussion of mental health correlates, a curvilinear relationship is suggested, with too much or too little self-disclosure detrimental to efficient reality testing. Additional comments about curvilinearity will be made later (see page 201).

To continue the discussion of reality testing, again consider self-disclosure's part in an individual's quest for greater self-acceptance. Roger's[12] view is that acceptance of self by others contributes to one's own acceptance of self. Conversely, other's acceptance of an individual's inauthentic or non-self-data hinders the process of real-self-acceptance. At this point, it is useful to compare the effects of two categories of data for self-disclosure. One category consists of data about which the communicator believes the receiver has no knowledge. The other contains data that the communicator believes will correct false impressions held by the receiver, impressions he has previously allowed to go uncorrected. To the extent that an individual believes elements of his self are totally unknown to others, he is unlikely to experience others as being acceptant of his self, no matter what they profess to know. To the extent a second individual is aware that his non-self *is* accepted by others, he is even less likely than the first to correct corresponding misimpressions. Self-disclosure under these circumstances entails more than the usual risks faced when an individual is not known; the discloser also runs the added risk of losing the acceptance he has already gained through non-self-data. However, when real-self-data are known by others, an individual is likely to view receiver acceptance as a valid response to his real-self. The discloser's perception of the validity of the response, of course, is contingent on what the discloser thinks is taking place inside the receiver—a consideration which would have to be made in either instance.

To summarize the above discussion on self-acceptance, real-self-disclosure is a necessary but not sufficient condition leading to real-self-acceptance. Failure to disclose at all makes it impossible to receive acceptance of one's self by others. Receiving acceptance for non-self-data—by which one has tacitly agreed to be known—decreases the likelihood that real-self-data, to correct these misimpressions, will eventually be disclosed.

Additional dimensions in self-disclosure

Many key dimensions of self-disclosure have already been identified. Others, highly relevant both to the interpersonal processes of self-disclosure and to the task of characterizing a given disclosure, remain to be discussed. In the service of clarity, these remaining dimensions will be discussed in compartment form. In terms of meaning, they are believed to be highly interdependent. Broadly, the following self-disclosure dimensions can be grouped under one of two headings, intrapersonal processes or interpersonal processes

Intrapersonal processes

The determinants or references for the following dimensions lie most centrally within the discloser. Each of them is relevant to the same issue; whether or not an individual will desire to make some self-information public. Five dimensions will be discussed: (1) the *intensity*, or subjective importance attributed to the self-disclosure; (2) the *modality* by which the disclosure is made; (3) the *type* of self-data being disclosed; (4) the *availability* of these self-data; and (5) the *content* or subject matter being disclosed.

1 Intensity—This construct characterizes the subjective importance an individual places on a given bit of self-data. Conveniently, intensity may be operationalized in at least three ways:

(a) The level of intimacy, or the number of others to whom the discloser has explicitly communicated the self-data; operationalized by asking the discloser either 'how many others know?' or 'what is your relationship to those others who know?' 'Number of others who know' or 'Closeness of others who know' would then be the index of *intensity*.

(b) The degree of emotional charging the discloser experiences while revealing the self-data; operationalized by having the discloser reveal self-data while recording GSRs, EKGs, or other suitable physiological measures.

(c) The risk entailed in making the self-data known; operationalized by asking the discloser for objective or subjective consequences he anticipates in making some self-data known and the likelihood that each consequence will take place. The index of *intensity* would then be the sum of the products of the probability that a given consequence might take place and a value assigned to indicate the subjective or objective magnitude of that consequence.

Intensity is affected by personality factors such as overall ease of disclosing. For example, it is likely that the earlier-mentioned differences which label some individuals 'revealers' and others 'concealers' may stem from the revealers' experiencing given bits of self-data at lower disclosure intensities than concealers' experiencing them. Intensity is also contingent on individual differences such as the intrapersonal dimension of *content* and the interpersonal dimension of *timing*. For example, while a 16-year-old girl may readily tell her age, a 45-year-old woman may go to great lengths to conceal hers. Furthermore, intensity is not independent of *contextual* considerations or personal *motivation*. (The just-mentioned 16-year-old may spontaneously find a need to conceal her age upon being attracted to a 20-year-old man.)

Occupying a special category of intensity is known-to-self information which has yet to be revealed to even one other person. Concealment over time sets into play dynamics that alter the intensity or emotional charging from that which was originally attached to the content. Frequently, the intensity increases with time. In such instances, the potential communicator experiences higher risk and therefore added difficulty in making the first-time disclosure. These feelings of high risk persist even though the more objective risks of the situation diminish. Consequently, first-time disclosures are often characterized by large amounts of intensity which generate high levels of emotionality during disclosure.

2 **Modality**—An individual may reveal personal information through a number of modalities—verbal, behavioral, or gesticulative. Different modalities carry different meanings for both discloser and receiver. These differences may be a function of any number of things: personality type, perceived directness, group norms, situational considerations, and so on. For the most part, the discloser determines the modalities of self-disclosure by which he will be known. Often, the choice is a function of personal preference. Some people, for example, prefer or find it easier to disclose through personal behavior than to explicitly state a bit of self-data in the first person. Intra-individual differences are also likely. For example, a typically 'verbal' person may be able to express tender feelings only in writing.

Also relevant to the modality of disclosure is the degree to which an individual needs to maintain control of the self-information by which others know him. Disclosers with relatively low needs for control are probably available to being known through a wider range of disclosure modalities and by the more subtle elements within any given modality. In contrast, disclosers with high needs for control are likely to be quite exacting about the self-data by which they agree to be known. This latter group appears to acknowledge only the more explicit or concrete elements of their behavior as self-disclosure.

The fact that a receiver may simultaneously receive discloser data through more than one modality and the fact that the discloser has the option to refuse to be known by a given bit of self-data together generate some interesting dynamics. In our society, for example, verbal behavior often is 'accepted' as comprising the total communication. That is, an implicit agreement seems to exist whereby the discloser and his receiver mutually accept each other at face value, regardless of how accompanying behavioral expressions may belie the spoken message. But the non-verbal expressions are being given off and received. Consequently, dual relationships are often created in which the participants have a greater private than public understanding of each other. There is little doubt that both participants experience added stress as a result of such duplicity.

3 **Type**—Thoughts, feelings, sensations, perceptions, judgement, intuitions, fantasies, desires, and actions—all are different types of self-information which an individual may choose to disclose. As is the case with disclosure modalities, large individual differences exist as to the significance attached to any given *type* of self-disclosure. The idea that individuals differ as to the specific type of expression they most often use, or typically rely upon, finds support in the theorizing of Jung.[16] Jung postulates four fundamental psychological functions: thinking, feeling, sensing, and intuiting, which every individual possesses in varying degrees of conscious dominance. Corresponding to a dominance of one function rather than another are individual preferences and competencies in attributing meaning to different *types* of behavior. A creditable amount of data is accumulating in support of Jung's theory (e.g., Myers[17]).

4 Availability—This dimension refers to differences in the self-information a person might *readily* have available for possible disclosure. Compare two hypothetical persons attempting to comment on a similar piece of self-data, such as a parental attitude. While one may have the attitude close at hand, *available*, and be able to present an insightful account of it, the other may be reportedly blocked on its content but go on to naively relate a dream which, to the trained listener, obviously communicates the attitude.

Availability of self-data, by definition, is the first requirement for self-disclosure. Hence, *availability* is closely tied to many other dimensions of self-disclosure. A particularly key linkage is found in the correlation between marginally available self-data—that is, data just at the threshold of consciousness and high levels of subjective importance, or intensity. The converse does not hold, however, as readily available material may or may not be accompanied by low levels of intensity. Frequently, material of the highest subjective importance to the communicator is very central within his daily span of awareness. In such instances, the communicator may be carrying out a vigil not to comment on this high intensity self-data lest he also encounter the vulnerability connected with its disclosure.

Individuals vary considerably with respect to the quantities of self-data they have available. Those with high quantities of data are often accorded high levels of 'psychological status', being called 'healthier', 'more likely to grow', and so on. But more relevant to the present discussion is that individuals possessing high levels of self-awareness are in preferred positions to make use of their abilities to self-disclose.

5 Content—Even with equal availability of self-information, individuals differ greatly in the *content* categories they choose to disclose. Content categories frequently referred to in the self-disclosure literature are personal values, religious beliefs, political ideologies, sexual practices, and finances. An individual's values, areas of guilt, needs for privacy, perceptions of societal or referent-group norms, needs for acceptance, perceptions of rewards and punishments, needs for safety, and doubts of personal adequacy are some of the factors contributing to the choice of content for disclosure.

In spite of the large number of reasons why one individual discloses a specific content and another does not, some generalizations can be made. Within a given population, it is likely that a specified set of content categories could be hierarchically arranged to construct a Guttman-type scale. For a standard situation, this scale might be used to predict that an individual would be willing to disclose self-data from all lower-ranked content categories given that he self-disclosed from a higher-ranked category. Some data supporting this prediction have already been collected by Rickers-Ovsiankina.[2]

Specific content categories provide rallying points for groups of individuals. In some instances, individuals define their specific relationships to a group in terms of their relationships to the content. Illustrative of such a relationship are participants in an Alcoholics Anonymous group. Here, the common disclosure *content,* 'I'm an alcoholic', serves as the group's purpose. Somewhat analagous are what Goffman[5] (page 140) terms 'dark secrets'. Dark secrets are facts that a collection of individuals know about themselves, but which are incompatible with the image of self they would like to present to some larger community. Examples are found in work teams when members gather to confess inadequacies, in groups of mothers sharing fears of pregnancy, and in off-the-record meetings where governmental representatives admit to the inappropriateness of the nationalistic policies employed by their respective countries.

Interpersonal processes

This paper has emphasized the interpersonal nature of self-disclosure. Even the intrapersonal processes described in the preceding section have interpersonal correlates; that is, each of the dimensions of intensity, modality, type, availability, and content is determined and regulated by the presence or absence of specific others. There are, however, a number of interpersonal dimensions that remain to be discussed. These dimensions include (1) the *appropriateness* of a self-disclosure, (2) the *motivation* prompting it; (3) the *timing* of its being made explicit; (4) the *tense* of the disclosure; (5) the communicator's *a priori* desire or *intention* in making it known; and (6) the *curvilinear relationship* thought to characterize the effectiveness of self-disclosure.

1 Appropriateness—This dimension refers to whether or not an individual discloses self-information with relevance and meaning for the events in which he is currently participating. Self-disclosure which changes a topic or mood without a reason, that is clearly understandable and/or acceptable to the intended receivers, is not likely to be considered *appropriate*. Relationships quickly establish norms or expectations that govern the appropriateness of the type of intensity of self-disclosures the participants anticipate exchanging. These norms may be unique to the specific relationship or, as in most instances, they mirror the norms that typically prevail in the back-home cultures of the participants.

A self-disclosure may deviate from agreed-upon norms; but to be appropriate within the context of a specific relationship, its discloser should acknowledge or be cognizant of the nature of these norms. Appropriateness of self-disclosure probably increases the likelihood of positive reactions from the other participants. This by no means implies that one should not 'risk' himself by going beyond such expectations. On the contrary, the *most* positive experiences emerge as a result of persons' taking risks. But essential to the meaning of 'risk' is that its effects may be far less than optimal, and the discloser must take the responsibility for risk-taking.

2 Motivation—The reasons, needs, or *motivations* which prompt the disclosure of personal information contribute to the overall meaning the disclosure has for others. When the communicator is seen as incongruent, then his stated motivation is not accepted by others to be the one he actually believes it to be, he elicits different reactions from those he elicits when he is seen as congruent. Communications viewed as incongruent usually evoke guarded reactions, at least until the

199

receiver can diagnose the situation and come up with some strategy that protects his participation. To the extent that the communicator is seen as congruent, the receiver is likely to accept his participation at face value and to be open to the possibility of viewing his communications favorably. Other types of reactions are elicited when the communicator's behavior is seen as consistent with the motivation he believes to be present but not with the one(s) his receivers perceive to be most salient. This situation frequently prompts receivers, first, to protect themselves and, once protected, to try to bring this discrepancy to the discloser's attention. The following seems reasonable as a working theorem: *Other variables held constant, to the extent that the communicator's verbal and/or physical actions are ostensibly representative of the inner motivations he experiences—and to the extent that his congruence is accepted by relevant others—the communicator will elicit, from these others, a receptive disposition for his disclosures.*

3 Timing—This dimension, closely linked to appropriateness and motivation, is simply the *when* of which something is said. This *when* dimension may, in large part, influence the communication's appropriateness as well as implicitly comment on the motivational factors underlying it. The content itself may take on entirely different meaning, depending on *when* it is entered into the discussion.

4 Tense—Self-disclosures are thought to differ importantly along the dimension of past, present, and future tenses. This dimension tells either when a given bit of self-data took place or when it was, is, or will be relevant to the relationship in which it is being disclosed. Not to be confused with the tense of the disclosure is the tense of the extra emotionality that communicators experience as a consequence of their self-disclosing activity. This emotionality is relevant to the tense of the disclosure *only* if the communicator explicitly acknowledges it in his self-disclosure.

There is no set format regarding the significance to be attached to any given tense, although disclosures in the past tense are more likely to be under the communicator's control than present- or future-tense disclosures. Many psychotherapies and most sensitivity training attribute key status to present-tense disclosures. They hold that such disclosures typically have the highest interpersonal relevance, generate the greatest amount of feedback, and make for the greatest receptivity to the feedback of others. Hence, present-tense disclosures, all other things being equal, are believed to possess the highest potential for increased self-awareness and personal growth.

5 Intention—This dimension describes a discloser's *a priori* intent to explicitly make a given bit of self-data known to some specified others. *Intention* has two implications for self-disclosure. One applies to a communicator's willingness to be known by the self-data he has revealed and the other to a communicator's willingness to have it known by the specific receivers who come to know them. Correspondingly, *unintentional* self-disclosure implies the discloser's reluctance to be known either by a given bit of self-data or by the specific receivers to whom he has revealed it. (The earlier discussion of 'What is meant by self-disclosure?' spells out a communicator's options in his after-the-fact dealings with unintentional disclosures.)

6 Curvilinear relation—This aspect of personal self-disclosure, initially suggested by Jourard[13] (page 15), relates amount or degree of self-disclosure with quality of interpersonal relationships formed. The disclosure of personal information is essential to a qualitatively rich interpersonal relationship, however it may be defined, and an insufficient amount of self-disclosure seems to settle this issue by default. The problem of too much disclosure is less clear-cut. What constitutes *too much*, under *what* circumstances, and by *whom* is a thoroughly complex issue. Appropriateness, motivation, timing, and tense all enter in. Moreover, what constitutes the *optimal* amount of self-disclosure is a no less complicated issue. The guideline for a first approximation to resolving this dilemma might lie in reasoning analogously to Speisman,[18] although he dealt with a somewhat different substantive issue. Such reasoning suggests that the way to a more open relationship is by one of the participant's making comments that are slightly more open and personally self-disclosing than the other and by continuing to respond at such a 'leading' level (sometimes at the same level as the other) until an optimal level of openness is mutually reached. If both participants are consistently responding at a low level of self-disclosure, there probably will be little impetus for either to be more open; one might expect such a relationship to most comfortably reach a stable equilibrium at this low level. On the other hand, the condition where one participant is too far ahead of the other in his personal openness could be perceived either by one or both of the participants as comprising an insurmountable breach in communications.

Conclusion

Implicit throughout the preceding discussion has been the assumption that self-disclosure is fundamentally an interpersonal process. Not only is the myriad of personal projects serviced by self-disclosure transactional in nature, but so is the meta-project of personal self-acceptance. The relationship between a communicator and his receiver(s) is critically important in assessing whether self-disclosure is either relevant or in the communicator's own best interests. The receiver is additionally important, for the accuracy of his perceptions is the key to giving a communicator feedback on his disclosures and acceptance for his real-self behavior. Thus, for self-disclosures in general and for disclosures aimed at servicing individual needs for self-acceptance in particular, the process is interpersonal: *It takes two to see one.*

References

1. LUFT, J., *Group processes: An introduction to group dynamics.* Palo Alto, Calif.: National Press, 1963.
2. RICKERS-OVSIANKINA, MARIA, 'Social accessibility in three age groups.' *Psychol. Rep.*, Vol. 2, 1956, pp. 283-96.

3. JOURARD, S. M. and LASAKOW, P., 'Some factors in self-disclosure.' *J. abn. soc. Psychol.*, Vol. 56, 1958, pp. 91-8.
4. BUGENTAL, DAPHNE E., TANNENBAUM, R. and BOBELE, H. K., 'Some causes and consequences in self-concealment.' Unpublished manuscript, U.C.L.A., 1965.
5. GOFFMAN, E., *The presentation of self in everyday life.* Garden City, N.Y.: Doubleday Anchor Books, 1959.
6. THIBAUT, J. W. and KELLEY, H. H., *The social psychology of groups.* N.Y.: Wiley, 1959.
7. FRENCH, J. R. P. and RAVEN, B., 'The basis of social power.' In D. Cartwright and A. Zander, eds., *Group dynamics research and theory.* Evanston, Ill.: Row Peterson, 1960.
8. BERNE, E., *The games people play.* N.Y.: Grove Press, 1964.
9. BUBER, M., *I and thou.* N.Y.: Scribner, 1937.
10. TILLICH, P., *The courage to be.* New Haven: Yale U.P., 1952.
11. FROMM, E., *The sane society.* N.Y.: Rinehart, 1955.
12. ROGERS, C. R. A., 'Theory of therapy, personality, and interpersonal relationships, as developed in the client-centered framework.' In S. Koch, ed *Psychology: A study of a science*, Vol. 3. N.Y.: McGraw-Hill, 1959.
13. JOURARD, S. M., *The transparent self.* Princeton, NJ: Van Nostrand, 1964.
14. MOWRER, O. H., *The new group therapy.* Princeton, NJ: Van Nostrand, 1964.
15. VOSEN, L. M., 'The relationship between self-disclosure and self-esteem.' Unpublished doctoral dissertation, U.C.L.A. 1966.
16. JUNG, C. G. 'Psychological types.' In V. S. de Laszlo, ed. *The basic writings of C. G. Jung.* New York: Modern Library, 1959. Pp 183-285.
17. MYERS, ISABEL B., *The Myers-Briggs type indicator manual.* Princeton, NJ: Educational Testing Service, 1962.
18. SPEISMAN, J. C., 'Depth of interpretation and verbal resistance in psychotherapy.' *J. consult. Psychol.*, Vol. 23, 1959, pp. 93-9.

14. Desiderata

Go placidly amid the noise and haste and remember what peace there may be in silence. As far as possible without surrender be on good terms with all persons. Speak your truth quietly and clearly, and listen to others, even the dull and ignorant; they too have their story. Avoid loud and aggressive persons, they are vexatious to the spirit. If you compare yourself with others you may become vain and bitter; for always there will be greater and lesser persons than yourself. Enjoy your achievements as well as your plans. Keep interested in your own career, however humble; it is a real possession in the changing fortunes of time. Exercise caution in your business affairs; for the world is full of trickery. But let this not blind you to what virtue there is; many persons strive for high ideals; and everywhere life is full of heroism. Be yourself. Especially, do not feign affection. Neither be cynical about love; for in the face of all aridity and disenchantment it is perennial as the grass. Take kindly the counsel of the years, gracefully surrendering the things of youth. Nurture strength of spirit to shield you in sudden misfortune. But do not distress yourself with imaginings. Many fears are born of fatigue and loneliness. Beyond a wholesome discipline, be gentle with yourself. You are a child of the universe, no less than the trees and the stars; you have a right to be here. And whether or not it is clear to you, no doubt the universe is unfolding as it should. Therefore be at peace with God, whatever you conceive Him to be, and whatever your labors and aspirations, in the noisy confusion of life keep peace with your soul. With all its sham, drudgery and broken dreams, it is still a beautiful world. Be careful. Strive to be happy.

(Found in Old Saint Paul's Church Baltimore; dated 1692)

PART SIX : Focus on context of learning and motivation

What needs to happen if adults are to alter their behaviour willingly? Telling a man to change his ways is so often not sufficient. Something more than cognitive and attitudinal changes are needed to effect the growth and direction of individual behaviour. Chapter 15, by Leland Bradford, draws attention to the environment necessary for effective learning. More than the man himself comes to the learning situation. He comes with all his own emotions and prejudices mindful also of the various groups to which he belongs back home. If a man is put in a position free to accept and free to reject new ways, why and how may he adopt new approaches? Chapter 16, the classical article 'Principles of Re-education' by Kurt Lewin and Paul Grabbe, states a number of important conditions if these hoped-for changes are to come about voluntarily. They affirm that he must be really involved in a social experience meaningful to him. In the process, he must be a member of a group disposed to be friendly. Furthermore, no man can learn if he feels at the time that he is being attacked. But through peer-education and mutual support he has the encouragement to try out new ways and to assess their benefits.

What mode of influence a management educator should adopt out of the many now available is taken up by Roger Harrison in chapter 17. He recognizes that sometimes the real target of change is a man's inner life. He sees that there are two overriding factors to be balanced, first, intervene at a level that effects enduring solutions, and, second, intervene at a level that mobilizes a man's own resources in solving problems. He accepts that the latter level may not be effective enough to resolve the organization issue—but it does not do violence to the person. The choice between these two issues is a matter of value judgement on the part of the consultant.

Chapter 18 places slightly more emphasis on the organization context within which individuals have to operate. Harold Bridger's contribution is based on his wide consulting experience. In 'Towards a Policy for Health of the Manager', he and Stephanie White emphasize the ubiquity of stress and conflict in managerial life. 'There is only one kind of person without conflicts—a dead one.' But how much stress? Of what kind? Maybe the most appropriate patterning of jobs means interpersonal difficulties for certain job holders. Family or work? Stay with the company or move? Get on, but at what price to health and social life? It is reminiscent of the Spanish proverb: 'He who buys, pays.' The more open organizations become the more stressful for some. But, as they point out, the nature and stress of the management job is subjective. It can only be discovered by actually doing it. Their article looks at the resultant of two forces—at issues concerning the inner man and at what must be asked of individual job-holders if the organization is to meet its objectives.

15. The teaching-learning transaction

Leland P. Bradford

A reexamination of the teaching-learning process is long overdue. Explorations into the many complex motivational, perceptual, and emotional forces in learning are needed even more than studies of procedures for presenting knowledge or methods of measuring recall. Analysis of the conditions which must be present before the individual can learn and change need also to be made.

An effective teaching-learning process should include two basic assumptions based on present research and experience with processes of learning and changing.

1 That the teaching-learning process is a human transaction involving the teacher, learner, and learning group, in a set of dynamic interrelationships. Teaching is a human relational problem. Teachers and learners engage together in a complex process of exploration and diagnosis of needs for and resistances to learning and change; of experimentation and fact-finding; of testing and planning for utilization of learning and change in the life of the individual. The relationships among learners and between teacher and learners have a great deal to do with the ultimate learning.

2 That the target of education is change and growth in the individual and his behavior; and thus in his worlds. This is a deeper and broader goal than cognitive learning only.

While cognitive and attitudinal learnings are basic aspects of individual growth and behavioral change, they do not guarantee that growth and change will occur. Each individual faces the task of continuously reorganizing, remaking and relating his internal and external worlds. His learning should be directed toward this task. Learning which remains merely cognitive and does not become part of his internal systems and external behavior, becomes compartmentalized and does not successfully affect his problems of living.

● From Leland P. Bradford, 'The Teaching-Learning Transaction.' *Adult Education*, Vol. 8, No. 3, Spring 1958, pp. 135-45. Published by the Adult Education Association of the USA, 1225 Nineteenth Street, Northwest, Washington, DC. Used by permission.

Creating learning conditions

These two assumptions lay a basis for a reexamination of a teaching-learning theory. They indicate the need to combine teaching procedures and understandings of the motivational, emotional and cognitive characteristics of the teacher and learners, with skills of working with learners and learning group in creating conditions for learning and change.

The following seven areas are some of those which must be examined in developing an effective teaching-learning theory.

1 What the learner brings to the transaction (in addition to ignorance and abilities).

2 What the teacher (helper) brings to the transaction (in addition to subject knowledge).

3 The setting in which learning and change takes place.

4 The interaction process.

5 The conditions necessary for learning and change.

6 The maintenance of change and utilization of learning in the life of the learner.

7 The establishment of the processes of continued learning.

What the learner brings

What, for example, are the learner's perceptions about the need for learning and change? How deep is his dissatisfaction with his present situation? How acutely, to use an analogy, does he feel pain? Are external pressures to learn and change reacted to but not really accepted internally? Where is the balance between desire for and resistance to learning and change?

What implicit theory about learning drawn from a variety of past experiences does the learner bring? If his concept is built around hearing lectures, reading, being quizzed, he will feel uneasy with and resist a learning process which more deeply involves him. If his concept of learning keeps him a passive recipient, he will fail to enter into an effective learning transaction. Perhaps the first major task of the teaching-learning transaction is to help the learner learn different ways of learning.

What are the learner's perceptions about the potentials for learning in himself, the teacher and the learning situation? Does he perceive the learning as abstract and irrelevant to his needs? Does he perceive the teacher as capable of understanding and helping him? To what extent does he even recognize the kinds of help he would most appreciate as well as most need? Does he feel acceptance or rejection from the teacher and the group? Does he have security in the learning situation and the learning group?

Inevitably, each person enters a change situation with actual or latent concerns and anxieties. To learn poses unknown possibilities. To change raises images of potential failure, discomfort, pain. What threats to self-image are present as the individual opens himself up to consideration of present inadequacies in knowledge or behavior? We all recall what fears and anxieties we can have in learning a new language or a different course in mathematics.

A perceptual screen

Each person has a perceptual screen filtering out or distorting communication to him. Information, too threatening for him to accept because it attacks his self-image, is blocked out or interpreted in such a way as to pose less of a threat. Adults, particularly, have self-images more resistant to the subordinating role of accepting knowledge from others. What information about personal performance does the learner accept or reject?

How much does he pigeon-hole knowledge, or turn it into abstractions, thus removing or modifying its threat to his self-image? To what extent does he maintain the ability of verbal recall but reject internalization into being and behaving? Does he have sufficient acceptance of himself as he is to accept need for improvement?

Motivation, perceptions, anxieties, all influence and affect the teaching-learning transaction. Self-perceived threats to the learner as a person become real blocks to learning.

Passive learning

Venturing into the unknown means leaving the tried and sure and safe, unsatisfactory as it may be. Resistance to leaving the safe, but at the same time wanting the new, frequently causes the learner to prefer the kind of presentation of knowledge which can be copied and recalled but never internalized, rather than a deeper process of learning involved in a program of change. Students frequently encourage more passive but less effective methods of learning and, by their satisfaction in being protected from important learning, reward teachers for ineffective teaching and thus perpetuate poor teaching.

Each learner brings to the learning situation his skills, or lack of skills, in group membership. If he lacks the ability to work effectively with others in a group situation, it is difficult for him to enter into the human transaction of learning.

Inadequate ability to listen or interact with others makes it less possible for him to learn from the learning group, thus increasing his tensions and anxieties about himself, decreasing his satisfaction with the learning transaction and very likely increasing his resistance to learning.

Approach to learning

Because the learner is one part of the human transaction of teaching-learning, his motivational, perceptual, emotional and attitudinal systems are very important factors in how he approaches learning and change and how open he is to them. It is the total individual, not just his mind, that comes to the learning experience. When only part of him is understood and approached, all of him is not reached, and learning does not get very deeply into him and his actions.

The emerging field of social science is beginning to contribute much to our total understanding of the process of learning and changing. From psychiatry and clinical psychology come knowledge of individual anxieties and concerns. From social psychology and sociology come knowledge about resistance to change and the process of changing. From psychology comes knowledge of motivation and perception. Educators need to utilize such knowledge in broadening and improving understanding of the teaching-learning transaction.

What the teacher brings

The teacher, like the learner, brings far more to the teaching-learning situation than a knowledge of the subject, skill in organizing and presenting material, or ability to test for recall.

First, he brings a certain degree of awareness or lack of awareness that the teacher-learning process is basically a delicate human transaction requiring skill and sensitivity in human relations.

The effective teacher's role is that of engaging in a relationship with the learner and the learning group in which the learners and the teacher go through the process of diagnosis of change needs and blocks together, of seeking and analyzing relevant information from outside sources and from the interaction of the learning group, of experimenting in new pathways of thought and behavior, and of planning for use of new behavior.

The teacher's role of helping in the complex process of learning and change, however, is based upon a set of human relationships precariously established with the learner and the learning group. These relationships are always precarious because of the anxieties of the learner, the threat of the teacher as a judge and expert, and the mixed feeling held by the learner about his dependency on the teacher. The teacher needs to be aware of the importance of these human relationships, sensitive to changes in them, and adept at repairing them.

Awareness of needs

Second, the teacher as a partner in the transaction of learning needs to be aware of his own needs and motivations, and of their consequences to the learning process. To what extent do his needs to control people, to maintain dependency upon himself, or to seek love and affection, distort and disturb his helper function and the learning transaction? To what extent does his fear of hostility develop repression in the learner so that healthy conflict as a basis of learning is lacking?

To what extent does his fear of relationship with people keep the learner at arm's length and thus reduce the possibility of an effective teaching-learning transaction? (This does not mean the other extreme of having to make himself love the learner. Rather it means the ability to enter planfully into a human transaction without need for either rejection or over-acceptance.) Knowing one's own motivations and their possible consequences on others better enables one to keep motivations under direction and control.

Acceptance as a person

Third, the teacher brings an ability, or lack of ability, to accept the learner as a person. Acceptance means ability to respect and listen to the other and to separate the person from unliked parts of his behavior. The physician who, hating disease, also hates and rejects the person who has the disease is not an effective doctor. Yet teachers frequently are not aware that they reject learners because of lack of knowledge, abilities, or effectiveness in relating to them. Acceptance does not mean approval of the present status of being and behaving of the learner. It rather marks the basic point from which the teacher tries to enter into a helping relationship.

The teacher works with a learning group. Good teacher-group relations are certainly as important as good teacher-student relations. The degree of ability in group leadership and membership skills on the part of the teacher has much to do with learning of the individuals in the class group.

The teacher is a second part of the teaching-learning transaction. His emotional, motivational, perceptual, and attitudinal systems, and his awareness of them and their consequences for learning and change are important forces in effective teaching-learning. Social science again has much to contribute in understanding the teacher.

Most education takes place in group situations. Thus, the teaching-learning transaction includes teacher, learner, and learning group. Each has its forces and impact on the learning outcome for the individuals. The class group is not merely an economical way of teaching. It should be at the heart of the learning process. Group impact and influence on its members can be a powerful force toward learning or toward supporting the learning process.

The teacher-learner transaction

Recent research into the dynamics of group behavior indicates how powerful group forces are in group and individual productivity. Some groups have the task of making machine parts, others of reaching decisions, and still others of increasing the learning of their members. In all instances, for the group to be successful, attention must be given to helping the group form, organize, grow and keep in good repair. Just as the leaders in work groups should assume responsibility for encouraging the growth and maintenance of the work group, so should the teacher of the learning group.

As teachers recognize emotional aspects of group behavior, individual anxieties and hidden motives, interpersonal threats and competition, problems of relations to leadership and authority, factors of individual involvement in groups, they will be better able to help classes become groups where the group task is individual learning and where group forces of cohesion are exerted on the learning of each individual.

As it is, group forces, inevitably present in all group situations, often work against the teacher and against learning. The class group bands against the teacher to reduce learning because the teacher did not know how to develop an effective learning group where members helped members and where morale was high.

How many teachers fail to encourage, or even allow, learners to help educate each other? If teachers were able to create learning groups in which member influenced and helped member, learning results would be far greater.

The learning group is the third part of the teaching-learning transaction. Educators are just beginning to realize the powerful forces present in groups which could measurably increase individual learning and change. Research in group dynamics in many university centers and experimentation with applied group dynamics carried out by the National Training Laboratories have much to offer an expanding teaching-learning theory.

The interaction process

The interaction process is basically a network of interactions taking place in a group setting. Teacher interaction with one student may be heard in many different ways and with different consequences by others. Praise or reward to one student may be heard as punishment to another because he was not selected for reward. To the learner, interactions of support and reaction from the group may be more valuable or more readily acceptable than from the teacher.

The teacher needs to be aware of the consequences of any interaction on all members of the learning group and on the group itself. Does an interaction designed to give needed knowledge to one learner create greater unhealthy dependency on the teacher by other group members?

The interaction process has two basic purposes: first, to establish and maintain relationships which reduce anxieties and defensiveness in the learner and help him open up for learning, and, second, to bring about learning and change.

A supportive climate

It is a false assumption, more common in secondary and higher than in elementary education, that the mature person does not need sensitive teacher-student relationships or group support. Fortunately, many adult educators have discovered the fallacies in this assumption and have come to realize the importance of developing a supportive climate that reduces resistance to learning.

With the interaction process basic in learning, the actual interventions of teachers and learners, and the response to them, are of critical importance.

What are the consequences, for example, of action or lack of action by the teacher on shifting the balances of motivation of the learner? What are the consequences in increasing or decreasing a feeling of support or of changing the perceptions of the learner? What are the consequences for the helping relationship between teacher and learner? Does any particular action create overdependency on the teacher?

It is unfortunate that there is a dearth of studies dealing with the effect of teacher intervention on the learning process. In the fields of consultation and therapy, much more has been done to train for sensitivity to the interaction process. In these fields, as well as in the field of medicine, the interaction process is recognized as basic in diagnosis and treatment.

If the interaction process is basic to learning, then experience in the area of consultation and therapy, and research in the social science fields of social and clinical psychology are important to a full development of a learning theory. Recent work on human relations training carried on by the various group development laboratories has been exploring the area of teacher intervention in the interaction process. Experience in clinical psychology is highly relevant to this area. Finally, recent studies in social psychology on the process of change and the function of helping with change have importance.

Learning and change

Learning and change take place most effectively only when certain conditions are present, making it possible for the learner to enter into a process of diagnosis, experimentation, information-finding, generalization, practice, and application, leading toward learning, growth and change.

1 Revealing thoughts, feelings, behavior—Until the thoughts, feelings, and behavior needing change are brought to the surface for the individual and made public to those helping him (in formal learning situations, the teacher and other members of the learning group), there is little likelihood of learning or change. Buried, they are blurred and indistinct for the learner, covered by misperceptions of adequacy, anxieties, defensiveness. Surfaced, they can be examined by learner, teacher and learning group in the light of greater reality.

Until thoughts and behavior are revealed and exposed, there is little that the learner or his helpers can take hold of to bring about improvement or change.

Not to fill a void

Learning is not a matter of filling a void with information. It is a process of internal organization of a complex of thought patterns, perceptions, assumptions, attitudes, feelings and skills, and of successfully testing this reorganization in relation to problems of living.

The basis for reorganization, and thus for learning, is diagnosis of inadequacy. Such diagnosis should be made collaboratively by the learner and those helping him. It is ineffectual for someone else to make the diagnosis for the learner—a frequent fault in education.

The diagnosis is never simply that of general inadequacy. It should include motivations, desires, anxieties, defensiveness, insecurities, perceptions. In combination, they create the normal ambivalences found in learning and change.

Diagnosis depends on having adequate data. Surfacing or revealing the thought, feeling and behavior patterns of the learner provides a common experience for learner, teacher, and learning group to make possible a collaborative diagnosis.

Group reactions

2 Seeking reactions to revealed ideas and behavior—Revealing inner thoughts, attitudes, behavior, without securing accurate and acceptable reactions from the teacher and learning group, from additional sources of information, or from self would be without much value. *We do not learn by doing only*. We learn by doing

213

under conditions in which relevant, accurate and acceptable reactions which we are able to use get through to us.

Increasingly, it is clear that the concept of feedback has important meaning for the educational process. Information following exposure which recognizes the individual's perceptual system, and which has for its purpose development rather than destruction, is the heart of learning. Feedback must be clearly and completely heard. Here is where the human relationship aspect of teaching-learning perhaps has greatest importance.

In an executive development program recently, one member told the group in various ways that he saw himself as a warm-hearted person who liked people and who was a democratic executive. His recital of his problems of apathy, irresponsibility and lack of creativity in his immediate subordinates revealed him as fearful and hostile toward people and certainly autocratic in his management.

Lectures or discussions about good executive behavior would have been heard by this man as referring to himself. Only as his behavior was revealed to himself and to other members of the learning group, and as he gradually received helpful feedback reactions enabling him to correct his perceptions of himself and, ultimately, some of his behavior, did real learning and change take place.

A climate for learning

3 Climate—Revealing thoughts and behavior and accepting reactions about them takes place effectively only when the atmosphere or climate in the learning group and the teaching-learning transaction is one which reduces threat and defensiveness and which also provides emotional support while the learner is undergoing the difficult process of changing patterns of thought and behavior.

The teacher has the important responsibility of helping to create a climate conducive to learning. It is crucial that the teacher *help the group* create this climate. The temptation to the teacher is to attempt to supply, himself, all the understanding and support necessary for each learner. This keeps the learner in the bondage of emotional dependency on the teacher.

If the climate is built by the group, with encouragement and assistance from the teacher, the individual learner can accept emotional support interdependently, rather than dependently, because he is contributing to the group support given to other members.

4 Information seeking and receiving—Knowledge from a variety of sources is vital to the learning process. Some comes from the analysis of the learning situation, some from immediate reactions of teacher and peers, some from experimentation and research results, some from past experiences of the individual and others, and some from the wide wisdom and vast experience of the past.

Knowledge-giving as a factor of learning, however, has attributes and consequences, all of which need much further exploration. The first is timing. Like a road map which is useless to the person who has made no decision to take a trip, information is often presented in teaching situations before the individual has made any personal decision about learning and change. Teachers need constantly to realize that attendance in a learning group does not necessarily mean commitment to the process of learning and change.

New ways of thinking

5 Experimentation and practice with new ways of thinking and doing—Knowledge, which remains basically outside the being and doing of the individual, is likely to become compartmentalized. Learning tends not to become a basic part of the being and doing of the individual until he has had opportunity to try out in practice situations new possibilities for thinking and doing. Experimentation and practice are important conditions in the total process of teaching-learning.

6 Application of change into the learning situation of the individual—Application of learning and change in the life of the individual is a far more difficult task than initial learning and change in a protected learning situation. Unless the teacher and the learning group give time and attention to individual problems of internalizing and using learning, regression and loss of the learning is likely.

These conditions need much further exploration and research in terms of completeness, relative importance, and integration. In various sections of the social sciences, some exploration is present. New research on feedback, or information theory, has immediate value for an enlarged concept of teaching-learning. The various approaches to counseling and therapy have developed experience in the area of establishing receptive climates. Research in human relations training has stressed the integration of these conditions and methods of training for application. Social psychology and sociology has worked on the problem of helping to apply and maintain change.

Overcoming resistance to change

Education has long recognized the importance of transfer of learning. Too frequently, such transfer has meant only the application of principles to new situations. This has ignored many of the problems of resistance to putting change into practice in the individual and in his worlds.

The problem of maintenance of change and utilization of learning have both emotional and cognitive aspects. The learner's motivations to maintain change in thought and behavior must be sufficiently strong to overcome his own hesitations and the forces in his environment pushing against change.

Many a summer school program has inspired teachers to want to improve teaching practices, only to find resistance among colleagues, students, and parents back in the school system. Change, to be maintained, must be well rooted in the individual and well supported by forces in his external worlds.

If maintenance of change and utilization of learning is a necessary part of a theory of teaching-learning, then efforts must be made during the process of formal

215

teaching-learning to prepare for the problem of maintenance. A number of helping steps can be taken at that time.

Steps toward change

1 Help needs to be given to the learner in diagnosing forces of resistance to change, and support for change likely to be found in himself and his environment. Basically, he needs help in locating and building supports in his internal and external worlds to maintain new learning and change.

2 Help needs to be given to the learner in assessing his own potential strengths and weaknesses in terms of support for change.

3 Help should be given the learner in planning how to reestablish himself in his outside worlds (after leaving the teaching-learning situation).

A few years ago, the author helped a team from Europe to develop skills in human relations training. It became clear, as the three-month training program came to an end, that their first and most crucial task back home was to gain reacceptance as Europeans. If they were seen as 'Americanized', any efforts to maintain changes in themselves and introduce changes in their situations would meet with strong resistances from those around them. Each person needs a foundation from which to encourage change in himself and his situations. Learning which totally removes such a foundation will not lead to continuing change.

4 Help needs to be given in planning how to create supports away from the learning situation. Supports for change in the situation must be matched by supports in the back-home situation.

5 Help needs to be given the individual to develop a continuing system of learning. Methods of experimentation and analysis can be taught which will encourage the person to continue to learn from a variety of experiences.

Only recently has systematic thought been given in the social sciences to the problem of maintenance of change. Lewin's earlier concept of the unfreezing-freezing-unfreezing-freezing cycle of change has had important implications in recent research. The National Training Laboratories efforts to develop methods for training change agents and of planning for back-home application of learning represents another area of experience and research.

Work in sociology as well as in social psychology has analyzed problems of change in relation to social system.

The teaching-learning process should endeavor to help the learner learn how to learn more effectively so that more of his experiences can lead toward learning and change.

As individuals learn to use scientific methods of experimentation, observation, and analysis in daily decision-making and problem-solving, instead of stereotypes, perceptual distortions, and closed eyes and ears, learning and changing from experiences can more likely become a continual process.

As individual learners become more aware, through an effective teacher-learner transaction, of their own anxieties and resistance to learning, they may be able to reduce them more frequently and thus enhance learning and change.

As individual learners become more accepting of themselves and gain more internal security, they will become less defensive and more able to perceive accurately and to use reactions to their thought and behavior patterns.

In brief, a basic purpose of education in all teaching-learning situations is first to help the individual learner open himself up for learning by being able to bring his problems and needs for learning to the surface, and to listen and accept relevant reactions about his problems and behavior. The second purpose is to help the learner gain methods of experimenting, analyzing and utilizing experiences and knowledge resulting from daily problem-solving.

Conclusion

An effective teaching-learning transactional process should include, in addition to the seven areas discussed above, pedagogical methods of presenting knowledge and developing experiences and methods of testing with the learners their learning and change.

As this broadened picture of teaching-learning is developed, it is obvious it has major implications for the entire field of teacher training. It will not be enough merely to add social science subject knowledge to what the prospective teacher is expected to 'learn'. Engaging in the complex human transaction of teaching-learning requires more than knowing about human behavior. It calls for sensitivity and awareness to on-going relationships and for skills of interacting with the learner and the learning group. These sensitivities and skills are not gained from traditional methods of teacher training. They will require a process of experiential learning in which the prospective teacher is helped to gain self-awareness, understanding of how others perceive his behavior (the consequences of his behavior on others), practice in diagnosing human relations and group problems, experience in sharpening sensitivity to what others are feeling and trying to communicate. These awarenesses and sensitivities are primary and teaching procedure secondary.

A healthy expansion of our knowledge of the teaching-learning process thus needs to be followed by an equally long overdue reexamination of methods of teacher training.

16. Principles of re-education

Kurt Lewin and Paul Grabbe

The re-educative process affects the individual in three ways. It changes his *cognitive* structure, the way he sees the physical and social worlds, including all his facts, concepts, beliefs, and expectations. It modifies his *valences and values*, and these embrace both his attractions and aversions to groups and group standards, his feelings in regard to status differences, and his reactions to sources of approval or disapproval. And it affects *motoric action*, involving the degree of the individual's control over his physical and social movements.

If all three of these effects (and the processes which give rise to them) were governed by the same laws, the practical task of re-education would be much simpler. Unfortunately, they are not, and the re-educator, in consequence, is confronted with certain contradictions. For instance, treatment involving the training of a thumb-sucking child in certain roundabout hand movements, designed to make the child aware of his thumb-sucking and thereby giving him more control over these movements, may set the child apart from other children and undermine his emotional security, the possession of which is a prerequisite for successful reeducation.

How these inner contradictions may be avoided is one of the basic problems of re-education. A correct sequence of steps, correct timing, and a correct combination of individual and group treatments are presumably essential. Most important, however, is a thorough understanding by the re-educator of the way in which each of these psychological components—the cognitive structure, valences and values, and motoric action—are affected by any specific step in reeducation.

The discussion that follows touches but two of the main problems here involved, one related to a change in cognition, the other, to the acceptance of new values.

Change in the cognitive structure

The difficulties encountered in efforts to reduce prejudices or otherwise to change the social outlook of the individual have led to a realization that re-education
● From 'Conduct, Knowledge, and Acceptance of New Values,' *The Journal of Social Issues*, Vol. 1, No. 3, August 1945, pp. 56-64. Reproduced with permission.

cannot merely be a rational process. . . . We know that lectures or other similarly abstract methods of transmitting knowledge are of little avail in changing his subsequent outlook and conduct. We might be tempted, therefore, to think that what is lacking in these methods is firsthand experience. The sad truth is that even firsthand experience will not necessarily produce the desired result. To understand the reasons, we must examine a number of premises which bear directly on the problem.

(1) Even extensive firsthand experience does not automatically create correct concepts (knowledge)

For thousands of years man's everyday experience with falling objects did not suffice to bring him to a correct theory of gravity. A sequence of very unusual, man-made experiences, so-called experiments, which grew out of the systematic search for truth were necessary to bring about a change from less adequate to more adequate concepts. To assume that first-hand experience in the social world would automatically lead to the formation of correct concepts (knowledge) or to the creation of adequate stereotypes seems therefore unjustifiable.

(2) Social action no less than physical action is steered by perception

In any situation, we cannot help but act according to the field we perceive, and our perception extends to two different aspects of this field. One has to do with facts, the other with values.

If we grasp an object, the movement of our hand is steered by its perceived position in the perceived surroundings. Likewise, our social actions are steered by the position in which we perceive ourselves and others within the total social setting. The basic task of re-education can thus be viewed as one of changing the individual's social perception. Only by this change in social perception can change in the individual's social action be realized.

Let us assume that inadequate information (knowledge) has somehow been replaced by more adequate knowledge. Does this suffice to change our perception? In answering this question, let us again take a lead from the field of physical perception by asking: How can false physical perception, for instance, visual illusions, be rectified?

(3) As a rule the possession of correct knowledge does not suffice to rectify false perception

Our insight into the conditions which determine the correctness or incorrectness of perception is still very limited. It is known that some relation exists between visual perception and knowledge. However, the lines which appear curved in an optical illusion do not straighten out as soon as we 'know' that they are straight. Even first-hand experience, the measuring of the distances in question, usually does not eliminate the illusion. As a rule, other types of change, such as the enlarging or the shrinking of the area perceived or a change in the visual frames of references, are needed to straighten out the lines.

When we consider resistances to re-education we usually think in terms of emotional obstacles. It is important, however, not to underestimate the difficulties inherent in changing cognition. If we keep in mind that even extensive experience with physical facts does not necessarily lead to correct physical perception, we will be less surprised at the resistances encountered when we attempt to modify inadequate social stereotypes. . . .

[French and Marrow tell the story of a forelady's attitude toward older workers. She clings to the conviction that older workers are no good, although she has older workers on her floor whom she considers very efficient. Her prejudices stand in direct opposition to all her personal experience.]

This example from industry is well in line with studies on Negro-White relations dealing with the effect of common schooling and with observations on the effect of mingling. They indicate that favorable experiences with members of another group, even if they are frequent, do not necessarily diminish prejudices towards that group.

Only if a psychological linkage is made between the image of specific individuals and the stereotype of a certain group, only when the individuals can be perceived as 'typical representatives' of that group, is the experience with individuals likely to affect the stereotype.

(4) Incorrect stereotypes (prejudices) are functionally equivalent to wrong concepts (theories)

We can infer, for instance, that the social experiences which are needed to change improper stereotypes have to be equivalent to those rare and specific physical experiences which cause a change in our theories and concepts about the physical world. Such experiences cannot be depended on to happen accidentally.

To understand the difficulties in the way of changing conduct, an additional point has to be considered:

(5) Changes in sentiments do not necessarily follow changes in cognitive structure

Even if the cognitive structure in regard to a group is modified in an individual, his sentiments toward this group may remain unchanged. The analysis of an opinion survey on the Negro problem, involving white respondents with varying educational backgrounds, shows that knowledge and sentiment are independent to a marked degree. The sentiments of the individual towards a group are determined less by his knowledge about that group than by the sentiments prevalent in the social atmosphere which surrounds him. Just as the alcoholic knows that he should not drink—and does not want to drink—so the white American soldier who observes a Negro dating a white girl in England may feel that he should not mind, and he might consciously condemn himself for his prejudices. Still he may frequently be helpless in the face of this prejudice since his perception and emotional reaction remain contrary to what he knows they ought to be.

Re-education is frequently in danger of reaching only the official system of values, the level of verbal expression and not of conduct; it may result in merely heightening the discrepancy between the super-ego (the way I ought to feel) and the ego (the way I really feel), and thus give the individual a bad conscience. Such a discrepancy leads to a state of high emotional tension, but seldom to correct conduct. It may postpone transgressions but is likely to make transgressions more violent when they occur. . . .

A factor of great importance in bringing about a change in sentiment is the degree to which the individual becomes actively involved in the problem. Lacking this involvement, no objective fact is likely to reach the status of a fact for the individual concerned and therefore influence his social conduct.

The nature of this interdependence becomes somewhat more understandable if one considers the relation between change in perception, acceptance, and group belongingness.

Acceptance of new values and group belongingness

Since action is ruled by perception, a change in conduct presupposes that new facts and values are perceived. These have to be accepted not merely verbally as an official ideology, but as an action-ideology, involving that particular, frequently non-conscious system of values which guides conduct. In other words:

(6) A change in action-ideology, a real acceptance of a changed set of facts and values, a change in the perceived social world—all three are but different expressions of the same process

By some, this process may be called a change in the culture of the individual; by others, a change of his super-ego.

It is important to note that re-education will be successful, i.e., lead to permanent change, only if this change in culture is sufficiently complete. If re-education succeeds only to the degree that the individual becomes a marginal man between the old and new system of values nothing worth while is accomplished.

One of the factors which has been shown to have a very important bearing on the success or failure of the re-educative process is the manner in which the new super-ego is introduced. The simplest solution seems to lie in outright enforcement of the new set of values and beliefs. In this case a new god is introduced who has to fight with the old god, now regarded as a devil. Two points may be made in this connection, illustrating the dilemma facing re-education in regard to the introduction of a new set of values.

1 **Loyalty to the old and hostility to the new values**—An individual who is forcibly moved from his own to another country, with a different culture, is likely to meet the new set of values with hostility. So it is with an individual who is made a subject of re-education against his will. Feeling threatened, he reacts with hostility. This threat is felt all the more keenly if the individual is not voluntarily exposing himself to re-education. A comparison of voluntary and involuntary migration from one culture to another seems to bear out this observation.

One would expect this hostility to be the more pronounced the greater the loyalty of the individual to the old system of values. Accordingly, persons who are more socially inclined, therefore less self-centred, can be expected to offer stronger resistances to re-education, for the very reason that they are more firmly anchored in the old system.

In any event, the re-educative process will normally encounter hostility. The task of breaking down this hostility becomes a paradox if one considers the relation between acceptance of new values and freedom of choice.

2 Re-education and freedom of acceptance—Much stress is laid on the creation, as part of the re-educative process, of an atmosphere of freedom and spontaneity. Voluntary attendance, informality of meetings, freedom of expression in voicing grievances, emotional security, and avoidance of pressure, all include this element. Carl Rogers's emphasis on self-decision by the patient stresses the same point for the psychotherapy of the individual.

There seems to be a paradox implied in this insistence on freedom of acceptance, and probably no other aspect of re-education brings more clearly into the open a basic difficulty of the process. Since re-education aims to change the system of values and beliefs of an individual or a group, to change it so as to bring it in line with society at large or with reality, it seems illogical to expect that this change will be made by the subjects themselves. The fact that this change has to be enforced on the individual from outside seems so obvious a necessity that it is often taken for granted. Many people assume that the creation, as part of the re-educative process, of an atmosphere of informality and freedom of choice cannot possibly mean anything else but that the re-educator must be clever enough in manipulating the subjects to make them think that they are running the show. According to such people, an approach of this kind is merely a deception and smoke-screen for what to them is the more honorable, straight-forward method of using force.

It may be pointed out, however, that if re-education means the establishment of a new super-ego, it necessarily follows that the objective sought will not be reached so long as the new set of values is not experienced by the individual as something freely chosen. If the individual complies merely from fear of punishment rather than through the dictates of his free will and conscience, the new set of values he is expected to accept does not assume in him the position of super-ego, and his re-education therefore remains unrealized.

From this we may conclude that social perception and freedom of choice are interrelated. Following one's conscience is identical with following the perceived intrinsic requirements of the situation. Only if and when the new set of values is freely accepted, only if it corresponds to one's super-ego do those changes in social perception occur which, as we have seen, are a prerequisite for a change in conduct and therefore for a lasting effect of re-education.

We can now formulate the dilemma which re-education has to face in this way: How can free acceptance of a new system of values be brought about if the person who is to be educated is, in the nature of things, likely to be hostile to the new values and loyal to the old?

(7) Acceptance of the new set of values and beliefs cannot usually be brought about item by item

Methods and procedures which seek to change convictions item by item are of little avail in bringing about the desired change of heart. This is found to be one of the most important experiences for those engaged in the field of re-education. Arguments proceeding logically from one point to another may drive the individual into a corner. But as a rule he will find some way—if necessary a very illogical way—to retain his beliefs. No change of conviction on any specific point can be established in more than an ephemeral way so long as the individual has not given up his hostility to the new set of values as a whole, to the extent of having changed from hostility at least to open-mindedness.

Step-by-step methods *are* very important in re-education. These steps, however, have to be conceived as steps in a gradual change from hostility to friendliness in regard to the new system as a whole, rather than as a conversion of the individual one point at a time. Of course, convictions in regard to certain points in the total system may play an important role in the process of conversion. It is, however, important for the overall planning of re-education not to lose sight of the fact that efforts directed toward bringing about a change from hostility to open-mindedness and to friendliness to the new culture as a whole be given priority over conversion in regard to any single item or series of items of the re-educative program.

How, then, can acceptance of the new values be established if not by an item by item change in conviction?

Creation of an in-group and the acceptance of a new value system

One of the outstanding means used today for bringing about acceptance in re-education, as discussed above, is the establishment of what is called an 'in-group', i.e., a group in which the members feel belongingness. Under these circumstances:

(8) The individual accepts the new system of values and beliefs by accepting belongingness to a group

... Allport formulates this point as a general principle of teaching people when he says, 'It is an axiom that people cannot be taught who feel that they are at the same time being attacked'. In other words, in spite of whatever status differences there might be between them, the teacher and the student have to feel as members of one group in matters involving their sense of values—the normal gap between teacher and student, doctor and patient, social worker and public, can be a real obstacle to acceptance of the advocated conduct.

The chances for re-education seem to be increased whenever a strong we-feeling is created. The establishment of this feeling that everybody is in the same boat, has gone through the same difficulties, and speaks the same language is stressed as one of the main conditions facilitating the re-education of the alcoholic and the delinquent.

When re-education involves the relinquishment of standards which are contrary to the standards of society at large (as in the case of delinquency, minority prejudices, alcoholism), the feeling of group belongingness seems to be greatly heightened if the members feel free to express openly the very sentiments which are to be dislodged through re-education. This might be viewed as another example of

223

the seeming contradictions inherent in the process of re-education: expression of prejudices against minorities or the breaking of rules of parliamentary procedures may in themselves be contrary to the desired goal. Yet a feeling of complete freedom and a heightened group identification are frequently more important at a particular stage of re-education than learning not to break specific rules.

This principle of in-grouping makes understandable why complete acceptance of previously rejected facts can be achieved best through the discovery of these facts by the group members themselves. Then, and frequently only then, do the facts become really *their* facts (as against other people's facts). An individual will believe facts he himself has discovered in the same way that he believes in himself or in his group. The importance of this fact-finding process for the group by the group itself has been recently emphasized with reference to re-education in several fields. It can be surmised that the extent to which social research is translated into social action depends on the degree to which those who carry out this action are made a part of the fact-finding on which the action is to be based.

Re-education influences conduct only when the new system of values and beliefs dominates the individual's perception. The acceptance of the new system is linked with the acceptance of a specific group, a particular role, a definite source of authority as new points of reference. It is basic for re-education that this linkage between acceptance of new facts or values and acceptance of certain groups or roles is very intimate and that the second frequently is a prerequisite for the first. This explains the great difficulty of changing beliefs and values in a piecemeal fashion. This linkage is a main factor behind resistance to re-education, but can also be made a powerful means for its success.

224

17. Choosing the depth of organizational intervention

Roger Harrison

There is a need for conceptual models which differentiate intervention strategies from one another in a way which permits rational matching of strategies to differing organizational change problems. A central concept in such a model could be the depth of individual emotional involvement in the change process. By depth we mean how deep, value-laden, emotionally charged, and central to the individual's sense of self are the issues and processes about which a consultant attempts directly to obtain information and which he seeks to influence. In order of increasing depth are the change strategies: Operations Analysis, Management by Objectives, the Managerial Grid, the T-Group, and Task Group Therapy.

As depth of intervention increases, so also do a number of concomitants of depth: dependence on the special competance of the change agent, centrality of the individual as the target of the change attempt, costs of intervention, and the risk of unintended consequences for individuals. These concomitants suggest a criterion for the depth of intervention: *to intervene at a level no deeper than that required to produce enduring solutions to the problems at hand.* However, a countervailing trend tends to push the level of intervention deeper as organizational systems shift from greater external control to more autonomy and internal control for members. As the individual becomes more important, the level at which the processes which effectively determine his behavior operate becomes deeper, and the individual has increasing influence over the success or failure of the intervention. A case is presented for a radical shift of consultant orientation in the direction of accepting a client's felt needs and presented problems as being real and of working on them at a level where the client can serve as a competent and willing collaborator. This leads to the second criterion: *to intervene at a level no deeper than that at which the energy and resources of the client can be committed to problem-solving and to change.*

• Reprinted with permission: *The Journal of Applied Behavioral Science*, Vol. 6, No. 2, 1970.

Since the Second World War, there has been a great proliferation of behavioral science-based methods by which consultants seek to facilitate growth and change in individuals, groups, and organizations. The methods range from operations analysis and manipulation of the organization chart, through the use of Grid laboratories, T-groups, and non-verbal techniques. As was true in the development of clinical psychology and psychotherapy, the early stages of this developmental process tend to be accompanied by considerable competition, criticism, and argument about the relative merits of various approaches. It is my conviction that controversy over the relative goodness or badness, effectiveness or ineffectiveness, of various change strategies really accomplishes very little in the way of increased knowledge or unification of behavioral science. As long as we are arguing about what method is better than another, we tend to learn very little about how various approaches fit together or complement one another, and we certainly make more difficult and ambiguous the task of bringing these competing points of view within one overarching system of knowledge about human processes.

As our knowledge increases, it begins to be apparent that these competing change strategies are not really different ways of doing the same thing—some more effective and some less effective—but rather that they are different ways of doing *different* things. They touch the individual, the group, or the organization in different aspects of their functioning. They require differing kinds and amounts of commitment on the part of the client for them to be successful, and they demand different varieties and levels of skills and abilities on the part of the practitioner.

I believe that there is a real need for conceptual models which differentiate intervention strategies from one another in a way which permits rational matching of strategies to organizational change problems. The purpose of this paper is to present a modest beginning which I have made toward a conceptualization of strategies, and to derive from this conceptualization some criteria for choosing appropriate methods of intervention in particular applications.

The point of view of this paper is that the depth of individual emotional involvement in the change process can be a central concept for differentiating change strategies. In focusing on this dimension, we are concerned with the extent to which core areas of the personality or self are the focus of the change attempt. Strategies which touch the more deep, personal, private, and central aspects of the individual or his relationships with others fall toward the deeper end of this continuum. Strategies which deal with more external aspects of the individual and which focus upon the more formal and public aspects of role behavior tend to fall toward the surface end of the depth dimension. This dimension has the advantage that it is relatively easy to rank change strategies upon it and to get fairly close consensus as to the ranking. It is a widely discussed dimension of difference which has meaning and relevance to practitioners and their clients. I hope in this paper to promote greater flexibility and rationality in choosing appropriate depths of intervention. I shall approach this task by examining the effects of interventions at various depths. I shall also explore the ways in which two important organizational processes tend to make demands and to set limits upon the depth of intervention which can produce effective change in organizational functioning. These two

226

processes are the autonomy of organization members and their own perception of their needs for help.

Before illustrating the concept by ranking five common intervention strategies along the dimension of depth, I should like to define the dimension somewhat more precisely. We are concerned essentially with how private, individual, and hidden are the issues and processes about which the consultant attempts directly to obtain information and which he seeks to influence. If the consultant seeks information about relatively public and observable aspects of behavior and relationship, and if he tries to influence directly only these relatively surface characteristics and processes, we would then categorize his intervention strategy as being closer to the surface. If, on the other hand, the consultant seeks information about very deep and private perceptions, attitudes, or feelings, and if he intervenes in a way which directly affects these processes, then we would classify his intervention strategy as one of considerable depth. To illustrate the surface end of the dimension, let us look first at operations research or operations analysis. This strategy is concerned with the roles and functions to be performed within the organization, generally with little regard to the individual characteristics of persons occupying the roles. The change strategy is to manipulate role relationships; in other words, to redistribute the tasks, the resources, and the relative power attached to various roles in the organization. This is essentially a process of rational analysis in which the tasks which need to be performed are determined and specified and then sliced up into role definitions for persons and groups in the organization. The operations analyst does not ordinarily need to know much about particular people. Indeed, his function is to design the organization in such a way that its successful operation does not depend too heavily upon any uniquely individual skills, abilities, values, or attitudes of persons in various roles. He may perform this function adequately without knowing in advance who the people are who will fill these slots. Persons are assumed to be moderately interchangeable, and in order to make this approach work it is necessary to design the organization so that the capacities, needs, and values of the individual which are relevant to role performance are relatively public and observable, and are possessed by a fairly large proportion of the population from which organization members are drawn. The approach is certainly one of very modest depth.

Somewhat deeper are those strategies which are based upon evaluating individual performance and attempting to manipulate it directly. Included in this approach is much of the industrial psychologist's work in selection, placement, appraisal, and counseling of employees. The intervener is concerned with what the individual is able and likely to do and achieve rather than with processes internal to the individual. Direct attempts to influence performance may be made through the application of rewards and punishments, such as promotions, salary increases, or transfers within the organization. An excellent illustration of this focus on end results is the practice of management by objectives. The intervention process is focused on establishing mutually agreed-upon goals for performance between the individual and his supervisor. The practice is considered to be particularly advantageous because it permits the supervisor to avoid a focus on personal

227

characteristics of the subordinate, particularly those deeper, more central characteristics which managers generally have difficulty in discussing with those who work under their supervision. The process is designed to limit information exchange to that which is public and observable, such as the setting of performance goals and the success or failure of the individual in attaining them.

Because of its focus on end results, rather than on the process by which those results are achieved, management by objectives must be considered less deep than the broad area of concern with work style which I shall term instrumental process analysis. We are concerned here not only with performance but with the process by which that performance is achieved. However, we are primarily concerned with styles and processes of work rather than with the processes of interpersonal relationships which I would classify as being deeper on the basic dimension.

In instrumental process analysis we are concerned with how a person likes to organize and conduct his work and with the impact which this style of work has on others in the organization. Principally, we are concerned with how a person perceives his role, what he values and disvalues in it, and with what he works hard on and what he chooses to ignore. We are also interested in the instrumental acts which the individual directs toward others: delegating authority or reserving decisions to himself, communicating or withholding information, collaborating or competing with others on work-related issues. The focus on instrumentality means that we are interested in the person primarily as a doer of work or a performer of functions related to the goals of the organization. We are interested in what facilitates or inhibits his effective task performance.

We are not interested *per se* in whether his relationships with others are happy or unhappy, whether they perceive him as too warm or too cold, too authoritarian or too *laissez faire*, or any other of the many interpersonal relationships which arise as people associate in organizations. However, I do not mean to imply that the line between instrumental relationships and interpersonal ones is an easy one to draw in action and practice, or even that it is desirable that this be done.

Depth gauges: Level of tasks and feelings

What I am saying is that an intervention strategy can focus on instrumentality or it can focus on interpersonal relationships, and that there are important consequences of this difference in depth of intervention.

When we intervene at the level of instrumentality, it is to change work behavior and working relationships. Frequently this involves the process of bargaining or negotiation between groups and individuals. Diagnoses are made of the satisfactions or dissatisfactions of organization members with one another's work behavior. Reciprocal adjustments, bargains, and trade-offs can then be arranged in which each party gets some modification in the behavior of the other at the cost to him of some reciprocal accommodation. Much of the intervention strategy which has been developed around Blake's concept of the Managerial Grid is at this level and involves bargaining and negotiation of role behavior as an important change process.

228

At the deeper level of interpersonal relationships the focus is on feelings, attitudes, and perceptions which organization members have about others. At this level we are concerned with the quality of human relationships within the organization, with warmth and coldness of members to one another, and with the experiences of acceptance and rejection, love and hate, trust and suspicion among groups and individuals. At this level, the consultant probes for normally hidden feelings, attitudes, and perceptions. He works to create relationships of openness about feelings and to help members to develop mutual understanding of one another as persons. Interventions are directed toward helping organization members to be more comfortable in being authentically themselves with one another, and the degree of mutual caring and concern is expected to increase. Sensitivity training using T-Groups is a basic intervention strategy at this level. T-Group educators emphasize increased personalization of relationships, the development of trust and openness, and the exchange of feelings. Interventions at this level deal directly and intensively with interpersonal emotionality. This is the first intervention strategy we have examined which is at a depth where the feelings of organization members about one another as persons are a direct focus of the intervention strategy. At the other levels, such feelings certainly exist and may be expressed, but they are not a direct concern of the intervention. The transition from the task orientation of instrumental process analysis to the feeling orientation of interpersonal process analysis seems, as I shall suggest later, to be a critical one for many organization members.

The deepest level of intervention which will be considered in this paper is that of intrapersonal analysis. Here, the consultant uses a variety of methods to reveal the individual's deeper attitudes, values, and conflicts regarding his own functioning, identity, and existence. The focus is generally on increasing the range of experiences which the individual can bring into awareness and cope with. The material may be dealt with at the fantasy or symbolic level, and the intervention strategies include many which are non-interpersonal and non-verbal. Some examples of this approach are the use of marathon T-Group sessions, the creative risk-taking laboratory approach of Byrd,[1] and some aspects of the task group therapy approach of Clark.[2] These approaches all tend to bring into focus very deep and intense feelings about one's own identity and one's relationships with significant others.

Although I have characterized deeper interventions as dealing increasingly with the individual's affective life, I do not imply that issues at less deep levels may not be emotionally charged. Issues of role differentiation, reward distribution, ability and performance evaluation, for example, are frequently invested with strong feelings. The concept of depth is concerned more with the *accessibility* and *individuality* of attitudes, values, and perceptions than it is with their strength. This narrowing of the common usage of the term, *depth*, is necessary to avoid the contradictions which occur when strength and inaccessibility are confused. For instance, passionate value confrontation and bitter conflict have frequently occurred between labor and management over economic issues which are surely toward the surface end of my concept of depth.

229

In order to understand the importance of the concept of depth for choosing interventions in organizations, let us consider the effects upon organization members of working at different levels.

The first of the important concomitants of depth is the degree of dependence of the client on the special competence of the change agent. At the surface end of the depth dimension, the methods of intervention are easily communicated and made public. The client may reasonably expect to learn something of the change agent's skills to improve his own practice. At the deeper levels, such as interpersonal and intrapersonal process analyses, it is more difficult for the client to understand the methods of intervention. The change agent is more likely to be seen as a person of special and unusual powers not found in ordinary men. Skills of intervention and change are less frequently learned by organization members, and the change process may tend to become personalized around the change agent as leader. Programs of change which are so dependent upon personal relationships and individual expertise are difficult to institutionalize. When the change agent leaves the system, he may not only take his expertise with him, but the entire change process as well.

A second aspect of the change process which varies with depth is the extent to which the benefits of an intervention are transferable to members of the organization not originally participating in the change process. At surface levels of operations analysis and performance evaluation, the effects are institutionalized in the form of procedures, policies, and practices of the organization which may have considerable permanence beyond the tenure of individuals. At the level of instrumental behavior, the continuing effects of intervention are more likely to reside in the informal norms of groups within the organization regarding such matters as delegation, communication, decision-making, competition and collaboration, and conflict resolution.

At the deepest levels of intervention, the target of change is the individual's inner life; and if the intervention is successful, the permanence of individual change should be greatest. There are indeed dramatic reports of cases in which persons have changed their careers and life goals as a result of such interventions, and the persistence of such change appears to be relatively high.

One consequence, then, of the level of intervention is that with greater depth of focus the individual increasingly becomes both the target and the carrier of change. In the light of this analysis, it is not surprising to observe that deeper levels of intervention are increasingly being used at higher organizational levels and in scientific and service organizations where the contribution of the individual has greatest impact.

An important concomitant of depth is that as the level of intervention becomes deeper, the information needed to intervene effectively becomes less available. At the less personal level of operations analysis, the information is often a matter of record. At the level of performance evaluation, it is a matter of observation. On the other hand, reactions of others to a person's work style are less likely to be discussed freely, and the more personal responses to his interpersonal style are even less likely to be readily given. At the deepest levels, important information may not be available to the individual himself. Thus, as we go deeper, the consultant must use more of his time and skill uncovering information which is ordinarily private and hidden. This is one reason for the greater costs of interventions at deeper levels of focus.

Another aspect of the change process which varies with the depth of intervention is the personal risk and unpredictability of outcome for the individual. At deeper levels, we deal with aspects of the individual's view of himself and his relationships with others which are relatively untested by exposure to the evaluations and emotional reactions of others. If in the change process the individual's self-perceptions are strongly disconfirmed, the resulting imbalance in internal forces may produce sudden changes in behavior, attitudes, and personality integration.

Because of the private and hidden nature of the processes into which we intervene at deeper levels, it is difficult to predict the individual impact of the change process in advance. The need for clinical sensitivity and skill on the part of the practitioner thus increases, since he must be prepared to diagnose and deal with developing situations involving considerable stress upon individuals.

The foregoing analysis suggests a criterion by which to match intervention strategies to particular organizational problems. It is *to intervene at a level no deeper than that required to produce enduring solutions to the problems at hand*. This criterion derives directly from the observations above. The cost, skill demands, client dependency, and variability of outcome all increase with depth of intervention. Further, as the depth of intervention increases, the effects tend to locate more in the individual and less in the organization. The danger of losing the organization's investment in the change with the departure of the individual becomes a significant consideration.

Autonomy increases depth of intervention

While this general criterion is simple and straightforward, its application is not. In particular, although the criterion should operate in the direction of less depth of intervention, there is a general trend in modern organizational life which tends to push the intervention level ever deeper. This trend is towards increased self-direction of organization members and increased independence of external pressures and incentives. I believe that there is a direct relationship between the autonomy of individuals and the depth of intervention needed to effect organizational change.

Before going on to discuss this relationship, I shall acknowledge freely that I cannot prove the existence of a trend toward a general increase in freedom in individuals within organizations. I intend only to assert the great importance of the degree of individual autonomy in determining the level of intervention which will be effective.

In order to understand the relationship between autonomy and depth of intervention, it is necessary to conceptualize a dimension which parallels and is implied by the depth dimension we have been discussing. This is the dimension of predictability and variability among persons in their responses to the different kinds of incentives which may be used to influence behavior in the organization. The key assumption in this analysis is that the more unpredictable and unique is the individual's response to the particular kinds of controls and incentives one can bring to bear upon him, the more one must know about that person in order to influence his behavior.

Most predictable and least individual is the response of the person to economic and bureaucratic controls when his needs for economic income and security are high. It is not necessary to delve very deeply into a person's inner processes in order to influence his behavior if we know that he badly needs his income and his position and if we are in a position to control his access to these rewards. Responses to economic and bureaucratic controls tend to be relatively simple and on the surface.

Independence of economic incentive

If for any reason organization members become relatively uninfluenceable through the manipulation of their income and economic security, the management of performance becomes strikingly more complex; and the need for more personal information about the individual increases. Except very generally, we do not know automatically or in advance what styles of instrumental or interpersonal interaction will be responded to as negative or positive incentives by the individual. One person may appreciate close supervision and direction; another may value independence of direction. One may prefer to work alone; another may function best when he is in close communication with others. One may thrive in close, intimate, personal interaction; while others are made uncomfortable by any but cool and distant relationships with colleagues.

What I am saying is that when bureaucratic and economic incentives lose their force for whatever reason, the improvement of performance *must* involve linking organizational goals to the individual's attempts to meet his own needs for satisfying instrumental activities and interpersonal relationships. It is for this reason that I make the assertion that increases in personal autonomy dictate change interventions at deeper and more personal levels. In order to obtain the information necessary to link organizational needs to individual goals, one must probe fairly deeply into the attitudes, values, and emotions of the organization members.

If the need for deeper personal information becomes great when we intervene at the instrumental and interpersonal levels, it becomes even greater when one is dealing with organization members who are motivated less through their transactions with the environment and more in response to internal values and standards. An example is the researcher, engineer, or technical specialist whose work behavior may be influenced more by his own values and standards of creativity or professional excellence than by his relationships with others. The deepest organizational interventions at the intra-personal level may be required in order to effect change when working with persons who are highly self-directed.

232

Let me summarize my position about the relationship among autonomy, influence, and level of intervention. As the individual becomes less subject to economic and bureaucratic pressures, he tends to seek more intangible rewards in the organization which come from both the instrumental and interpersonal aspects of the system. I view this as a shift from greater external to more internal control and as an increase in autonomy. Further shifts in this direction may involve increased independence of rewards and punishments mediated by others, in favor of operation in accordance with internal values and standards.

I view organizations as systems of reciprocal influence. Achievement of organization goals is facilitated when individuals can seek their own satisfactions through activity which promotes the goals of the organization. As the satisfactions which are of most value to the individual change, so must the reciprocal influence systems, if the organization goals are to continue to be met.

If the individual changes are in the direction of increased independence of external incentives, then the influence systems must change to provide opportunities for individuals to achieve more intangible, self-determined satisfactions in their work. However, people are more differentiated, complex, and unique in their intangible goals and values than in their economic needs. In order to create systems which offer a wide variety of intangible satisfactions, much more private information about individuals is needed than is required to create and maintain systems based chiefly on economic and bureaucratic controls. For this reason, deeper interventions are called for when the system which they would attempt to change contains a high proportion of relatively autonomous individuals.

There are a number of factors promoting autonomy, all tending to free the individual from dependence upon economic and bureaucratic controls, which I have observed in my work with organizations. Wherever a number of these factors obtain, it is probably an indication that deeper levels of intervention are required to effect lasting improvements in organizational functioning. I shall simply list these indicators briefly in categories to show what kinds of things might signify to the practitioner that deeper levels of intervention may be appropriate.

The first category includes anything which makes the evaluation of individual performance difficult:

A long time span between the individual's actions and the results by which effectiveness of performance is to be judged.

Non-repetitive, unique tasks which cannot be evaluated by reference to the performance of others on similar tasks.

Specialized skills and abilities possessed by an individual which cannot be evaluated by a supervisor who does not possess the skills or knowledge himself.

The second category concerns economic conditions:

Arrangements which secure the job tenure and/or income of the individual.

A market permitting easy transfer from one organization to another (e.g., engineers in the US aerospace industry).

Unique skills and knowledge of the individual which make him difficult to replace.

233

The third category includes characteristics of the system or its environment which lead to independence of the parts of the organization and decentralization of authority such as:

An organization which works on a project basis instead of producing a standard line of products.

An organization in which subparts must be given latitude to deal rapidly and flexibly with frequent environmental change.

The ethics of delving deeper

I should like to conclude the discussion of this criterion for depth of intervention with a brief reference to the ethics of intervention, a problem which merits considerably more thorough treatment than I can give it here.

There is considerable concern in the United States about invasion of privacy by behavioral scientists. I would agree that such invasion of privacy is an actual as well as a fantasied concomitant of the use of organizational change strategies of greater depth. The recourse by organizations to such strategies has been widely viewed as an indication of greater organizational control over the most personal and private aspects of the lives of the members. The present analysis suggests, however, that recourse to these deeper interventions actually reflects the greater *freedom* of organization members from traditionally crude and impersonal means of organizational control. There is no reason to be concerned about man's attitudes or values or interpersonal relationships when his job performance can be controlled by brute force, by economic coercion, or by bureaucratic rules and regulations. The 'invasion of privacy' becomes worth the cost, bother, and uncertainty of outcome only when the individual has achieved relative independence from control by other means. Put another way, it makes organizational sense to try to get a man to *want* to do something only if you cannot *make* him do it. And regardless of what intervention strategy is used, the individual still retains considerably greater control over his own behavior than he had when he could be manipulated more crudely. As long as we can maintain a high degree of voluntarism regarding the nature and extent of an individual's participation in the deeper organizational change strategies, these strategies can work toward adapting the organization to the individual quite as much as they work the other way around. Only when an individual's participation in one of the deeper change strategies is coerced by economic or bureaucratic pressures, do I feel that the ethics of the intervention clearly run counter to the values of a democratic society.

Role of client norms and values in determining depth

So far our attention to the choice of level of intervention has focused upon locating the depth at which the information exists which must be exchanged to facilitate system improvement. Unfortunately, the choice of an intervention strategy cannot practically be made with reference to this criterion alone. Even if a correct diagnosis is made of the level at which the relevant information lies, we may not be able to work effectively at the desired depth because of client norms, values, resistances, and fears.

In an attempt to develop a second criterion for depth of intervention which takes such dispositions on the part of the client into account, I have considered two approaches which represent polarized orientations to the problem. One approach is based upon analyzing and overcoming client resistance; the other is based upon discovering and joining forces with the self-articulated wants or 'felt needs' of the client.

There are several ways of characterizing these approaches. To me, the simplest is to point out that when the change agent is resistance-oriented he tends to lead or influence the client to work at a depth greater than that at which the latter feels comfortable. When resistance-oriented, the change agent tends to mistrust the client's statement of his problems and of the areas where he wants help. He suspects the client's presentation of being a smoke screen or defense against admission of his 'real' problems and needs. The consultant works to expose the underlying processes and concerns and to influence the client to work at a deeper level. The resistance-oriented approach grows out of the work of clinicians and psycho-therapists, and it characterizes much of the work of organizational consultants who specialize in sensitivity training and deeper intervention strategies.

On the other hand, change agents may be oriented to the self-articulated needs clients. When so oriented, the consultant tends more to follow and facilitate the client in working at whatever level the latter sets for himself. He may assist the client in defining problems and needs and in working on solutions, but he is inclined to try to anchor his work in the norms, values, and accepted standards of behavior of the organization.

I believe that there is a tendency for change agents working at the interpersonal and deeper levels to adopt a rather consistent resistance-oriented approach. Consultants so oriented seem to take a certain quixotic pride in dramatically and self-consciously violating organizational norms. Various techniques have been developed for pressuring or seducing organization members into departing from organizational norms in the service of change. The 'marathon' T-Group is a case in point, where the increased irritability and fatigue of prolonged contact and lack of sleep move participants to deal with one another more emotionally, personally, and spontaneously than they would normally be willing to do.

I suspect that unless such norm-violating intervention efforts actually succeed in changing organizational norms, their effects are relatively short-lived, because the social structures and interpersonal linkages have not been created which can utilize for day-to-day problem-solving the deeper information produced by the inter-vention. It is true that the consultant may succeed in producing information, but he is less likely to succeed in creating social structures which can continue to work in his absence. The problem is directly analogous to that of the community developer who succeeds by virtue of his personal influence in getting villagers to build a school or a community center which falls into disuse as soon as he leaves because of the lack of any integration of these achievements into the social structure and day-to-day needs and desires of the community. Community developers have had to learn through bitter failure and frustration that ignoring or subverting the standards and norms of a social system often results in temporary success followed by a reactionary increase in resistance to the influence of the change agent. On the other hand, felt needs embody those problems, issues, and difficulties which have a high conscious priority on the part of community or organization members. We can expect individuals and groups to be ready to invest time, energy, and resources in dealing with their felt needs, while they will be relatively passive or even resistant toward those who attempt to help them with externally defined needs. Community developers have found that attempts to help with felt needs are met with greater receptivity, support, and integration within the structure and life of the community than are intervention attempts which rely primarily upon the developer's value system for setting need priorities.

The emphasis of many organizational change agents on confronting and working through resistances was developed originally in the practice of individual psychoanalysis and psychotherapy, and it is also a central concept in the conduct of therapy groups and sensitivity training laboratories. In all of these situations, the change agent has a high degree of environmental control and is at least temporarily in a high status position with respect to the client. To a degree that is frequently underestimated by practioners, we manage to create a situation in which it is more unpleasant for the client to leave than it is to stay and submit to the pressure to confront and work through resistances. I believe that the tendency is for behavioral scientists to overplay their hands when they move from the clinical and training situations where they have environmental control to the organizational consulting situation, where their control is sharply attenuated.

This attenuation derives only partially from the relative ease with which the client can terminate the relationship. Even if this most drastic step is not taken, the consultant can be tolerated, misled, and deceived in ways which are relatively difficult in the therapeutic or human relations training situations. He can also be openly defied and blocked if he runs counter to the strongly shared group norms, whereas when the consultant is dealing with a group of strangers, he can often utilize differences among the members to overcome this kind of resistance. I suspect that, in general, behavioral scientists underestimate their power in working with individuals and groups of strangers, and overestimate it when working with individuals and groups in organizations. I emphasize this point because I believe that a good many potentially fruitful and mutually satisfying consulting relationships are terminated early because of the consultant's taking the role of overcomer of resistance to change rather than that of collaborator in the client's attempts at solving his problems. It is these considerations which lead me to suggest my second criterion for the choice of organization intervention strategy: *to intervene at a level no deeper than that at which the energy and resources of the client can be committed to problem-solving and to change.* These energies and resources can be mobilized through obtaining legitimation for the intervention in the norms of the organization and through devising intervention strategies which have clear relevance to consciously felt needs on the part of the organization members.

The consultant's dilemma: felt needs v. deeper levels

Unfortunately, it is doubtless true that the forces which influence the conditions we desire to change often exist at deeper levels than can be dealt with by adhering to the criterion of working within organization norms and meeting felt needs. The level at which an individual or group is willing and ready to invest energy and resources is probably always determined partly by a realistic assessment of the problems and partly by a defensive need to avoid confrontation and significant change. It is thus not likely that our two criteria for selection of intervention depth will result in the same decisions when practically applied. It is not the same to intervene at the level where behavior-determining forces are most potent as it is to work on felt needs as they are articulated by the client. This, it seems to me, is the consultant's dilemma. It always has been. We are continually faced with the choice between leading the client into areas which are threatening, unfamiliar, and dependency-provoking for him (and where our own expertise shows up to best advantage) or, on the other hand, being guided by the client's own understanding of his problems and his willingness to invest resources in particular kinds of relatively familiar and non-threatening strategies.

When time permits, this dilemma is ideally dealt with by intervening first at a level where there is good support from the norms, power structure, and felt needs of organizational members. The consultant can then, over a period of time, develop trust, sophistication, and support within the organization to explore deeper levels at which particularly important forces may be operating. This would probably be agreed to, at least in principle, by most organizational consultants. The point at which I feel I differ from a significant number of workers in this field is that I would advocate that interventions should *always* be limited to the depth of the client's felt needs and readiness to legitimize intervention. I believe we should always avoid moving deeper at a pace which outstrips a client system's willingness to subject itself to exposure, dependency, and threat. What I am saying is that if the dominant response of organization members indicates that an intervention violates system norms regarding exposure, privacy, and confrontation, then one has intervened too deeply and should pull back to a level at which organization members are more ready to invest their own energy in the change process. This point of view is thus in opposition to that which sees negative reactions primarily as indications of resistances which are to be brought out into the open, confronted, and worked through as a central part of the intervention process. I believe that behavioral scientists acting as organizational consultants have tended to place overmuch emphasis on the overcoming of resistance to change and have underemphasized the importance of enlisting in the service of change the energies and resources which the client can consciously direct and willingly devote to problem solving.

What is advocated here is that, in general, we accept the client's felt needs or the problems he presents as real, and that we work on them at a level at which he can serve as a competent and willing collaborator. This position is in opposition to one which sees the presenting problem as more or less a smoke screen or barrier. I am

237

not advocating this point of view because I value the right to privacy of organization members more highly than I value their growth and development or the solution of organizational problems. (This is an issue which concerns me, but it is enormously more complex than the ones with which I am dealing in this paper.) Rather, I place first priority on collaboration with the client, because I do not think we are frequently successful consultants without it.

In my own practice, I have observed that the change in client response is frequently quite striking when I move from a resistance-oriented approach to an acceptance of the client's norms and definitions of his own needs. With quite a few organizational clients in the United States, the line of legitimacy seems to lie somewhere between interventions at the instrumental level and those focused on interpersonal relationships. Members who exhibit hostility, passivity, and dependence, when I initiate intervention at the interpersonal level, may become dramatically more active, collaborative, and involved when I shift the focus to the instrumental level. ,

If I intervene directly at the level of interpersonal relationships, I can be sure that at least some members, and often the whole group, will react with anxiety, passive resistance, and low or negative commitment to the change process. Furthermore, they express their resistance in terms of norms and values regarding the appropriateness or legitimacy of dealing at this level. They say things like, 'It isn't right to force people's feelings about one another out into the open'; 'I don't see what this has to do with improving organizational effectiveness'; 'People are being encouraged to say things which are better left unsaid.'

If I then switch to a strategy which focuses on decision-making, delegation of authority, information exchange, and other instrumental questions, these complaints about illegitimacy and the inappropriateness of the intervention are usually sharply reduced. This does not mean that the clients are necessarily comfortable or free from anxiety in the discussions, nor does it mean that strong feelings may not be expressed about one another's behavior. What is different is that the clients are more likely to *work with* instead of *against* me, to feel and express some sense of ownership in the change process, and to see many more possibilities for carrying it on among themselves in the absence of the consultant.

What I have found is that when I am resistance-oriented in my approach to the client, I am apt to feel rather uncomfortable in 'letting sleeping dogs lie'. When, on the other hand, I orient myself to the client's own assessment of his needs, I am uncomfortable when I feel I am leading or pushing the client to operate very far outside the shared norms of the organization. I have tried to indicate why I believe the latter orientation is more appropriate. I realize, of course, that many highly sophisticated and talented practitioners will not agree with me.

In summary, I have tried to show in this paper that the dimension of depth should be central to the conceptualization of intervention strategies. I have presented what I believe are the major consequences of intervening at greater or lesser depths, and from these consequences I have suggested two criteria for choosing the appropriate depth of intervention: first, *to intervene at a level no deeper than that required to produce enduring solutions to the problems at hand*;

and second, *to intervene at a level no deeper than that at which the energy and resources of the client can be committed to problem-solving and to change.*

I have analyzed the tendency for increases in individual autonomy in organizations to push the appropriate level of intervention deeper when the first criterion is followed. Opposed to this is the countervailing influence of the second criterion to work closer to the surface in order to enlist the energy and support of organization members in the change process. Arguments have been presented for resolving this dilemma in favor of the second, more conservative, criterion. The dilemma remains, of course; the continuing tension under which the change agent works is between the desire to lead and push, or to collaborate and follow. The middle ground is never very stable, and I suspect we show our values and preferences by which criterion we choose to maximize when we are under the stress of difficult and ambiguous client-consultant relationships.

References

1. BYRD, R. E. 'Training in a non-group'. *J. humanistic Psychol.*, Vol. 7, No. 1, 1967, pp. 18-27.
2. CLARK, J. V. 'Task group therapy'. Unpublished manuscript, U.C.L.A., 1966.

18. Towards a policy for health of the manager

Harold Bridger and Stephanie White

Appropriate and inappropriate stress

Much has already been written about the health of the manager or the executive, particularly in terms of stress diseases such as peptic ulcer and coronary thrombosis. There is evidence to suggest, however, that professional groups may be as liable to the latter disease, and in some cases more so. It is by no means true, in any case, that symptoms of overt physical illness are the sole indicators of stress or, so-called, fatigue. (The latter term is really a misnomer as was 'exhaustion' during the last war when cases of breakdown were given this euphemistic title.)

Attitudes to problems of emotional health are extremely diverse. For many, such problems do not exist except as something to do with neurotics and psychotics—and if not these, then one only has to 'pull one's socks up', 'pull oneself together' or 'put it out of one's mind'. The conception of the normal as only a difference of degree, rather than of kind, is becoming more current, despite its more painful implications. There is a reality about physical medicine, and it is socially acceptable to visit the doctor on that score. The same does not necessarily apply to psychological medicine, although together with the increase in jokes and cartoons about 'trick-cyclists' and informative programmes on radio and TV, there has been a growing understanding.

Apprehension lest strain or tension suggest that a manager is not fit to continue or be considered for promotion is an inhibiting factor in seeking help. Top management sanction is required if counselling facilities are to operate successfully, and even then they will need to earn the right to become a socially acceptable and necessary step to take in relevant circumstances. Few people realize that the insights and awareness to be gained in working through a problem of relationships in work or outside it may be a capital gain.

There is no suggestion here that stress is a bad thing. There is only one kind of person without conflicts—a dead one. It is, however, the degree of stress conducive to effective work and living which is the essential issue to be examined. To be

240

somewhat more exact, it is the external environment and circumstances which by their nature face the person with stresses of one kind or another. These may be tolerated more easily in one situation than in another. Strain will be felt by the person when he has difficulty in dealing with the particular task. Whether he succeeds in coping will depend on the degree of internal conflict aroused by the external situation and the capacity to tolerate it.

The changing nature of the manager's job

In all the various studies of stress all too little account has been taken of the process of interaction between the man and the organization—as he proceeds up the ladder, moves from one field of activity to another or from one country to another.[1]

As a manager he may be changing his job to a far greater extent when he moves from one level to another than he does by moving from one side of the business to another. This is especially true, however, of the three phases of management usually referred to as junior, middle, and senior. The demands made on managers in transition from one phase to another can be more clearly seen by examining the extent to which certain types of functions performed by all managers in their jobs are present and vary in each phase. These functions do not, of course, appear in isolation, but managers exercise them in the course of their work:

1 Policy formation and decision-making.
2 Taking, and giving advice.
3 Taking, and delegating, executive action.
4 Coordinating one's own actions with those of other managers.
5 Bringing on subordinates.
6 Taking into account the effects of political, social, economic, and techno-logical change on one's own activities and plans.

With each succeeding phase, these functions increase in complexity and import-ance for the manager and the business. For example, little or no policy formation is present in junior management work, but it is a *sine qua non* for senior managers in their jobs.

The term 'general manager' is usually applied to those who manage a group of managers. The diversity of specialities controlled by this group of managers make it impossible for the general manager to operate satisfactorily in any one of them himself; even if he has once managed in a specialist position he cannot be in touch with the immediate situations without bypassing the manager concerned and neglecting his own job.

Two of the main problems which face a man moving into a general management position are those of relinquishing a specialized technical, commercial, or marketing skill and developing the capacity to handle relationships, which forms a major part of the general manager's job. This involves moving away from a situation in which the manager can have a relatively high degree of certainty about the outcome of his decisions, to one in which much more ambiguity and uncertainty are involved. The manager is required to pay more attention to the specifically managerial component of his role, and can no longer rely to the same extent on technical expertise.

Managers spend much more time on problems related to the personnel function and in handling personal and intergroup relationships both inside and outside the business than they recognize. One investigation[2] has demonstrated this fact in a very interesting way. Although the junior manager is primarily concerned with specialist responsibilities in a narrowly delineated field, he is also responsible for the interrelationships between himself and other members of his team, and for the team's relationship with other subgroups of the organization. At middle levels of management, the responsibility for intergroup relations within the organization increases, and the senior manager is also responsible for relations between the organization and other groups in its environment. The handling of the complex relationships can be a very stressful task. The high level manager's involvement with groups outside the orbit of his own company brings him into contact with people from different backgrounds, holding different values, with whom communication is correspondingly more difficult. In these negotiations, he must be conscious of himself as a *representative* of his own organization. This means, first, that his conduct and comportment will be noted and taken to convey an impression of the company as a whole; second, that his representative status will involve responsibility for reconciling the interests of opposing groups—for reaching agreement with the 'outsiders' without losing the support of his sponsoring group.

Whether recognized or not, the strain on managers derives considerably from this context, and it is one that deserves greater acknowledgement and respect. The isolation and loneliness implicit in the general manager's job can too easily be glossed over by observing only the outward signs of relationships and apparent freedom which he has over his movements. From middle management upwards, this element of loneliness increases—not simply as a function of remoteness from the shop floor, but because of the importance of the decisions he is taking and, however friendly and cooperative his colleagues, superiors, and subordinates may be, he is always having to recognize the high attainment and experience they hold in their own right.

Top management and senior management make the broad policies and decisions which affect all the rest; they are ultimately responsible for ensuring that plans are carried out. Since they determine the main form and direction of the business, they are crucial to the organization. The care and attention given by managers to the emotional and physical well-being of people within their companies and departments requires that the organization invests as much and more in those who not only exercise such responsibilities, but are exposed to far greater stresses and strains.

From a health point of view as well, as from the need to develop the manager more adequately for his future, the greater the attention which can be paid to the stages of transition between one phase of management to another the better. While the same is true of movement from one job to another, the quality and amount of attention is different when considering movement from junior to middle, or middle to senior management. Stress is greatest at these points in time by the very nature of the change in quality of the roles assumed. No set pattern of methods can be given since the needs of people will vary. It is however all too easy to assume that because the person is ready and able to make the change that it is merely a question of taking another job. There will always be the question of how much can be left to the man and how much he requires help. As an example, one might suggest that the timing of management courses designed to assist in cases such as these should, whenever possible, be arranged to precede anticipated transition of a manager from one phase to another. Yet further assistance of another kind, e.g., tutorials with senior managers, counselling, etc., could be of help once the manager has had the chance of trying himself out in his new appointment.

The job and the manager

No job can be described *in vacuo*. The scope provided by a job is determined by the purpose and policies of the organization of which it is part, by the structure of that organization and the nature of other jobs in it; and not least, by the way those jobs are related to one another and the people occupying them. There is evidence to suggest that an inappropriately designed managerial job (e.g., which involves work relationships which cut across one another) will, of its own accord, affect adversely the performance of the manager occupying the job. In any situation of stress, it is therefore important to be able to assess how far the job divorced of its present job-holder is a viable one and not merely to treat it solely as a personal problem. Similarly, an inappropriate patterning of jobs can create greater interpersonal difficulties between the managers concerned than there might otherwise be.

Temporary or long-term pressures and policies, both internal and external, may, however, force an organization to adapt itself to certain less appropriate forms. But this is quite different from the much more dangerous situation when jobs are determined by a need to avoid interpersonal difficulties rather than by the functions they are intended to perform for the organization. This danger is reduced if the situation is clearly recognized, and the reasons known and accepted. While an organization may be flexible enough to contain inappropriate jobs and patterns of jobs, there is a distinct limit to the number and quality which can be maintained at any one time. An emergency or crisis allows for some tolerance in this connection, but under conditions of normal working the degree of tolerance required should be as low as possible.

In any intra- or inter-job conflict, repercussions on managers occupying such jobs—and others in the organization—will be inevitable, even with the best intentions and goodwill. Conscious stress can be appreciated and tackled to a degree, but unrecognized or unconscious stresses and their various forms of expression are much more difficult to spot and trace. In fact, such symptoms or 'forms of expression' are too often treated as if they were the real problems, and far from settling the issue, people are, without being at all aware of it, driven to use less obvious and less desirable channels for dealing with that stress.

While, therefore, it may be necessary to accept pressures and responsibilities which entail adaptation to less appropriate patterns of jobs, every example of it deserves examination with a view to deciding the course to be adopted. In some cases there will be no option, in others it may be a choice between (a) having the appropriate pattern of jobs and taking the risk of interpersonal difficulties, and (b) having inappropriate pattern of jobs in an attempt to avoid interpersonal problems. Best of all, it may be possible to redistribute functions and roles in such a way as not merely to avoid difficulties, but to create better jobs and patterns of jobs for all concerned.

However, where the job design is not at fault, stress may still arise because a particular manager is inappropriately placed. In this situation, it is not always the placement itself which gives rise to the greatest danger. Stress is certain to occur before very long, but the major problem is the length of time the manager remains in the job. Unless the difficulties are seen in reasonable time and alternative arrangements made, there are bound to be repercussions, not only on the effectiveness with which the tasks are carried out, but on subordinates as well. The manager may himself take steps to effect a change but often he may consider the job, however inappropriate, as a challenge which threatens his assessment as a manager—either in his own eyes or those of others.

The stress may for a long time have been noted by subordinates without it appearing so clear to his superior. Alternatively, it may be the reverse, or more apparent to colleagues. This may be because he presents himself differently to various executives by reason of the work he is doing with them. Generally speaking, however, the stress is perceived in different forms by all. He may, however, all too easily be written off as 'that kind of chap'—he may be—but an opportunity to reassess his position and to be redeployed where possible does more than change his job; those who remain know that something has been done by 'the concern'.

The capacity of the individual to fulfil the requirements of the roles appropriate to the level and responsibilities of the job may not always be available. Certain of the roles may be more readily assumed than others. Awareness of strengths and limitations will play an essential part in delegating and accepting delegation, effectively.* Failure to recognize the way he matches the requirements of his roles at the level and in the job he is doing must involve a degree of stress for the manager.

In an attempt to avoid stress, he may, for example, compensate by delegating overmuch of the role he dislikes, and too little of what he prefers, to others. Although it may appear to complicate matters, some managers may act on the reverse basis. In the former example, though oversimplified, we can at least become aware of the tendency to abdicate rather than delegate in certain roles. The more usual and better-known situation occurs when the manager or general manager is unable to delegate—very often without being aware of it. Many might be surprised or even shocked to learn that they are failing to do so in certain areas of their work, because they can always point to some delegated authority and responsibility. Where the manager delegates little, he is usually considering his subordinates as

---

* There is some danger of making a moral issue of delegation. The 'dynamics' of delegation are not the mystery they are sometimes made out to be—the real need is to discover why and how delegation may be more difficult for some than for others.

'hived off' parts of himself and not as independent managers in their own right whose activities he is coordinating and directing through his relationships with the group and each one of them. It must, however, be recognized that it is not only the subordinate managers who are operating under stress in these circumstances. The superior will also experience strain though he may well attribute it to other factors.

The manager is responsible not only for seeing that a given task is performed, but also for maintaining a satisfactory pattern of relationships within the group of people whom he works with. The pattern of delegation he adopts will have implications for the structure of the group as illustrated in the following section.

Forms of delegation

Whatever pattern he adopts, his relationship to his subordinates will be significantly affected by the extent to which both of them feel free to express to each other their feelings about their relationship. Where the superior and subordinate share responsibility for the task which the subordinate is doing they should examine what they are *doing together* to fulfil this responsibility.

Since no manager is perfect—or should be expected to be—it is necessary to differentiate between the more and less insightful managers; those who are more realistically aware of personal attributes and lacks—and those who project or displace their deficiencies on external events, subordinates, colleagues, superiors, etc. It is possible to make a hypothesis at this point—the greater the awareness, the less the stress. A corollary of this assumption would be that the manager who can make or accept (not simply because he is told) a realistic appraisal of his capacities is more likely to delegate appropriate parts of all his roles than others.

The variations on the above theme are, of course, infinite. But in the activities of managers performing the functions outlined in 'Changing Nature of the Manager's Job' above, we can observe the degree to which the nature of delegating authority and responsibility is defensive (against stress—and awareness) or realistic. Nor should we forget that every manager and general manager is part of yet another group responsible to a more senior manager—and at the very top, responsible to a board and shareholders. Managers, therefore, need to be able to accept delegated powers. Corresponding problems exist in the relationship between line (executive) managers and those operating in advisory and service departments, even though the character of the problems is different.

Finally, it is salutary to bear in mind that the nature of a management job can only be discovered through the manager occupying it and through those with whom he comes into contact in the course of his work. This, in turn, suggests that managers have much to gain from training and experience in studying jobs. This is far from the simple exercise it may seem to be at first sight since besides the technical and other aspects of the functions concerned there are the social and psychological consequences which need to be taken into account.

The individual and the organization

It is all too seldom taken into account that the personal image of a company, the wider concern, their respective objectives, methods of functioning, and so on, varies considerably from manager to manager. Even where the same words are used, the 'music behind the words' convey the personal differences in interpretation. This is to be expected since, with vastly different histories of experience in terms of relationships established, function, side of the business, level and responsibilities as well as personal fantasies which everyone gives the organization to which one belongs, there will be a perception of the company which is the person's own. People expect those outside the company to have a different perception of it, but they like to think that those 'in it' have the same perception, and the degree to which it is commonly felt as 'good' provides the basis for the 'loyalty'. The degree to which the perception is held in common is an important factor, not only in the morale, but in the capacity to operate as an integrated force to achieve objectives. This does not mean, as is suggested by W. H. Whyte,[1] that people have to lose their personal independence and identities. Where the accent is on perception as distinct from denial of it, the gain is worth the effort necessary to provide people with the means of deepening and widening their perceptions. This does not suggest that managers should be given more to see, but rather that they be given the opportunity to develop the capacity to perceive.

Policies designed to increase the managers' awareness that they have a shared 'holding' in the company are far from the idea of attempting to create the 'organization man'—that is, so long as the methods used do not by inference, as distinct from intention, implicitly convey the 'organization man' message. Respect for the personal image allows for freedom of ideas, creativity and purposeful action to be consistent with the attainment of common objectives. In technical (social science) language, this personal image is called the 'reference group'. It is introduced here because it also describes the process by which people compare and assess what they are doing, and try to determine the degree to which they might 'succeed' in the organization. Consciously (and unconsciously), the manager is continually confronted by the realities of the organization, and often by decisions, attitudes and behaviour of other managers which do not always fit the pattern of 'his concern'. I am not here speaking of business decisions on which he might have other views, but of those actions which surprise him—one way or the other: 'I would not have believed such a thing could happen', 'It was far too generous', and so on. The personal fantasy which plays such an important part of the personal image derives from the same source as the imaginative and creative powers which the manager can apply in the course of his work. Enhancement or damage to 'his concern' (it is worth noting that the word 'concern' has both its meanings here) can therefore act as an encouragement or constraint on the use of his attributes. Hence the importance of the message (or 'music' as it was referred to earlier) conveyed by the observations he is able to make of the relationships existing between senior managers, between the units they control, and so on.

His own senior managers are, of course, in a special position in this respect. They represent the 'example' and standard against which personal images are matched. Their policies and actions in achieving objectives and dealing with people and especially their way of going about things, may convey much more than is said in words. On the one hand, ineffectual compromise, a failure to take advice, not

246

taking appropriate executive action or other negative approaches to the functions already mentioned may cause stress or even teach the lesson: 'So it is all right for me to do that, too.' Sympathy and understanding may be there, too, but, as distinct from this, a weak concession is a yielding up of a personal standard. On the other hand, imaginative pursuit of a manager's roles to the best of the individual's capacity is the real answer to dangers of complacency, cynicism, contempt, scapegoating, and similar responses. Nor must this aspect be considered only from the point of view of colleagues and subordinates. Every manager is in the limelight in this connection—and the glare becomes greater the more senior he becomes.

In the efforts made to create a sense of unified purpose and to induce cooperation in common objectives, much emphasis is laid by top managements on loyalty to the concern. Moral pressure is often added to personal and group loyalties already present in the individual. The 'fringe' and welfare benefits gained by being a member of an organization can, in this sense, be experienced as predominantly binding and restrictive, rather than as opportunities conferred on the individual which allow him to mobilize his capacities more easily and effectively. Where morale is high, emphasis placed on such 'loyalties' is likely to coincide with the individual's own wish to accentuate the attribute. Where morale is lower, such emphasis may well be felt as a sign of top management's uncertainty of the organization's cohesion. The constituent units within a large decentralized organization may vary considerably in the degree to which these loyalties operate.

Reconciling objectives, values, and attitudes to authority

Conflict of loyalties within an organization is much less of a problem for those who will not expect to go much further than junior management than it is for those who have the potential to enter wider orbits. Many senior managers, who themselves have moved up the ladder by steps in different companies, may tend to rationalize their overlong retention of promising managers who should be getting wider experience. The senior managers are often aware of the implicit contradiction in their actions, and use loyalty to the company as a means of coping with the problem. The subordinate managers concerned, on the other hand, may collude with this approach, not because they agree with it, but because they fear to 'cross' their superior who they feel can further or mar their future career. Both levels, in these and similar circumstances are operating under stress.

William M. Evan[3] has suggested that the failure to develop appropriate machinery for assessing the performance of junior and middle managers may give rise to some of the syndromes of the organization man mentality. The manager becomes too tied to the good opinion of his superior, loyalty to the organization is too highly valued, and conformist attitudes are fostered.

At some time in his career, every manager reaches a ceiling, even if it is the 'top'. The measure of satisfaction with the position attained depends not only on the degree to which the job meets capacities as perceived by superiors, but how far the individual can accept it, too. The manager himself may really agree with the decision in one part of himself yet be unable to accept a situation which is not commensurate with the personal aspirations he holds in yet another part. He may otherwise experience the family pressure from a wife whose aspirations for him are greater than his own. There is also the not infrequent case of the manager who, for various reasons, gets overlooked at an important stage in his career and may later be too old to take into consideration.

It is far from unusual for a manager or senior manager to wonder at some stage in his career whether he could not find greater satisfaction or scope with another company. The large, decentralized organization, particularly one of an international character, provides opportunities for change which allows for job and company change depending on the needs of the business and the suitability of the manager. On the other hand, tempting offers, not necessarily or entirely financial, sometimes give the manager food for thought. Family considerations may play a part in this, too, as for example, when the place would enable the family to settle in a known social setting. In the United States, the culture pattern supports the move from organization to organization as an accepted form of development and experience. In this country, there is still evidence of the tradition of remaining with one particular company. While this may be strongest at lower levels, it is also true of managers. The decision to stay or leave is never an easy one, even if it is made quickly. The pros and cons are probably discussed with the manager's wife and his intimate friends, but it is not easy for the manager to discuss them with colleagues or superiors, though he may have a close friend elsewhere in the business. The manager has to assess his prospects with his present company—which in themselves have no certainty—with those in an unknown company. The situation involves much more, however, than balancing one set of advantages and disadvantages against another. Feelings and conflicts may be aroused which may have little to do with the real nature of the decision. It might be better for the manager and the concern if he were able to be more aware of what was at stake—whether he decided to stay or leave. Opportunities taken to work through problems of this kind have done much more than enable the manager to reach his decision.

Family and social life

When a woman marries a sailor she often feels she is competing with his ship in his affections, and, to some extent, this is true of many men's work. It is particularly true of the wife and growing family of a man who enters industry and progressively moves upwards in commerce or industry. Although he may stay in the same organization, he is, for them, continually 'changing his job'. The family has then to accept conditions imposed by his advancement, and to observe his increasing emotional and time investment in his business affairs. Depending on the original background circumstances of husband and wife, there may also be the problems of adaptation to a new economic status. Geographical moves may involve more of a domestic upheaval than the moving operation. Many other real life issues of this kind could be listed with their corresponding meanings for the family.

Educational requirements for the children should, however, receive special mention. They do not usually impinge on the family in the early stage of the man's career, but, from a financial point of view, it is frequently budgeted for from birth of the child—and future career aspirations are emotionally 'mortgaged' to provide opportunities for the children, consistent with parental wishes and knowledge of educational conditions. The awareness of what is happening in recruitment and selection schemes, the rapid trend of industrial management itself towards becoming a profession, all form part of the base line from which considerations of future possibilities for children can stem. The children may not enter industry, but comparisons will be made with it when considering other vocations. In one sense, the preoccupation with the right schooling for the children and later the appropriate exploration and direction towards a career is common to most families, but these considerations mean, understandably, even more for managers and professional families. There is a greater need to have the best advice—as they are used to in their own activities—and in dealing with family affairs generally, it is to be expected that a 'transfer' of experience and training takes place. It is not crudely a question of taking one's management methods home and being the 'manager', but using one's knowledge as a resource for family well-being. In any case, being a husband and a father means being a manager, though of a different kind. Being one half of the management team is not possible in a family group where there is a distinct limit to the number of separate responsibilities possible; the common ground is the most vital, however the rest may be dealt with.

In our counselling experience and vocational guidance work, experience shows how important the need is to have the chance of giving the kind of advice which allows parents and children to make up their own minds—not to be told what to do.[4] It is disastrous for counselling consultants to take away from parents the most important common grounds—and one of these is joint decisions about their children—even when parents appear to want it. At the same time, there are often occasions when such parents are faced with various courses, the implications of which they cannot easily discover. These do not just simply relate to this or that school, but much more frequently to reaching the best decisions for future development in various circumstances. Among these come problems of separation and any symptoms which may indicate emotional disturbance.

The manager, like other fathers, needs to be responsible for his own family affairs in association with his wife, but there are circumstances and points at which the opportunity to have the appropriate counselling would enable them to retain their responsibilities, without displacing their worries onto each other or the children, or undermining their effectiveness in their independent and respective fields. The facilities for finding the appropriate source to handle difficulties at the right time—and not, as so often happens, so late that a relatively accessible problem has become much more difficult—is a very necessary provision.

As his career develops, the manager or professional man tends more and more to pay for services in the home to leave himself free to devote his interests towards the business and towards the family itself. His work becomes more and more his hobby. Those interested in art, music, etc., do retain some measure of relaxation from these sources—but often as much because they are common grounds with their wives—and later, the children. Other forms of relaxation are seldom so much sought as accepted through opportunities offered by friends. Later on in life, when he faces retirement, he has to take stock, and may find himself relatively unprepared for the next phase. This is becoming less true as managers realize that outside interests—social and community ones—can offer tremendous opportunities for people with their experience and knowledge. The main difficulty lies in the fact that they have so little chance—or even incentive—to grow the roots necessary while they are still occupied fully in business affairs. Not a little depends on their capacity to face the implications of retirement when they are still in middle age.

Women experience an overt sign in the menopause which, with its psychological consequences, helps them to realize the sequence of events. The fortunate ones are able to face their depression and cope with it effectively; others need more help to deal with the situation effectively. It is not so widely recognized that, even though the overt sign is not present, the psychological equivalents occur in men, but progression at work and very often moving to the height of his powers at the time, as well as family and social interests, provide the man with valuable defences in continuing to fulfil his creative drives. On the other hand, these defences can also prevent him from making constructive use of depressive feelings associated with the inevitable process of life and death. In managers who have reached their ceiling some time beforehand, the effects are more apparent, and not an uncommon feature is the unrest and dissatisfaction with themselves and their careers at this point. The organization may be used for displacement of emotional forces—as may the family itself. Much needs to be explored in this field and it has only been touched on here, but there is every reason to suggest that this phase in a man's life needs special consideration by the organization as well as by the man himself. The senior general managers may appear to be 'better off' in this respect and may even find it difficult to understand why a good subordinate manager should behave in such or such a way. Of course, it will not always be for the reasons under discussion, but very often attempts will be made to deal with a particular difficulty presented, the solution of which is only part of the problem.

Reverting to more general issues in family life, there are usually areas in which the manager or professional man likes to make his contribution—whether it is to gardening or some other activity which can represent the 'home'. He may have been a do-it-yourself fan in the early days, but as time goes on this frequently diminishes. At the same time as he wishes to pay for more services (and in one sense is able to do so), there is the growing need for money to pay for the domestic, educational, social, and other commitments, consistent with the society in which he lives. This conflict is a very real one for managers whose incomes are heavily taxed and who, however senior, are not owners of the business in which they carry such heavy responsibilities. Except in terms of assurance policies and pension schemes, additional income provides diminishing returns.

Of course, family life and the capacity of the family to meet and change with the manager's own development depends a great deal on the personalities of husband and wife—but even more so on their mature basic relationship. The willingness and preparedness of the wife to adjust and make family and personal sacrifices for her husband's career are not, however, always the simple answer.

There would be no solution in suggesting that managers marry women with a capacity for 'resignation'. Developing interests in the home, children, and outside interests naturally play a considerable part, but consciously or unconsciously there is a need for the extent of the common ground to be adequate in the wife's terms as well as the husband's. Interest in the career and business activities may play their part early on and even continue in one way or another, but even where this happens, it is impossible to bridge the real gap created by an independent, full, and complex management job. The capacity to respect the husband's independent career involves more than conscious effort. Coming to terms with rivalry with the organization, or even with the husband, is not an easy matter for many wives. For some, it is sufficient to have the occasional grumble or 'family joke' about the organization's demands. These are the expressions of feeling which help to attack or laugh off the problem together, but they are also signs of the effort required to keep the relationship and the career 'good'.

There is one matter which deserves special attention in this context. The overseas appointment, when there are possibilities for development and where actual promotion may be involved, carries special implications for the family. Again, there will be tremendous variations, but the case of the husband who wants to go and cannot because of his wife is not uncommon—and provides an example of many problems in this sphere. While the decision itself may be solved by his not going, there remains the wife's knowledge that but for her he would have had a wonderful opportunity, and there is his knowledge that but for her he would have gone. The family carries a heavy burden, perhaps some form of predecision and postdecision counselling should be available to the family if required: in very many, if not all, cases this should be available when there is agreement to go together. On what basis has the decision been reached? The senior management concerned has to determine how far a particular manager will be suitable for the overseas post which will require the most effective use of his capacities. It may be that besides providing candidates with the opportunity for exploring the nature of the job and the responsibilities involved and deciding which one would appear to fit it best, that the organization might offer facilities to enable the man and, if desired, his wife to assess the family position more fully. It would naturally be imperative that in the latter case professional confidence was maintained.

When stress occurs between husband and wife, it does not always appear directly as such. Problems in the home, emotional disturbance in a child, external situations with friends and relatives—all very real in themselves—can also be used unconsciously to require the husband's personal attention and signify that the common ground is felt to be invaded. This is not abnormal and, in fact, the absence of such problems would not only raise questions about the relationship, but would be quite remarkable. Again, the matter of quality and degree of the situations presented is the relevant issue. Beyond a certain point, the husband may begin to feel 'pestered' and the wife unhappy about 'bothering' him. The solution of one problem is followed by another. The wife may herself develop a 'complaint' or illness. Variations are, of course, infinite, but all of them indicate a syndrome which merits more attention. It is difficult to determine, as in all similar situations, at what point

251

the need for help begins. The greatest danger lies in the time and effort spent by the husband and wife in endeavouring unsuccessfully to sort it out for themselves. Capacity to do so with awareness and success—by effective, not ineffectual, compromise or rationalization—can be of immense value to both. On the other hand, the damage done can at times be irreversible unless assistance is sought.

Dr Bott[5] has shown how the 'normal' family varies in its pattern of living and how the pattern developed relates to the patterns of the families in which husband and wife grew up. She also indicates the way in which the family, through its own course of development, husband's career, and so on, determines its own pattern, based on the extent to which independent or joint connections are made with groups in the other's 'networks'.

When one considers the importance assigned to the recruitment, selection, training and development of managers, because of the comparative rarity of men with the capacity to fill the complex management tasks of today and tomorrow, it becomes equally important not to waste or neglect the investment of resources made by the manager and the organization. The manager's family plays a vital part in the maintenance and success of his endeavours. While there should never be any invasion of a man's private life, nor should he have his responsibility for his family taken away, the interaction of the manager's family and his career can be a crucial factor. His emotional health is as vital to the ultimate objectives of the organization as is his physical health and his capacity to use his intellectual powers and the roles described earlier in this paper. It is not that the industrial manager's family is different from any other, but rather that some industrial organizations have matured faster than professional associations in being prepared to consider these issues.

Considerations in developing a policy for the health of managers

The organization's investment in managers at all levels is high, as is the managers' investment of themselves in the business. It is important for everyone in it, and for large numbers of people outside it, that the management force should be fully effective. No one can take away the inevitable stress involved by a general manager having to take a 'calculated risk' in the course of his responsibilities, but the business does provide him with numerous resources (e.g., in the shape of advisory and service departments) which not only enable him to come to better decisions, but can also have the effect (whether initially intended or not) of coping with the stress. For although the general manager still has to take the decision himself, there is a sharing of the problems with others in a constructive way. (This assumes relationships to match the intention.) In the same way, there are many features within the working life of the organization which though not instituted for the primary purpose of diminishing or preventing undue strain in the manager, do in fact make a significant contribution in that regard. A few further examples are listed below, to which will be added a comment on the 'emotional health component'.

The selection procedure itself can be designed in such a way as to increase the candidate's knowledge of himself and the organization. It can elucidate the 'psychological contract' which the individual is making with the organization. It can help the candidate to understand himself and his aspirations more fully, and at the same time increase his knowledge of the organization. He is then in a position to see how far what it can offer matches his own aspirations. Whereas the immediate task of the selection board is that of seeing each candidate against the demands of management roles in various sides and functions of the business it can provide an educational experience for selectors, too.

Although the contribution to the development of those taking part could rightly be said to be all too brief, it does represent the type and quality of experience which, if reproduced in other directions and ways, can add to management education generally. It also contributes, however, to an awareness of the aetiology and growth of stress conditions with their consequent effects on the individual and the business. In such a process, there must also occur an implicit awareness of personal attitudes through comparing individual observations and perceptions. The preparedness to take part in such a process should not be regarded as an easy matter. To express views and opinions on candidates involves declaring personal predelictions and personal conceptions of management.

Study groups, courses, and conferences held by the organization can be said to contribute towards health. This is particularly true of group methods (so long as the 'gang' dynamic is not in operation) and tutoring of the best kind. The growth of sincerity and tolerance under conditions of learning with and from each other can be as important a source of awareness as it can be an opportunity to acquire knowledge. At the same time, it cannot be said that all opportunities of this kind achieve this objective. It is also possible to derive the right kind of technical information under conditions—in groups or otherwise—which are the reverse of therapeutic.

The management appraisal procedure can be a tremendous force for better understanding between superior and subordinate. The interviews cannot by reason of the relationship involved, really be counselling interviews in the professional sense, but they can achieve a direct mutual appreciation and a healthy working relationship provided the participants are capable of it.

Professional counselling can be of distinct value to those who are able to make the initial approach. We have learned that where possibilities of this kind exist, the result is to increase the capacity of the manager to deal with his work and relationships both inside and outside the business—not simply to lessen or prevent stress. Equally, when counselling has taken the form of providing educational, vocational, or personal help for a child or wife it could also be regarded as contributing to the manager's development—and not just providing him with a fringe benefit.

The development of a policy of health for managers is not solely a medical problem—it concerns the managers themselves and how far they perceive it as making a valuable contribution to their organization and themselves. The role of the medical officer in industry is growing in importance. To an increasing extent, he has become the adviser more easily and satisfactorily consulted by the manager in preference to his GP. Naturally, this depends considerably upon the relationship between the manager and his GP, but the National Health Service has probably intensified this trend. Even the senior manager today, for example, has seriously to consider economies, since he is likely to have aspirations for his children and heavy expenses in various family commitments, and will therefore have a NHS doctor, but, for certain kinds of advice, they will turn to a doctor who can understand their problems. Whether justifiable or not, it is often the case that the manager feels that the company doctor is more likely to be in touch with the situation and with the most relevant sources for handling problems which do not come within his immediate medical capacity. The doctor, besides being in charge of the company medical service and having a personnel function role, has an increasingly important counselling role for the managers as individuals. In many circumstances, the doctor can do much on his own account but, as in the case of psychological problems, he may not always be the most appropriate adviser. Although, however, psychological treatment might be outside the medical officer's sphere by reason of his role in the company, irrespective of other considerations, there is a case for considering postgraduate training in this subject which would enable doctors to handle relevant issues themselves. Ultimately, therefore, the doctor must be concerned with the problem of discovering the most appropriate methods of dealing with stress situations, with the prevention of stress in managers and having the resources on which to draw in this regard, as well as dealing with strictly medical problems.

Where the medical adviser has a thorough knowledge of the working community, and the structure and roles within it, he may be in a position to indicate contributory factors to stress which can be remedied and prevented for the future. In this area, the doctor contributes to company, or departmental, policy and in particular, plays his special part as a manager.

Conclusion: change and the future

Stress must be understood in relation to the context in which it arises. Any attempt to cope with the overt signs of stress which does not tackle the underlying problems which have given rise to the symptoms, will be inadequate. The external pressures which the manager experiences as stressful may derive from the work situation, from his family life, or from the interface between these two and any others affecting his career or identity as a person.

There are relatively few men—if any—who are not 'adaptable to change' in one direction or another, but the capacity to adapt will vary enormously in different people. The so-called 'resistance to change' is really too general a term to be of much use in determining how to help people adapt to new situations. The components of such 'resistance' require to be identified in the case of groups as well as in individuals.

The increasing 'openness' of organizations to environments which are themselves subject to rapid change and turbulence, leads to the need for increasing complexity of junctions within the organizations, in an attempt to control those different aspects of the external world. Growth involves the management of uncertainty. Combined with the necessity of managing the internal interdependence of functions and activities, while coping with external economic and social change and technological and information 'explosions'. The division between 'challenge' and 'undue stress' will be increasingly less clear as we move into the 'seventies. Unless the health of the enterprise is good, even the younger men and women developing in the new environments and culture will find it difficult to adapt satisfactorily. Indeed, their hope must lie in members of the older generation who have the foresight not to retain the earlier structure of organization and authority patterns, but can engage with greater participation in the achievement of objectives.

References

1. WHYTE, W. H., *Organization Man,* London: Jonathan Cape, 1957, has some salutory things to say about the effect of the 'organization' on the manager, but it takes little account of the organization as a living organism affected by its structure and people occupying roles in it.
2. BURNS, T., 'The Directions of Activity and Communication on a Departmental Executive Group.' *Human Relations,* Vol. 7, 1954, p. 73.
3. EVAN, WILLIAM M., 'Organization Man and One Process of Law.' *American Sociological Review,* Vol. 26, 1961, pp. 540-7.
4. BRIDGER, HAROLD, 'From School to Work: A Process not a Procedure.' *New Era,* May 1952.
5. BOTT, ELIZABETH, *Family and Social Network.* London: Tavistock Publications, 1957.

PART SEVEN: Focus on improving the organization

To a few managers, organization effectiveness implies reaching a particular finite pitch of competitive performance. The four contributors in this final part, however, all suggest quite a different meaning. They put the emphasis on the *process* of improvement rather than on a specific product, or level of competence. More specifically they think in terms of organizations learning how to improve their own ways of managing themselves. In essence, they are concerned with the management of change.

One reading of the contemporary management scene is that everything seems to be in flux. It is not difficult to see that almost all organizations are working in an external environment that is becoming increasingly turbulent, while internally, work relations are becoming more ambiguous, and the available technology more complex. Furthermore, their workforce is more educated and perceptibly less willing to carry out instructions just because they have been told to do so.

Many organizations already accept the need to operate a different management style, if they are to generate the kind of decisions that will give them the quality of products their customers want. The problem is not whether to change, but how to change. The most obvious way for some is to tell their managers to operate differently; yet the limitations of cognitive changes by themselves have been demonstrated in previous articles. Moreover, it might flummox a theory X manager (and many others who believe they are not theory X by inclination) to be propositioned that they personally can obtain better results by adopting a more participative approach to man-management and the control of work groups. An outsider can say in good faith that they need to go through a process of conviction, and that a real change in behaviour will not come from being lectured. 'A man persuaded against his will, is of the same opinion still' But put oneself in the shoes of such theory X managers: they sense they are being asked to forego the security of their legitimate official authority. They believe they will be personally uncomfortable at being exposed to having their decisions contested by their subordinates.

All four chapters speak to this general concern. The organization wants better results: the individual needs assurance of the kind mentioned in chapter 16, if he is to consider changing his ways. So both the organization and the individual are the targets of change—though of different kinds. In chapter 19, William Eddy shows the necessity for taking learning into the organization and treating organization subunits as the critical targets for change; this may mean questioning the power base. In that case, what kinds of support are there inside the organization for such an attempt? He also itemizes some of the significant changes in training approaches between traditional training and organization development.

In chapter 20, Sheldon Davis asserts rightly that organization development is much more than sensitivity training. The need is for an organization to develop an internal capability to solve its own problems. Change must become self-supporting. This calls for a new kind of executive capable of confronting and working on difficult organization issues. Talking about the problem is by no means sufficient; he must also care for the individuals affected. He must be task-minded, outgoing, and capable, not defensive or agreeable. He must involve those very managers in fashioning ways to improve their management situation—ways which they will maintain when he has moved on to other problem areas.

The last two chapters can be seen as essays in 'responsible involvement'. They have been chosen because they demonstrate success experiences. Each, however, points to something much more than that. Chapter 21, by Alistair Mant is almost a kind of real-time education. Course curriculum and problems with business school staff can so easily be seen by MBA students as problems 'out there', which allows them to go on bitching at the authorities. When staff and students jointly attempt to look at the issue of a man being really responsible for his own learning, they are opening up new educational vistas. As one student said, 'learning about authority really matters in a management career. We spend one week on this and the remainder of the two years getting subject inputs that will soon be obsolete.' Is there something here that a young MBA can learn about himself and his learning which will stop him becoming outdated in ways that have befallen all recent management generations?

William J. Crockett illustrates so many points in chapter 22. At an experiential learning course for Presidents of US corporations, he had the mirror, 'It takes two to see one' (Samuel Culbert), placed before him. He saw that a change was needed in himself, first, before he could hope that new procedures and improvements, good in themselves, would be accepted and operated by others. As Deputy Under Secretary of State, US State Department, using, in his own terms, theory X approaches, he had already achieved much. This new knowledge about himself helped him to make far-reaching and effective departmental changes. The essential step was his ability to apply these insights about himself and his effect on others to his operational setting—to move from private thoughts to public works. Points of substance made by almost all the other writers about effective organizations and their managers are to be found in this successful organization development programme.

19. Management issues in organization development

William B. Eddy

The training function in business and public organizations has gained almost as much acceptance as has the field of education in American society. Yet organizational training is currently in a state of uncertainty and re-examination. It is common to find major discrepancies between the training director's aspirations and level of accomplishment, between the training curriculum and behavior change, and between program goals and organizational outcomes. A part of the difficulty involves attempts to move from a traditional personnel training function toward broader programs of organization development and change.

This paper examines some of the characteristics of organization development programs, as contrasted with more traditional efforts, and some of the issues which these new kinds of programs raise for management.

Traditionally, the training function in organizations has been viewed primarily as a segment of the operation designed to upgrade the skill levels of employees, both at the beginning of their employment and, later, as they changed roles or as new work methods were introduced. Upper level managers were rarely involved in the training programs. This view began to change with the appearance of 'executive development programs' sponsored by universities, the American Management Association, and other groups. The focus at this stage, however, was still primarily upon individual growth in special areas of competence, so that the individual could make a more significant contribution to the organization by exerting better judgement, making better decisions, bringing more knowledge to bear on problems, or dealing with people more diplomatically.

This philosophy of training is currently being re-examined. The potentials of training, or management development, or organization development, as instruments for changing not only individual components, but also the climate and operation of the entire organizational system, are being explored.

● Reproduced by special permission from *Behavioral Science and the Manager's Role,* Selected Readings, Series No. 9 1969.

Organizations as social systems

Before examining these efforts and their rationale, it may be useful to review some of the characteristics and implications of earlier practices in training. Many organizations were built upon the principles of bureaucratic structure and administrative management. The goal of the manager was to set up the organization as a rational, efficient system with rules, procedures, and authority to hold the system together and direct the work behavior of employees. Employees were viewed largely as individual components who bartered their job skills and energies in return for wages. Training was primarily on the job and was oriented towards bringing the level of technical skill performance up to acceptable standards. Preparation for management came through achievement of technical skills plus experience.

As more and more researchers became interested in the processes of organization and management, as the practice of management became better understood, and as the direction of more and more organizations was taken over by professional managers, the concept of the organization began to change—and with it the concept of training. Beginning with such projects as the Hawthorne Western Electric studies, it became clear that for purposes of understanding and dealing with the behavior of employees, it is more useful and valid to view the organization as a 'social system' than as a set of technical skills directed by rational rules. The factors which frequently make the difference in the total performance and effectiveness of the organization include not only the individual skill levels or work methods, but also the overall functioning of the organization as a series of interdependent parts. Some characteristics which often influence performance include the quality of communication in all directions, clarity and acceptance of individual and organizational objectives and goals, cooperation among laterally-related units, trust level, distribution and use of power, effectiveness in resolving intra-organizational conflict, and adaptability to change. These findings influenced organizations to shift a part of their training focus to the skill areas that have to do with effective human relationships and team conditions. Thus, many programs in leadership, human relations, and motivation and group dynamics have been developed. The problem with these programs is that they do not deal effectively with the system, but, again, work with individuals and hope that their behavior will influence or contribute to the overall situation. Follow-up research has demonstrated that this occurrence is somewhat unlikely to happen. Job performance is a result not only of individual competence, but also of the 'social role' of the employee as he operates within a framework of authority relationships, collaborative relationships, and communication patterns. Individuals who are taught new ideas or attitudes about organizational behavior outside the context of their own job often find it difficult and sometimes threatening to try to implement these new behaviors in the work setting. Thus, the focus has begun to shift towards organizational sub-units rather than individuals as the objects of training effort.

This organizational focus has encouraged training directors and consultants to look for new approaches to training and development. The traditional classroom techniques for transferring knowledge remain useful, but do not provide the entire

260

answer because they are not attuned to the need to bring about changes in social system behavior. Likewise, training methods based on individual learnings, separate and independent from the learnings of other members of the unit (as seen in the university classroom), have not proven particularly useful, because it is not the individual learnings, but the shared learnings, attitudes, and feelings that provide a basis for productive cooperation.

Another impetus for the search for new approaches to organizational training has been the recognition of a series of new, or at least newly recognized, conditions confronting organizations. These have been described in detail by Bennis[2] and others. Technology is advancing so rapidly that older more rigid organizational forms are sorely taxed. New approaches, such as project management, place a premium on such skill areas as rapid adaptation to change, teamwork, and temporary system (committee and task force) formation. Emerging societal values and the rise of professionalism influence employees to be less willing to be excluded from participation in goal-setting and decision-making. Complex products or functions require the pooling of varied technical resources into workable units. These and other developments have spurred the search for techniques useful in changing not only individual skill levels, but also the process of the organization.

The organizational development process

As the need to devise new ways of improving human effectiveness in organizations has become pressing, training directors, consultants, and social scientists have looked for educational approaches which are able to intervene at the system level. Ideas from the social psychology of attitude and social system change, group dynamics techniques, consulting and change agent skills, counselling, and personality theory currently form the nucleus of the field called 'organization development' or 'OD'. The term refers to no formal set of techniques—there are none—but to a general point of view which may be implemented in a variety of ways.

Case descriptions of organizational development programs and their rationale and methodology are beginning to appear. Events at Union Carbide (Burck[4]), TRW Systems (Davis[5]), Harwood Manufacturing Company (Marrow, Bowers and Seashore,[8]), and Esso Standard (Buchanan[3]), along with organizations studied by Argyris,[1] Mann,[7] and others, have been documented. Warren Bennis, Gordon Lippitt, Floyd Mann, Chris Argyris, Edgar Schein, and Robert Blake and Jane Mouton, are among those who have contributed to the literature in this field. Some of the common characteristics of many OD programs are listed.

1 They focus on the total organization or natural sub-organizational groupings (work units, teams, management levels) rather than individual employees as the object of training.

2 They emphasize experiential learning techniques (role-playing, problem-solving exercises, T-Groups) in addition to traditional lecture methods.

3 Their subject matter includes real problems and events that exist in the organization and often in the training group, rather than hypothetical cases or

examples. Often, there is gathering and analysis of organizational data—either formally or informally.

4 Emphasis is placed upon competence in interpersonnel relationships rather than upon task skills. Much of the content and method is based on the behavioral sciences rather than upon administrative management theory, operations research or personnel techniques—although these may be included as part of the program. The methodologies of the National Training Laboratories, Managerial Grid training, survey-feedback techniques and industrial psychology are often used.

5 Goals frequently have to do with developing group behavioral competence in areas such as communication, decision-making, and problem-solving, rather than understanding and retention of principles and theories. The trainer often sees himself more as consultant or change agent than expert-teacher.

6 They are frequently anchored in a humanistic value system which is committed to integrating individual needs and management goals, maximizing opportunity for human growth and development, and encouraging more open, authentic human relationships.

7 They are not intended to refute the traditional structural-functional conception of the organization, but to help remedy some of its major dysfunctions.

Many training directors and managers are aware of the increasing interest in organization development programs and would like to try them. However, they frequently run into significant difficulty in convincing top management of the value of this approach and in developing financial and policy support. Thus, many OD efforts never get off the ground, while others get watered down to impotent proportions. A part of this circumstance is doubtless due to unfamiliarity or lack of appreciation of the problem by managers—as is often asserted. But another significant part is probably due to more subtle forces. While traditional training was assumed to deal primarily with relatively 'safe' areas of technical job skills, OD evokes the specters of *influence* and *change*. It deals not only with *how* a particular individual does a job, but puts that job in its context in the total organizational system and claims as its legitimate domain the confrontation of such questions as *why* the job is structured as it is, organizational policy that relates to that job, and the behavior of other people who relate to that job—including managers. In other words, it brings organizational members at all levels in on issues that heretofore were considered to be the exclusive province of top management. Furthermore, it legitimizes the opportunity for employees to react openly to aspects of the social system which impinge upon them, and to attempt counter-influence in order to change organizational forces surrounding their roles.

It may be useful to compare the foregoing description of organization development with 'management development', as the term is currently used. Management development, as described by House,[6] refers to 'any attempt to improve current or future managerial performance by imparting information, conditioning attitudes, or increasing skills. Hence, management development includes such efforts as on-the-job coaching, counseling, classroom training, job rotation, selected readings, planned experience, and assignment to understudy

Dimension	Traditional Training	Organization Development
Unit of focus	The individual	Groups—teams or work units
Content of training	Technical and administrative skills	Interpersonal and group membership competence
Target subjects	Primarily first line employees and supervisors, managers trained outside organization	All levels, frequent initial intervention with upper management in-house
Conception of learning process	Cognitive and rational	Cognitive, rational, and emotional-motivational
Teaching style	Subject matter and teacher centered	Participant, immediate experience, and subject matter centered
Learning goals	Rationality and efficiency	Awareness and adaptation
View of organization	Discrete functional skill units	Social system

Figure 19.1
A Comparison of Traditional Training and Organization Development

positions.' (page 13.) The focus is primarily upon the manager and his behavior. The major contribution of current books and programs related to management development is that of presenting a more sophisticated and complete approach to training in the skill areas related to management. Such programs may be a major component of an organizational development effort.

Problems and issues in implementation

Organizations considering embarking on OD programs should seriously review their development needs, possible impacts of such programs upon the organization, their readiness for self-examination and change, and the willingness of management to open up organizational issues which may be affecting employees' performance. Below are listed some points worthy of consideration by organizations contemplating a broad development program.

1 Significant development programs are rarely successful without continued *active* support and involvement from top management. Total responsibility cannot be vested in a middle level staff person. Upper managers must be involved in formulating training goals, must participate in the training themselves, and must reinforce the behaviors sought after in training in their everyday managerial behaviors. They should also be involved in the evaluation of training.

2 The goal and probable impact of a development program is *change*—and to change the thoughts and feelings of members of the organization will likely result in changes in their behavior, relationships, and attitudes about the organization. Outcomes of OD may challenge and call into question existing policies, structure, and managerial performance.

263

3 Training cannot realistically be expected to solve all the 'people problems' of an organization, and attempts to raise morale, develop loyalty, or 'sell the company' through training may be risky at best.

4 The outcomes of training will be influenced by the total organization system. The 'climate' of the organization may encourage and reinforce changes aimed at in the training, or it may make these changes impossible and frustrate the trainees. The organization must be willing to look at its climate to see if it fosters development, growth, and change.

5 The organization must be willing to accept the fact that some of the people in whom it invests training resources may leave the organization and utilize their learning elsewhere. This possibility has kept more than one organization from instituting a significant development program.

6 There is evidence to suggest that underlying the substance of many discussions that take place in training sessions are basic employee concerns about such factors as interpersonal relationships, status, and career potential. Many consultants who are involved in development programs try to build into the programs the possibility for these basic concerns to be legitimized and dealt with in the training situation. It is not realistic in organization development to expect to 'keep feelings out of it', or to deal only with abstract principles.

7 The relatively early state of development of management theory leaves us with differing opinions about successful management approaches and with no right or wrong answers or no magic keys to success. No training or development program can provide quick and easy solutions which can be readily implemented tomorrow.

8 Some organizations make the mistake of confusing development programs with show business. For example, the training director may become saddled with the responsibility for attracting and holding the audience on a volunteer basis, or making programs entertaining or 'satisfying' as rated by participants. While participant feedback is an important aspect of a development program, the organization has no more responsibility to entertain its employees in training sessions than it does in budget conferences or planning meetings. The onus should be just as much on the participants as it is on the trainer to create conditions for productive learning, and the appropriate criterion is more effective managerial behavior—not satisfaction.

If a decision is made to pursue an organizational development program, its success can be enhanced by building it into the management process. It may be useful to establish a permanent advisory group made up of management personnel from various parts of the organization. This group can work with the designated staff person or department in formulating, implementing, and evaluating the program. And the advisory group can participate in the development of a comprehensive long-range plan for the program and can periodically review and revise the program, if necessary.

Probably, the second most difficult aspect of implementing an OD program—after getting the organization to accept and integrate the concept—is to locate training resources. If the training department carries the responsibility for implementation, some readjustments may be necessary. One area of readjustment

264

may be the attitudes and skills of the training staff itself. Staff members, whose experience and attitudes indicate a role of teacher, audio-visual expert, or administrator of skill training classes may need a considerable amount of retraining themselves in order to perform roles more akin to change agents in the management process.

Another area of readjustment relates to the way the trainer is perceived by other members of the organization. The roles of many training directors are viewed as roles of relatively low power whose legitimate domain does not include managerial behavior and organizational operation. As long as these perceptions exist, whether they be valid or invalid, the incumbent will have difficulty administering an OD program.

A well-reasoned training and development program can often utilize a combination of internal and external resources. Few companies can accumulate a large and well-qualified staff of trainers to meet all needs. Yet a willy-nilly mix of visiting speakers, professional meetings, and canned programs will probably not be effective. Depending on the size and characteristics of the organizations, some programs that are recurrent and specific to the organization, such as supervisory training, can often be best handled in-house. Other programs can be developed out of regular visits by consultants, planned attendance at university or professional society conferences and management study seminars, and with regular reinforcement on the job through meetings, reports, etc. The distinguishing characteristic of most OD programs is a series of sessions for teams of employees in which consultants (either internally or externally based) assist participants in combining training with problem-solving and planning. No available program can realistically expect to meet all training needs. Most packages are based on certain premises and aimed at certain problem areas. They should be used to deal with certain organization problems or in tandem with other training approaches.[10]

In summary, moving from a traditional skill training program to a program of organization development may well mean that the organization has to deal with issues which are easy to ignore or avoid, but crucial to the success of the program. These issues have to do with the emphasis to be placed on the development program and the resources to be devoted to it, with the implications of the program in regard to basic and sometimes uncomfortable issues such as influence, with change in behavior and attitude, and with the roles and competencies of the staff of the program. Unless these issues are confronted and dealt with, the organization is likely to find that it is extremely difficult to sustain a meaningful development program.

References

1. ARGYRIS, C., *Interpersonal Competence and Organizational Effectiveness.* Homewood, Illinois: Dorsey-Irwin, 1962.
2. BENNIS, WARREN G., *Changing Organizations.* N.Y.: McGraw-Hill, 1966.
3. BUCHANAN, P. C., 'Training Laboratories in Organization Development.' in *Issues in Human Relations Training,* I. R. Weschler and E. H. Schein, eds. Washington, DC: N.T.L. Institute, 1962.
4. BURCK, G., 'Union Carbide's Patient Schemers.' *Fortune Magazine,* December, 1965.

5. DAVIS, SHELDON A., 'An Organic Problem-Solving Method of Organizational Change.' *Journal of Applied Behavioral Science.* Vol. 3, Jan.-March, 1967.
6. HOUSE, R. J., *Management Development: Design, Evaluation and Implementation.* Ann Arbor: University of Michigan, 1967.
7. MANN, F. C., 'Studying and Creating Change: A Means to Understanding Social Organization. In D. M. Arensberg, *et al., Research in Industrial Human Relations.* N.Y.: Harper, 1957.
8. MARROW, A. J., BOWERS, D. G. and SEASHORE, STANLEY, *Management by Participation.* N.Y.: Harper, 1967.
9. ROETHLISBERGER, F. J., and DICKSON, W. J., *Management and the Worker.* Cambridge, Mass.: Harvard U. P., 1939.
10. A discussion of the application of several OD programs can be found in *What's Wrong With Work?* New York: National Association of Manufacturers, 1967.

20. An organic problem-solving method of organizational change

Sheldon A. Davis

In the opinion of the author, behavioral science literature does not give proper emphasis to the principle of confrontation as it relates to the improvement and development of organizations. Furthermore, sensitivity training is not effectively put into a larger context as a means to an end. This paper describes an extensive organizational development effort within TRW Systems which places a heavy emphasis on confrontation and the use of sensitivity training as part of an effort to improve the culture of an organization. The improvement focuses on the quality of working relationships between interdependent individuals and groups. The elements of this organic approach to organizational change are discussed and a generalized time-phased model is presented.

Some time ago, I learned from a vice-president of a large national corporation that two of the three top executives in his company had recently participated in a Presidents' Conference on Human Behavior conducted by the National Training Laboratories. I learned further that, both before and after attending the conference, these two persons were highly committed to theory Y notions, as described by Douglas McGregor in *The Human Side of Enterprise.* My acquaintance expressed concern, however, with the form this commitment was taking. He mentioned that one of these two men had chaired a meeting during which he expressed his commitment to those assumptions stated by McGregor. As a concrete example of this commitment, he said that a few days earlier a key subordinate presented some work for approval. The 'boss' did not like the quality of the work and said so. The subordinate pointed out that his people had worked very hard in producing the

• Reproduced by special permission from *The Journal of Applied Behavioral Science,* Vol. 3, No. 1, 1967.

work and were highly committed to it. The top executive said, 'OK. In that case, let's go ahead.'

To me, this is *not* an example of what McGregor meant. It is an example of very soft human relationships that are not task-oriented and, therefore, in my opinion, are irrational. It does represent, however, a problem presented in laboratory training. How can we eliminate some of the soft, mushy, 'sweetness and light' impressions that some people feel are implicit in sensitivity training?

An example of a different approach recently took place within TRW Systems.

A section head, the lowest managerial level in the organization, discovered that a certain quality control procedure for manufacturing hampered his effectiveness. He sought to get the procedure modified, only to be told that this was impossible because it covered all of the divisions and therefore could not be modified. He was further told that a change would raise the ire of at least one general manager of another division. The section head refused to accept the explanation and personally called a meeting of the general manager identified, the manager of manufacturing—both vice-presidents of the company, and four levels above the section head—and the director of product assurance. Within an hour the procedure was modified in the direction desired by the section head.

The foregoing vignettes dramatize the differences which can occur because of markedly different applications of behavioral science theories within an organization. In both instances, the individuals involved were convinced that they were using the best of behavioral science techniques. The consequence of their interpretation and application had decidedly different payoffs.

Confrontation: the missing element in behavioral science literature

The values that Douglas McGregor stood for and articulated regarding organizational development have within them a very real toughness: in dealing with one another, we will be open, direct, explicit. Our feelings will be available to one another, and we will try to problem-solve rather than be defensive. These values have within them a very tough way of living—not a soft way. But, unfortunately, in much of the behavioral science literature, the messages come out sounding soft and easy, as if what we are trying to do is to build happy teams of employees who feel 'good' about things, rather than saying we are trying to build effective organizations with groups who function well and can zero in quickly on their problems and deal with them rationally, in the very real sense of the word. As an example of this kind of softness, I do not remember reading in any book in the field that one of the alternatives in dealing with a problem person is the possibility of discharging him.

There is no real growth—there is no real development—in the organization or in the individuals within it if they do not confront and deal directly with their problems. They can get together and share feelings, but if that is all they do, it is merely a catharsis. While this is useful, it has relatively minimal usefulness compared with what can happen if they start to relate differently within the organizational setting around task issues.

Laboratories are not enough

I think one important theme of the nearly four-year organizational change effort at TRW Systems is that of using laboratory training (sensitivity training, T-Grouping) clearly as a means to an end—that of putting most of our energy into on the job situations, real-life intergroup problems, real-life job-family situations, and dealing with them in the here and now. This effort has reached a point where sensitivity training, *per se*, represents only 10 to 15 per cent of the effort in our own program. The rest of the effort, 85 to 90 per cent, is in on the job situations, working real problems with the people who are really involved in them. This has led to some very important, profound, and positive changes in the organization and the way it does many things, including decision-making, problem-solving, and supervisory coaching of subordinates.

One generalization I would draw from this and other similar experiences is that laboratory training in and of itself is not enough to really make the kind of difference that might be made in an organization forcefully trying to become more rational in its processes of freeing the untapped potential of its people and of dealing more sensibly with its own realities. Attending a strangers' laboratory or, in our case, a cousins' laboratory (that is, being in a T-Group with people who are not necessarily from the same job-family, but are from the same company) is a very useful, important experience. Most people learn much in laboratory training, as has been well documented and discussed. However, this is not enough.

We have felt that the laboratory experience (the sensitivity training experience itself) should not be just three days or a week or whatever is spent in the off-site laboratory. As a result, we have undertaken important laboratory prework as well as postwork. The prework typically consists of an orientation session where the staff very briefly presents some of the theoretical aspects of the program and an explanation of why we do laboratories. During this time, participants in the coming laboratory can ask any kind of question, such as: Is this therapy? Is the company going to evaluate my performance? And so on.

Also, we typically hand out a questionnaire to the participants for their own use (they are not asked to turn it in). It presents questions such as: 'What are the three most pressing problems you feel you pose for those who have to work with you?' It is an attempt to get the person to become introspective about his own particular work situation, to begin his articulation process within himself.

Then there is the laboratory itself. This is followed up by on-site sessions several weeks apart, perhaps one evening every other week for three or four sessions. At this time a variety of actions are taken in an attempt to help people phase into their work situation. There is continued working in the small training groups; there can be exercises such as intergroup competition.

The laboratory is a highly intensive experience. Attitudes towards it can be extremely euphoric, and people can experience tremendous letdowns when they return to the ongoing culture—even a highly supportive one. Therefore, there is major emphasis on working in the ongoing situation in real-life job families as well as in intergroup situations and mergers, for example.

269

Recently, we have added to the follow-on work an opportunity for the wives of the participants to experience a micro-laboratory. This might be a 1.0-5.0 p.m. session on a Saturday for the wives, with a staff available to give some feel for the laboratory experience.

One of the problems many people have as a result of laboratory training is returning to their continuing organizational culture and finding it quite hostile to the values learned and to the approaches they would like to try. The notion very early in the TRW Systems effort was to focus on changes in the ongoing culture itself: the norms, values, rewards, systems, and processes. If all we did was to have a lot of people attend sensitivity training, this might indeed be useful to them as individuals, but its usefulness would be quite limited with respect to the total organization.

We have had other kinds of concerns with laboratory training. We have tried hard not to *send* people to a laboratory, but to make it as voluntary as possible. People who are *sent* usually spend much of their time wondering why they were sent instead of working on relevant issues.

If we look at the process of change itself, it is quite clear that it is not enough for an individual to gain enormous insight into his own situation, his own dynamics, and his own functioning. Granted, this will help him develop a better understanding of how groups work and of the complexity of communication processes. However, if he cannot take this understanding and turn it into action in the on the job situation, if he cannot find other people who are interested in trying some of the same ideas, if he cannot bring about a difference in his real life, the value of the laboratory is very severely minimized. In real life, what do we find? We find organizations, typically, with highly traditional methods of management and with very unrealistic assumptions about people (the kind of theory X assumptions that Douglas McGregor stated). There has to be an emphasis on changing the ongoing organization. The direction has to be towards working in the organization on a day to day basis.

Organizational setting and development of program

I should like to describe the program under way at TRW Systems as an example of this kind of effort—of a non-mechanical, organic approach to career development— the development of the careers of the individuals in the organization and the career of the organization itself, both inextricably tied.

TRW Systems currently employs about 13 300 persons. About one-third are professional engineers, and half of these have advanced degrees. It is an organization with products of tremendous innovation and change. It is an organization that is highly interdependent. We have a matrix organization: there are project offices and functional areas of technical capabilities, such as structures, dynamics, guidance, and control. A project office, to perform its task, must call upon capabilities and people throughout the organization. This is a highly complicated matrix of interdependencies. No one can really get his job done in this kind of system without working with others. As a result, problems of relationships, of communication,

270

of people being effectively able to problem-solve with one another are extremely critical.

The program started at a time when the company was going through a significant change in its role—from an organization with essentially one air force contract for systems engineering on ballistic missile programs (Thor, Atlas, Titan, and Minuteman) to a company that would be fully competitive in the aerospace market. This has indeed happened over the past six years. We now have many contracts, many customers. Most of our work is done under fixed-price and incentive contracts; we produce hardware, such as unmanned scientific satellites, propulsion engines for the Apollo mission, as well as other types of hardware. The company has become exceedingly more complex in its product lines and its mix of business.

All through this growth and diversification, there has been a concern about the careers of the people in the organization, about trying to maintain certain qualities within the organization. On page 278, there is a list of these qualities which was prepared in September of 1965 and is an attempt to list qualities which seem to have a direct bearing on the kind of success we have been having over the past six years. That success has been quite striking: a tremendous increase in sales, in the number of contracts, a good record in competitions for programs in our industry, and a large increase in the number of employees.

In the middle of 1961, TRW Systems, then called Space Technology Laboratories, began to think about organizational development. At that time, Herbert Shepard, then on the faculty at Case Institute of Technology, spent a portion of the summer at TRW, including some time with key executives. The following summer he spent a month with the organization. Just prior to this vist, the director of Industrial Relations and his associate attended a laboratory conducted by the University of California at Los Angeles.

Shepard's visit and discussions centering around it led to a growing articulation of what we might want to do with respect to career development. A number of things happened in the next several months.

One was the preparation of a white paper on career development—a statement of how we might approach the subject. The paper discussed why a program was needed, assumptions to be made about employees (a paraphrase of McGregor's theory Y), the type of organizational climate and training needed, as well as some general indications of how we might proceed.

An assumption we made was that most of the people in the organization were highly competent, very intelligent, and certainly experimental. If they could be freed up enough to look at some of their behavior, to question some of their assumptions, to look at assumptions other people were making, to try new approaches, this group could, within limits, develop their own specific management theory.

The white paper was circulated to a number of key persons. Interviews were then conducted to determine possible next steps. A series of events led from this point.

One event was the first of many team development laboratories. (By team development laboratory, I mean an activity which might, for example, be a three

271

day off-site meeting involving a supervisor and the people who immediately report to him. The agenda for the meeting would be 'How can we improve our own effectiveness?') The first team meeting involved one of the program offices in the company. It turned out to be quite successful. With this experience under our belts, we had further discussions to formulate what we wanted to do as an organization with respect to the careers of the people comprising it.

Employees within the personnel organization began attending sensitivity training laboratories such as the Arden House Management Work Conferences, conducted by National Training Laboratories.

A very significant event in the total development of this change effort occurred in May of 1963, when a group of 12 key executives attended a laboratory. Their co-trainers were Herbert Shepard (an outside consultant) and myself (a member of the TRW Systems organization).*

The participants in this first laboratory were quite positive in their feedback to the director of industrial relations and to the president of the company, who himself was very much interested in how people were reacting to the training. The president had given support for us to be experimental: 'Let's try things. If they work, continue them. If they don't, modify them, improve them, or drop them.'

A consulting team evolved over time. The consultants were not used in any one-shot way, but were asked to make a significant commitment of time over a long-term period. They have become involved with us. They have learned our culture and our problems. While our consultants are all qualified T-Group trainers, most of their time is spent in on the job situations. There is a need to function as a team, since we are all dealing with one organization, one culture, one social system. The kind of cohesiveness that takes place during consulting team meetings has been a critical part of the program here at TRW Systems.

In one sense, we started at the top of the organization, and in another we did not. In the beginning, there was a shared general understanding between the president and the key people in industrial relations about the type of program we wanted. There were some shared values about the organization we had and wanted to maintain, build, and develop. So in McGregor's term, this was not theory X management and theory Y training effort. Both had a theory Y quality.

In another sense, we did not start at the top: the president and others of the top management team were relatively late in becoming involved in laboratory training and in applying this training to their own job families. The president of the company attended an NTL Presidents' Conference on Human Behavior early in 1965. Directly after that experience, his top team had an off-site team development meeting in March of 1965. In April 1966, they had a follow-up meeting.

Prior to this top team activity many other things had happened with a number of other people in other job families. In fact, this other activity helped us get to the

* This has been one of the important notions in the approach at TRW Systems. We use, at this point, about nine consultants who are members of the NTL Network—people like Richard Beckhard, Michael Blansfield, James Clark, Charles Ferguson, Jack Gibb, George Lehner, Herbert Shepard, Robert Tannenbaum, and others. These people are *always* coupled in their work, either in T-Group training or on the job consulting, with someone inside the organization, typically a personnel manager in one of the line operating units.

point where the top management team became interested in trying to apply some of these techniques. Since the program started, more than 500 key persons in the organization have attended sensitivity training laboratories, primarily laboratories conducted by the company. The staff of these laboratories is drawn from our consultants, the personnel organization, and, more recently, from skilled and interested employees in line management positions.

We have also conducted more than 85 team development efforts. These vary in format, but a typical one involves interviews with each of the members of the team (a job family consisting of a supervisor and his immediate subordinates) and then, perhaps, a three day off-site meeting where the interview data are fed back for the groups to work with. The team ends the meeting with explicit action items. Follow-on to the off-site meeting involves implementing the many action items.

We have been devoting much effort to intergroup problems: relationships between manufacturing and engineering, between product assurance and other parts of the organization, between various interfacing elements in the engineering organizations. We have found that these efforts have a great deal of leverage. We have done some work on facilitating mergers and with key people on approaching satellite launches. The latter become very tense, tight operations where people can become extremely competitive and behave in ways which clearly get in the way of having an effective launch.

Characteristics of the process

We wound up with a number of notions. We did not want to have a program that was canned, but one that was experimental. We wanted participation to be voluntary rather than something that the company forced upon employees. We did not want it to be a crash program (in our industry there are many crash programs). We wanted the training to be highly task-oriented. (If it were not relevant to making a difference on today's problems, it would not be a successful program.) We wanted to have the emphasis on experience-based learning, which implies, in a very general sense, the use of laboratory methods, of people really looking at how they are doing, examining the assumptions behind their management style, identifying alternate ways of problem solving, and making choices based on a wider range of possibilities. We wanted to be concerned with the careers of all employees, not those of key people only. We wanted to be concerned about company goals and the actual, on the job work environment, since this has a profound effect on the careers of people. We wanted to place the emphasis on measuring ourselves against our potential, on being quite introspective on how we were doing. So, for example, if there were an either/or situation (and there usually is not), we would rather not have someone come in and lecture on how to conduct staff meetings, but would have ourselves look introspectively at the conduct of our own staff meetings. And we wanted to do continuous research on how we were faring so that it could be fed back into the program for further development.

I should like to describe what I think we have come to mean by an organic approach to organizational change within TRW Systems. There are a number of points which, at least for me, tend to describe what is meant by organic methods.

1 There is a notion that if you are interested in improving a particular culture—a particular social system—you must be able to step out of it in the sense of being very analytical about it, of understanding what is going on, by not being trapped within the culture and its own particular values. If you look at a culture from the viewpoint of its own values, you are not going to come up with anything very startling and different for it to do. You have got to be able to step out of it and say, 'What really would make sense here?' This ability to step out of the culture and yet not leave it, not become alienated from it, is a very important one.

2 A bias toward optimism regarding the chances for meaningful organizational development to take place increases the psychological freedom for those trying to introduce the change. There is certainly a tremendous amount of evidence at this point that significant, even profound, changes can occur in the behavior of individuals and organizations.

3 Taking a systems engineering approach to the effort (i.e., looking at the totality of the system, dealing with fundamentals within it, considering how a change in one part affects parts elsewhere) provides an analytical approach which increases the conceptual freedom.

4 The extensive use of third-party facilitation is made with respect to interpersonal and organizational problems. A consultant who is not directly involved in an emotional sense in a situation can be useful just by that fact.

5 Direct confrontation of relevant situations in an organization is essential. If we do not confront one another, we keep the trouble within ourselves and we stay in trouble. With respect to confrontation, the whole notion of feedback is crucial. Giving persons feedback on how they are doing gives them a choice to do better. Caring plays an important part. Confronting without caring can be a rather destructive process. (See Albee's *Who's Afraid of Virginia Woolf?*) It does turn out that people in general can be very caring of one another.

6 Becoming the 'other' is an important part of the organic method. This is the empathic notion that Carl Rogers and others have developed. To have a really meaningful exchange, one somehow has to look at the situation as the other sees it. For a consultant to work effectively with an organization, he has to be perceptive and understanding about the organization and its people from *their* point of view.

7 Dealing with the here and now and increasing the ability of people within the organization to do the same have a great deal of leverage. It is important in an organizational development effort to start with what is going on now within the organization and to deal with those things effectively. One of our objectives is to help the organization build its own capability, to deal with its problems as they emerge. Problems are constantly emerging in any live organization, and so our objective is *not* to end up with an organization that has no problems: that would be a very fat, dumb, and happy kind of place.

8 Multiplier planning is rather crucial in the early stages of introducing organizational change. What can we next do that will have the largest effect? There is always a wide range of alternatives and possibilities; there is never enough time,

money, or energy to do all the things we might do, so we are constantly picking and choosing.

9 Fanning-out is coupled with the multiplier-planning aspect. It is important in an effort of this kind—if it is not to be subversive, *sub rosa*, hidden, squashed out—to be something that does fan out: someone does something that leads to others doing something that leads to still others doing something.

10 A person can act, then act again and then act again; or he can act, critique what he just did, then act, then critique, then act. And that is the whole notion of going back and forth between content and process, between doing the job and then looking at how we are doing it. Building that into the day to day culture is a major objective.

11 Finally, there is the notion of testing of choices. One always has choices within any particular situation. However, it is typically true that we do not test the choices we have. So someone might say, 'Well, I really can't do that because these fellows won't let me,' or 'Yes, I would very much like to do the following, but I can't because of so and so.' Given these limits, some choices do not get tested. One of the efforts is to get people to be aware of the various possibilities they have and to test them—not to accept the stereotypes in the situation, the sacred cows, that exist in any kind of organization, but to say, 'OK, this is what makes sense to me in working that problem. This is what I want to try to do.'

Underpinnings to the effort

The principles of confrontation—that laboratory training must be seen as a means to an end, that most of the effort has to be done after people have attended the laboratory, and not in the laboratory itself—have been central to this effort. This has affected the way we budget time, the way we spend money, the assumptions we make about what we are doing.

Another significant development in this large-scale effort has been a deliberate, successful attempt to build up the internal resources to carry out the program. Two years ago, in a sensitivity training laboratory put on by the company, there would have been a staff of six, four or five of whom were outside consultants. This situation has completely reversed itself. Today, when a T-Group cousins' laboratory is conducted, four or five of the persons are from inside the organization, and only one or two are external consultants.

Furthermore, in the on the job aspects of the program, the effort is carried on by people within the organization, primarily individuals in personnel and, increasingly, managers from the line organization.

A very interesting aspect of the program has focused on the question of risk-taking. In my opinion, those of us engaged in this kind of work are quite often too cautious, too constrained, and not experimental enough in trying out things within the organization. We do not behave as though we fully believe the implications of McGregor's theory Y formulation: that people are creative, that they are strong, that they are motivated, that they want to make a difference. We tend sometimes to approach them gingerly and tentatively. These are constraints more within ourselves than within others or within the situation.

Many times our consultants have reported that their experience at TRW Systems has been a very 'stretching' one: they have been fully challenged; people at TRW Systems are experimental, want to try things, are saying, 'OK, that was useful, what should we do next?' Much of the effort in the consulting team meetings has been to push ourselves to be more developmental, more experimental in the approaches that we take within the effort.

For example, until quite recently, many people in the field felt that laboratory training was not something one could do within a job-family. It seems to me that the whole objective of sensitivity training is to develop an on the job culture within which we can relate to one another interpersonally just the way we do in a T-Group. We at TRW want to make that transfer; we do not want the T-Group to be a separate, special kind of experience. We prefer to say: 'All right, let's sit down and really level with one another. Let's do this on the job, and from day to day.' That is the objective. It leads to a more effective, efficient, problem-solving organization.

Working with teams in real life situations is exactly what we are after. Otherwise, the program can be ethereal—not particularly related to the company's real life situations It cannot be 'gutty' if it does not come to grips with some of the tougher issues, pinpoint and deal with them, and cause people to become involved and to work actively to solve problems.

In September 1963, I put together a short paper which conceptualized several plateaux that we might be moving through as an organization in this change effort.

The first one is characterized as problem awareness—that point in time during which there is general recognition and awareness on the part of some people within the organization that there are crucial interdependencies which exist in order for us to function and that there are problems due to inappropriate means of dealing with these interdependencies.

The second plateau, the identification and freeing of key people within the organization, is seen as consisting of two parts. The first part is an effort to identify key people in the organization who seem to be perceptive about the problems the company is experiencing and have a desire to work on them. They are key people in the sense that their efforts to deal with organizational problems could produce a multiplier effect that would lead others to similar action.

The second part of this particular phase of the program is characterized by an effort to provide a situation that would initiate the process of freeing up these potential multipliers from the organizational and personal constraints which, in the past, kept them from responding effectively to their awareness of the problems. Here, the strangers' laboratories, the cousins' laboratories conducted by the company, and the team development laboratories are seen as being especially relevant.

The third phase, or plateau, involves action steps to follow-up—experimental steps stimulated by a participation in the various kinds of laboratories that are taking place. These action steps have taken many forms: a supervisor holding a team development laboratory within his own job family; a family group diagnosing the kinds of interaction problems it has with other parts of the organization and beginning to resolve these problems in an open, direct manner in search of a creative solution rather than an avoidance compromise; two persons at odds moving in on the problem of relating and communicating with each other; new ways of looking at functions in the organization.

The fourth plateau occurs when the effort itself gains an independent status and becomes a self-supporting system. At this plateau there are norms within the organization that support open, direct confrontation of conflict, resolution of conflict without resorting to the power structure unless there is somehow a failure in the process, and a shared commitment to objectives as a consequence of being interdependent. These organizational norms would support the giving and receiving of feedback, openness, experimentation, and day to day problem-solving.

In this fourth phase, we are trying to build procedures into the day to day situation which hopefully, put into concrete terms some of the things we have learned in the earlier phases. For example, when a new project office is started it is probably useful to program some team building early in its life. When there is a new merger within the organization, particular attention can be paid to the merger process. One of the things we have learned is that specific attention should continuously be paid to the processes within the organization: how we make decisions, how we fill key spots, how we communicate with one another, how we decide to reorganize, how we make other important decisions. There is a heavy people involvement in these processes, and, typically, they do not get enough legitimate attention. If I am concerned about the quality of staff meetings I attend, I tend to talk about them in the hallways or go home and kick the dog and tell my wife about them. I do not exert effort during the staff meetings to try to change their quality and improve them, because somehow that is not legitimate. 'Let's keep personalities out of it. Don't get emotional.' These are the kinds of expressions that inhibit me from dealing with the problem.

Development through the four plateaux requires considerable invention because the state of the art of organizational change, in my opinion, is such that one cannot program in advance everything he is going to do within the organization. There are some people who approach organizational change this way. I believe their efforts tend to be mechanical and relatively superficial.

Another important aspect of this effort which I think is particularly consistent with theory Y formulation is that the direction and pace that the effort takes should be meaningful to the members who are participating in it. The consultant in any particular situation has to get in touch with the needs and concerns of the people involved from *their* point of view, not from *his*.

I have tried to suggest that, in many situations in which behavioral scientists are trying to apply their principles, the really serious limitations are not within the people or the organizations they are working with, but within themselves —their own skills and ability and courage to act. Theory Y has deeply ingrained in it a profound belief in the abilities, strengths, and motivations of people in general and specifically. Many times, we do not act as if we fully believe or understand that set of formulations.

Next steps

In TRW Systems, we are now moving in a number of directions, some of which I should like to describe. We are moving more towards day to day coaching—on the job feedback, if you will—with or without consultants and without calling special meetings, but just as we work together. We are paying continuing attention to process as a way of doing business. We are moving more and more toward using third-party facilitation as a standard operating procedure.

So far there has not been a heavy involvement of the rank and file. The first several years in the effort were specifically biased toward working with key people. These are the ones who have a large effect upon the culture, upon the processes of the organization, upon the tone of the climate. But we are now at a point where we want to get more and more involvement of all the employees within the organization.

I think that the experience of the past several years within TRW Systems has rather clearly demonstrated the potential high leverage of applying some of the behavioral science formulations of people like McGregor, Lewin, and Likert. I think it has also demonstrated that there needs to be much more organizational theory development based upon experience, not upon someone's sitting in a room by himself and thinking about the topic. Some of the statements written about organizational development are to me naive, impractical, unrealistic, and unrelated to organizational problems as they actually exist. Through experiences gained at TRW Systems and many other places, we should be able to develop a more sophisticated understanding of organizational development.

In my opinion, there is great potential in the development of this theory and in its application with organizations. That seems to me to be one of the leading edges within the field of behavioral science.

Qualities of TRW Systems which have a direct bearing on its success

In thinking about the problems associated with the very dramatic growth of TRW Systems, I attempted to identify those qualities which have had a great deal to do with our success in the past and ought therefore to be maintained in the future.

1 The individual employee is important, and focus is on providing him the tools and other things that he needs to carry out his assignments.

2 The systems within the organization (policies, procedures, practices) have been designed to be a platform *from which* the individual operates rather than a set of ground rules *within which* he must confine himself.

3 One objective of the organization has been this: The work we do ought to be fun (personally rewarding, meaningful, enjoyable), and this has had a direct effect on assignments, among other things.

4 There is a great deal of trust displayed in the individual person: a minimum of rules, controls, and forces outside the individual telling him what to do and how to do it.

5 'Technical democracy': a society of peers rather than a rigid hierachy. There is a relative lack of social distance between employees and managers and among the various echelons of management. There have been a spontaneous willingness and an interest in keeping social distance at a minimum; and while managers enjoy the accoutrements of rank, they are not used as barriers between themselves and others at lower levels of the organization.

6 A heavy emphasis on quality: Attract best people, give them excellent working conditions, provide them with challenging assignments, demonstrate that paramount importance is placed on the professional and technical excellence of work assignments.

7 Although, within TRW Systems, there has been continuous and rapid change, the organization as a whole has been relatively stable, providing long-term career opportunities for a high percentage of our key people who are positive about the emphasis on internal, upward mobility and individual chance for many diversified job assignments. This is career development in a very literal sense.

8 In giving responsibility to individuals, we have had a bias toward giving 'too much responsibility too soon' rather than being conservative. This has 'stretched' the individual and, for those who are capable, it has led to rapid growth and outstanding performance.

9 There is, in a relative sense, less organization 'politics' (e.g., people ruthlessly working at getting ahead, back-stabbing) and more focus on task. Part of the language is 'working the problem'.

10 On task issues there is a great deal of direct confrontation rather than 'passing the buck', maneuvering, and so on.

11 There is a great deal of delegation downward within the organization, so that a relatively large number of persons find themselves assigned to tasks with relatively high responsibility.

12 The management group has been quite experimental in its approach to its task rather than generally traditional.

13 The individual employee enjoys relative freedom to be personally responsible for himself and his job. The job is generally seen as an important one and as making a significant contribution to the noteworthy technological advances in our society.

14 People who will be markedly affected by decisions feel that they will have the opportunity, to a greater degree than is customary elsewhere, to participate in the decision-making process.

21. Learning to cope with a management career: Preparation not salvage

Alistair D. Mant

A brief examination of the range of management education today shows some interesting divergencies between the preparation of young men for a management career and what is sometimes seen by teachers as the 'salvaging' of older executives. The two are connected, if only because, on any available evidence, many of the recipients of the former will end up requiring the latter in a few years' time.

This chapter looks at the character of the 'salvaging' job via a programme of the preparation kind. The logic of this approach is as follows:

To an increasing extent the efforts of management development specialists in companies and in schools seem to be turning towards the use of the relatively new practice of organizational development. This, in turn, means that practitioners are becoming increasingly concerned with how experienced executives can be helped to *manage their own learning* over time (rather than submit like children to teacher practices that have remained basically unchanged for hundreds of years). Additionally, teachers are worrying more about what form of 'teaching' will make *action* more comprehensible to the learner.

These are fundamental questions for any teacher, and it is by no means clear how many management developers realize the significance of them. For example, to 'learn how to learn' implies self-insight beyond that exhibited by most executives; to understand action, in the fullest sense, means a grasp of the psychology of organizations and authority structures at a very high level indeed. In short, the management developer is setting out, however unconsciously, to remedy the deficiencies of the educational system as a whole. This deduction is based on the simplest definition of what an education is for and recognizing that the aims of any education system are complex. For example, small children may be sent to school to learn certain 'things' like the three Rs, but, in fact, the mechanism of the school will probably retard their rate of learning compared with other approaches. The benefit is, of course, the socialization for a wider role which takes place in a hundred informal ways.

Similarly, it should be argued that secondary and tertiary education are to 'prepare' young people for a productive life. For the sake of such a statement, whether 'productive' means for the individual or for the community or state, or both, must be determined by individual conscience; the aim is essentially practical. It might, for example, be practical, in a sense, for Oxbridge to produce nothing but argument-loving theorists without a whiff of action in them, if the kind of society we had was enriched and developed, on the whole, by their presence. Nobody seems to be arguing thus nowadays, and plenty of critics would diagnose the real failings of the educational system as the inability to teach individuals how to manage their own actions and learning.

We come therefore to a point where management development specialists in the OD business have more to learn (about teaching) from primary school practice and psychoanalytic theory than from the universities. The question then arises: if we really want to tackle the job on a broad front, at what point in the total educational edifice is it possible to inject a kind of 'action-learning', so that the later 'salvage' job becomes less necessary. An obvious point of entry is the postgraduate school of administration, where many students have already tasted action, and may have in their memories the spectre of a few 'obsolescent' executives to further motivate them to avoid the same fate.

The Conference on organization and authority

This chapter therefore describes one programme, of one week's duration, constructed for the specific purpose of inoculating a group of young men against the ailments that management developers are now diagnosing in older executives— rigidity, dependency, and fear.

For the last three years, staff members at the Manchester Business School have run a one week Conference on Organization and Authority for volunteers from the first and second year MBA students. The design has altered over these years, but the basic objective has been an 'institution building' exercise in which real preoccupations of the students about their education and their careers can be worked through in a totally dynamic atmosphere. (The discussion below assumes a level of knowledge of such Conferences.[1]) The Conferences have contained small groups (T-Groups, about 9 to 11 people), large groups, (about 30 or more) with the purpose of studying the behaviour of the group as it happens, and also an intergroup exercise to study relations between groups.

The first of the three Conferences was held at the end of the academic year, with the effect that, within the total design, the small groups assumed the greatest importance for participants because of their concern with ending relationships. The most recent of the continuing series, the subject of this article, was held at the end of the first term to ensure a maximum spin-off from the Conference to the subsequent life of the school.

Without a useful spin-off, the Conference, as an institution-builder, at least, must be adjudged a failure. Even when multiple effects have been observed, it is far too early to claim any lasting successes. This simple account of the events is meant to serve as an example of the *kinds* of experiments that schools of administration must engage in if they expect to contribute to broad-based learning in their students. The significance of what results have been observed is that they appear to redress the deficiences in the educational system as a whole which were noted above.

Before the last Conference began, there had been little significant political activity on the students' part in that first term (most of them had had some years of industrial experience) due, in part, to the suggestion of the director of studies that the first-term representative structure might usefully be a temporary arrangement to be re-evaluated after the Conference. At the suggestion of staff, a representative committee had formed at the beginning of the year to 'speak for' the student body on matters of curriculum, and so on. The committee, eight strong, had been largely self-appointed, as few students understood so early in the year what its functions might be. By the time the Conference took place at the end of the first term, the committee members had had time to become locked into their respective roles, and some doubt had built up in the other students' minds as to the suitability of their representatives.

No useful evidence is available about the composition of the Conference membership. It is probably fair to assume some important differences between those who volunteered to attend and those who did not. The narrative below refers simply to those who did.

Specific concerns of the Conference

As each Conference has developed, the overriding questions causing concern to the participants have tended to be:

1 What kind of Institution am I in? How can I influence it to help me ascertain my needs for development and to meet those needs?

2 What kind of a career have I chosen? Whatever my skill level, will I be able, in the long term, to justify a business career to myself and my friends, even if I prove competent?

This does not imply that the students at any of the conferences were necessarily *eager* to tackle these questions, nor that they were especially grateful for being placed in a setting where it was virtually impossible to dodge them.

The more specific concerns which were worked through as follows.

The apparent fragility and discontinuity in the Business School structure

Plainly, many of the students had half-expected a business school life of serenity somewhere between Ivy League and Oxbridge. In the state of business school growth in Britain they found themselves grappling, along with their teachers, with all the problems of growth and change. In practice, this meant a fast turnover of some of the best staff, passing on sometimes to greater prizes in the academic

282

reward system, but more frequently a peripatetic leap ahead of the others. It meant, further, an apparent conflict in the career messages propounded by staff, from the hard line ('If you haven't made the board by 35, forget it!') to the soft ('Business comprises dense and complex organizational systems, and there is a good deal of luck about success in it').

Within the school the physical exigencies of temporary accommodation had meant the exile of MBA students' recreation facilities from the main building to an auxiliary one. In theory, they were the academic first-class citizens in the school; in practice, they were not so sure. (The intergroup exercise in the most recent Conference 'replayed' the reality to an uncanny extent, as one of the intergroup rooms happened to be isolated from the main conference, and its occupiers reacted to the Conference in much the way the MBA students as a whole had dealt with isolation from the school proper.)

Overriding all these preoccupations with the school and its staff, were feelings about the fragility of the MBA degree itself. It was all very well to assume responsibility for changing the school, but what were the implications of *that* for the degree? Whatever complaint one might make about the fundamental worth of, for example, a Harvard MBA, *that* degree was worth a thousand or two extra in salary, whether or not you played an active part in the education process. To play too active a part in the process might jeopardize one's examination performance. In short, those students who cared most about the Conference values were faced with the necessity of balancing two quite different values.

In all this there is not much doubt that the real issues facing a growing business school were illuminated, including the very considerable constraints on faculty. After the Conference, the students could no longer comfort themselves that somehow it could be left to a hard worked staff to put matters right.

The pervasive character of 'authority'

The model employed in the Conference calls for a 'staff group' representing the authority and responsibility for Conference events. (In this particular Conference, this group contained, of course, a number of people who represented 'authority' in the wider university sphere.) No instructions as to what they should discuss were given to participants, save a statement of the rules the *staff* would adhere to. The staff thereafter devote themselves unswervingly to their primary task of, within the Conference design, helping students to understand the dynamics of what happens.

The predictable effect of this approach was, in a business school, where there is an understandable desire to be 'taught what I need to know', acute frustration and even anger because (forgetting what staff had *explicity* committed themselves to) the staff did not behave the way authorities are 'supposed to'. Afterwards, one student confessed himself astounded at the extent to which 'authority is attributed rather than earned'. This realization, combined with an insight into the 'fragility' referred to above, apparently stripped away some of the participants' determination that those in charge could, or in this case *should*, be relied on to put everything right.

Competition

The large and small groups, which always present testing opportunities for personal exposure and bids for influence, had the effect of showing the extent to which the students had been avoiding issues of power and influence within their own ranks. The Conference repeatedly returned to the reassuring theme that *all* the participants belong to an elite (one application in ten to the Business School succeeds) and they therefore had nothing to fear from one another.

As the students came to face differentials in competence, and feelings of dislike and affection, they came closer to facing some of the realities of a business career. Some openly asked themselves whether, in pursuing a postgraduate qualification, they were not simply postponing the competition that faced them, whether or not they were likely to be the victors in the larger conflict.

The relevance of the curriculum

The most pungent commentary on the experience came from one participant near the end of the week. After a steady diet of confronting the authority, both within and, by extension, without the Conference, and testing out in a dynamic and apparently threatening setting how it feels to *assume* authority, he said in a bemused tone: 'If you think about it, we are now spending a week learning about things that will *really* matter in a management career, and we will spend the rest of the two years on getting inputs that will soon be obsolete. Wouldn't it be more sensible to do it the other way round?' (This was inaccurate, but it appeared that, in nearly 20 years of schooling, this was the first revelation he had experienced about his own learning and about his own responsibility to make choices about it.) This question had as much, or more, relevance for staff, as it did for the students, and, in a way, crystallized the dilemma of a business school trying to bridge the disparate worlds of university and big business. Plainly, the traditional methods left a good deal to be desired so far as students of management were concerned. On the other hand, some of the values of the traditional system had enduring relevance for management; but the real issue facing the staff was the extent to which they were really constrained by the oligarchical properties of the university system. In designing an experience which challenged the students to assume responsibility for their own affairs and to do away with authority fantasies, the staff were challenging themselves to do the same within the larger university framework.

The above represents a very short list of major preoccupations during the few days of the Conference. It can be seen that what began, at one level, as an opportunity for the students to appraise T-Group methods, had, at another level, a great deal in common with organizational development projects in industry. But then, no one can be expected to learn much about OD by reading books about how *other* organizations learn to face up to *their* problems.

Apart from the issues listed above, much else happened, especially in the development of interpersonal relationships between students and between staff and students. This chapter is devoted to the *system* learning aspects; this does not imply that the interpersonal development might not stand on its own as a proper purpose for such events.

After the Conference

An obvious presumption for an institution-building Conference, which aims to develop a sense of responsibility, is that it *ought* to produce a sense of responsibility for *institution-building* on the part of its participants. An observable outcome ought to be self-initiated *activities* within the school which are *seen* as relevant learning.

The paragraphs below list the actual events in the school which followed on the conference. This is essentially a listing, because it is impossible to tie down causal links. The fact that most of the activities listed were initiated by those students who elected to join the Conference is impressive; but it might equally be argued that they were prone to engage in political activity anyway. The facts are presented for what relevance they may have.

Representation

The pattern of representation changed considerably after the Conference, with the formation of a new students' committee. Its areas of operation were defined more precisely, numbers were reduced to five, and the emergent leaders during the Conference assumed major positions on the committee. In the main, the new committee directed itself to a variety of housekeeping tasks (library procedures, arranging vacation work relevant for dissertations, and so on) but, in the period after its formation, had to withstand two additional challenges. One took the form of a student paper on *The Role of a Business School in a Changing Society* which was an unofficial (i.e., not committee) contribution which was sent direct to the governing council of the school. The other concerned the issue of direct feedback (in the form of written reports) to teachers from the students. This proposal was firmly opposed by the committee chairman against some odds. On the whole, however, the chairman was used actively as a representative and spokesman for the student body.

Confrontation

Plainly, the Conference had brought to the surface a number of apprehensions about the purposes of the school, the design of its courses and the way in which it was working for the students' benefit. (During the Conference, one participant had stated 'It is pointless to argue whether we [the post-graduate students] or the post-experience students are "firstclass citizens" in the school; the only firstclass citizens are staff!')

The result of these apprehensions was a 'confrontation meeting', partly initiated by the students, between the student committee and the school director and his senior staff. This had been preceded by a plenary meeting of staff to discuss the School's structure and objectives, and which had led to the commissioning of a major study of the issue by a staff member. The purpose of the meeting was to look at the perceived 'fragility' of the school's operation and to thrash out a clear statement of the 'Management model' on which the school was working. The meeting was not particularly successful, to some extent because the student committee went into it unprepared for the confrontation process, but it at least succeeded in looking realistically at questions of course design, the availability of faculty, and so on.

All this indicated a heightened awareness *about* the educational process on the part of some of the students. It is true to say that a majority of the total student body continued to strive for the paper qualification without worrying too much about the process, but for some, notably Conference members, working at the educational process had somehow become a legitimate *part* of education.

Responsibility and involvement

Three months after the Conference, the University of Manchester was stunned by the first active student demonstration in its history. At the centre of the manifestation was a sit-in over the question of the alleged keeping of political files on activist students. (The Business School occupies separate premises, off-campus.) It seemed to Conference members that, at a distance, they understood the dynamics of the sit-in very well, particularly in respect of the motives and tactics of the most activist students, and also the increasingly panic-stricken and reactionary behaviour of the University authorities. In fact, the whole affair looked like an analogy of the Conference structure, with student leaders attributing totally unrealistic motives and aims to 'authority'.

So far so good. Conference staff were pleased that active experience at the Conference helped the students to understand some of the complexities of the phenomenon 'down the road'. However, the Conference had aimed to generate a sense of responsibility to complement any understanding; the large question became—what would they *do* about it? (Staff had fresh in their minds stories of the almost total disinterest of the Harvard Business School, both staff and students, in respect of the large-scale student revolution at that university.)

In the event, some students, primarily Conference members, decided for themselves that intervention 'down the road' was an appropriate component of their education as administrators. Accordingly, they devoted time to speech-making, joined in some of the main student activities, in an attempt to enlighten the student body on appropriate tactics as they saw it, for the confrontation. In this, they appeared to have some success, but the principal outcome was that most confessed themselves 'astounded' at the extent to which their predictions about the course of the sit-in, based on the Conference, came true.

The Business School students' motives bear examining, because there is not much doubt that their real concern for the students in the University proper was overlaid by a fairly obvious desire for dominance and control. This would seem not to matter so long as the students recognized it (they did) and were able to relate this awareness to the task in hand and to their careers in industry.

All the events described above were discussed at a brief Conference follow-up meeting at which participants and staff members came together to discuss the usefulness of the Conference design and the ways in which it might be improved. This meeting was too short to achieve much, largely because of the logistics of bringing Conference staff together in one location.

This serves to underline the extent to which the Conference as a whole 'belonged' to the school, or was dependent on outside help in the form of consultants who had insufficient time to follow through and consolidate the outcomes. It is certainly arguable that such events do not permit a *formal* follow-up, at least in anything like the original conference form; by that time, events have taken over and the follow-up is already in the bloodstream of the school, so to speak.

Conclusion

At the time of writing, the one week Conference on Organization and Authority is a familiar but by no means established feature of the end of the first term of the postgraduate programme at Manchester, and the fourth in the series is drawing near. The description above proves nothing scientifically, but should at least pose some searching questions for the administrators of courses in administration.

First, it seems timely to question the value of any business school education which does not address problems of value, morality, and responsibility. The typical consumer of a business school education may be prepared to ignore such problems in his, or her, quest for a high standard of living, and there is evidence to show a preponderant conservatism of the group as a whole. It can be argued that the output of today's primary schools will be better equipped to design their own curricula, but they will be a long time coming, by which time the present crop may be filling positions of power as amorally as some of their predecessors.

Not all old-fashioned businessmen are amoral, of course, but many are puzzled at the way in which their motives are misunderstood and derided, especially by their teenage children. One can sympathize with them in this, remembering that most of the nonsense they have learned of systems, leadership and authority they have learned passively from books, if they had a formal management education, or else from the behaviour of their parents, commanding officers and teachers in rigid authoritarian settings. Whatever the deficiencies of their education they now seem to be boxed-in at the tops of their organizations and strangely insulated by their systems from further learning.

Learning is a habit we may lose easily and at different points of our life. For many people, learning about oneself and one's contract with the world cuts off in primary school. What is the role of the school of administration when confronted with very intelligent and eager students prepared to learn anything which will fit their vocation, *except* a revelation about themselves and their career choices? Can the schools simply bow to the superficial requirements of the consumer?

The simple idea behind the Manchester experiment is the conviction that today's business school graduates represent, because of their opportunities, an immense force for reaction, on the one hand, or inspired change on the other. No matter what the sophistication of their technical preparation for the management job, management teachers will probably have failed in the larger task if students leave postgraduate courses:

Without having taken active choices about their learning.
Without having some revelation about their own processes of continuous learning and adaptation.
Without a feel for how they 'use' themselves and their beliefs and values in testing and uncertain situations.

The Conference on Organization and Authority does not *replace* traditional MBA content or method: it *should* provide an educational framework within which intelligent young adults can take some *choices* about content and method. It should also produce MBA's capable of integrating themselves more sensitively and effectively with some of the older 'casualities' referred to in the opening paragraph.

The wider question raised by this kind of approach has to do with student 'unrest'. It is important, once again, to distinguish between the content and the method of student revolt. If one examines the content, there are plainly some real grievances that the university establishment seems infuriatingly incompetent to cope with. The methods, however, look disturbingly and uncannily like the tantrums of children who have been given no moral sense by their parents, and whose antics seem to be a *cri de coeur* for *any* kind of involvement, commitment, and moral discipline.

If we really want students to behave responsibly, (that is, to use political systems creatively rather than to smash them, as a child might a toy), we will have to give them some realistic chance to learn how.

The attempt to do so described above represents the efforts of a small group of staff and outside collaborators, initiated primarily by the director of studies of the MBA course. Whether, in the long run, such programmes can exist as *part* of the curriculum must be doubtful if only because of the risk of culture-clash within the school. A real attack on management and political skills and sensitivity probably has to be launched on a broad front, embracing top management at the school, a synergystic qualtity of the faculty, and a commitment to research in learning effectiveness.

REFERENCE

1. For a full description of the Tavistock Institute model used, see RICE, A. K., *Learning for Leadership*. London: Tavistock Publications, 1965.

22. Introducing change to a complex organization

William J. Crockett

Change is neither automatic nor easy

Much of our contemporary thought and writing in the field of management, both in its theory and its practice, is devoted to the subject of change. A casual observer might therefore come to a number of erroneous conclusions. For example, he might well conclude that our public and private institutions are in active, throbbing, vibrant pursuit of change. He might conclude that the managers of these institutions are, in fact, modern revolutionaries who are masterminding a bureaucratic revolution that is actively being pursued in their institutions. He might conclude that all an institution must do in order to bring about change is simply to open its doors and let change flow into it. And, finally, he might conclude that all of the people in the institution are eager, willing, and able to formally embrace the new procedures and techniques, concepts and organization that change entails. But none of these conclusions would be totally valid.

From my own experience in a large and traditional public institution (U.S. Department of State), I know that the process of bringing about change to such an institution—its people, its processes, its organization, its attitudes, its objectives, and its way of life—is neither casual, nor automatic, nor easy. Many managers who are responsible for the day to day operations have little time and little motivation to pursue change, for change is often disruption, effort, and trouble for them.

I am therefore concerned about the easy connotations of the pat phrases we use in describing the way we organize to effect change. We call it 'the management of change' or 'the management for change', as if change itself were a dynamic force knocking on our doors, and all we had to do was to channel and guide it through our institutions. A phrase more suited to the process might well be 'the agony of change'. This is more descriptive of what happens, both in the institution and to the individuals in the institution, when change is brought about by the methods often employed by management today. In the normal institutional setting, even the smallest change is often brought about by an authoritarian directive imposed in an atmosphere of suspicion, misunderstanding, controversy, threat, and distrust. It can be an agonizing experience for the people who are caught up in its process, and it may result in tearing the fabric of the institution itself.

In this paper I would like to describe the various processes that we used to effect change in the Department of State over the five years that I was in charge of its management, first as Assistant Secretary of State for Administration and then as Deputy Under Secretary of State for Administration. This period started in the early days of the Kennedy Administration and ended in the early months of 1967 in the Johnson Administration.

A commitment to change

The Kennedy Administration was committed to bringing extensive change to the executive branch of government. The principal mandate I was given by Mr Kennedy at the time of my appointment was to help his administration achieve a more dynamic and effective Department of State.

After the election and before the inauguration, Mr Kennedy set up numerous task forces composed of important private citizens to look into the administrative and management problems, as well as the political and functional problems of many agencies of the Federal Government. The State Department was one of the agencies selected for this kind of preliminary review; and while some aspects of policy were considered by the task force, they concentrated most of their interests in the field of management, and specifically, on how to make the State Department function more effectively. As a result, when I took over the State Department's administration early in 1961, we had numerous ideas to pursue on how to improve its management, modernize its organization, and speed up its operations.

The development of a program for change

Soon after my appointment, I made a worldwide inspection trip with Under Secretary of State, Chester Bowles. We talked to ambassadors and foreign service officers around the world about the problems they were having in those outposts of the State Department in operating effectively and in carrying out their duties. As a result of this trip, some 150 action items were identified for changes that should be considered in order to improve our operations abroad.

A project was started early in 1961 to develop a comprehensive list of all the subjects that had been suggested for us to look into, and to establish priorities for further study. We finally identified 136 major and minor items that warranted further work. For example, the first one on the list reads as follows:

1 Interdepartmental leadership in foreign affairs and relationships with other agencies—develop a program for better interdepartmental leadership in the foreign affairs field and liaison in relationships with other agencies, including arrangements for general direction of certain functions transferred from the Operations Coordination Board. Time to complete: 60 days. Resources: Part time of one officer.

The list involved such areas as the State Department's relationships with other agencies; its leadership role in the Federal Government; the leadership role of the ambassadors abroad, as well as the whole bureaucratic process in the State and its effect upon the individuals and the institutions it was supposed to serve.

These projects were published in a booklet called, *Work Improvement Plans for the Department of State*, dated May 1961. It might be interesting to look at a couple of paragraphs in the foreword of this document:

> Management improvements do not just happen—they must be planned and developed systematically. Areas in need of improvement must be identified, objectives established, and resources marshalled to convert plans into realized accomplishments.
>
> If we are to be effective in our efforts, we must be aware of the pace of change and plan to meet new and evolving needs with expedition and resourcefulness.
>
> We have a responsibility to improve organizational structure, delegate adequate authority, eliminate unnecessary procedures and checkpoints, simplify procedures, and reduce costs through effective utilization of manpower, materials, and money.

Brave and bold words and perhaps also naïve and overly optimistic words as well.

The objectives

There were numerous blueprints developed over the years by which we hoped to bring about the change we desired, but in this paper I shall speak briefly about only the most important ones. We were determined to relax the Department's bureaucracy and to cut out the underbrush of regulations that produced its slow and sometimes ponderous action. We were determined to find and to eliminate unnecessary requirements which bogged people down with paperwork and secondary activity, rather than letting them get at the real issues of their jobs. We saw this program as a means of giving people time to think and time to do the more essential parts of their duties.

Change did occur

A great many changes were brought about in the Department of State by our authoritarian process, for there was no dearth of ideas. The only problem was to get the bureaucracy to do something about accepting the ideas. Our solution, as we practised it in those days, was to study the idea, and if top management thought it made sense, then top management simply told the bureaucracy to do it, and we had enough pressure to get the job done in many cases.

A great deal of change was actually brought about during this period of theory X management. In a report dated March 1966, more than 1200 recommendations for analysis and study had been suggested and actually looked into. The first annual report in 1962 showed that 109 committees had been formally terminated, and 86

291

other groups were removed from the committee register. Ninety-five reoccurring reports had been eliminated, and 30 others were simplified. The report went on to say that, 'through work simplification, decentralization of authority, and the reduction or elimination of marginal services, the Bureau of Administration effected a net reduction of 132 positions in its own organization in the first year.'

If the average salary for each of the jobs eliminated was approximately $15 000 then this alone represented a considerable accomplishment.

One tactic: 'Directed change'

In the early days, a great deal of this change came about as a result of large doses of theory X. It was not until later, much later, after much superficial success, accompanied by a nagging sense of something lacking in the whole endeavor, that we decided to change our tactics and use McGregor's theory Y as a better means of accomplishing our ends. One way we used theory X to bring about change was by the arbitrary elimination of a function, a process, an agency, or an operation.

The most dramatic example of this method was the announcement by President Kennedy of the abolition of the OCB (Operations Coordinating Board) early in his administration. The OCB was established in the Eisenhower Administration to act as a staff arm of the President with the responsibility for bringing about inter-agency coordination and to monitor action decisions in the field of foreign policy. It was often cumbersome and sometimes bureaucratic, but it did serve the useful function of follow-up. In the abolition of this board, the Kennedy Administration simply stated that they would look to the State Department to fulfil the foreign affairs responsibilities formerly carried on by the board, and that they would look to the other agencies of government for action, as a matter of policy might fall within their area of interest. And so, by this dramatic and arbitrary order, an agency and its function was eliminated, and change was indeed brought about.

But the mere abolition of a function does not automatically cause the operational and organizational substitutions to be made that are required in order to make the new machinery operate, and for a long period of time no substitute organization was established to insure that coordination, action, and follow-up were taking place. There was no formal system established to fulfill the functions that the OCB had formerly fulfilled, even though the item appeared as number one on our priority list of action. (See page 290.) The failure of the Federal agencies to develop an alternative system for coordination was clearly observable in the Bay of Pigs incident. During that dramatic and tragic time, it was obvious that there had been a failure on the part of the agencies to coordinate their policies and actions; they had left all of the necessary coordination to the President himself.

As a direct outgrowth of the Bay of Pigs, the Operations Center in Department of State was established to provide the coordinating function formerly performed by the OCB. This War Room or Situation Room had the responsibility for pulling together all the communications and action responsibilities bearing upon a crisis. People from all of the other foreign affairs agencies of the Government, including the military, were brought into this center and served on a 24 hour, round the clock basis. This group was responsible for monitoring all of the interlocking areas of responsibility in the field of foreign affairs of all of the agencies that were involved in a particular problem, and to insure that all information of military, political, economic, and intelligence nature, relevant to it was available to the President and his staff for decision-making purposes.

In the State Department we used this process (arbitrarily eliminating a function) extensively and effectively in reducing reports, in eliminating committees, and in eliminating unnecessary operations. One way we used it would be to send a cable to the embassies instructing them that, as of such and such a date, they would no longer be required to send in a certain report. Then we would inform the State Department bureaux and offices that had had the responsibility for processing the information contained in these reports, that, as of such and such a date, they would no longer have the reports for their functions.

This kind of authoritarian change was controversial and arbitrary, threatening, and stressful, because it did not give people a chance to discuss the issues or to become involved in the change. We did not ask people for their views. We told them what to eliminate without questions. People were displaced and frustrated. Ill feeling was created by this sometimes ruthless means of bringing about reform.

Building upon crisis

Another way we used theory X to bring about change in the State Department during this time was in taking advantage of and building upon crisis situations. Often, it was not the crisis itself, but the way the crisis was handled, or the deficiency in the way it was handled, which taught us the most.

An illustration of how a crisis was used to trigger change occurred during the second Cuban incident, the Missile Crisis. For many months, we had been concerned with the antiquated communication system of the Department of State. For many months, we had studied the possibility of establishing a modern worldwide network. We had come to the conclusion that we must take action to coordinate the communications systems of the Department of State with those of the CIA and the military, into an integrated overseas communications network for all foreign affairs agencies. But other problems and other requirements pushed this project into the background, until the Missile Crisis. During this crisis, our communications facilities were swamped; they were unable to transmit to all of the US embassies around the world, the text of President Kennedy's speech to the American people before the speech was given here at home. It was intended that all our ambassadors around the world should have a text of the speech in advance, so that they could have informed the friendly nations about the crisis and of the contents of the President's message before it was made public in his report to the American people. Our inability to fulfill this mission was of great concern at the time, and as a direct result of this crisis, the State Department (by authoritarian directive) developed and put into operation a multi-million dollar worldwide computerized communications system.

Change through systems development

In our direct line operation where the change was not too complex, and where the authority was without challenge, the authoritarian process did bring about significant changes. Our attitude then was to sweep all of the opposition under the rug, and go ahead and accomplish things. But we were not nearly so effective in bringing about change by this means when the authority was not so clear and direct. In a complex organization, we found that it was difficult to bring about change, even by authoritarian means, when we had to move across the borders of our own line authority and operate in a staff capacity within the authority of another's bailiwick. Then, the authoritarian process and the force it carries fall off greatly and opposition may form that prevents the change from coming into being at all. A few examples serve to illustrate this point.

Very early in our program, we determined that one of our most pressing priorities was to develop systems that would enable the Department of State to attain an important and much needed leadership role in foreign policy and overseas operations. To achieve this objective we devised a four pronged strategy made up of:

1 A policy-planning council which would establish one comprehensive, total statement of US foreign policy for each country, which would involve all agencies of the US Government (including the Department of State) in its development, and which all would support and follow.

2 A 'comprehensive country programming system' which would evaluate every 'agency' program in each country in relationship to our policy for that country, and then establish priorities among the agencies involved for program and resource allocation.

3 A reorganization within the State Department (Senior Interdepartmental Group and Interdepartmental Regional Group and Country Directors) which would give the State Department in Washington the same overall control of foreign affairs planning and operations that the ambassadors enjoyed abroad.

4 A comprehensive foreign affairs personnel system operated by the Secretary of State, which would give all US personnel working abroad the identical status, benefits, and prerogatives of the foreign service.

The Policy-Planning Council operated fairly well with outward support from the agencies, but we were always discovering special 'Agency policies' for various countries that were sometimes in addition to the master plan, but were sometimes contrary to the planning. But unenthusiastic support is as an effective means of killing an idea as is overt opposition. The State Department operational officers saw little use in the plans, and despite Secretary Rusk's active participation in the planning process, they actually were but nice documents in desk drawers. We knew this and were not surprised. But we were determined to make them become powerful forces in the system. And the way we believed this could be achieved was to make all US agencies programs in the foreign affairs field be measured against these policies, country by country. In this way, we envisaged that the total US program in a country (all countries virtually) would be developed, funded, and evaluated, in order to support the central US policy for that country. Obviously, a very dangerous and revolutionary idea. Using this system, the State would draw evaluative conclusions about the operational and cost effectiveness of every overseas program and could determine priorities for resource allocation country by country and agency by agency. In other words, we were trying to bring about a 'McNamara analytical process' for the foreign policy agencies, with the State Department doing the analysis.

To achieve this objective, we developed a model of a programming system, which we called 'The Comprehensive Country Programming System'. We selected and trained a cadre of enthusiastic young officers to install the program at selected embassies. They were to develop input data for the system by examining, country by country, all US programs, probing deeply into issues, and seeking answers from US agency program directors as to how they were using their money in a country, how they were carrying out their programs, and how these programs were related to or were accomplishing United States foreign policy objectives for that country.

We had no lack of support from the top for all of these strategies. For example, in 1965, President Johnson directed all US agencies to conduct an evaluative experiment in 13 countries, based on this model. The project was strongly supported by Secretary Rusk.

But we had initiated, developed, and established the whole strategy of change in an authoritarian, directive way. We used all the force at our command to get the system installed and accepted; it was shoved down the throats of anyone who objected, without much involvement of the people concerned. In the end, all four efforts to accomplish our overall objective failed to become operational. And they failed, I am convinced, because of the *way* we went about bringing them into being and trying to use them, rather than because of their lack of merit.

They were all good ideas and ones that should be done sometime. The problem was, however, that there was no commitment on the part of the people involved: in fact, in most cases there was much opposition. The programs were imposed upon the embassies and the other US government agencies, and we did not have enough authority over the other agencies nor enough commitment from even the State Department people to enforce the directives that were issued. Every matter was controversial. If we wanted a decision, we had to carry it high enough to get it the attention of the Secretary of State or the President before we could get action. There were just too many issues that could not be solved at lower levels, because the people at those levels did not want the system to succeed, and as a result, the programs did not get off the ground. Despite their potential, their high quality, and the great need for them, the programs failed. And they failed principally, I am convinced, because they were imposed and implemented only by authoritarian means—theory X.

Change without commitment

Those experiences convinced us that because of the complexities of human relationships and reactions, the authoritarian method (theory X) of changing operational responsibilities and systems in an organization was not always the most effective method. It could not insure the acceptance of change, nor doing the new tasks with enthusiasm and effectiveness. In fact, change imposed in this way generated hostility, suspicion, and defensiveness, and mobilized both covert and overt opposition. In the end, we were not successful, despite our best efforts. We established strong follow-up systems—we set up thorough inspections and controls, and we received inputs directly from many outside sources, but I felt that there was often surface change without commitment. There seemed to be a change of organization without there being a change in people's attitude. I felt skeptical that we were accomplishing as much as we ought to be, or as much as we thought we were. I was skeptical that the changes were really being put into the fabric of the system, or into the hearts of people. I doubted that the changes would endure over a long period of time, because there was too much evidence of opposition—and we had had too many failures.

The use of theory Y to bring about change

After a time, we came to the conclusion that there was surely a better way of bringing about change in a complex organization than the authoritarian approach we had used in the past. Surely there was a way which would take into consideration the feelings and ideas of the people concerned; a way which would get them involved in wanting the change, and in planning the methods that were to be used in effecting it. We needed a style of management which would cause people not only to change a procedure, but would cause them to change their own behavior, their commitments, their attitudes, and their outlook as well. We needed a management system where we would not be dependent upon a crisis as the catalyst, but a system in which the people themselves would become the prime sources for change because they could see that it would improve their own situations as well as the situation of the institution. The answer seemed to be in using McGregor's concept of theory Y as a management style. This would mean using involvement and participation, team-building, and organizational development as the style by which we would try to bring about change.

The impact of a lab (T-Group) experience on management style

At about this time, I attended my first T-Group—a NTL President's Lab in Florida. It was led by Dr Herbert Shepard and Dr Jack Gibb.

While I had some deferential feelings toward the businessmen who were the principal participants in the lab, I personally felt that I was one of the best administrators (managers) in the whole Federal Government. I had been selected from the career service (Foreign Service of the United States) from a relatively junior level, jumped over a great many of my more senior colleagues, and been appointed by President Kennedy to the top management job in the entire Department of State and Foreign Service—first as Assistant Secretary of State and then as Deputy Under Secretary of State for Administration. I frankly felt pretty satisfied with myself. I thought that I knew all of the problems, that I knew all of the answers, and that what I primarily needed to 'straighten out the Department' was a group of loyal subordinates to carry out my policies and directives.

After a few days at the lab, I was surprised, to say the least, by the feedback I was receiving. I recall sharing it with my wife, Verla, who was there with me at the time, and curiously, it was very much like some of the feedback she had given me from time to time and which I had pooh-poohed as being just the usual 'woman's bias'. But to have a group of strangers tell me such things was tough to take, such things as:

'You are devious and manipulative.'

'You are authoritarian and controlling.'

'You don't listen.'

'You intellectualize all feelings and refuse to deal with people on a feelings level.'

'You are sly, and we don't totally trust you, nor would we want to work for you.'

Finally, it began to dawn upon me that maybe the problems we were having in gaining acceptance for our new programs and philosophies in the Department of State might, to some extent at least, be because of my own personal management style and the way we were trying to bring them about.

But even more importantly, I saw (had mirrored for me) a side of myself and my behavior that I did not like and determined to change.

One of the first things I did after returning home from this lab was to have a team-building meeting with my principal subordinates. In this meeting, we did expose and solve many of our own interpersonal problems and developed a general style and strategy for bringing about (introducing) change in the Department by using the concepts of theory Y instead of theory X.[1]

ACORD

I felt, as a matter of pride and satisfaction, that I had always tried to work *for* the people of the foreign service, as well as for the best interest of the Department of State. But despite the many positive things we had accomplished over the years, they had been brought about in an authoritarian manner, with arrogance and hardness: theory X. As a result, even the beneficial programs, were often suspected and even rejected.

We changed to the theory Y style of management in 1965. In many ways, this was the most rewarding and most interesting part of my State Department tenure. It was the part where I received the most satisfaction because I think it was during this period that we tried to work *with* people rather than *against* them. I believed this style of management had the best chance of achieving the objectives of change, for it was the most effective, the most interesting, and the least harmful way of bringing change to the institution and to the people in the institution. This new approach to organizational change was called 'ACORD', an 'Action Program of Organizational Development'.

The ACORD program was a multi-faceted program designed to not only bring change in the Department of State, but it was also designed to expose a wide

297

variety of State Department people to a new style of management. It used the insights and the knowledge of the social and behavioral sciences.

The administrative area of the Department of State, for which I had management responsibility, with its 2500 people, was conceived as being a management laboratory for this program. We wanted to be able to observe the new management process, and to be able to determine the effectiveness of our new methods and organization. We wanted to be able to observe the commitment of the people involved and the problems they had so that we could from this learning, develop valid programs and methods that could be used in other areas of the Department of State which were not directly under my responsibility.

The first activity, which was a cornerstone of the ACORD program, was the organization of the whole administrative area of the Department of State under the concept of management by objectives and programs (MOP). The essential feature of this idea was to eliminate as much of the vertical hierarchy and layering as possible. It had long been the conviction of Secretary Rusk that we should eliminate layering and establish a wide lateral organization in order to improve performance (particularly in the policy areas). His idea was that we ought to have 'a great many chiefs' who knew their jobs, who had well-established policy guidance, who had adequate resources, who had some mutually determined goals and objectives and who, as a consequence, would have a great deal of operational leeway—freedom in how they did their jobs. The Secretary often said that in this way each person could 'live up to the horizons of his job' as he saw fit and as the needs of the day dictated.

This was the spirit which motivated us in decentralizing a great deal of authority to the embassies; this was the spirit through which we eliminated seven layers of hierarchy in the administrative area of the State Department; and this was the spirit by which we tried to free the administrative managers from the confinement of their bureaucracies and infuse in them the entrepreneurial spirit. To do this we established some 35 operating groups in administration to whom we gave almost total operational freedom on such things as operations, objectives to be achieved within a certain timetable, resources that were to be used, and other activities they would like to fulfill in order to accomplish their objectives.

We learned from the experiment that some people did operate and manage better, were more agressive and more dynamic under the MOP management style. The Secretary's general goal of eliminating layers was validated and the tone and quality of operations were improved.

Training

We established several training concepts. Our people went to outside laboratory (sensitivity) training in the NTL programs. Some of our people went to the Organizational Development Programs at Bethel and UCLA. We felt that it was important for our leaders to understand the concepts and the theory of this new management style which we were all trying to use. These trained people were seeded throughout the areas where changes in management style, organization, and MOP were to occur. We established special 'in-house' one week seminars on organizational development to teach those management concepts. The seminars were conducted by NTL trainers about once every two months for State Department personnel. Some of the participants were 'cousin groups', where people in the Department were selected at random, while others were vertical slices within the same organization. Others were peer groups within the same organization. By this means, we spread the theory deeply within the organization as well as beyond its borders to the other organizations with whom it had to deal.

Team-building

Another means we used to carry out the program was to hold what we call 'Team-building' (problem-solving) sessions. These were short, off-site meetings of from one to three days in length, conducted by a behavioral scientist trainer. These meetings provided a closer look at the problems of the group than the other kinds of training and seminars did for they involved people who were working together in an organizational unit.

In these meetings, we considered the actual problems of the organization, both substantive and process. The agenda also centered around the difficulties the group members had of working together as a group and the things within the group that were getting in the way of effective operations. Sometimes, they came together after a trainer had done quite extensive research questioning each of the individuals in the group, discussing their problems and their interpersonal relationships. When this occurred, the trainer brought to the meeting deep insights about the group and the issues which could be discussed. Other times, the teams would get together without such preliminary research and through their discussion bring the issues that were bothering them into the open. In this way, they could get an understanding of what it was that was holding back their effective operation.

Another part of the ACORD development program was the formation of sub-groups for team-building sessions. We felt it important for the people to decide whether or not they, too, would like to have such meetings of their own. Some of the people in the session would decide that they would like to go off-site with their own subordinates for a team-building meeting of their own. In this way, the effect cascaded downwards so that there were sub-groups and sub-sub-groups, etc., all down the management line having these meetings. Each group would use a behavioral scientist as a trainer and would meet to talk about how they worked together, what their problems were and how they could solve their problems better.

An external consulting team

An important ingredient in insuring the effectiveness of the ACORD program was building an external consulting team. This was a professional group of behavioral scientists that could come in to work with us as we needed them. This association of top-flight social and behavioral scientists from the NTL network with the State Department was an important part of the program.

In addition to serving as a training staff in the special seminars, in team-building and problem-solving sessions, these professionals worked closely with line operators to help form a strong link between *training* and *follow-up* action within the organizations. For example, these men were available to attend staff meetings, to attend problem-solving meetings, and were on hand to observe the process of the group in other operational modes. They would report back to each of the individuals on his attitude, his behavior, and how he came through to the group. They would call attention to their conduct in the group. They would often stop the group in its work to have it focus its attention on the process within the group, as well as upon the problem under discussion. They coached and counselled with the leader and his members.

Internal change agents

As a part of the ACORD project, we developed internal change agents or consulting teams. Staff members of the ACORD program were identified and trained to act as internal consultants. They were assigned to our program managers and assisted them on all kinds of organizational development matters. They were available on a full-time basis to meet with operators and their staffs when they were holding meetings. They could talk with them about their problems, do research with their people, and then they could feed this research back to the manager so that he could see what he was doing and how it was affecting his staff and his internal operations.

These internal change agents (or 'internal consultant staff', as they were sometimes called) were sometimes linked to specific external consultants, in which case they would be assigned special organizational units to work with as clients. When an organizational unit in their care needed help, these people would call in a professional behavioral scientist—to sit in a meeting and talk through the issues. This permitted an increased involvement and a better continuity between the individual consultants from the outside and the organization to which they were assigned on the inside.

Changes in organization require systems development

I mentioned earlier that we changed the structure of the organization. When we established the program of management by objectives and programs, it became evident that structural and procedural change should be made in order to make the whole organization function better. But just as we had learned that it was not enough to work on the structure without regard to interpersonal relationships, we also learned that changes in the structure required changes in procedures and systems. In other words, people had to work within the structure (organization) and the structure could not be effectively changed without involving the people, but in all cases procedures and systems also had to be changed for the system to work.

These elements are so interrelated—structure, interpersonal relationships and the procedures (the system)—that all have impact on the overall goal of improving organizational effectiveness, and all must be given attention to almost simultaneously.

Therefore, a 'systems approach' was extensively used. By this means we tried to take into account not only interpersonal relationships, but also the whole life of the organization, the way the staff meetings were conducted, the way people were promoted and compensated, the way the organizational parts linked together, the way information flowed, the ways decisions were made, who needed to see whom about what, etc. We found out very early that a significant change in one part of the system directly affected another part of the system which would then require systems development. We discovered that the failure to bring about a procedural revision in one part of the system after we had changed another part seriously inhibited the whole process. Therefore, as part of the ACORD program, we had a group working only on systems and systems modifications. Their job was to insure that the system, *as a whole,* was linked together with common procedures and that all the interfaces were provided for in order to make a complex organization work.

Research

Another ingredient that played an important part of the program was research. A general body of theory, which we put vigorously into practice, required some research in order to give us insights into our progress. But it also gave us quick knowledge of what new problems our organization was causing. We felt a need for carrying on a variety of action-oriented research efforts in conjunction with the programs themselves. These activities included such things as pre-meeting interviews, open discussions by participants in off-site meetings, written surveys to determine the effect of major organizational changes upon people, etc. By these constant patterns of research, we were able to ascertain the development of the program, its progress, the effect of the program upon people, the commitment of people, the problems they had with the efforts we were making, and so on. Research gave us the insights in diagnosing the real life situations we faced in fulfilling our program objectives and provided specific targets that we could aim at in our meetings, to solve problems without wasting time or without beating about the bush.

This research effort was carried on under contract with the Center for Research on Utilization of Scientific Knowledge, Institute for Social Research, The University of Michigan, Lansing, Michigan.

Public advisors

Another important part of the ACORD program, although it is perhaps not as important in a business institution as it was in a public institution, was our Board of Public Advisors. Early on in the establishment of the program, I felt it important that we have a group of businessmen, who had experience with an OD program in their own organizations and who were committed to the process, to advise me as to the methods of accomplishing the program in the Department of State.

We had three eminent businessmen—Ed Fogel, Vice-President, Union Carbide Corporation, New York; Fred Holloway, Vice-President, Esso Research, New York; and Alfred Marrow, Chairman of the Board, Harwood Manufacturing Company, New York—who were faithful, farsighted, and helpful to me in organizing and developing the program. A great deal of the success of the program is theirs to claim.

Objective: involvement

By coupling all of these activities (as well as a great many others) into a program which we called ACORD, and by earnestly trying to use the humanistic management concepts of theory Y, we tried to provide a climate within the organization that involved the people who were to be most affected by the change in the change process itself. We hoped by this means to secure more commitment to the objectives we were trying to achieve. We tried to make people feel that they had a personal stake in the results. We tried to insure that the personal goals of people were consistent with the organizational goals and vice versa, and therefore to avoid the conflicts of interest the individual might have had in pursuing the corporate goals versus the pursuit of his own goals.

Excitement and commitment

There were irritations because the old ways of getting the job done no longer were in existence. There were frustrations because the new systems needed to nourish the whole took time to develop and install. There were mistakes because we were all people. But there was excitement, fun, commitment, enthusiasm, and a sense of freedom that I had never before experienced in a large institution.

ACORD—the involvement of people in their own change—was a tremendously exciting adventure in a new management and organizational style.

Conclusions

1 Among the things we validated in our organizational development program, although we already believed it, was the fact that nowhere in the body of organizational theory or literature are there ready formulas and pat answers to the enormously complex problems of organizational change and the development of people.

ACORD was but one, albeit comprehensive, approach to the problem. But it is not the only approach, for there are other activities that might have been added to the things that made our program as good as it was. But the ACORD program did help stimulate gradual and positive change toward a new style of management, to new organizational patterns and to improved interpersonal relationships. It did contribute toward greater responsiveness within the organization, better communications among its membership, higher commitment on the part of the people to the objectives, and, accordingly, it did produce a more effective and efficient operation. The entrepreneurial spirit even in such a traditional organization as State was not dead!

2 I felt that the T-Group was a valuable tool in helping the people get started and in providing a focal point for disseminating information about the program and its objectives. It did help to create a receptive attitude and a climate of trust and commitment that somehow must take place in an organization before it can move forward effectively in its own renewal and in changing its organizational structure. The laboratory training laid the foundation for subsequent team-building and problem-solving meetings that were essential to the success of the program, and, perhaps, did as much as any one single thing in the making for the success of the program. But it was my belief that sending people to stranger labs, or to training sessions outside of the living environment of the organization was not the most effective way of bringing about organizational change. This alone will not bring about a change of climate or development within the organization.

It was my belief that learning and development can best be a group experience. Group growth, and the creating of new group norms, can best be achieved by group activity where the organizational unit or entity experiences the new concepts and moves forward together as a group.

3 Our organizational development program was under constant experimentation. We changed the activities a little bit here and there as we went along. The organizational development program had to be flexible enough to meet the new situations that came up, meet the new problems that people faced and move to any new situation that emerged.

4 For any organizational development program to really succeed, it was (is) my feeling that it must involve the top of the organization and move down, rather than moving from the bottom up. I think one of the problems of our program was that it started too low in the organizational structure and worked down. It never got the top involved.

This failure to get the top involved created uneasiness on the part of some of the managers who were involved, and it gave them the impression that there was a lack of sincerity, a lack of purpose, and lack of commitment to the whole program. This caused the program to lack some of the validity that it might have had if top management had been more personally and directly involved.

5 I am convinced that a program of organizational change, no matter what its specific agenda of action may be, is best for the living organization and for the people involved, when it works *with* people in the spirit of theory Y. This means trying to bring about change in the structure of the organization, change in methods and procedures of operation, change in outlook and climate within the organization, increased effectiveness of operations, etc., by working with people and working through people rather than arbitrarily making the decisions and then trying to force the people down the line to fulfill the decisions someone above has made for them.

The authoritarian method of change creates emotional disturbance, animosities, schisms within the group, which sometimes are never healed. It builds up distrust, frustration, and lack of commitment, which can mean that the change is never effective and is never really implemented. It is my conviction that a good OD program does give people an opportunity to work together in groups to solve their own problems and the problems of the group. This is the only way that a change can succeed.

6 When embarking upon a comprehensive change program (structure, organization, climate, training, etc.) I believe it is important to have some kind of a scientifically based research group to monitor the progress and the impact of the change upon people, so that management can know its progress, but also so that problems, errors, and false starts can be quickly caught and corrected.

7 It is my belief that an organizational change program of this magnitude should be linked to an outside consulting staff of professional behavioral scientists and other consultants who can provide resources and advice as they are needed.

8 I believe that the internal and external change agents must design a total program that fits the institution—that relates itself to the people, to the needs of both people and organization, and builds upon the reality of the organization as it is.

9 The various efforts to achieve a more effective Department of State which I have described in this paper were not developed at any one time, but were things that had been in progress within the Department of State for a number of years. But all of them put together indicate a consistency of approach and a unity of purpose and a climate for inquiry that, to me, is impressive.

Many of the objectives were so illusive, albeit important, that they will probably never be fully achieved. Others, while temporarily achieved, will have to be redone as conditions and environment and management change. But all of our efforts toward this organizational renewal were important for the simple reason that if people—management and staff alike—do not make an effort to improve themselves and their operations, then their people and their operations will become outmoded and archaic. Management, like the rest of man's activities and disciplines, is not static. Management, through various kinds of organizational programs, must endeavor to be ready to take advantage of the new concepts and theories wherever they emerge, and, hopefully, management will be in the vanguard of helping to test, experiment and even create the new.

Reference

1. CROCKETT, WILLIAM J., 'Team Building, One Approach to Organizational Development'. See *Journal of Applied Behavioral Science,* Vol. 6, No. 3, 1970, p. 291.

Printed by William Clowes & Sons Limited, London, Colchester and Beccles